Living Books
of Moses

Living Books of Moses

A Paraphrase of
Genesis—Exodus—Leviticus
Numbers—Deuteronomy

TYNDALE HOUSE PUBLISHERS
Wheaton, Illinois

Coverdale House Publishers
London and Eastbourne, England

Distributed in Canada by
Home Evangel Books Ltd., Toronto, Ontario

Third printing, November 1970
478,000 copies in print

Library of Congress Catalog Card No. 70-93076
SBN No. 8423-2301-5, Paper
SBN No. 8423-2300-7, Cloth

Contents

From Wm. Tyndale's Prologue to the First Printed English New Testament:

Exhortynge instantly and besechynge those that are better sene in the tongues than I, and that have higher gifts of grace to interpret the sense of Scripture, and meaning of the Spirit, than I, to consider and ponder my labor, and that with the spirit of meekness. And if they perceive in any places that I have not attained the very sense of the tongue, or meaning of the Scripture, or have not given the right English word, that they put to their hands to amend it, remembering that so is their duty to do. For we have not received the gifts of God for ourselves only, or for to hide them; but for to bestow them unto the honoring of God and Christ and edifying of the congregation, which is the body of Christ.

Some thoughts from the translator:

This book is the next to the last volume in the *Living* Series of Paraphrased Scriptures. Hopefully, the final volume, *The Living History of Israel,* will follow within a year.

The right title for this book was a problem! Among the suggestions considered and the reactions to the suggestions were: *Living Pentateuch* ("What's *that*?"), *Living Laws* ("But aren't the Mosaic ordinances *dead*?"), and *Living Beginnings* (How odd!"). So we have decided on the prosaic but descriptive title, *Living Books of Moses.* This will not satisfy those who doubt Moses' authorship, but for the rest of us, it is beautifully apt.

And now a few words about my own feelings as to the value of reading these five ancient documents. In what sense are they *living?* My reply is first, that they are given by the living God to man for his edification: "The whole Bible was given to us by inspiration from God and is useful to teach us what is true and to make us realize what is wrong in our lives; it straightens us out and helps us do what is right. It is God's way of making us well prepared at every point, fully equipped to do good to everyone" (2 Timothy 3:16,17).

So these books, like all other parts of the Scripture, are alive with the power of God. For they are parts of His Word—the Holy Spirit's sword that lays bare the thoughts and intents of the heart—mine and yours.

What I found in my own heart, when reading these books, is but a reflection of the utter stubbornness of the Israeli here described. How often, as I was preparing these pages, I cried out in angry reproach at those who had such opportunities to know and love God, but refused. And then I looked at myself. It is a sobering experience.

Secondly, these books live as history, and history is indeed His Story—the story of the power of God reaching into the lives of all mankind. These five Books of Moses record the profound beginnings of the earth and of all mankind, and of the thin red line of crimson blood that starts just outside the garden of Eden and extends through the entire Scriptures, from one end to the other. God's eternal purposes become at least clearer, if not entirely clear, when reading these books.

But many of the laws recorded here are obsolete, now that Christ has come. So why read them? One reason is that we can rejoice in being free from them! For Christ has set us free. Well does the old hymn remind us: "Free from the law, oh, happy condition!"

But with this freedom from legalism, there is an obligation to internal purity, love, and truth. The external ordinances have been laid aside, but the internal necessity remains adamant: we are to love God, obey Him, rejoice in Him, worship Him, be cleansed by Him. As you read these ancient ordinances, do not only think, "Oh, boy, I'm glad I'm free from having to follow all those weird rules!" But also think, "What was the purpose of those rules? How can I follow their intent? Those rules required external purification rites—how can I now be cleansed within? They required sacrifices—how can I truly find the sacrificial Lamb? They required rigid forms of worship—how can I find joyous communion?

When read in this way, these books are worth their weight in gold as devotional guides.

Finally, the greatest inspirational value in the entire Bible probably will be found by many readers in the true stories of faith contained herein—the faith of Abraham, Moses, Joseph, and a host of minor characters. If you pattern your faith after theirs, even for a few minutes, it can be a life-shaking experience.

And faith comes to those who read these accounts, for "faith comes by hearing and hearing by the Word of God." Do you need more faith? Here it is, all ready and packaged for you! Read, and grow.

K. N. T.

Genesis

CHAPTER 1

When God began creating[1] the heavens and the earth,

2 The earth was at first[2] a shapeless, chaotic mass,[3] with the Spirit of God brooding over the dark vapors.[4]

3 Then[2] God said, "Let there be light." And light appeared.

4, 5 And God was pleased with it, and divided the light from the darkness. So He let it shine for awhile, and then there was darkness again. He called the light "daytime," and the darkness "nighttime." Together they formed the first day.[5]

6 And God said, "Let the vapors separate[6] to form the sky above and the oceans below."

7, 8 So God made the sky, dividing the vapor above from the water below. This all happened on the second day.[7]

9, 10 Then God said, "Let the water beneath the sky be gathered into oceans so that the dry land will emerge." And so it was. Then God named the dry

[1]Or, "In the beginning God created . . ."
[2]Implied.
[3]Or, "shapeless and void."
[4]Or, "over the cloud of darkness," or, "over the darkness and waters," or even, "over the dark, gaseous mass." There is no "right" way to translate these words.
[5]Literally, "And there was evening and there was morning, one day (or, 'period of time')."
[6]Literally, "Let there be a dome to divide the waters."
[7]Literally, "There was evening and there was morning, a second day (or, 'period of time')."

land "earth," and the water "seas." And God was pleased.

11, 12 And He said, "Let the earth burst forth with every sort of grass and seed-bearing plant, and fruit trees with seeds inside the fruit, so that these seeds will produce the kinds of plants and fruits they came from." And so it was, and God was pleased.

13 This all occurred on the third day.[8]

14, 15 Then God said, "Let there be bright lights in the sky to give light to the earth and to identify the day and the night; they shall bring about the seasons on the earth, and mark the days and years." And so it was.

16 For God made two huge lights, the sun and moon, to shine down upon the earth—the larger one, the sun, to preside over the day and the smaller one, the moon, to preside through the night; He also made the stars.

17 And God set them in the sky to light the earth,

18 And to preside over the day and night, and to divide the light from the darkness. And God was pleased.

19 This all happened on the fourth day.[9]

20 Then God said, "Let the waters teem with fish and other life, and let the skies be filled with birds of every kind."

21, 22 So God created great sea creatures, and every sort of fish and every kind of bird. And God looked at them with pleasure, and blessed them all. "Multiply and stock the oceans," He told them, and

---

[8]Literally, "And there was evening and there was morning, a third day (or, 'period of time')."
[9]Literally, "And there was evening and there was morning, a fourth day (or, 'period of time')."

to the birds He said, "Let your numbers increase. Fill the earth!"

23 That ended the fifth day.[10]

24 And God said, "Let the earth bring forth every kind of animal—cattle and reptiles and wildlife of every kind." And so it was.

25 God made all sorts of wild animals and cattle and reptiles. And God was pleased with what He had done.

26 Then God said, "Let us make a man[11]—someone like ourselves,[12] to be the master of all life upon the earth and in the skies and in the seas."

27 So God made man like his Maker.
Like God did God make man;
Man and maid did He make them.

28 And God blessed them and told them, "Multiply and fill the earth and subdue it; you are masters of the fish and birds and all the animals.

29 And look! I have given you the seed-bearing plants throughout the earth, and all the fruit trees for your food.

30 And I've given all the grass and plants to the animals and birds for their food."

31 Then God looked over all that He had made, and it was excellent in every way. This ended the sixth day.[13]

CHAPTER 2

Now at last the heavens and earth were successfully completed, with all that they contained.

---

[10]Literally, "And there was evening and there was morning, a fifth day (or, 'period of time')."
[11]Literally, "men."
[12]Literally, "Let us make man in our image, in our likeness."
[13]Literally, "And there was evening and there was morning, a sixth day (or, 'period of time')."

2 So on the seventh day, having finished His task, God ceased from this work He had been doing,

3 And God blessed the seventh day and declared it holy, because it was the day when He ceased this work of creation.

* * * * *

4 Here is a summary of the events in the creation of the heavens and earth which the Lord God made.

5 There were no plants or grain sprouting up across the earth at first, for the Lord God hadn't sent any rain; nor was there anyone to farm the soil.

6 (However, water welled up from the ground at certain places and flowed across the land.)

7 The time came when the Lord God formed a man's body from the dust of the ground[1] and breathed into it the breath of life. And man became a living person.

8 Then the Lord God planted a garden in Eden, to the east, and placed in the garden the man He had formed.

9 The Lord God planted all sorts of beautiful trees there in the garden, trees producing the choicest of fruit. At the center of the garden He placed the Tree of Life, and also the Tree of Conscience, giving knowledge of Good and Bad.

10 A river from the land of Eden flowed through the garden to water it; afterwards the river divided into four branches.

11, 12 One of these was named the Pishon; it winds across the entire length of the land of Havilah,[2]

---

[1]Or, "from a lump of soil," or, "from clods in the soil," or, "from a clod of clay."
[2]Located along the border of Babylonia.

where nuggets of pure gold are found, also beautiful bdellium and even lapis lazuli.

13   The second branch is called the Gihon, crossing the entire length of the land of Cush.

14   The third branch is the Tigris, which flows to the east of the city of Asher. And the fourth is the Euphrates.

15   The Lord God placed the man in the Garden of Eden as its gardener, to tend and care for it.

16, 17   But the Lord God gave the man this warning: "You may eat any fruit in the garden except fruit from the Tree of Conscience—for its fruit will open your eyes to make you aware of right and wrong, good and bad. If you eat its fruit, you will be doomed to die."

18   And the Lord God said, "It isn't good for man to be alone; I will make a companion for him, a helper suited to his needs."

19, 20   So the Lord God formed from the soil every kind of animal and bird, and brought them to the man to see what he would call them; and whatever he called them, that was their name. But still there was no proper helper for the man.

21   Then the Lord God caused the man to fall into a deep sleep, and took one of his ribs and closed up the place from which He had removed it,

22   And made the rib into a woman, and brought her to the man.

23   "This is it!" Adam exclaimed. "She is part of my own bone and flesh! Her name is 'woman' because she was taken out of a man."

24   This explains why a man leaves his father and mother and is joined to his wife in such a way that the two become one person.[3]

---

[3]Literally, "one flesh."

25 Now although the man and his wife were both naked, neither of them was embarrassed or ashamed.

CHAPTER 3

The serpent was the craftiest of all the creatures the Lord God had made. So the serpent came to the woman. "Really?" he asked. *"None* of the fruit in the garden? God says you mustn't eat *any* of it?"

2, 3 "Of course we may eat it," the woman told him. "It's only the fruit from the tree at the *center* of the garden that we are not to eat. God says we mustn't eat it or even touch it, or we will die."

4 "That's a lie!" the serpent hissed. "You'll not die!

5 God knows very well that the instant you eat it you will become like Him, for your eyes will be opened—you will be able to distinguish good from evil!"

6 The woman was convinced. How lovely and fresh looking it was! and it would make her so wise! So she ate some of the fruit and gave some to her husband, and he ate it too.

7 And as they ate it, suddenly they became aware of their nakedness, and were embarrassed. So they strung fig leaves together to cover themselves around the hips.

8 That evening they heard the sound of the Lord God walking in the garden; and they hid themselves among the trees.

9 The Lord God called to Adam, "Why are you hiding?"[1]

10 And Adam replied, "I heard You coming and didn't want You to see me naked. So I hid."

[1]Or, "Where are you?"

11 "Who told you you were naked?" the Lord God asked. "Have you eaten fruit from the tree I warned you about?"

12 "Yes," Adam admitted, "but it was the woman You gave me who brought me some, and I ate it."

13 Then the Lord God asked the woman, "How could you do such a thing?"

"The serpent tricked me," she replied.

14 So the Lord God said to the serpent, "This is your punishment: you are singled out from among all the domestic and wild animals of the whole earth— to be cursed. You shall grovel in the dust as long as you live, crawling along on your belly.

15 From now on you and the woman will be enemies, as will all of your offspring and hers. And I will put the fear of you into the woman, and between your offspring and hers. He shall strike you on your head, while you will strike at His heel."

16 Then God said to the woman, "You shall bear children in intense pain and suffering; yet even so, you shall welcome your husband's affections, and he shall be your master."

17 And to Adam, God said, "Because you listened to your wife and ate the fruit when I told you not to, I have placed a curse upon the soil. All your life you will struggle to extract a living from it.

18 It will grow thorns and thistles for you, and you shall eat its grasses.

19 All your life you will sweat to master it, until your dying day. Then you will return to the ground from which you came. For you were made from the ground, and to the ground you will return."

* * * * *

20　The man named his wife Eve (meaning[2] "The life-giving one"), for he said, "She shall become the mother of all mankind";

21　And the Lord God clothed Adam and his wife with garments made from skins of animals.

22　Then the Lord said, "Now that the man has become as we are, knowing good from bad, what if he eats the fruit of the Tree of Life and lives forever?"

23　So the Lord God banished him forever from the Garden of Eden, and sent him out to farm the ground from which he had been taken.

24　Thus God expelled him, and placed mighty angels at the east of the garden of Eden, with a flaming sword to guard the entrance to the Tree of Life.

CHAPTER 4

Then Adam had sexual intercourse with Eve his wife, and she conceived and gave birth to a son, Cain (meaning "I have created"). For, as she said, "With God's help, I have created a man!"

2　Her next child was his brother, Abel. Abel became a shepherd, while Cain was a farmer.

3　At harvest time Cain brought the Lord a gift of his farm produce,

4　And Abel brought the fatty cuts of meat from his best lambs, and presented them to the Lord. And the Lord accepted Abel's offering,

5　But not Cain's. This made Cain both dejected and very angry, and his face grew dark with fury.

6　"Why are you angry?" the Lord asked him. "Why is your face so dark with rage?

---

[2]Many Hebrew names are based on puns. In this case for instance, the Hebrew word for *Eve* sounds similar to a Hebrew word that means "life-giving."

7   It can be bright with joy if you will do what you should! But if you refuse to obey, watch out. Sin is waiting to attack you, longing to destroy you. But you can conquer it!"

8   One day Cain suggested to his brother, "Let's go out into the fields." And while they were together there, Cain attacked and killed his brother.

9   But afterwards the Lord asked Cain, "Where is your brother? Where is Abel?"

"How should I know?" Cain retorted. "Am I supposed to keep track of him wherever he goes?"

10   But the Lord said, "Your brother's blood calls to Me from the ground. What have you done?

11   You are hereby banished from this ground which you have defiled with your brother's blood.

12   No longer will it yield crops for you, even if you toil on it forever! From now on you will be a fugitive and a tramp upon the earth, wandering from place to place."

13   Cain replied to the Lord, "My punishment is greater than I can bear.

14   For You have banished me from my farm and from You, and made me a fugitive and a tramp; and everyone who sees me will try to kill me."

15   The Lord replied, "They won't kill you, for I will give seven times your punishment to anyone who does." Then the Lord put an identifying mark on Cain as a warning not to kill him.

16   So Cain went out from the presence of the Lord and settled in the land of Nod, east of Eden.

17   Then Cain's wife conceived and presented him with a baby son named Enoch; so when Cain founded

a city, he named it Enoch, after his son.

18   Enoch was the father[1] of Irad;
Irad was the father[1] of Mehujael;
Mehujael was the father[1] of Methusael;
Methusael was the father[1] of Lamech;

19 Lamech married two wives—Adah and Zillah.

20 To Adah was born a baby named Jabal. He became the first of the cattlemen and those living in tents.

21 His brother's name was Jubal, the first musician—the inventor[2] of the harp and flute.

22 To Lamech's other wife, Zillah, was born Tubal-cain. He opened the first foundry[3] forging instruments of bronze and iron.

23 One day Lamech said to Adah and Zillah, "Listen to me, my wives. I have killed a youth who attacked and wounded me.

24 If anyone who kills Cain will be punished seven times, anyone taking revenge against me for killing that youth should be punished seventy-seven times!"

25 Later on Eve gave birth to another son and named him Seth (meaning "Granted"); for, as Eve put it, "God has granted me another son for the one Cain killed."

26 When Seth grew up, he had a son and named him Enosh. It was during his lifetime[4] that men first began to use the name "Jehovah" when speaking to God.

---

[1]Or, "the ancestor of."
[2]Literally, "He was the father of all such as handle the harp and pipe."
[3]Literally, "He was the father of all metal workers in bronze and iron."
[4]Or, "This man was the first to invoke the name of Jehovah."

CHAPTER 5

Here is a list of some[1] of the descendants of Adam —the man who was like[2] God from the day of his creation.

2 God created man and woman and blessed them, and called them Man from the start.

3 *Adam:*

Adam was 130 years old when his son[3] Seth was born, the very image of his father in every way.[4]

4, 5 After Seth was born,[5] Adam lived another 800 years, producing sons and daughters, and died at the age of 930.

6 *Seth:*

Seth was 105 years old when his son Enosh was born.

7 Afterwards he lived another 807 years, producing sons and daughters,

8 And died at the age of 912.

9 *Enosh:*

Enosh was ninety years old when his son Kenan was born.

10 Afterwards he lived another 815 years, producing sons and daughters,

11 And died at the age of 905.

12 *Kenan:*

Kenan was seventy years old when his son

[1] Literally, "This is the roll of Adam's descendants."
[2] Literally, "In the likeness of God."
[3] Or, by Hebrew usage, "When his son, the *ancestor* (of Seth) was born." So also in verses 6, 9, 12, 15, 18, 21, 25, 28, 32.
[4] Literally, "In his own likeness, after his image."
[5] Or, by Hebrew usage, "After this ancestor of Seth was born."

Mahalalel was born.

13 Afterwards he lived another 840 years, producing sons and daughters,

14 And died at the age of 910.

15 *Mahalalel:*

Mahalalel was sixty-five years old when his son Jared was born.

16 Afterwards he lived 830 years, producing sons and daughters,

17 and died at the age of 895.

18 *Jared:*

Jared was 162 years old when his son Enoch was born.

19 Afterwards he lived another 800 years, producing sons and daughters,

20 And died at the age of 962.

21 *Enoch:*

Enoch was sixty-five years old when his son Methuselah was born.

22 Afterwards he lived another 300 years in fellowship with God, and produced sons and daughters;

23 Then, when he was 365,

24 And in constant touch with God, he disappeared, for God took him!

25 *Methuselah:*

Methuselah was 187 years old when his son Lamech was born;

26 Afterwards he lived another 782 years, producing sons and daughters,

27 And died at the age of 969.

28, 29 *Lamech:*

Lamech was 182 years old when his son

Noah was born. Lamech named him Noah (meaning "Relief") because he said, "He will bring us relief from the hard work of farming this ground which God has cursed."

30   Afterwards Lamech lived 595 years, producing sons and daughters,

31   And died at the age of 777.

32 *Noah:*

Noah was 500 years old and had three sons, Shem, Ham, and Japheth.

CHAPTER 6

Now a population explosion took place upon the earth. It was at this time that beings from the spirit world[1] looked upon the beautiful earth women and took any they desired to be their wives.

3   Then Jehovah said, "My Spirit must not forever be disgraced in man, wholly evil as he is. I will give him 120 years to mend his ways."

4   In those days, and even afterwards, when the evil beings from the spirit world were sexually involved with human women, their children became giants, of whom so many legends are told.

5   When the Lord God saw the extent of human wickedness, and that the trend and direction of men's lives were only towards evil,

6   He was sorry He had made them. It broke His heart.

7   And He said, "I will blot out from the face of the earth all mankind that I created. Yes, and the

---

[1] Literally, "sons of God" used here in the sense of His created, supernatural beings, but no longer godly in character (verse 3).

animals too, and the reptiles and the birds. For I am sorry I made them."

8   But Noah was a pleasure to the Lord. Here is the story of Noah:

9, 10   He was the only truly righteous man living on the earth at that time. He tried always to conduct his affairs according to God's will. And he had three sons—Shem, Ham, and Japheth.

11   Meanwhile, the crime rate was rising rapidly across the earth, and, as seen by God, the world was rotten to the core.

12, 13   As God observed how bad it was, and saw that all mankind was vicious and depraved, He said to Noah, "I have decided to destroy all mankind; for the earth is filled with crime because of man. Yes, I will destroy mankind from the earth.

14   Make a boat from resinous wood, sealing it with tar; and construct decks and stalls throughout the ship.

15   Make it 450 feet long, 75 feet wide, and 45 feet high.

16   Construct a skylight all the way around the ship, eighteen inches below the roof; and make three decks inside the boat—a bottom, middle, and upper deck—and put a door in the side.

17   Look! I am going to cover the earth with a flood and destroy every living being—everything in which there is the breath of life. All will die.

18   But I promise to keep you safe in the ship, with your wife and your sons and their wives.

19, 20   Bring a pair of every animal—a male and a female—into the boat with you, to keep them alive through the flood. Bring in a pair of each kind of bird and animal and reptile.

21   Store away in the boat all the food that they and you will need."

22   And Noah did everything as God commanded him.

CHAPTER 7

Finally the day came when the Lord said to Noah, "Go into the boat with all your family, for among all the people of the earth, I consider you alone to be righteous.

2   Bring in the animals, too—a pair of each, except those kinds I have chosen for eating and for sacrifice: take seven pairs of each of them,

3   And seven pairs[1] of every kind of bird. Thus there will be every kind of life reproducing again after the flood has ended.

4   One week from today I will begin forty days and nights of rain; and all the animals and birds and reptiles I have made will die."

5   So Noah did everything the Lord commanded him.

6   He was 600 years old when the flood came.

7   He boarded the boat with his wife and sons and their wives, to escape the flood.

8, 9   With him were all the various kinds of animals—those for eating and sacrifice, and those that were not, and the birds and reptiles. They came into the boat in pairs, male and female, just as God commanded Noah.

*   *   *   *   *

10, 11, 12   One week later, when Noah was 600 years, two months, and seventeen days old, the rain

---

[1]Literally, "the male and female."

came down in mighty torrents from the sky, and the subterranean waters burst forth upon the earth for forty days and nights.

13 But Noah had gone into the boat that very day with his wife and his sons, Shem, Ham, and Japheth, and their wives.

14, 15 With them in the boat were pairs of every kind of animal—domestic and wild—and reptiles and birds of every sort.

16 Two by two they came, male and female, just as God had commanded. Then the Lord God[2] closed the door and shut them in.

17 For forty days the roaring floods prevailed, covering the ground and lifting the boat high above the earth.

18 As the water rose higher and higher above the ground, the boat floated safely upon it;

19 Until finally the water covered all the high mountains under the whole heaven,

20 Standing twenty-two feet and more above the highest peaks.

21 And all living things upon the earth perished— birds, domestic and wild animals, and reptiles and all mankind—

22 Everything that breathed and lived upon dry land.

23 All existence on the earth was blotted out— man and animals alike, and reptiles and birds. God destroyed them all, leaving only Noah alive, and those with him in the boat.

24 And the water covered the earth 150 days.

_____
[2]Literally, "Jehovah."

CHAPTER 8

God didn't forget about Noah and all the animals in the boat! He sent a wind to blow across the waters, and the floods began to disappear,

2 For the subterranean water sources ceased their gushing, and the torrential rains subsided.

3, 4 So the flood gradually receded until, 150 days after it began, the boat came to rest upon the mountains of Ararat.

5 Three months later,[1] as the waters continued to go down, other mountain peaks appeared.

6 After another forty days, Noah opened a porthole

7 And released a raven that flew back and forth[2] until the earth was dry.

8 Meanwhile he sent out a dove to see if it could find dry ground,

9 But the dove found no place to light, and returned to Noah, for the water was still too high. So Noah held out his hand and drew the dove back into the boat.

10 Seven days later Noah released the dove again,

11 And this time, towards evening, the bird returned to him with an olive leaf in her beak. So Noah knew that the water was almost gone.

12 A week later he released the dove again, and this time she didn't come back.

---

[1]Literally, "on the first day of the tenth month."
[2]Apparently lighting from time to time upon carcasses of dead animals floating on the water. The dove which Noah next dispatched would not alight on such floating carrion, and was thus a good indication of the water level.

13 Twenty-nine days after that,[3] Noah opened the door to look, and the water was gone.

14 Eight more weeks went by. Then at last the earth was dry.

15, 16 Then God told Noah, "You may all go out.

17 Release all the animals, birds, and reptiles, so that they will breed abundantly and reproduce in great numbers."

18, 19 So the boat was soon empty. Noah, his wife, and his sons and their wives all disembarked, along with all the animals, reptiles, and birds—all left the ark in pairs and groups.

20 Then Noah built an altar and sacrificed on it some of the animals and birds God had designated[4] for that purpose.

21 And Jehovah was pleased with[5] the sacrifice and said to Himself, "I will never do it again—I will never again curse the earth, destroying all living things, even though man's bent is always toward evil from his earliest youth, and even though he does such wicked things.

22 As long as the earth remains, there will be springtime and harvest, cold and heat, winter and summer, day and night."

CHAPTER 9

G od blessed Noah and his sons and told them to have many children and to repopulate the earth.

---

[3]Literally, "in the 601st year, in the first month, the first day of the month."
[4]Literally, "clean," i.e., ritually approved by God.
[5]Literally, "and Jehovah smelled the delicious odor and said . . ."

2, 3 "All wild animals and birds and fish will be afraid of you," God told him; "for I have placed them in your power, and they are yours to use for food, in addition to grain and vegetables.

4 But never eat animals unless their life-blood has been drained off.

5, 6 And murder is forbidden. Man-killing animals must die, and any man who murders shall be killed; for to kill a man is to kill one made like God.

7 Yes, have many children and repopulate the earth and subdue it."

8 Then God told Noah and his sons,

9, 10, 11 "I solemnly promise you and your children[1] and the animals you brought with you—all these birds and cattle and wild animals—that I will never again send another flood to destroy the earth.

12 And I seal this promise with this sign:

13 I have placed My rainbow in the clouds as a sign of My promise until the end of time, to you and to all the earth.

14 When I send clouds over the earth, the rainbow will be seen in the clouds,

15 And I will remember My promise to you and to every being, that never again will the floods come and destroy all life.

16, 17 For I will see the rainbow in the cloud and remember My eternal promise to every living being on the earth."

18 The names of Noah's three sons were Shem, Ham, and Japheth. (Ham is the ancestor of the Canaanites.)[2]

---

[1]Literally, "your seed."
[2]Ham was not the ancestor of the Negro, as was once erroneously supposed.

19 From these three sons of Noah came all the nations of the earth.

20, 21 Noah became a farmer and planted a vineyard, and he made wine. One day as he was drunk and lay naked in his tent,

22 Ham, the father of Canaan, saw his father's nakedness and went outside and told his two brothers.

23 Then Shem and Japheth took a robe and held it over their shoulders and, walking backwards into the tent, let it fall across their father to cover his nakedness as they looked the other way.

24, 25 When Noah awoke from his drunken stupor, and learned what had happened and what Ham, his younger son had done, he cursed Ham's descendants:[3]

> "A curse upon the Canaanites," he swore.
> "May they be the lowest of slaves
> To the descendants of Shem and Japheth."

26, 27 Then he said,

> "God bless Shem,
> And may Canaan be his slave.[4]
> God bless Japheth,
> And let him share the prosperity of Shem,
> And let Canaan be his slave."

28 Noah lived another 350 years after the flood,

29 And was 950 years old at his death.

CHAPTER 10

These are the families of Shem, Ham, and Japheth, who were the three sons of Noah; for sons were born to them after the flood.

---

[3]Literally, "cursed be Canaan." The Canaanites were Ham's descendants.
[4]Or, "Blessed be Jehovah, the God of Shem . . . and may the Canaanites be Shem's slaves."

* * * * *

2 The sons[1] of Japheth were:
Gomer,
Magog,
Madai,
Javan,
Tubal,
Meshech,
Tiras.

3 The sons of Gomer:
Ashkenaz,
Riphath,
Togarmah.

4 The sons of Javan:
Elishah,
Tarshish,
Kittim,
Dodanim.

5 Their descendants became the maritime nations in various lands, each with a separate language.

* * * * *

6 The sons of Ham were:
Cush,
Mizraim,
Put,
Canaan.

7 The sons of Cush were:
Seba,
Havilah,
Sabtah,
Raamah,
Sabteca.

---

[1]"descendants."

The sons of Raamah were:
Sheba,
Dedan.

8 One of the descendants[2] of Cush was Nimrod, who became the first of the kings.

9 He was a mighty hunter, blessed of God, and his name became proverbial. People would speak of someone as being "like Nimrod—a mighty hunter, blessed of God."

10 The heart of his empire included Babel, Erech, Accad, and Calneh in the land of Shinar.

11, 12 From there he extended his reign to Assyria. He built Nineveh, Rehoboth-Ir, Calah, and Resen (which is located between Ninevah and Calah), the main city of the empire.

13 Mizraim was the ancestor[3] of the people inhabiting these areas:
Ludim,
Anamim,
Lehabim,
Naphtuhim,
14   Pathrusim,
Casluhim (from whom came the
Philistines), and
Caphtorim.

15 Canaan's oldest son was Sidon, and he was also the father of Heth;

16 From Canaan descended these nations:
Jebusites,
Amorites,
Girgashites,

[2]Or, "the son of Cush."
[3]Or, "father."

17   Hivites,
            Arkites,
            Sinites,
18, 19   Arvadites,
            Zemarites,
            Hamathites.

Eventually the descendants of Canaan spread from Sidon all the way to Gerar, in the Gaza strip; and to Sodom, Gomorrah, Admah, and Zeboim, near Lasha.

20   These, then, were the descendants of Ham, spread abroad in many lands and nations, with many languages.

*   *   *   *   *

21   Eber descended from Shem, the oldest brother of Japheth.

22   Here is a list of Shem's other descendants:
            Elam,
            Asshur,
            Arpachshad,
            Lud,
            Aram.

23   Aram's sons[4] were:
            Uz,
            Hul,
            Gether,
            Mash.

24   Arpachshad's son was Shelah, and Shelah's son was Eber.

25   Two sons were born to Eber:
            Peleg (meaning "Division," for during his lifetime the people of the world were separated and dispersed), and

----

[4]Or, "descendants."

Joktan (Peleg's brother).

26 Joktan was the father[5] of
Almodad,
Sheleph,
Hazarmaveth,
Jerah.
27 Hadoram,
Uzal,
Diklah,
28 Obal,
Abima-el,
Sheba,
29, 30 Ophir,
Havi-lah,
Jobab.

These descendants of Joktan lived all the way from Mesha to the eastern hills of Sephar.

31 These, then, were the descendants of Shem, classified according to their political groupings, languages, and geographical locations.

* * * * *

32 All of the men listed above descended from Noah, through many generations, living in the various nations that developed after the flood.

CHAPTER 11

At that time all mankind spoke a single language.

2 As the population grew and spread eastward, a plain was discovered in the land of Babylon,[1] and was soon thickly populated.[2]

3, 4 The people who lived there began to talk

---

[5]Or, "ancestor."
[1]Literally, "the land of Shinar," located at the mouth of the Persian Gulf.
[2]Literally, "and they settled there."

about building a great city, with a temple-tower reaching to the skies—a proud, eternal monument to themselves. "This will weld us together," they said, "and keep us from scattering all over the world." So they made great piles of hard-burned brick, and collected bitumen to use as mortar.

5 But when God came down to see the city and the tower mankind was making,

6 He said, "Look! If they are able to accomplish all this when they have just *begun* to exploit their linguistic and political unity, just think of what they will do later! Nothing will be unattainable for them![3]

7 Come, let us go down and give them different languages, so that they won't understand each other's words!"

8 So, in that way, God scattered them all over the earth; and that ended the building of the city.

9 That is why the city was called Babel (meaning "confusion"), because it was there that Jehovah confused them by giving them many languages, thus widely scattering them across the face of the earth.

* * * * *

10, 11 Shem's line of descendants included Arpachshad, born two years after the flood when Shem was 100 years old; after that he lived another 500 years, and had many sons and daughters.

12, 13 When Arpachshad was thirty-five years old, his son[4] Shelah was born, and after that he lived another 403 years, and had many sons and daughters.

---

[3]Language is the basis on which science feeds upon itself and grows. This was the beginning of an explosion of knowledge, nipped in the bud because of wrong motives and wrong use of the knowledge gained. Similarity with today's world is significant.
[4]Or, by Hebrew usage, "there was born to him the ancestor of Shelah, and after that . . ." So also throughout the remainder of the chapter.

14, 15   Shelah was thirty years old when his son Eber was born, living 403 years after that, and had many sons and daughters.

16, 17   Eber was thirty-four years old when his son Peleg was born. He lived another 430 years afterwards and had many sons and daughters.

18, 19   Peleg was thirty years old when his son Reu was born. He lived another 209 years afterwards, and had many sons and daughters.

20, 21   Reu was thirty-two years old when Serug was born. He lived 207 years after that, with many sons and daughters.

22, 23   Serug was thirty years old when his son Nahor was born. He lived 200 years afterwards, with many sons and daughters.

24, 25   Nahor was twenty-nine years old at the birth of his son Terah. He lived 119 years afterwards, and had sons and daughters.

26   By the time Terah was seventy years old, he had three sons, Abram, Nahor, and Haran.

27   And Haran had a son named Lot.

28   But Haran died young, in the land where he was born (in Ur of the Chaldeans), and was survived by his father.

29   Meanwhile, Abram married his half-sister[5] Sarai, while his brother Nahor married their orphaned niece Milcah,[6] who was the daughter of their brother
[6]Implied.
Haran; and she had a brother named Iscah.

30   But Sarai was barren; she had no children.

31   Then Terah took his son Abram, his grandson Lot (his son Haran's child), and his daughter-in-law

---

[5]Implied. See Genesis 20:12.

Sarai, and left Ur of the Chaldeans to go to the land of Canaan; but they stopped instead at the city of Haran and settled there.

32　And there Terah died at the age of 205.[7]

CHAPTER 12

After the death of Abram's father, God told him, "Leave your own country behind you, and your own people, and go to the land I will guide you to.

2　If you do, I will cause you to become the father of a great nation; I will bless you and make your name famous, and you will be a blessing to many others.[1]

3　I will bless those who bless you and curse those who curse you; and the entire world will be blessed because of you."[2]

4　So Abram departed as the Lord had instructed him, and Lot went too; Abram was seventy-five years old at that time.

5　He took his wife Sarai, his nephew Lot, and all his wealth—the cattle and slaves he had gotten in Haran—and finally arrived in Canaan.

6　Traveling through Canaan, they came to a place near Shechem, and set up camp beside the oak at Moreh. (This area was inhabited by Canaanites at that time.)

7　Then Jehovah appeared to Abram and said, "I am going to give this land to your descendants." And Abram built an altar there to commemorate Jehovah's visit.

---

[7]Implied. The Samaritan Pentateuch says that Terah died when he was 145 years old, so that his death occurred in the year of Abraham's departure from Haran. This is more consistent with Genesis 11:26 and 12:4. See also Acts 7:4.
[1]Or, "I will make your name so famous that it will be used to pronounce blessings on others."
[2]Or, "The nations will bless themselves because of you."

8   Afterwards Abram left that place and traveled southward³ to the hilly country between Bethel on the west and Ai on the east. There he made camp, and made an altar to the Lord and prayed to Him.

9   Thus he continued slowly southward to the Negeb, pausing frequently.

10   There was at that time a terrible famine in the land: and so Abram went on down to Egypt to live.

11, 12, 13   But as he was approaching the borders of Egypt, he asked Sarai his wife to tell everyone that she was his sister! "You are very beautiful," he told her, "and when the Egyptians see you they will say, 'This is his wife. Let's kill him and then we can have her!' But if you say you are my sister, then the Egyptians will treat me well because of you, and spare my life!"

14   And sure enough, when they arrived in Egypt everyone spoke of her beauty.

15   When the palace aides saw her, they praised her to their king, the Pharaoh, and she was taken into his harem.⁴

16   Then Pharaoh gave Abram many gifts because of her—sheep, oxen, donkeys, men and women slaves, and camels.

17   But the Lord sent a terrible plague upon Pharaoh's household on account of her being there.

18   Then Pharaoh called Abram before him and accused him sharply. "What is this you have done to me?" he demanded. "Why didn't you tell me she was your wife?

19   Why did you let me marry her, saying she

---

³Implied.
⁴Literally, "into the household of Pharaoh."

was your sister? Here, take her and be gone!"

20　And Pharaoh sent them out of the country under armed escort—Abram, his wife, and all his household and possessions.

CHAPTER 13

S o they left Egypt and traveled north into the Negeb —Abram with his wife, and Lot, and all that they owned, for Abram was very rich in livestock, silver, and gold.

3, 4　Then they continued northward toward Bethel where he had camped before, between Bethel and Ai—to the place where he had built the altar. And there he again worshiped the Lord.

5　Lot too was very wealthy, with sheep and cattle and many servants.[1]

6　But the land could not support both Abram and Lot with all their flocks and herds. There were too many animals for the available pasture.

7　So fights broke out between the herdsmen of Abram and Lot, despite the danger they all faced[2] from the tribes of Canaanites and Perizzites present in the land.

8　Then Abram talked it over with Lot. "This fighting between our men has got to stop," he said. "We can't afford to let a rift develop between our clans. Close relatives such as we are must present a united front!

9　I'll tell you what we'll do. Take your choice of any section of the land you want, and we will separate. If you want that part over there to the east, then

---

[1]Implied. Literally, "many tents."
[2]Implied.

I'll stay here in the western section. Or, if you want the west, then I'll go over there to the east."

10 Lot took a long look at the fertile plains of the Jordan River, well watered everywhere (this was before Jehovah destroyed Sodom and Gomorrah): the whole section was like the Garden of Eden,[3] or like the beautiful countryside around Zoar in Egypt.

11 So that is what Lot chose—the Jordan valley to the east of them. He went there with his flocks and servants, and thus he and Abram parted company.

12 For Abram stayed in the land of Canaan, while Lot lived among the cities of the plain, settling at a place near the city of Sodom.

13 The men of this area were unusually wicked, and sinned greatly against Jehovah.

14 After Lot was gone, the Lord said to Abram, "Look as far as you can see in every direction,

15 For I am going to give it all to you and your descendants.

16 And I am going to give you so many descendants that, like dust, they can't be counted!

17 Hike in all directions and explore the new possessions I am giving you."

18 Then Abram moved his tent to the oaks of Mamre, near Hebron, and built an altar to Jehovah there.

CHAPTER 14

Now war filled the land—
      Amraphel, king of Shinar,
      Arioch, king of Ellasar,
      Ched-or-laomer, king of Elam, and

---

[3] Literally, "the Garden of Jehovah."

Tidal, king of Goiim
2   Fought against:
Bera, king of Sodom,
Birsha, king of Gomorrah,
Shinab, king of Admah,
Shemeber, King of Zeboiim, and
The king of Bela (later called Zoar).

3   These kings (of Sodom, Gomorrah, Admah, Zeboiim, and Bela) mobilized their armies in Siddim Valley (that is, the valley of the Salt Sea).

4   For twelve years they had all been subject to King Ched-or-laomer, but now in the thirteenth year, they rebelled.

5   One year later, Ched-or-laomer and his allies arrived and the slaughter began. For they were victorious over the following tribes at the places indicated:
The Rephaim in Ashteroth-karnaim;
The Zuzim in Ham;
The Emim in the plain of Kiriathaim,

6   The Horites in Mount Seir, as far as El-paran at the edge of the desert.

7   Then they swung around to Enmishpat (later called Kadesh) and destroyed the Amalekites, and also the Amorites living in Hazazan-tamar.

8, 9   But now the other army, that of the kings of Sodom, Gomorrah, Admah, Zeboiim, and Bela (Zoar), unsuccessfully[1] attacked Ched-or-laomer and his allies as they were in the Salt Sea Valley (four kings against five).

10   As it happened, the valley was full of asphalt pits. And as the army of the kings of Sodom and

[1]Implied.

Gomorrah fled, some slipped into the pits, and the remainder fled to the mountains.

11 Then the victors plundered[2] Sodom and Gomorrah and carried off all their wealth and food, and went on their homeward way,

12 Taking with them Lot—Abram's nephew[3] who lived in Sodom—and all he owned.

13 One of the men who escaped came and told Abram the Hebrew, who was camping among the oaks belonging to Mamre the Amorite (brother of Eshcol and Aner, Abram's allies).

14 When Abram learned that Lot had been captured, he called together the men born into his household, 318 of them in all, and chased after the retiring army as far as Dan.

15 That night he successfully attacked them and pursued the fleeing army to Hobah, north of Damascus,

16 And recovered everything—the loot that had been taken, his relative Lot, and all of Lot's possessions, including the women and other captives.

17 As Abram returned from his strike against Ched-or-laomer and the other kings at the Valley of Shaveh (later called King's Valley), the king of Sodom came out to meet him,

18 And Melchizedek, the king of Salem (Jerusalem), who was a priest of the God of Highest Heaven, brought him bread and wine.

19 Then Melchizedek blessed Abram with this blessing:

> "The blessing of the supreme God, Creator
> of heaven and earth, be upon you, Abram;

---

[2]Implied from context.
[3]Literally, "Abram's brother's son."

20   And blessed be God, who has delivered your enemies over to you."

Then Abram gave Medchizedek a tenth of all the spoils.

21   The king of Sodom told him, "Just give me back my people who were captured; keep for yourself the booty stolen from my city."

22   But Abram replied, "I have solemnly promised Jehovah, the supreme God, Creator of heaven and earth,

23   That I will not take so much as a single thread from you, lest you say, 'Abram is rich because of what I gave him!'

24   All I'll accept is what these young men of mine have eaten: but give a share of the booty to Aner, Eshcol, and Mamre, my allies."

CHAPTER 15

A fterwards Jehovah spoke to Abram in a vision, and this is what He told him: "Don't be fearful, Abram, for I will defend you. And I will give you great blessings."

2   But Abram replied, "O Lord Jehovah, what good are all Your blessings when I have no son? For without a son, some other member of my household[1] will inherit all my wealth."

4   Then Jehovah told him, "No, no one else will be your heir, for you will have a son to inherit everything you own."

5   Then God brought Abram outside beneath the nighttime sky and told him, "Look up into the heavens and count the stars if you can. Your descendants will be like that—too many to count!"

[1]Or, "Eliezer of Damascus."

6   And Abram believed God; then God considered him righteous on account of his faith.

7   And He told him, "I am Jehovah who brought you out of the city of Ur of the Chaldeans, to give you this land forever."

8   But Abram replied, "O Lord Jehovah, how can I be sure that You will give it to me?"

9   Then Jehovah told him to take a three-year-old heifer, a three-year-old female goat, a three-year-old ram, a turtle-dove and a young pigeon,

10   And to slay them and to cut them apart down the middle, and to separate the halves, but not to divide the birds.

11   And when the vultures came down upon the carcasses, Abram shooed them away.

12   That evening as the sun was going down, a deep sleep fell upon Abram, and a vision of terrible foreboding, darkness, and horror.

13   Then Jehovah told Abram, "Your descendants will be oppressed as slaves in a foreign land for 400 years.

14   But I will punish the nation that enslaves them, and at the end they will come away with great wealth.

15   (But you will die in peace, at a ripe old age.)

16   After four generations they will return here to this land; for the wickedness of the Amorite nations living here now[2] will not be ready for punishment until then."

17   As the sun went down and it was dark, Abram saw a smoking fire-pot and a flaming torch that passed between the halves of the carcasses.

18   So that day Jehovah made this covenant with

[2]Implied.

Abram: "I have given this land to your descendants from the Wadi-el-Arish[3] to the Euphrates River.

19 And I give to them these nations:

       Kenites,

       Kenizzites,

       Kadmonites,

20   Hittites,

       Perizzites,

       Rephaim,

21   Amorites,

       Canaanites,

       Girgashites,

       Jebusites."

CHAPTER 16

But Sarai and Abram had no children. So Sarai took her maid, an Egyptian girl named Hagar,

2, 3 And gave her to Abram to be his second wife. "Since the Lord has given me no children," Sarai said, "you may sleep with my servant girl, and her children shall be mine." And Abram agreed. (This took place ten years after Abram had first arrived in the land of Canaan.)

4 So he slept with Hagar, and she conceived; and when she realized she was pregnant, she became very proud and arrogant toward her mistress Sarai.

5 Then Sarai said to Abram, "It's all your fault. For now this servant girl of mine despises me, though I myself gave her the privilege of being your wife. May the Lord judge you for doing this to me!"[1]

6 "You have my permission to punish the girl as

---

[3]Literally, "River of Egypt," at the southern border of Judah.
[1]Literally, "Let the Lord judge between me and you."

you see fit," Abram replied. So Sarai beat her and she ran away.

7 The Angel of the Lord found her beside a desert spring along the road to Shur.

8 *The Angel:* "Hagar, Sarai's maid, where have you come from, and where are you going?"

Hagar: "I am running away from my mistress."

9 *The Angel:* "Return to your mistress and act as you should,

10 For I will make you into a great nation.

11 Yes, you are pregnant and your baby will be a son, and you are to name him Ishmael ("God hears"), because God has heard your woes.

12 This son of yours will be a wild one—free and untamed as a wild ass! He will be against everyone, and everyone will feel the same towards him. But he will live near the rest of his kin."

13 Thereafter[2] Hagar spoke of Jehovah—for it was He who appeared to her—as "the God who looked upon me," for she thought, "I saw God and lived to tell it."

14 Later that well was named "The Well of the Living One Who Sees Me." It lies between Kadesh and Bered.

15 So Hagar gave Abram a son, and Abram named him Ishmael.

16 (Abram was eighty-six years old at this time.)

---

[2]Implied.

CHAPTER 17

When Abram was ninety-nine years old, God appeared to him and told him, "I am the Almighty; obey Me and live as you should.

2, 3, 4 I will prepare a contract between us, guaranteeing to make you into a mighty nation. In fact you shall be the father of not only one nation, but a multitude of nations!" Abram fell face downward in the dust as God talked with him.

5 "What's more," God told him, "I am changing your name. It is no longer 'Abram' ('Exalted Father'), but 'Abraham' ('Father of Nations')—for that is what you will be. I have declared it.

6 I will give you millions of descendants who will form many nations! Kings shall be among your descendants!

7, 8 And I will continue this agreement between us generation after generation, forever, for it shall be between Me and your children as well. It is a contract that I shall be your God and the God of your posterity. And I will give all this land of Canaan to you and them, forever. And I will be your God.

9, 10 Your part of the contract," God told him, "is to obey its terms. You personally and all your posterity have this continual responsibility: that every male among you shall be circumcised;

11 The foreskin of his penis shall be cut off. This will be the proof that you and they accept this covenant.

12 Every male shall be circumcised on the eighth day after birth. This applies to every foreign-born slave as well as to everyone born in your household. This is a permanent part of this contract, and it applies

to all your posterity.

13 All must be circumcised. Your bodies will thus be marked as participants in My everlasting covenant.

14 Anyone who refuses these terms shall be cut off from his people; for he has violated My contract."

15 Then God added, "Regarding Sarai your wife— her name is no longer 'Sarai' but 'Sarah' ('Princess').

16 And I will bless her and give you a son from her! Yes, I will bless her richly, and make her the mother of nations! Many kings shall be among your posterity."

17 Then Abraham threw himself down in worship before the Lord, but inside he was laughing in disbelief! "Me, be a father?" he said in amusement, "Me— 100 years old? And Sarah, to have a baby at 90?"

18 And Abraham said to God, "Yes, do bless Ishmael!"

19 "No," God replied, "that isn't what I said. *Sarah* shall bear you a son; and you are to name him Isaac ('Laughter'), and I will sign My covenant with him forever, and with his descendants.

20 As for Ishmael, all right, I will bless him also, just as you have asked Me to. I will cause him to multiply and become a great nation. Twelve princes shall be among his posterity.

21 But My contract is with Isaac, who will be born to you and Sarah next year at about this time."

22 That ended the conversation and God left.

23 Then, that very day, Abraham took Ishmael his son and every other male—born in his household or bought from outside—and cut off their foreskins, just as God had told him to.

24, 25, 26, 27 Abraham was ninety-nine years old at that time, and Ishmael was thirteen. Both were circumcised the same day, along with all the other men and boys of the household, whether born there or bought as slaves.

CHAPTER 18

The Lord appeared again to Abraham while he was living in the oak grove at Mamre. This is the way it happened: One hot summer afternoon as he was sitting in the opening of his tent,

2 He suddenly noticed three men coming toward him. He sprang up and ran to meet them and welcomed them.

3, 4 "Sirs," he said, "please don't go any further. Stop awhile and rest here in the shade of this tree while I get water to refresh your feet,

5 And a bite to eat to strengthen you. Do stay awhile before continuing your journey."

"All right," they said, "do as you have said."

6 Then Abraham ran back to the tent and said to Sarah, "Quick! Mix up some pancakes![1] Use your best flour, and make enough for the three of them!"

7 Then he ran out to the herd and selected a fat calf and told a servant to hurry and butcher it.

8 Soon, taking them cheese and milk and the roast veal, he set it before the men and stood beneath the tree beside them as they ate.

9 "Where is Sarah, your wife?" they asked him.

"In the tent," Abraham replied.

10 Then the Lord said, "Next year[2] I will give you

---

[1] Probably some sort of *tortilla*.
[2] Literally, "when life would be due."

and Sarah a son!" (Sarah was listening from the tent door behind him.)

11 Now Abraham and Sarah were both very old, and Sarah was long since past the time when she could have a baby.

12 So Sarah laughed silently. "A woman my age have a baby?" she scoffed to herself. "And with a husband as old as mine?"

13 Then God said to Abraham, "Why did Sarah laugh? Why did she say 'Can an old woman like me have a baby?'

14 Is anything too hard for God? Next year, just as I told you, I will certainly see to it that Sarah has a son."

15 But Sarah denied it. "I didn't laugh," she lied, for she was afraid.

16 Then the men stood up from their meal and started on toward Sodom; and Abraham went with them part of the way.

17 "Should I hide my plan from Abraham?" God asked.

18 "For Abraham shall become a mighty nation, and he will be a source of blessing for all the nations of the earth.

19 And I have picked him out to have godly descendants and a godly household—men who are just and good—so that I can do for him all I have promised."

20 So the Lord told Abraham, "I have heard that the people of Sodom and Gomorrah are utterly evil, and that everything they do is wicked.

21 I am going down to see whether these reports are true or not. Then I will know."

22, 23 So the other two went on toward Sodom, but the Lord remained with Abraham a while. Then Abraham approached Him and said, "Will you kill good and bad alike?

24 Suppose you find fifty godly people there within the city—will You destroy it, and not spare it for their sakes?

25 That wouldn't be right! Surely You wouldn't do such a thing, to kill the godly with the wicked! Why, You would be treating godly and wicked exactly the same! Surely You wouldn't do that! Should not the Judge of all the earth be fair?"

26 And God replied, "If I find fifty godly people there, I will spare the entire city for their sake."

27 Then Abraham spoke again. "Since I have begun, let me go on and speak further to the Lord, though I am but dust and ashes.

28 *Suppose there are only forty-five?* Will You destroy the city for lack of five?"

And God said, "I will not destroy it if I find forty-five."

29 Then Abraham went further with his request. *"Suppose there are only forty?"* And God replied, "I won't destroy it if there are forty."

30 "Please don't be angry," Abraham pleaded. "Let me speak: *suppose only thirty are found there?"*

And God replied, "I won't do it if there are thirty there."

31 Then Abraham said, "Since I have dared to speak to God, let me continue—*Suppose there are only twenty?"*

And God said, "Then I won't destroy it for the sake of the twenty."

32   Finally, Abraham said, "Oh, let not the Lord be angry; I will speak but this once more! *Suppose only ten are found?"*

And God said, "Then, for the sake of the ten, I won't destroy it."

33   And the Lord went on His way when He had finished His conversation with Abraham. And Abraham returned to his tent.

CHAPTER 19

That evening the two angels came to the entrance of the city of Sodom, and Lot was sitting there as they arrived. When he saw them he stood up to meet them, and welcomed them.

2   "Sirs," he said, "come to my home as my guests for the night; you can get up as early as you like and be on your way again."

"Oh, no thanks," they said, "we'll just stretch out here along the street."

3   But he was very urgent, until at last they went home with him, and he set a great feast before them, complete with freshly baked unleavened bread. After the meal,

4   As they were preparing to retire for the night, the men of the city—yes, Sodomites, young and old from all over the city—surrounded the house

5   And shouted to Lot, "Bring out those men to us so we can rape them."

6   Lot stepped outside to talk to them, shutting the door behind him.

7   "Please, fellows," he begged, "don't do such a wicked thing.

8 Look—I have two virgin daughters, and I'll surrender them to you to do with as you wish. But leave these men alone, for they are under my protection."

9 "Stand back," they yelled. "Who do you think you are? We let this fellow settle among us and now he tries to tell us what to do! We'll deal with you far worse than with those other men." And they lunged at Lot and began breaking down the door.

10 But the two men reached out and pulled Lot in and bolted the door,

11 And temporarily blinded the men of Sodom so that they couldn't find the door.

12 "What relatives do you have here in the city?" the men asked. "Get them out of this place—sons-in-law, sons, daughters, or anyone else.

13 For we will destroy the city completely. The stench of the place has reached to heaven and God has sent us to destroy it."

14 So Lot rushed out to tell his daughters' fiancés, "Quick, get out of the city, for the Lord is going to destroy it." But the young men looked at him as though he had lost his senses.

15 At dawn the next morning the angels became urgent. "Hurry," they said to Lot, "take your wife and your two daughters who are here and get out while you can, or you will be caught in the destruction of the city."

16 When Lot still hesitated, the angels seized his hand and the hands of his wife and two daughters and rushed them to safety, outside the city, for the Lord was merciful.

17 "Flee for your lives," the angels told him. "And don't look back. Escape to the mountains. Don't stay down here on the plain or you will die."

18, 19, 20 "Oh no, sirs, please," Lot begged, "since you've been so kind to me and saved my life, and you've granted me such mercy, let me flee to that little village over there instead of into the mountains, for I fear disaster in the mountain. See, the village is close by and it is just a small one. Please, please, let me go there instead. Don't you see how small it is? And my life will be saved."

21 "All right," the angel said, "I accept your proposition and won't destroy that little city.

22 But hurry! For I can do nothing until you are there." (From that time on that village was named Zoar, meaning "Little City.")

23 The sun was rising as Lot reached the village.

24 Then the Lord rained down fire and flaming tar from heaven upon Sodom and Gomorrah,

25 And utterly destroyed them, along with the other cities and villages of the plain, eliminating all life—people, plants, and animals alike.

26 But Lot's wife looked back as she was following along behind him, and became a pillar of salt.

27 That morning Abraham was up early and hurried out to the place where he had stood before the Lord.

28 He looked out across the plain to Sodom and Gomorrah and saw columns of smoke and fumes, as from a furnace, rising from the cities there.

29 So God heeded Abraham's plea and kept Lot safe, removing him from the maelstrom of death that engulfed the cities.

30   Afterwards Lot left Zoar, fearful of the people there, and went to live in a cave in the mountains with his two daughters.

31   One day the older girl said to her sister, "There isn't a man anywhere in this entire area that our father would let us marry. And our father will soon be too old for having children.

32   Come, let's fill him with wine and then we will sleep with him, so that our clan will not come to an end."

33   So they got him drunk that night, and the older girl went in and had sexual intercourse with her father; but he was unaware of her lying down or getting up again.

34   The next morning she said to her younger sister, "I slept with my father last night. Let's fill him with wine again tonight, and you go in and lie with him, so that our family line will continue."

35   So they got him drunk again that night, and the younger girl went in and lay with him, and, as before, he didn't know that anyone was there.

36   And so it was that both girls became pregnant from their father.

37   The older girl's baby was named Moab; he became the ancestor of the nation of the Moabites.

38   The name of the younger girl's baby was Ben-ammi; he became the ancestor of the nation of the Ammonites.

CHAPTER 20

Now Abraham moved south to the Negeb, and settled between Kadesh and Shur. One day, when visiting the city of Gerar,

2   He remarked that Sarah was his sister! Then King Abimelech sent for her, and had her brought to him at his palace.

3   But that night God came to him in a dream and told him, "You are a dead man, for that woman you took is married."

4   But Abimelech hadn't slept with her yet, so he said, "Lord, will You slay an innocent man?

5   He told me, 'She is my sister,' and she herself said, 'Yes, he is my brother.' I hadn't the slightest intention of doing anything wrong."

6   "Yes, I know," the Lord replied. "That is why I held you back from sinning against Me; that is why I didn't let you touch her.

7   Now restore her to her husband, and he will pray for you (for he is a prophet) and you shall live. But if you don't return her to him, you are doomed to death along with all your household."

8   The king was up early the next morning, and hastily called a meeting of all the palace personnel and told them what had happened. And great fear swept through the crowd.

9, 10   Then the king called for Abraham. "What is this you've done to us?" he demanded. "What have I done that deserves treatment like this, to make me and my kingdom guilty of this great sin? Who would suspect that you would do a thing like this to me? Whatever made you think of this vile deed?"

11, 12   "Well," Abraham said, "I figured this to be a godless place. 'They will want my wife and will kill me to get her,' I thought. And besides, she *is* my sister —or at least a half-sister (we both have the same father)—and I married her.

13 And when God sent me traveling far from my childhood home, I told her, 'Have the kindness to mention, wherever we come, that you are my sister.' "

14 Then King Abimelech took sheep and oxen and servants—both men and women—and gave them to Abraham, and returned Sarah his wife to him.

15 "Look my kingdom over, and choose the place where you want to live," the king told him.

16 Then he turned to Sarah. "Look," he said, "I am giving your 'brother' a thousand silver pieces as damages for what I did, to compensate for any embarrassment and to settle any claim against me regarding this matter. Now justice has been done."

17 Then Abraham prayed, asking God to cure the king and queen and the other women of the household, so that they could have children;

18 For God had stricken all the women with barrenness to punish Abimelech for taking Abraham's wife.

CHAPTER 21

Then God did as He had promised, and Sarah became pregnant and gave Abraham a baby son in his old age, at the time God had said;

3 And Abraham named him Isaac (meaning "Laughter!").

4, 5 Eight days after he was born, Abraham circumcised him, as God required. (Abraham was 100 years old at that time.)

6 And Sarah declared, "God has brought me laughter! All who hear about this shall rejoice with me.

7 For who would have dreamed that I would ever have a baby? Yet I have given Abraham a child in

his old age!"

8   Time went by and the child grew and was weaned; and Abraham threw a big party to celebrate the happy occasion.

9   But when Sarah noticed Ishmael—the son of Abraham and the Egyptian girl Hagar—playing[1] with Isaac,

10   She turned upon Abraham and demanded, "Get rid of that slave girl and her son. He is not going to share your property with my son. I won't have it."

11   This upset Abraham very much, for after all, Ishmael too was his son.

12   But God told Abraham, "Don't be upset over the boy or your slave-girl wife; do as Sarah says, for Isaac is the son through whom My promise will be fulfilled.

13   And I will make a nation of the descendants of the slave-girl's son, too, because he also is yours."

14   So Abraham got up early the next morning, prepared food for the journey, and strapped a canteen of water to Hagar's shoulders and sent her away with their son. She hiked out into the wilderness of Beer-sheba, wandering aimlessly.

15   When the water was gone she left the child beneath a bush

16   And went off and sat down a hundred yards or so away. "I don't want to watch him die," she said, and burst into tears, sobbing wildly.

17   Then God answered the lad's cries, and the Angel of God called to Hagar from the sky, "Hagar, what's wrong? Don't be afraid! For God has heard the

---

[1] Or, "teasing" or "mocking"; whether in innocent fun or otherwise is not clear in the text.

lad's cries as he is lying there.

18   Go and get the boy and comfort him, for I will make a great nation from his descendants."

19   Then God opened her eyes and she saw a well; so she refilled the canteen and gave the lad a drink.

20, 21   And God blessed the boy and he grew up in the wilderness of Paran, and became an expert archer. And his mother arranged a marriage for him with a girl from Egypt.

*   *   *   *   *

22   About this time King Abimelech, and Phicol, commander of his troops, came to Abraham and said to him, "It is evident that God helps you in everything you do;

23   Swear to me by God's name that you won't defraud me or my son or my grandson, but that you will be on friendly terms with my country, as I have been toward you."

24   Abraham replied, "All right, I swear to it!"

25   Then Abraham complained to the king about a well the king's servants had taken violently away from Abraham's servants.

26   "This is the first I've heard of it," the king exclaimed, "and I have no idea who is responsible. Why didn't you tell me before?"

27   Then Abraham gave sheep and oxen to the king, as sacrifices to seal their pact.

28, 29   But when he took seven ewe lambs and set them off by themselves, the king inquired, "Why are you doing that?"

30   And Abraham replied, "They are my gift to you as a public confirmation that this well is mine."

31   So from that time on the well was called Beer-

sheba ("Well of the Oath"), because that was the place where they made their covenant.

32　Then King Abimelech, and Phicol, commander of his army, returned home again.

33　And Abraham planted a tamarisk tree beside the well, and prayed there to the Lord, calling upon the Eternal God [to witness the covenant[1]].

34　And Abraham lived in the Philistine country for a long time.

CHAPTER 22

Later on, God tested Abraham's [faith and obedience[1]].

"Abraham!" God called.

"Yes, Lord?" he replied.

2　"Take with you your only son—yes, Isaac whom you love so much—and go to the land of Moriah and sacrifice him there as a burnt offering upon one of the mountains which I'll point out to you!"

3　The next morning Abraham got up early, chopped wood for a fire upon the altar, saddled his donkey, and took with him his son Isaac and two young men who were his servants, and started off to the place where God had told him to go.

4　On the third day of the journey Abraham saw the place in the distance.

5　"Stay here with the donkey," Abraham told the young men, "and the lad and I will travel yonder and worship, and then come right back."

6　Abraham placed the wood for the burnt offering upon Isaac's shoulders, while he himself carried the

---

[1]Implied.

knife and the flint for striking a fire. So the two of them went on together.

7 "Father!" Isaac asked, "we have the wood and the flint to make the fire, but where is the lamb for the sacrifice?"

8 "God will see to it, my son," Abraham replied. And they went on.

9 When they arrived at the place where God had told Abraham to go, he built an altar and placed the wood in order, ready for the fire, and then tied Isaac and laid him on the altar over the wood.

10 And Abraham took the knife and lifted it up to plunge it into his son, to slay him.

11 At that moment the Angel of God shouted to him from heaven, "Abraham! Abraham!"

"Yes, Lord!" he answered.

12 "Lay down the knife; don't hurt the lad in any way," the Angel said, "for I know that God is first in your life—you have not withheld even your beloved son from Me."

13 Then Abraham noticed a ram caught by its horns in a bush. So he took the ram and sacrificed it, instead of his son, as a burnt offering on the altar.

14 Abraham named the place "Jehovah Sees"— and it still goes by that name to this day.

15 Then the Angel of God called again to Abraham from heaven.

16 "I, the Lord, have sworn by Myself that because you have obeyed Me and have not withheld even your beloved son from Me,

17 I will bless you with incredible blessings and multiply your descendants into countless thousands and millions, like the stars above you in the sky, and like

the sands along the seashore. These descendants of
yours will conquer their enemies,

18   And be a blessing to all the nations of the earth
—all because you have obeyed Me."

19   So they returned to his young men, and traveled home again to Beer-sheba.

20   After this, a message arrived that Milcah, the
wife of Abraham's brother Nahor, had borne him eight
sons. Their names were:

21   Uz, the oldest,
          Buz, the next oldest,
          Kemuel (father of Aram),
22, 23   Chesed,
          Hazo,
          Pildash,
          Jidlaph,
          Bethuel (father of Rebekah).

24   He also had four other children from his concubine, Reumah:

          Tebah,
          Gaham,
          Tahash,
          Maacah.

CHAPTER 23

When Sarah was 127 years old, she died in Hebron
in the land of Canaan; there Abraham mourned
and wept for her.

3   Then, standing beside her body, he said to the
men of Heth:

4   "Here I am, a visitor in a foreign land, with
no place to bury my wife. Please sell me a piece of
ground for this purpose."

5, 6 "Certainly," the men replied, "for you are an honored prince of God among us; it will be a privilege to have you choose the finest of our sepulchres, so that you can bury her there."

7 Then Abraham bowed low before them and said,

8 "Since this is your feeling in the matter, be so kind as to ask Ephron, Zohar's son,

9 To sell me the cave of Mach-pelah, down at the end of his field. I will of course pay the full price for it, whatever is publicly agreed upon, and it will become a permanent cemetery for my family."

10 Ephron was sitting there among the others, and now he spoke up, answering Abraham as the others listened, speaking publicly before all the citizens of the town:

11 "Sir," he said to Abraham, "please listen to me. I will give you the cave and the field without any charge. Here in the presence of my people, I give it to you free. Go and bury your dead."

12 Abraham bowed again to the men of Heth,

13 And replied to Ephron, as all listened: "No, let me buy it from you. Let me pay the full price of the field, and then I will bury my dead."

14, 15 "Well, the land is worth 400 pieces of silver," Ephron said, "but what is that between friends? Go ahead and bury your dead."

16 So Abraham paid Ephron the price he had suggested—400 pieces of silver, as publicly agreed.

17, 18 This is the land he bought: Ephron's field at Mach-pelah, near Mamre, and the cave at the end of the field, and all the trees in the field. They became his permanent possession, by agreement in the presence of the men of Heth at the city gate.

19, 20 So Abraham buried Sarah there, in the field and cave deeded to him by the men of Heth as a burial plot.

CHAPTER 24

A braham was now a very old man, and God blessed him in every way.

2 One day Abraham said to his household administrator, who was his oldest servant,

3 "Swear by Jehovah, the God of heaven and earth, that you will not let my son marry one of these local girls, these Canaanites.

4 Go instead to my homeland, to my relatives, and find a wife for him there."

5 "But suppose I can't find a girl who will come so far from home?" the servant asked. "Then shall I take Isaac there, to live among your relatives?"

6 "No!" Abraham warned, "Be careful that you don't do that under any circumstance.

7 For the Lord God of heaven told me to leave that land and my people, and promised to give me and my children this land. He will send His angel on ahead of you, and He will see to it that you find a girl from there to be my son's wife.

8 But if you don't succeed, then you are free from this oath; but under no circumstances are you to take my son there."

9 So the servant vowed[1] to follow Abraham's instructions.

10 He took with him ten of Abraham's camels

---

[1]Literally, "put his hand under the thigh of Abraham his master and swore to him that . . ."

loaded with samples of the best of everything his master owned, and journeyed to Iraq, to Nahor's village.

11 There he made the camels kneel down outside the town, beside a spring. It was evening, and the women of the village were coming to draw water.

12 "O Jehovah, the God of my master," he prayed, "show kindness to my master Abraham and help me to accomplish the purpose of my journey.

13 See, here I am, standing beside this spring, and the girls of the village are coming out to draw water.

14 This is my request: when I ask one of them for a drink and she says, 'Yes, certainly, and I will water your camels too!'—let her be the one You have appointed as Isaac's wife. That is how I will know."

15, 16 As he was still speaking to the Lord about this, a beautiful young girl[2] named Rebekah arrived with a water jug on her shoulder and filled it at the spring. (Her father was Bethuel the son of Nahor[3] and his wife Milcah.)

17 Running over to her, the servant asked her for a drink.

18 "Certainly, sir," she said, and quickly lowered the jug for him to drink.

19 Then she said, "I'll draw water for your camels, too, until they have enough!"

20 So she emptied the jug into the watering trough and ran down to the spring again and kept carrying water to the camels until they had enough.

21 The servant said no more, but watched her carefully to see if she would finish the job,[4] so that

---

[2]Literally, "a virgin."
[3]Abraham's brother.
[4]Implied.

he would know whether she was the one.

22　Then at last, when the camels had finished drinking, he produced a quarter-ounce gold earring[5] and two five-ounce golden bracelets for her wrists.

23　"Whose daughter are you, miss?" he asked. "Would your father have any room to put us up for the night?"

24　"My father is Bethuel, the son of Milcah, the wife of Nahor," she replied.

25　"Yes, we have plenty of straw and food for the camels, and a guest room."

26　The man stood there a moment with head bowed, worshiping Jehovah.

27　"Thank You, Lord God of my master Abraham," he prayed; "thank You for being so kind and true to him, and for leading me straight to the family of my master's relatives."

28　The girl ran home to tell her folks,[6]

29, 30　And when her brother Laban saw the ring, and the bracelets on his sister's wrists, and heard her story, he rushed out to the spring where the man was still standing beside his camels, and said to him,

31　"Come and stay with us, friend;[7] why stand here outside the city when we have a room all ready for you, and a place prepared for the camels!"

32　So the man went home with Laban, and Laban gave him straw to bed down the camels, and feed for them, and water for the camel drivers to wash their feet.

33　Then supper was served. But the old man said,

---

[5]Literally, "nose-ring."
[6]Doubtless to tell them that a messenger had arrived from her great-uncle.
[7]Literally, "blessed of Jehovah."

"I don't want to eat until I have told you why I am here."

"All right," Laban said, "Tell us your errand."

34   "I am Abraham's servant," he explained.

35   "And Jehovah has overwhelmed my master with blessings so that he is a great man among the people of his land. God has given him flocks of sheep and herds of cattle, and a fortune in silver and gold, and many slaves and camels and donkeys.

36   Now when Sarah, my master's wife, was very old, she gave birth to my master's son, and my master has given him everything he owns.

37   And my master made me promise not to let Isaac marry one of the local girls,[8]

38   But to come to his relatives here in this far-off land, to his brother's[9] family, and to bring back a girl from here to marry his son.

39   'But suppose I can't find a girl who will come?' I asked him.

40   'She will,' he told me—'for my Lord, in whose presence I have walked, will send His angel with you and make your mission successful. Yes, find a girl from among my relatives, from my brother's family.

41   You are under oath to go and ask. If they won't send anyone, then you are freed from your promise.'

42   Well, this afternoon when I came to the spring I prayed this prayer: 'O Jehovah, the God of my master Abraham, if You are planning to make my mission a success, please guide me in this way:

43   Here I am, standing beside this spring. I will say to some girl who comes out to draw water, "Please

---

[8]Literally, "daughters of the Canaanites."
[9]Literally, "go into my father's house."

give me a drink of water!"

44 And she will reply, "Certainly! And I'll water your camels too!" Let that girl be the one You have selected to be the wife of my master's son.'

45 Well, while I was still speaking these words, Rebekah was coming along with her water jug upon her shoulder; and she went down to the spring and drew water and filled the jug. I said to her, 'Please give me a drink.'

46 She quickly lifted the jug down from her shoulder so that I could drink, and told me, 'Certainly, sir, and I will water your camels too!' So she did!

47 Then I asked her, 'Whose family are you from?' And she told me, 'Nahor's. My father is Bethuel, the son of Nahor and his wife Milcah.' So I gave her the ring and the bracelets.

48 Then I bowed my head and worshiped and blessed Jehovah, the God of my master Abraham, because He had led me along just the right path to find a girl from the family[10] of my master's brother.

49 So tell me, yes or no. Will you or won't you be kind to my master and do what is right? When you tell me, then I'll know what my next step should be, whether to move this way or that."

50 Then Laban and Bethuel replied, "The Lord has obviously brought you here, so what can we say?

51 Take her and go! Yes, let her be the wife of your master's son, as Jehovah has directed."

52 At this reply, Abraham's servant fell to his knees before Jehovah.

53 Then he brought out jewels set in solid gold and silver for Rebekah, and lovely clothing; and he

---

[10]Literally, "my master's brother's daughter."

gave many valuable presents to her mother and brother.

54 Then they had supper, and the servant and the men with him stayed there overnight. But early the next morning he said, "Send me back to my master!"

55 "But we want Rebekah here at least another ten days or so!" her mother and brother exclaimed. "Then she can go."

56 But he pleaded, "Don't hinder my return; the Lord has made my mission successful, and I want to report back to my master."

57 "Well," they said, "we'll call the girl and ask her what she thinks."

58 So they called Rebekah. "Are you willing to go with this man?" they asked her.

And she replied, "Yes, I will go."

59 So they told her goodbye, sending along the woman who had been her childhood nurse,

60 And blessed her with this blessing as they parted:

> "Our sister,
> May you become
> The mother of many millions!
> May your descendants
> Overcome all your enemies."

61 So Rebekah and her servant girls mounted the camels and went with him.

62 Meanwhile, Isaac, whose home was in the Negeb, had returned to Beer-lahai-roi.

63 One evening as he was taking a walk out in the fields, meditating, he looked up and saw the camels coming.

64 Rebekah noticed him and quickly dismounted.

65 "Who is that man walking through the fields to

meet us?" she asked the servant.

And he replied, "It is my master's son!"[11] So she covered her face with her veil.

66 Then the servant told Isaac the whole story,

67 And Isaac brought Rebekah into his mother's tent, and she became his wife. He loved her very much, and she was a special comfort to him after the loss of his mother.

CHAPTER 25

N ow Abraham married again. Keturah was his new wife, and she bore him several children:

2   Zimran,

       Jokshan,

       Medan,

       Midian,

       Ishbak,

       Shuah.

3 Jokshan's two sons were Sheba and Dedan. Dedan's sons were Asshurim, Letushim, and Leummim.

4 Midian's sons were Ephah, Epher, Hanoch, Abida, and Eldaah.[1]

5 Abraham deeded everything he owned to Isaac;

6 However, he gave gifts to the sons of his concubines and sent them off into the east, away from Isaac.

7, 8 Then Abraham died, at the ripe old age of 175,

9, 10 And his sons Isaac and Ishmael buried him in the cave of Mach-pelah near Mamre, in the field Abraham had purchased from Ephron the son of Zohar, the Hethite, where Sarah, Abraham's wife was buried.

---

[11]Literally, "It is my master."
[1]The text adds, "all these were the children of Keturah."

11 After Abraham's death, God poured out rich blessings upon Isaac. (Isaac had now moved south to Beer-lahai-roi in the Negeb.)

12 Here is a list, in the order of their births, of the descendants of Ishmael, who was the son of Abraham and Hagar the Egyptian, Sarah's slave girl:

13   Nebaioth,
           Kedar,
           Abdeel,
           Mibsam,
14   Mishma,
           Dumah,
           Massa,
15   Hadad,
           Tema,
           Jetur,
           Naphish,
           Kedemah.

16 These twelve sons of his became the founders of twelve tribes that bore their names.

17 Ishmael finally died at the age of 137, and joined his ancestors.[3]

18 These descendants of Ishmael were scattered across the country from Havilah to Shur (which is a little way to the northeast of the Egyptian border in the direction of Assyria). And they were constantly at war with one another.

*   *   *   *   *

19 This is the story of Isaac's children:

20 Isaac was forty years old when he married Rebekah, the daughter of Bethuel the Aramean from Paddam-aram, sister of Laban.

---

[3]Literally, "and was gathered to his people."

21 Isaac pleaded with Jehovah to give Rebekah a child, for even after many years of marriage[4] she had no children. Then at last she became pregnant.

22 And it seemed as though children were fighting each other inside her! "I can't endure this," she exclaimed. So she asked the Lord about it.

23 And He told her, "The sons in your womb shall become two rival nations. One will be stronger than the other; and the older shall be a servant of the younger!"

24 And sure enough, she had twins.

25 The first was born so covered with reddish hair that one would think he was wearing a fur coat! So they called him "Esau."[5]

26 Then the other twin was born with his hand on Esau's heel! So they called him Jacob (meaning "He grabs heels!"). Isaac was 60 years old when the twins were born.

27 As the boys grew, Esau became a skillful hunter, while Jacob was a quiet sort who liked to stay at home.

28 Isaac's favorite was Esau, because of the venison he brought home, and Rebekah's favorite was Jacob.

29 One day Jacob was cooking stew when Esau arrived home exhausted from the hunt.

30 *Esau:* "Boy, am I starved! Give me a bite of that red stuff there!" (From this came his nickname "Edom," which means "Red Stuff.")

31 *Jacob:* "All right, trade me your birthright for it!"

---

[4] Implied in verses 20 and 26.
[5] Which sounds a little like the Hebrew word for "hair."

32 *Esau:* "When a man is dying of starvation, what good is his birthright?"

33 *Jacob:* "Well then, vow to God that it is mine!"

And Esau vowed, thereby selling all his eldest-son rights to his younger brother.

34 Then Jacob gave Esau bread, peas, and stew; so he ate and drank and went on about his business, indifferent to the loss of the rights he had thrown away.[6]

CHAPTER 26

Now a severe famine overshadowed the land, as had happened before, in Abraham's time, and so Isaac moved to the city of Gerar where Abimelech, king of the Philistines, lived.

2 Jehovah appeared to him there and told him, "Don't go to Egypt.

3 Do as I say and stay here in this land. If you do, I will be with you and bless you, and I will give all this land to you and to your descendants, just as I promised Abraham your father.

4 And I will cause your descendants to become as numerous as the stars! And I will give them all of these lands; and they shall be a blessing to all the nations of the earth.

5 I will do this because Abraham obeyed My commandments and laws."

6 So Isaac stayed in Gerar.

7 And when the men there asked him about Rebekah, he said, "She is my sister!" For he feared for his life if he told them she was his wife; he was afraid they would kill him to get her, for she was very attractive.

---

[6]Literally, "thus did Esau consider his birthright to be of no value."

8 But sometime later, King Abimelech, king of the Philistines, looked out of a window and saw Isaac petting with Rebekah.

9 Abimelech called for Isaac and exclaimed, "She is your wife! Why did you claim she is your sister?"

"Because I was afraid I would be murdered if I did," Isaac replied. "I thought someone would kill me to get her from me."

10 "How could you treat us this way?" Abimelech exclaimed. "Someone might carelessly have raped her, and we would be doomed."

11 Then Abimelech made a public proclamation: "Anyone harming this man or his wife shall die."

12 That year Isaac's crops were tremendous—100 times the grain he sowed. For Jehovah blessed him.

13 He was soon a man of great wealth, and became richer and richer.

14 He had large flocks of sheep and goats, great herds of cattle, and many servants. And the Philistines became jealous of him.

15 So they filled up his wells with earth—all those dug by the servants of his father Abraham.

16 And King Abimelech asked Isaac to leave the country. "Go somewhere else," he said, "for you have become too rich and powerful for us."

17 So Isaac moved to Gerar Valley and lived there instead.

18 And Isaac redug the wells of his father Abraham, the ones the Philistines had filled after his father's death, and gave them the same names they had had before, when his father had named them.

19 His shepherds also dug a new well in Gerar Valley, and found a gushing underground spring.

20   Then the local shepherds came and claimed it. "This is our land and our well," they said, and argued over it with Isaac's herdsmen. So he named the well, "The Well of Argument!"[1]

21   Isaac's men then dug another well, but again there was a fight over it. So he called it, "The Well of Anger."[2]

22   Abandoning that one, he dug again, and the local residents finally left him alone. So he called it, "The Well of Room Enough for Us at Last!"[3]

"For now at last," he said, "the Lord has made room for us and we shall thrive."

23   When he went to Beer-sheba,

24   Jehovah appeared to him on the night of his arrival. "I am the God of Abraham your father," He said. "Fear not, for I am with you and will bless you, and will give you so many descendants that they will become a great nation—because of My promise to Abraham, who obeyed Me."

25   Then Isaac built an altar and worshiped Jehovah; and he settled there, and his servants dug a well.

26   One day Isaac had visitors from Gerar. King Abimelech arrived with his advisor, Ahuzzath, and also Phicol, his army commander.

27   "Why have you come?" Isaac asked them; "this is obviously no friendly visit, since you kicked me out in a most uncivil way."

28   "Well," they said, "we can plainly see that Jehovah is blessing you. We've decided to ask for a treaty between us.

29   Promise that you will not harm us, just as we

---

[1] Eseb.
[2] Sitnah.
[3] Rehoboth.

have not harmed you, and in fact, have done only good to you and have sent you away in peace; we bless you in the name of the Lord."

30 So Isaac prepared a great feast for them, and they ate and drank in preparation for the treaty ceremonies.

31 In the morning, as soon as they were up, they each took solemn oaths to seal a non-aggression pact. Then Isaac sent them happily home again.

32 That very same day Isaac's servants came to tell him, "We have found water"—in the well they had been digging.

33 So he named the well, "The Well of the Oath,"[4] and the city that grew up there was named "Oath,"[5] and is called that to this day.

*   *   *   *   *

34 Esau, at the age of forty, married a girl named Judith, daughter of Be-eri the Hethite; and he also married Basemath, daughter of Elon the Hethite.

35 But Isaac and Rebekah were bitter about his marrying them.

CHAPTER 27

One day, in Isaac's old age when he was half-blind, he called for Esau his oldest son.

    Isaac: "My son?"

    Esau: "Yes, father?"

2   *Isaac:* "I am an old man now, and expect
           to die 'most any day.

3   Take your bow and arrows out into the
         fields and get me some venison,

---

[4]Shibah.
[5]Beer-sheba.

4   And prepare it just the way I like it—
           savory and good—and bring it here for me
           to eat, and I will give you the blessings
           that belong[1] to you, my first-born son,[1]
           before I die."

5   But Rebekah overheard the conversation. So
when Esau left for the field to hunt for the venison,

6, 7   She called her son Jacob and told him what
his father had said to his brother.

8   *Rebekah:* "Now do exactly as I tell you.

9   Go out to the flocks and bring me two
           young goats, and I'll prepare your father's
           favorite dish from them.

10   Then take it to your father, and after he has
           enjoyed it he will bless *you* before his
           death, instead of Esau!"[2]

11   *Jacob:* "But mother! He won't be fooled that
           easily.[1] Think how hairy Esau is, and how
           smooth my skin is!

12   What if my father feels me? He'll think I'm
           making a fool of him, and curse me instead
           of blessing me!"

13   *Rebekah:* "Let his curses be on me, dear son.
           Just do what I tell you. Go out and get the
           goats."

14   So Jacob followed his mother's instructions,
bringing the dressed kids, which she prepared in his
father's favorite way.

15   Then she took Esau's best clothes—they were
there in the house—and instructed Jacob to put them
on.

---

[1]Implied.

16   And she made him a pair of gloves from the hairy skin of the young goats, and fastened a strip of the hide around his neck;

17   Then she gave him the meat, with its rich aroma, and some fresh-baked bread.

18   Jacob carried the platter of food into the room where his father was lying.

*   *   *   *   *

Jacob: "Father?"

Isaac: "Yes? Who is it, my son—Esau or Jacob?"

19   *Jacob:* "It's Esau, your oldest son. I've done as you told me to. Here is the delicious venison you wanted. Sit up and eat it, so that you will bless me with all your heart!"

20   *Isaac:* "How were you able to find it so quickly, my son?"

Jacob: "Because Jehovah your God put it in my path!"

21   *Isaac:* "Come over here. I want to feel you, and be sure it really is Esau!"

22   (Jacob goes over to his father. He feels him!)

Isaac: (to himself) "The voice is Jacob's, but the hands are Esau's!"

23   (The ruse convinces Isaac and he gives Jacob his blessings):

24   *Isaac:* "Are you really Esau?"

Jacob: "Yes, of course."

25   *Isaac:* "Then bring me the venison, and I will eat it and bless you with all my heart."

(Jacob takes it over to him and Isaac eats; he also drinks the wine Jacob brings him.)

26   *Isaac:* "Come here and kiss me, my son!"

(Jacob goes over and kisses him on the cheek. Isaac sniffs his clothes, and finally seems convinced.)

27   *Isaac:* "The smell of my son is the good smell of the earth and fields that Jehovah has blessed.

28   May God always give you plenty of rain for your crops, and good harvest of grain, and new wine.

29   May many nations be your slaves. Be the master of your brothers. May all your relatives bow low before you. Cursed are all who curse you, and blessed are all who bless you."

30   (As soon as Isaac has blessed Jacob, and almost before Jacob leaves the room, Esau arrives, coming in from his hunting.

31   He also has prepared his father's favorite dish and brings it to him.)

Esau: "Here I am, father, with the venison. Sit up and eat it so that you can give me your finest blessings!"

32   *Isaac:* "Who is it?"
Esau: "Why, it's me, of course! Esau, your oldest son!"

33   (Isaac begins to tremble noticeably.)
Isaac: "Then who is it who was just here with venison, and I have already eaten it and blessed him with irrevocable blessing?"

34   (Esau begins to sob with deep and bitter sobs.)
Esau: "O my father, bless me, bless me too!"

35   *Isaac:* "Your brother was here and tricked me

and has carried away your blessing."

36　*Esau:* (Bitterly) "No wonder they call him "The Cheater."[2] For he took my birthright, and now he has stolen my blessing. Oh, haven't you saved even one blessing for me?"

37　*Isaac:* "I have made him your master, and have given you yourself and all of his relatives as his servants. I have guaranteed him abundance of grain and wine—what is there left to give?"

38　*Esau:* "Not one blessing left for me? O my father, bless me too."

(Isaac says nothing[3] as Esau weeps.)

39　*Isaac:* "Yours will be no life of ease and luxury,
40　　　　But you shall hew your way with your sword. For a time you will serve your brother, but you will finally shake loose from him and be free."

41　So Esau hated Jacob because of what he had done to him. He said to himself, "My father will soon be gone, and then I will kill Jacob."

42　But someone got wind of what he was planning, and reported it to Rebekah. She sent for Jacob and told him that his life was being threatened by Esau.

43　"This is what to do," she said. "Flee to your Uncle Laban in Haran.

44　Stay there with him awhile until your brother's fury is spent,

45　And he forgets what you have done. Then I will send for you. For why should I be bereaved of both of you in one day?"

46　Then Rebekah said to Isaac, "I'm sick and tired

---

[2]"Jacob" means "Cheater."
[3]This clause appears in some versions, not in others.

of these local girls. I'd rather die than see Jacob marry one of them."

CHAPTER 28

So Isaac called for Jacob and blessed him and said to him, "Don't marry one of these Canaanite girls.

2   Instead, go at once to Paddan-aram, to the house of your grandfather[1] Bethuel, and marry one of your cousins—your Uncle[2] Laban's daughters.

God Almighty bless you and give you many children; may you become a great nation of many tribes!

4   May God pass on to you and to your descendants the mighty blessings promised to Abraham. May you own this land where we now are foreigners, for God has given it to Abraham."

5   So Isaac sent Jacob away, and he went to Paddan-aram to visit his Uncle Laban, his mother's brother—the son of Bethuel the Aramean.

6, 7, 8   Esau realized that his father despised the local girls, and that his father and mother had sent Jacob to Paddan-aram, with his father's blessing, to get a wife from there, and that they had strictly warned him against marrying a Canaanite girl, and that Jacob had agreed and had left for Paddan-aram.

9   So Esau went to his Uncle Ishmael's family and married two additional wives from there, besides the wives he already had. One of these new wives was Mahalath, the sister of Nebaioth, and daughter of Ishmael, Abraham's son.

10   So Jacob left Beer-sheba and journeyed toward Haran.

11   One night, when he stopped to camp at sun-

[1] Literally, "your mother's father."
[2] Literally, "your mother's brother."

down, he found a rock for a headrest and lay down to sleep,

12 And dreamed that a staircase[3] reached from earth to heaven, and he saw the angels of God going up and down upon it.

13 At the top of the stairs stood the Lord. "I am Jehovah," He said, "the God of Abraham, and of your father Isaac. The ground you are lying on is yours! I will give it to you and to your descendants.

14 For you will have descendants as many as dust! They will cover the land from east to west and from north to south; and all the nations of the earth will be blessed through you and your descendants.

15 What's more, I am with you, and will protect you wherever you go, and will bring you back safely to this land; I will be with you constantly until I have finished giving you all I am promising."

16, 17 Then Jacob woke up. "God lives here!" he exclaimed in terror. "I've stumbled into His home! This is the awesome entrance to heaven!"

18 The next morning he got up very early and set his stone headrest upright as a memorial pillar, and poured olive oil over it.

19 He named the place Bethel ("House of God"), though the previous name of the nearest village[4] was Luz.

20 And Jacob vowed this vow to God: "If God will help and protect me on this journey and give me food and clothes,

21 And will bring me back safely to my father, then I will choose Jehovah as my God!

---

[3]Literally, "ladder."
[4]Literally, "of the city."

22   And this memorial pillar shall become a place for worship; and I will give You back a tenth of everything You give me!"

CHAPTER 29

Jacob traveled on, finally arriving in the land of the East.

2   He saw in the distance three flocks of sheep lying beside a well in an open field, waiting to be watered. But a heavy stone covered the mouth of the well.

3   (The custom was that the stone was not removed until all the flocks were there. After watering them, the stone was rolled back over the mouth of the well again.)

4   Jacob went over to the shepherds and asked them where they lived. "At Haran," they said.

5   "Do you know a fellow there named Laban, the son of Nahor?"

"We sure do."

6   "How is he?"

"He's well and prosperous. Look, there comes his daughter Rachel with the sheep."

7   "Why don't you water the flocks so they can get back to grazing?" Jacob asked. "They'll be hungry if you stop so early in the day!"

8   "We don't roll away the stone and begin the watering until all the flocks and shepherds are here," they replied.

9   As this conversation was going on, Rachel arrived with her father's sheep, for she was a shepherdess.

10   And because she was his cousin—the daughter of his mother's brother—and because the sheep were

his uncle's, Jacob went over to the well and rolled away the stone and watered his uncle's flock.

11 Then Jacob kissed Rachel and started crying!

12, 13 He explained about being her cousin on her father's side, and that he was her Aunt Rebekah's son. She quickly ran and told her father, Laban, and as soon as he heard of Jacob's arrival, he rushed out to meet him and greeted him warmly and brought him home. Then Jacob told him his story.

14 "Just think, my very own flesh and blood," Laban exclaimed.

After Jacob had been there about a month,

15 Laban said to him one day, "Just because we are relatives is no reason for you to work for me without pay. How much do you want?"

16 Now Laban had two daughters, Leah, the older, and her younger sister, Rachel.

17 Leah had lovely eyes, but Rachel was shapely, and in every way a beauty.

18 Well, Jacob was in love with Rachel. So he told her father, "I'll work for you seven years if you'll give me Rachel as my wife."

19 "Agreed!" Laban replied. "I'd rather give her to you than to someone outside the family."

20 So Jacob spent the next seven years working to pay for Rachel. But they seemed to him but a few days, he was so much in love.

21 Finally the time came for him to marry her. "I have fulfilled my contract," Jacob said to Laban. "Now give me my wife, so that I can sleep with her."

22 So Laban invited all the men of the settlement to celebrate with Jacob at a big party.

23 Afterwards, that night, when it was dark, Laban

took Leah to Jacob, and he slept with her.

24 (And Laban gave to Leah a servant girl, Zilpah, to be her maid.)

25 But in the morning—it was Leah!

"What sort of trick is this?" Jacob raged at Laban.

"I worked for seven years for Rachel. What do you mean by this trickery?"

26 "It's not our custom to marry off a younger daughter ahead of her sister," Laban replied smoothly.[1]

27 "Wait until the bridal week is over and you can have Rachel too—if you promise to work for me another seven years!"

28 So Jacob agreed to work seven more years. Then Laban gave him Rachel, too.

29 And Laban gave to Rachel a servant girl, Bilhah, to be her maid.

30 So Jacob slept with Rachel, too, and he loved her more than Leah, and stayed and worked the additional seven years.

31 But because Jacob was slighting Leah, Jehovah let her have a child, while Rachel was barren.

32 So Leah became pregnant and had a son, Reuben (meaning "God has noticed my trouble"), for she said, "Jehovah has noticed my trouble—now my husband will love me."

33 She soon became pregnant again and had another son and named him Simeon (meaning "Jehovah heard"), for she said, "Jehovah heard that I was unloved, and so He has given me another son."

34 Again she became pregnant and had a son, and named him Levi (meaning "Attachment") for she said,

---

[1] Implied from context.

"Surely now my husband will feel affection for me, since I have given him three sons!"

35 Once again she was pregnant and had a son and named him Judah (meaning "Praise"), for she said, "Now I will praise Jehovah!" And then she stopped having children.

CHAPTER 30

Rachel, realizing she was barren, became envious of her sister. "Give me children or I'll die," she exclaimed to Jacob.

2 Jacob flew into a rage. "Am I God?" he flared. "He is the one who is responsible for your barrenness."

3 Then Rachel told him, "Sleep with my servant-girl Bilhah, and her children will be mine."

4 So she gave him Bilhah to be his wife, and he slept with her,

5 And she became pregnant and presented him with a son.

6 Rachel named him Dan (meaning[1] "Justice"), for she said, "God has given me justice, and heard my plea and given me a son."

7 Then Bilhah, Rachel's servant-girl, became pregnant again and gave Jacob a second son.

8 Rachel named him Naphtali (meaning "Wrestling"), for she said, "I am in a fierce contest with my sister and I am winning!"

9 Meanwhile, when Leah realized that she wasn't getting pregnant anymore, she gave her servant-girl

---

[1]The meaning is not of the actual Hebrew name, but of a Hebrew word sounding like the name. The name given is a Hebrew pun. An example in English might be, "Because of the large hospital bill the child was named 'Bill'!"

Zilpah to Jacob, to be his wife,

10   And soon Zilpah presented him with a son.

11   Leah named him Gad (meaning "My luck has turned!").

12   Then Zilpah produced a second son,

13   And Leah named him Asher (meaning "Happy"), for she said, "What joy is mine! The other women will think me blessed indeed!"

14   One day during the wheat harvest, Reuben found some mandrakes[2] growing in a field and brought them to his mother Leah. Rachel begged Leah to give them to her,

15   But Leah angrily replied, "Wasn't it enough to steal my husband? And now will you steal my son's mandrakes too?"

Rachel said sadly, "He will sleep with you tonight when you give him the mandrakes your son found."

16   That evening as Jacob was coming home from the fields, Leah went out to meet him. "You must sleep with me tonight!" she said; "for I am hiring you with some mandrakes my son has found!" So he did.

17   And God answered her prayers and she become pregnant again, and gave birth to her fifth son.

18   She named him Issachar (meaning "Wages"), for she said, "God has repaid me for giving my slave-girl to my husband."

19   Then once again she became pregnant, with a sixth son.

20   She named him Zebulon (meaning "Gifts"),

---

[2]A leafy plant eaten by peasant women in the belief that this would aid them in becoming pregnant.

for she said, "God has given me good gifts for my husband. Now he will honor me, for I have given him six sons."

21 Afterwards she gave birth to a daughter and named her Dinah.

22 Then God remembered about Rachel's plight, and answered her prayers by giving her a child.

23, 24 For she became pregnant and gave birth to a son. "God has removed the dark slur against my name," she said. And she named him Joseph (meaning "May I also have another!"), for she said, "May Jehovah give me another son."

* * * * *

25 Soon after the birth of Joseph to Rachel, Jacob said to Laban, "I want to go back home.

26 Let me take my wives and children—for I earned them from you—and be gone, for you know how fully I have paid for them with my service to you."

27 "Please don't leave me," Laban replied, "for a fortune-teller that I consulted[3] told me that the many blessings I've been enjoying are all because of your being here.

28 How much of a raise do you need to get you to stay? Whatever it is, I'll pay it."

29 Jacob replied, "You know how faithfully I've served you through these many years, and how your flocks and herds have grown.

30 For it was little indeed you had before I came, and your wealth has increased enormously; Jehovah has blessed you from everything I do! But now, what about me? When should I provide for my own family?"

---

[3]Literally, "I have learned by divination."

31, 32 "What wages do you want?" Laban asked again.

Jacob replied, "If you will do one thing, I'll go back to work for you. Let me go out among your flocks today and remove all the goats that are speckled or spotted, and all the black sheep. Give them to me as my wages.

33 Then if you ever find any white goats or sheep in my flock, you will know that I have stolen them from you!"

34 "All right!" Laban replied. "It shall be as you have said!"

35, 36 So that very day Laban went out and formed a flock for Jacob of all the male goats that were ringed and spotted, and the females that were speckled and spotted with any white patches, and all of the black sheep. He gave them to Jacob's sons to take them three day's distance, and Jacob stayed and cared for Laban's flock.

37 Then Jacob took fresh shoots from poplar, almond, and plane trees, and peeled white streaks in them,

38 And placed these rods beside the watering troughs so that the flocks would see them when they came to drink; for that is when they mated.

39, 40 So the flocks mated before the white-streaked rods, and their offspring were streaked and spotted, and Jacob added them to his flock. Then he divided out the ewes from Laban's flock and segregated them from the rams, and let them mate only with Jacob's black rams. Thus he built his flocks from Laban's.

41　Moreover, he watched for the stronger animals to mate, and placed the peeled branches before them,

42　But didn't with the feebler ones. So the less healthy lambs were Laban's and the stronger ones were Jacob's!

43　As a result, Jacob's flocks increased rapidly and he became very wealthy, with many servants, camels, and donkeys.

CHAPTER 31

B ut Jacob learned that Laban's sons were grumbling, "He owes everything he owns to our father. All his wealth is at our father's expense."

2　Soon Jacob noticed a considerable cooling in Laban's attitude towards him.

3　Jehovah now spoke to Jacob and told him, "Return to the land of your fathers, and to your relatives there; and I will be with you."

4　So one day Jacob sent for Rachel and Leah to come out to the field where he was with the flocks,

5　To talk things over with them. "Your father has turned against me," he told them, "and now the God of my fathers has come and spoken to me.

6　You know how hard I've worked for your father,

7　But he has been completely unscrupulous and has broken his wage contract with me again and again and again. But God has not permitted him to do me any harm!

8　For if he said the speckled animals would be mine, then all the flock produced speckled; and when he changed and said I could have the streaked ones, then all the lambs were streaked!

9   In this way God has made me wealthy at your father's expense.

10   And at the mating season, I had a dream, and saw that the he-goats mating with the flock were streaked, speckled, and mottled.

11   Then, in my dream, the Angel of God called to me

12   And told me that I should mate the white[1] nanny goats with streaked, speckled, and mottled he-goats. 'For I have seen all that Laban has done to you,' the Angel said.

13   'I am the God you met at Bethel,' He continued, 'the place where you anointed the pillar and made a vow to serve me. Now leave this country and return to the land of your birth.' "

14   Rachel and Leah replied, "That's fine with us! There's nothing for us here—none of our father's wealth will come to us anyway!

15   He has reduced our rights to those of foreign women; he sold us, and what he received for us has disappeared.

16   The riches God has given you from our father were legally ours and our children's to begin with! So go ahead and do whatever God has told you to."

17, 18, 19, 20   So one day while Laban was out shearing sheep, Jacob set his wives and sons on camels, and fled without telling Laban his intentions. He drove the flocks before him—Jacob's flocks he had gotten there at Padan-aram—and took everything he owned and started out to return to his father Isaac in the land of Canaan.

---

[1]Implied. Literally, "notice that all the mating males are speckled, streaked, and mottled."

21 So he fled with all of his possessions (and Rachel stole her father's household gods and took them with her) and crossed the Euphrates River and headed for the territory of Gilead.

22 Laban didn't learn of their flight for three days.

23 Then, taking several men with him, he set out in hot pursuit and caught up with them seven days later, at Mount Gilead.

24 That night God appeared to Laban in a dream. "Watch out what you say to Jacob," he was told. "Don't give him your blessing and don't curse him."

25 Laban finally caught up with Jacob as he was camped at the top of a ridge; Laban, meanwhile, camped below him in the mountains.

26 "What do you mean by sneaking off like this?" Laban demanded. "Are my daughters prisoners, captured in a battle, that you have rushed them away like this?

27 Why didn't you give me a chance to have a farewell party, with singing and orchestra and harp?

28 Why didn't you let me kiss my grandchildren and tell them goodbye? This is a strange way to act.

29 I could crush you, but the God of your father appeared to me last night and told me, 'Be careful not to be too hard on Jacob!'

30 But see here—though you feel you must go, and long so intensely for your childhood home—why have you stolen my idols?"

31 "I sneaked away because I was afraid," Jacob answered. "I said to myself, 'He'll take his daughters from me by force.'

32 But as for your household idols, a curse upon

anyone who took them. Let him die! If you find a single thing we've stolen from you, I swear before all these men, I'll give it back without question." For Jacob didn't know that Rachel had taken them.

33 Laban went first into Jacob's tent to search there, then into Leah's, and then searched the two tents of the concubines, but didn't find them. Finally he went into Rachel's tent.

34 Rachel, remember, was the one who had stolen the idols; she had stuffed them into her camel saddle and now was sitting on them! So although Laban searched the tents thoroughly, he didn't find them.

35 "Forgive my not getting up, father," Rachel explained, "but I'm pregnant."[2]

36, 37 Now Jacob got mad at Laban. "What did you find?" he demanded. "What is my crime? You have come rushing after me as though you were chasing a criminal and have searched through everything. Now put everything I stole out here in front of us, before your men and mine, for all to see and to decide whose it is!

38 Twenty years I've been with you, and all that time I cared for your ewes and nanny goats so that they produced healthy offspring, and I never touched one ram of yours for food.

39 If any were attacked and killed by wild animals, did I show them to you and ask you to reduce the count of your flock? No, I took the loss. You made me pay for every animal stolen from the flocks, whether I could help it or not.[3]

---

[2]Implied. Literally, "The manner of women is upon me." She was pregnant with Benjamin, but nevertheless may have been falsely claiming her menstrual period, which, under the later Mosaic law, caused ceremonial defilement of all that was sat upon. See Leviticus 15.
[3]Literally, "stolen by day or by night."

40 I worked for you through the scorching heat of the day, and through the cold and sleepless nights.

41 Yes, twenty years—fourteen of them earning your two daughters, and six years to get the flock! And you have reduced my wages ten times!

42 In fact, except for the grace of God—the God of my grandfather Abraham, even the glorious God of Isaac, my father—you would have sent me off without a penny to my name. But God has seen your cruelty and my hard work, and that is why He appeared to you last night."

43 Laban replied, "These women are my daughters, and these children are mine, and these flocks and all that you have—all are mine. So how could I harm my own daughters and grandchildren?

44 Come now and we will sign a peace pact, you and I, and will live by its terms."

45 So Jacob took a stone and set it up as a monument,

46 And told his men to gather stones and make a heap, and Jacob and Laban ate together beside the pile of rocks.

47, 48 They named it "The Witness Pile"—"Jegar-sahadutha," in Laban's language, and "Galeed" in Jacob's.

"This pile of stones will stand as a witness against us [if either of us trespasses across this line[4]]," Laban said.

49 So it was also called "The Watchtower" (Mizpah). For Laban said, "May the Lord see to it that we keep this bargain when we are out of each other's sight.

---

[4]Implied.

50 And if you are harsh to my daughters, or take other wives, I won't know, but God will see it.

51, 52 This heap," Laban continued, "stands between us as a witness of our vows that I will not cross this line to attack you and you will not cross it to attack me.

53 I call upon the God of Abraham and Nahor, and of their father, to destroy either one of us who does." So Jacob took oath before the mighty God of his father Isaac, to respect the boundary line.

54 Then Jacob presented a sacrifice to God there at the top of the mountain, and invited his companions to a feast, and afterwards spent the night with them on the mountain.

55 Laban was up early the next morning and kissed his daughters and grandchildren, and blessed them, and returned home.

CHAPTER 32

So Jacob and his household[1] started on again. And the angels of God came to meet him. When he saw them he exclaimed, "God lives here!" So he named the place "God's territory!"[2]

3 Jacob now sent messengers to his brother Esau in Edom, in the land of Seir,

4 With this message: "Hello from Jacob! I have been living with Uncle Laban until recently,

5 And now I own oxen, donkeys, sheep, and many servants, both men and women. I have sent these messengers to inform you of my coming, hoping that you will be friendly to us."

[1]Implied.
[2]Literally, "Two encampments."

6 The messengers returned with the news that Esau was on the way to meet Jacob—with an army of 400 men!

7 Jacob was frantic with fear. He divided his household, along with the flocks and herds and camels, into two groups;

8 For he said, "If Esau attacks one group, perhaps the other can escape."

9 Then Jacob prayed, "O God of Abraham my grandfather, and of my father Isaac—O Jehovah who told me to return to the land of my relatives, and said that You would do me good—

10 I am not worthy of the least of all Your loving kindnesses shown me again and again just as You promised me. For when I left home[3] I owned nothing except a walking stick! And now I am two armies!

11 O Lord, please deliver me from destruction at the hand of my brother Esau, for I am frightened—terribly afraid that he is coming to kill me and these mothers and my children.

12 But You promised to do me good, and to multiply my descendants until they become as the sands along the shores—too many to count."

13 Jacob stayed where he was for the night, and prepared a present for his brother Esau:

14	200	nanny goats,
	20	billy goats,
	200	ewes,
	20	rams,
15	30	milk camels, with their colts,
	40	cows,
	10	bulls,

---

[3]Literally, "passed over this Jordan."

> 20 female donkeys,
> 10 male donkeys.

16 He instructed his servants to drive them on ahead, each group of animals by itself, separated by a distance between.

17 He told the men driving the first group that when they met Esau and he asked, "Where are you going? Whose servants are you? Whose animals are these?"—

18 They should reply: "These belong to your servant Jacob. They are a present for his master Esau! He is coming right behind us!"

19 Jacob gave the same instructions to each driver, with the same message.

20 Jacob's strategy was to appease Esau with the presents before meeting him face to face! "Perhaps," Jacob hoped, "he will be friendly to us."

21 So the presents were sent on ahead, and Jacob spent that night in the camp.

22, 23, 24 But during the night he got up and wakened[4] his two wives and his two concubines and eleven children, and took them across the Jordan River at the Jabbok ford, then returned again to the camp and was there alone; and a Man wrestled with him until dawn.

25 And when the Man saw that he couldn't win the match, He struck Jacob's hip, and knocked it out of joint at the socket.

26 Then the Man said, "Let me go, for it is dawn."

But Jacob panted, "I will not let you go until you bless me."

27 "What is your name?" the Man asked.

---

[4] Implied.

"Jacob," was the reply.

28 "It isn't anymore!" the Man told him. "It is Israel—one who has power with God. Because you have been strong with God, you shall prevail with men."

29 "What is *your* name?" Jacob asked Him.

"No, you mustn't ask," the Man told him.

And He blessed him there.

30 Jacob named the place "Peniel" ("The Face of God"), for he said, "I have seen God face to face, and yet my life is spared."

31 The sun rose as he started on, and he was limping because of his hip.

32 (That is why the people of Israel still do not eat the sciatic muscle where it attaches to the hip.)

CHAPTER 33

Then, far in the distance, Jacob saw Esau coming with his 400 men.

2 Jacob now arranged his family into a column, with his two concubines and their children at the head, Leah and her children next, and Rachel and Joseph last.

3 Then Jacob went on ahead. As he approached his brother he bowed low seven times before him.

4 And then Esau ran to meet him and embraced him affectionately and kissed him; and both of them were in tears!

5 Then Esau looked at the women and children and asked, "Who are these people with you?"

"My children," Jacob replied.

6 Then the concubines came forward with their children, and bowed low before him.

7   Next came Leah with her children, and bowed, and finally Rachel and Joseph came and made their bows.

8   "And what were all the flocks and herds I met as I came?" Esau asked.

And Jacob replied, "They are my gifts, to curry your favor!"

9   "Brother, I have plenty," Esau laughed. "Keep what you have."

10   "No, but please accept them," Jacob said, "for what a relief it is to see your friendly smile! I was as frightened of you as though approaching God![1]

11   Please take my gifts. For God has been very generous to me and I have enough." So Jacob insisted, and finally Esau accepted them.

12   "Well, let's be going," Esau said. "My men and I will stay with you and lead the way."

13   But Jacob replied, "As you can see,[2] some of the children are small, and the flocks and herds have their young, and if they are driven too hard, they will die.

14   So you go on ahead of us and we'll follow at our own pace and meet you at Seir."

15   "Well," Esau said, "at least let me leave you some of my men to assist you and be your guides."

"No," Jacob insisted, "we'll get along just fine. Please do as I suggest."

16   So Esau started back to Seir that same day.

17   Meanwhile Jacob and his household went as far as Succoth. There he built himself a camp, with pens for his flocks and herds. (That is why the place

---

[1]Literally, "forasmuch as I have seen your face as one sees the face of God."
[2]Implied.

is called Succoth, meaning "huts.")

18 Then they arrived safely at Shechem, in Canaan, and camped outside the city.

19 (He bought the land he camped on from the family of Hamor, Shechem's father, for 100 pieces of silver.

20 And there he erected an altar and called it "El-Elohe-Israel," "The Altar to the God of Israel.")

CHAPTER 34

One day Dinah, Leah's daughter, went out to visit some of the neighborhood girls,

2 But when Shechem, son of King Hamor the Hivite, saw her, he took her and raped her.

3 He fell deeply in love with her, and tried to win her affection.

4 Then he spoke to his father about it. "Get this girl for me," he demanded. "I want to marry her."

5 Word soon reached Jacob of what had happened, but his sons were out in the fields herding cattle, so he did nothing until their return.

6, 7 Meanwhile King Hamor, Shechem's father, went to talk with Jacob, arriving just as Jacob's sons came in from the fields, too shocked and angry to overlook the insult, for it was an outrage against all of them.

8 Hamor told Jacob, "My son Shechem is truly in love with your daughter, and longs for her to be his wife. Please let him marry her.

9, 10 Moreover, we invite you folks to live here among us and to let your daughters marry our sons, and we will give our daughters as wives for your young men. And you shall live among us wherever you wish and carry on your business among us and become rich!"

11   Then Shechem addressed Dinah's father and brothers. "Please be kind to me and let me have her as my wife," he begged. "I will give whatever you require.

12   No matter what dowry or gift you demand, I will pay it—only give me the girl as my wife."

13   Her brothers then lied to Shechem and Hamor, acting dishonorably because of what Shechem had done to their sister.

14   They said, "We couldn't possibly. For you are not circumcised. It would be a disgrace for her to marry such a man.

15   I'll tell you what we'll do—if every man of you will be circumcised,

16   Then we will intermarry with you and live here and unite with you to become one people.

17   Otherwise we will take her and be on our way."

18, 19   Hamor and Shechem gladly agreed, and lost no time in acting upon this request, for Shechem was very much in love with Dinah, and could, he felt sure, sell the idea to the other men of the city—for he was highly respected and very popular.

20   So Hamor and Shechem appeared before the city council[1] and presented their request.

21   "Those men are our friends," they said. "Let's invite them to live here among us and ply their trade. For the land is large enough to hold them, and we can intermarry with them.

22   But they will only consider staying here on one condition—that every one of us men be circumcised, the same as they are.

23   But if we do this, then all they have will be-

---

[1] Literally, "came into the gate of their city."

come ours and the land will be enriched. Come on, let's agree to this so that they will settle here among us."

24   So all the men agreed, and all were circumcised.

25   But three days later, when their wounds were sore and sensitive to every move they made, two of Dinah's brothers, Simeon and Levi, took their swords, entered the city without opposition, and slaughtered every man there,

26   Including Hamor and Shechem. They rescued Dinah from Shechem's house and returned to their camp again.

27   Then all of Jacob's sons went over and plundered the city because their sister had been dishonored there.

28   They confiscated all the flocks and herds and donkeys—everything they could lay their hands on, both inside the city and outside in the fields,

29   And took all the women and children, and wealth of every kind.

30   Then Jacob said to Levi and Simeon, "You have made me stink among all the people of this land —all the Canaanites and Perizzites. We are so few that they will come and crush us, and we will all be killed."

31   "Should he treat our sister like a prostitute?" they retorted.

CHAPTER 35

Move on to Bethel now, and settle there," God said to Jacob, "and build an altar to worship the God who appeared to you when you fled from your brother Esau."

2   So Jacob instructed all those in his household to destroy the idols they had brought with them, and

to wash themselves and to put on fresh clothing.

3   "For we are going to Bethel," he told them, "and I will build an altar there to the God who answered my prayers in the day of my distress, and was with me on my journey."

4   So they gave Jacob all their idols and their earrings, and he buried them beneath the oak tree near Shechem.

5   Then they started on again. And the terror of God was upon all the cities they journeyed through, so that they were not attacked.

6   Finally they arrived at Luz (also called Bethel), in Canaan.

7   And Jacob erected an altar there and named it "The altar to the God who met me here at Bethel"[1] because it was there at Bethel that God appeared to him when he was fleeing from Esau.

8   Soon[2] after this, Rebekah's old nurse Deborah died and was buried beneath the oak tree in the valley below Bethel. And ever after it was called "The Oak of Weeping."

9   Upon Jacob's arrival at Bethel, en route from Paddam-aram, God appeared to him once again and blessed him.

10   And God said to him, "You shall no longer be called Jacob ("Cheater"),[3] but Israel ("One who prevails with God").[3]

11   "I am God Almighty," the Lord said to him, "and I will cause you to be fertile and to multiply and to become a great nation, yes, many nations; many kings shall be among your descendants.

[1]Literally, "The God of Bethel."
[2]Implied.
[3]Cf. Genesis 32:28. Literally, "shall no longer be called Jacob, but Israel."

12　And I will pass on to you the land I gave to Abraham and Isaac. Yes, I will give it to you and to your descendants."

13, 14　Afterwards Jacob built a stone pillar at the place where God had appeared to him; and he poured wine over it as an offering to God, and then anointed the pillar with olive oil.

15　Jacob named the spot Bethel ("House of God"), because God had spoken to him there.

16　Leaving Bethel, he and his household traveled on toward Ephrath (Bethlehem). But Rachel's pains of childbirth began while they were still a long way away.

17　After a very hard delivery, the midwife finally exclaimed, "Wonderful—another boy!"

18　And with Rachel's last breath (for she died) she named him "Ben-oni" ("Son of my sorrow"); but his father called him "Benjamin" ("Son of my right hand").

19　So Rachel died, and was buried near the road to Ephrath (also called Bethlehem).

20　And Jacob set up a monument of stones upon her grave, and it is there to this day.

21　Then Israel journeyed on and camped beyond the Tower of Eder.

22　It was while he was there that Reuben slept with Bilhah, his father's concubine, and someone told Israel about it.

Here are the names of the twelve sons of Jacob:

23　The sons of Leah:

　　　　Reuben, Jacob's oldest child,
　　　　Simeon,
　　　　Levi,

Judah,
Issachar,
Zebulun.

24 The sons of Rachel:
Joseph,
Benjamin.

25 The sons of Bilhah, Rachel's servant-girl:
Dan,
Naphtali.

26 The sons of Zilpah, Leah's servant-girl:
Gad,
Asher.

All these were born to him at Paddan-aram.

27 So Jacob came at last to Isaac his father at Mamre in Kiriath-arba (now called Hebron), where Abraham too had lived.

28, 29 Isaac died soon afterwards, at the ripe old age of 180. And his sons Esau and Jacob buried him.

CHAPTER 36

Here is a list of the descendants of Esau (also called Edom):

2, 3 Esau married three local girls from Canaan:
Adah (daughter of Elon the Hethite),
Oholibamah (daughter of Anah and granddaughter of Zibeon the Hivite),
Basemath (his cousin[1]—she was a daughter of Ishmael—the sister of Nebaioth).

4 Esau and Adah had a son named Eliphaz.
Esau and Basemath had a son named Reuel.

5 Esau and Oholibamah had sons named Jeush,

---

[1]Implied. Literally, "the daughter of Ishmael."

Jalam, and Korah. All these sons were born to Esau in the land of Canaan.

6, 7, 8   Then Esau took his wives, children, household servants, cattle and flocks—all the wealth he had gained in the land of Canaan—and moved away from his brother Jacob to Mount Seir. (For there was not land enough to support them both because of all their cattle.)

9   Here are the names of Esau's descendants, the Edomites, born to him in Mount Seir:

10, 11, 12   Descended from his wife Adah, born to her son Eliphaz were:

> Teman,
> Omar,
> Zepho,
> Gatam,
> Kenaz,
> Amalek, (born to Timna, Eliphaz' concubine).

13, 14[2]   Esau also had grandchildren from his wife Basemath. Born to her son Reuel were:

> Nahath,
> Zerah,
> Shammah,
> Mizzah.

15, 16   Esau's grandchildren[3] became the heads of clans, as listed here:

> The clan of Teman,
> The clan of Omar,
> The clan of Zepho,
> The clan of Kenaz,

---

[2]Verse 14 is a repetition of the names listed in verse 5.
[3]Implied.

  The clan of Korah,
  The clan of Gatam,
  The clan of Amalek.

The above clans were the descendants of Eliphaz, the oldest son of Esau and Adah.

17 The following clans were the descendants of Reuel, born to Esau and his wife Basemath while they lived in Canaan:

  The clan of Nahath,
  The clan of Zerah,
  The clan of Shammah,
  The clan of Mizzah.

18, 19 And these are the clans named after the sons of Esau and his wife Oholibamah (daughter of Anah):

  The clan of Jeush,
  The clan of Jalam,
  The clan of Korah.

20 These are the names of the tribes that descended from Seir, the Horite—one of the native families of the land of Seir:

  The tribe of Lotan,
  The tribe of Shobal,
  The tribe of Zibeon,
  The tribe of Anah,
21 The tribe of Dishon,
  The tribe of Ezer,
  The tribe of Dishan.

22 The children of Lotan (the son of Seir) were Hori and Heman. (Lotan had a sister, Timna.)

23 The children of Shobal:

  Alvan,
  Manahath,

Ebal,
Shepho,
Onam.

24 The children of Zibeon:
Aiah,
Anah. (This is the boy who discovered a
hot springs in the wasteland while he
was grazing his father's donkeys.)

25 The children of Anah:
Dishon,
Oholibamah.

26 The children of Dishon:
Hemdan,
Eshban,
Ithran,
Cheran.

27 The children of Ezer:
Bilhan,
Zaavan,
Akan.

28, 29, 30[4] The children of Dishan:
Uz,
Aran.

31 These are the names of the kings of Edom
(before Israel had her first king):

32 King Bela (son of Beor), from Dinhabah
in Edom.
Succeeded[5] by:

33 King Jobab (son of Zerah), from the city[6]
of Bozrah.
Succeeded by:

---

[4]Verses 29 and 30 repeat the names listed in verses 20, 21.
[5]More literally, "succeeded at his death by . . ."
[6]Implied.

34   King Husham, from the land of the Temanites.

Succeeded by:

35   King Hadad (son of Bedad), the leader of the forces that defeated the army of Midian when it invaded Moab. His city was Avith.

36   Succeeded by:

King Samlah, from Masrekah.

37   Succeeded by:

King Shaul, from Rehoboth-by-the-River.

38   Succeeded by:

King Baal-hanan (son of Achbor).

39   Succeeded by:

King Hadad, from the city of Pau.

King Hadad's wife was Mehetabel, daughter of Matred and granddaughter of Mezahab.

40 Here are the names of the sub-tribes of Esau, living in the localities named after themselves:

The clan of Timna,

The clan of Alvah,

The clan of Jetheth,

41   The clan of Oholibamah,

The clan of Elah,

42   The clan of Pinon,

The clan of Kenaz,

The clan of Teman,

The clan of Mibzar,

43   The clan of Magdiel,

The clan of Iram.

These, then, are the names of the sub-tribes of Edom, each giving its name to the area it occupied. (All were Edomites, descendants of Esau.)

CHAPTER 37

So Jacob settled again in the land of Canaan, where his father had lived.

* * * * *

2 Jacob's son Joseph was now seventeen years old. His job, along with his half-brothers, the sons of his father's wives Bilhah and Zilpah, was to shepherd his father's flocks. But Joseph tattled to his father about some of the things they were doing.

3 Now as it happened, Israel loved Joseph more than any of his other children, because Joseph was born to him in his old age. So one day Jacob gave him a special gift—a brightly-colored coat.[1]

4 His brothers of course noticed their father's partiality, and consequently hated Joseph; they couldn't say a kind word to him.

5 One night Joseph had a dream and promptly reported the details to his brothers, causing even deeper hatred.

6 "Listen to this," he proudly announced.

7 "We were out in the field binding sheaves, and my sheaf stood up, and your sheaves all gathered around it and bowed low before it!"

8 "So you want to be our king, do you?" his brothers derided.

And they hated him both for the dream and for his cocky attitude.

9 Then he had another dream and told it to his brothers. "Listen to my latest dream," he boasted. "The sun, moon, and eleven stars bowed low before me!"

10 This time he told his father as well as his

---

[1]More literally, "an ornamented tunic," or "long-sleeved tunic."

brothers; but his father rebuked him. "What is this?" he asked. "Shall I indeed, and your mother and brothers come and bow before you?"

11   His brothers were fit to be tied concerning this affair, but his father gave it quite a bit of thought and wondered what it all meant.

12   One day Joseph's brothers took their father's flocks to Shechem to graze them there.

13, 14   A few days later Israel called for Joseph, and told him, "Your brothers are over in Shechem grazing the flocks. Go and see how they are getting along, and how it is with the flocks, and bring me word."

"Very good," Joseph replied. So he traveled to Shechem from his home at Hebron Valley.

15   A man noticed him wandering in the fields. "Who are you looking for?" he asked.

16   "For my brothers and their flocks," Joseph replied. "Have you seen them?"

17   "Yes," the man told him, "they are no longer here. I heard your brothers say they were going to Dothan." So Joseph followed them to Dothan and found them there.

18   But when they saw him coming, recognizing him in the distance, they decided to kill him!

19, 20   "Here comes that master-dreamer," they exclaimed. "Come on, let's kill him and toss him into a well and tell father that a wild animal has eaten him. Then we'll see what will become of all his dreams!"

21, 22   But Reuben hoped to spare Joseph's life. "Let's not kill him," he said; "we'll shed no blood— let's throw him alive into this well here; that way he'll die without our touching him!" (Reuben was planning to get him out later and return him to his father.)

23 So when Joseph got there, they pulled off his brightly-colored robe,

24 And threw him into an empty well—there was no water in it.

25 Then they sat down for supper. Suddenly they noticed a string of camels coming towards them in the distance, probably Ishmaelite traders who were taking gum, spices, and herbs from Gilead to Egypt.

26, 27 "Look there," Judah said to the others. "Here come some Ishmaelites. Let's sell Joseph to them! Why kill him and have a guilty conscience? Let's not be responsible for his death, for, after all, he is our brother!" And his brothers agreed.

28 So when the traders[2] came by, his brothers pulled Joseph out of the well and sold him to them for twenty pieces of silver, and they took him along to Egypt.

29 Some time later, Reuben (who was away when the traders came by)[3] returned to get Joseph out of the well. When Joseph wasn't there, he ripped at his clothes in anguish and frustration.

30 "The child is gone; and I, where shall I go now?" he wept to his brothers.

31 Then the brothers killed a goat and spattered its blood on Joseph's coat,

32 And took the coat to their father and asked him to identify it.

"We found this in the field," they told him. "Is it Joseph's coat or not?"

---

[2]Literally, "Midianites."
[3]Implied.

33 Their father recognized it at once. "Yes," he sobbed, "it is my son's coat. A wild animal has eaten him. Joseph is without doubt torn in pieces."

34 Then Israel tore his garments and put on sackcloth and mourned for his son in deepest mourning for many weeks.

35 His family all tried to comfort him, but it was no use. "I will die in mourning for my son," he would say, and then break down and cry.

36 Meanwhile, in Egypt, the traders sold Joseph to Potiphar, an officer of the Pharaoh—the king of Egypt. Potiphar was captain of the palace guard, the chief executioner.

CHAPTER 38

About this time, Judah left home and moved to Adullam and lived there with a man named Hirah.

2 There he met and married a Canaanite girl—the daughter of Shua.

3, 4, 5 They lived at Chezib and had three sons, Er, Onan, and Shelah. These names were given to them by their mother, except for Er, who was named by his father.

6 When his oldest son Er grew up, Judah arranged for him to marry a girl named Tamar.

7 But Er was a wicked man, and so the Lord killed him.

8 Then Judah said to Er's brother, Onan, "You must marry Tamar, as our law requires of a dead man's brother; so that her sons from you will be your brother's heirs."

9 But Onan was not willing to have a child who would not be counted as his own, and so, although he

married her,[1] whenever he went in to sleep with her, he spilled the sperm on the bed[2] to prevent her from having a baby which would be his brother's.

10 So far as the Lord was concerned, it was very wrong of him [to deny a child to his deceased brother],[3] so He killed him, too.

11 Then Judah told Tamar, his daughter-in-law, not to marry again at that time, but to return to her childhood home and to her parents, and to remain a widow there until his youngest son Shelah was old enough to marry her.

(But he didn't really intend for Shelah to do this, for fear God would kill him, too, just as He had his two brothers.) So Tamar went home to her parents.

12 In the process of time Judah's wife died. After the time of mourning was over, Judah and his friend Hirah, the Adullamite, went to Timnah to supervise the shearing of his sheep.

13 When someone told Tamar that her father-in-law had left for the sheep-shearing at Timnah,

14 And realizing by now that she was not going to be permitted to marry Shelah, though he was fully grown, she laid aside her widow's clothing and covered herself with a veil to disguise herself, and sat beside the road at the entrance to the village of Enaim, which is on the way to Timnah.

15 Judah noticed her as he went by and thought she was a prostitute, since her face was veiled.

16 So he stopped and propositioned her to sleep with him, not realizing of course that she was his own daughter-in-law.

---

[1]Implied.
[2]Literally, "spilled it on the ground."
[3]Implied.

"How much will you pay me?" she asked.

17 "I'll send you a young goat from my flock," he promised.

"What pledge will you give me, so that I can be sure you will send it?" she asked.

18 "Well, what do you want?" he inquired.

"Your identification seal and your walking stick," she replied. So he gave them to her and she let him come and sleep with her; and she became pregnant as a result.

19 Afterwards she resumed wearing her widow's clothing as usual.

20 Judah asked his friend Hirah the Adullamite to take the young goat back to her, and to pick up the pledges he had given her, but Hirah couldn't find her!

21 So he asked around of the men of the city, "Where does the prostitute live who was soliciting out beside the road at the entrance of the village?"

"But we've never had a public prostitute here," they replied.

22 So he returned to Judah and told him he couldn't find her anywhere, and what the men of the place had told him.

23 "Then let her keep them!" Judah exclaimed. "We tried our best. We'd be the laughingstock of the town to go back again."

24 About three months later word reached Judah that Tamar, his daughter-in-law, was pregnant, obviously as a result of prostitution. "Bring her out and burn her," Judah shouted.

25 But as they were taking her out to kill her she sent this message to her father-in-law: "The man who owns this identification seal and walking stick is the

father of my child. Do you recognize them?"

26   Judah admitted that they were his and said, "She is more in the right than I am, because I refused to keep my promise to give her to my son Shelah." But he did not marry her.

27   In due season the time of her delivery arrived and she had twin sons.

28   As they were being born, the midwife tied a scarlet thread around the wrist of the child who appeared first,

29   But he drew back his hand and the other baby was actually the first to be born. "Where did *you* come from!" she exclaimed. And ever after he was called Perez (meaning "Bursting Out").

30   Then, soon afterwards, the baby with the scarlet thread on his wrist was born, and he was named Zerah.

CHAPTER 39

When Joseph arrived in Egypt as a captive of the Ishmaelite traders, he was purchased from them by Potiphar, a member of the personal staff of Pharaoh, the king of Egypt. Now this man Potiphar was the captain of the king's bodyguard and his chief executioner.

2   The Lord greatly blessed Joseph there in the home of his master, so that everything he did succeeded.

3   Potiphar noticed this and realized that the Lord was with Joseph in a very special way.

4   So Joseph naturally became quite a favorite with him. Soon he was put in charge of the administration of Potiphar's household, and all of his business affairs.

5   At once the Lord began blessing Potiphar for Joseph's sake. All his household affairs began to run smoothly, his crops flourished and his flocks multiplied.

6   So Potiphar gave Joseph the complete administrative responsibility over everything he owned. He hadn't a worry in the world with Joseph there, except to decide what he wanted to eat! Joseph, by the way, was a very handsome young man.

7   One day at about this time Potiphar's wife began making eyes at Joseph, and suggested that he come and sleep with her.

8   Joseph refused. "Look," he told her, "my master trusts me with everything in the entire household;

9   He himself has no more authority here than I have! He has held back nothing from me except you yourself because you are his wife. How can I do such a wicked thing as this? It would be a great sin against God."

10   But she kept on with her suggestions day after day, even though he refused to listen, and kept out of her way as much as possible.

11   Then one day as he was in the house going about his work—as it happened, no one else was around at the time—

12   She came and grabbed him by the sleeve[1] demanding, "Sleep with me." He tore himself away, but as he did, his jacket[1] slipped off and she was left holding it as he fled from the house.

13   When she saw that she had his jacket, and that he had fled,

14, 15   She began screaming; and when the other men around the place came running in to see what had

---

[1]The Hebrew word is not specific.

happened, she was crying hysterically. "My husband had to bring in this Hebrew slave to insult us!" she sobbed. "He tried to rape me, but when I screamed, he ran, and forgot to take his jacket."

16   She kept the jacket, and when her husband came home that night,

17   She told him her story. "That Hebrew slave you've had around here tried to rape me,

18   And I was only saved by my screams. He fled, leaving his jacket behind!"

19   Well, when her husband heard his wife's story, he was furious.

20   He threw Joseph into prison, where the king's prisoners were kept in chains.

21   But the Lord was with Joseph there, too, and was kind to him by granting him favor with the chief jailer.

22   In fact, the jailer soon handed over the entire prison administration to Joseph, so that all the other prisoners were responsible to him.

23   The chief jailer had no more worries after that, for Joseph took care of everything, and the Lord was with him so that everything ran smoothly and well.

CHAPTER 40

Some time later it so happened that the king of Egypt became angry with his chief baker and his wine taster, so he jailed them both in the prison where Joseph was, in the castle of Potiphar, the captain of the guard, who was the chief executioner.

4   They remained under arrest there for quite some time, and Potiphar assigned Joseph to wait on them.

5   One night each of them had a dream.

6   The next morning Joseph noticed that they looked dejected and sad.

7   "What in the world is the matter?" he asked.

8   And they replied, "We both had dreams last night, but there is no one here to tell us what they mean."

"Interpreting dreams is God's business," Joseph replied. "Tell me what you saw."

9, 10   The wine taster told his dream first. "In my dream," he said, "I saw a vine with three branches that began to bud and blossom, and soon there were clusters of ripe grapes.

11   I was holding Pharaoh's wine cup in my hand, so I took the grapes and squeezed the juice into it, and gave it to him to drink."

12   "I know what the dream means," Joseph said. "The three branches mean three days!

13   Within three days Pharaoh is going to take you out of prison and give you back your job as his wine taster.

14   And please have some pity on me when you are back in his favor, and mention me to Pharaoh, and ask him to let me out of here.

15   For I was kidnapped from my homeland among the Hebrews, and now this—here I am in jail when I did nothing to deserve it."

16   When the chief baker saw that the first dream had such a good meaning, he told his dream to Joseph, too.

"In my dream," he said, "there were three baskets of pastries on my head.

17   In the top basket were all kinds of bakery goods

for Pharaoh, but the birds came and ate them."

18, 19 "The three baskets mean three days," Joseph told him. "Three days from now Pharaoh will take off your head and impale your body on a pole, and the birds will come and pick off your flesh!"

20 Pharaoh's birthday came three days later, and he gave a big party for all of his officials and household staff. He sent for his wine taster and chief baker, and they were brought to him from the prison.

21 Then he restored the wine taster to his former position;

22 But he sentenced the chief baker to be impaled, just as Joseph had predicted.

23 Pharaoh's wine taster, however, promptly forgot all about Joseph, never giving him a thought.

CHAPTER 41

One night two years later, Pharaoh dreamed that he was standing on the bank of the Nile River,

2 When suddenly, seven sleek, fat cows came up out of the river and began grazing in the grass.

3 Then seven other cows came up from the river, but they were very skinny and all their ribs stood out. They went over and stood beside the fat cows.

4 Then the skinny cows ate the fat ones! At which point, Pharaoh woke up!

5 Soon he fell asleep again and had a second dream. This time he saw seven heads of grain on one stalk, with every kernel well formed and plump.

6 Then, suddenly, seven more heads appeared on the stalk, but these were shrivelled and withered by the east wind.

7 And these thin heads swallowed up the seven plump, well-formed heads! Then Pharaoh woke up again and realized it was all a dream.

8 Next morning, as he thought about it, he became very concerned as to what the dreams might mean; he called for all the magicians and sages of Egypt and told them about it, but not one of them could suggest what his dreams meant.

9 Then the king's wine taster spoke up. "Today I remember my sin!" he said.

10 "Some time ago when you were angry with a couple of us and put me and the chief baker in jail in the castle of the captain of the guard,

11 The chief baker and I each had a dream one night.

12 We told the dreams to a young Hebrew fellow there who was a slave of the captain of the guard, and he told us what our dreams meant.

13 And everything happened just as he said: I was restored to my position of wine taster, and the chief baker was executed, and impaled on a pole."

14 Pharaoh sent at once for Joseph. He was brought hastily from the dungeon, and after a quick shave and change of clothes, came in before Pharaoh.

15 "I had a dream last night," Pharaoh told him, "and none of these men can tell me what it means. But I have heard that you can interpret dreams, and that is why I have called for you."

16 "I can't do it by myself," Joseph replied, "but God will tell you what it means!"

17 So Pharaoh told him the dream. "I was standing upon the bank of the Nile River," he said,

18 "When suddenly, seven fat, healthy-looking

cows came up out of the river and began grazing along the river bank.

19 But then seven other cows came up from the river, very skinny and bony—in fact, I've never seen such poor-looking specimens in all the land of Egypt.

20 And these skinny cattle ate up the seven fat ones that had come out first,

21 And afterwards they were still as skinny as before! Then I woke up.

22 A little later I had another dream. This time there were seven heads of grain on one stalk, and all seven heads were plump and full.

23 Then, out of the same stalk, came seven withered, thin heads.

24 And the thin heads swallowed up the fat ones! I told all this to my magicians, but not one of them could tell me the meaning."

25 "Both dreams mean the same thing," Joseph told Pharaoh. "God was telling you what He is going to do here in the land of Egypt.

26 The seven fat cows (and also the seven fat, well-formed heads of grain) mean that there are seven years of prosperity ahead.

27 The seven skinny cows (and also the seven thin and withered heads of grain) indicate that there will be seven years of famine following the seven years of prosperity.

28 So God has showed you what He is about to do:

29 The next seven years will be a period of great prosperity throughout all the land of Egypt;

30 But afterwards there will be seven years of famine so great that all the prosperity will be forgotten and wiped out; famine will consume the land.

31 The famine will be so terrible that even the memory of the good years will be erased.

32 The double dream gives double impact, showing that what I have told you is certainly going to happen, for God has decreed it, and it is going to happen soon.

33 My suggestion is that you find the wisest man in Egypt and put him in charge of administering a nation-wide farm program.

34, 35 Let Pharaoh divide Egypt into five administrative districts,[1] and let the officials of these districts gather into the royal storehouses all the excess crops of the next seven years,

36 So that there will be enough to eat when the seven years of famine come. Otherwise, disaster will surely strike."

37 Joseph's suggestions were well received by Pharaoh and his assistants.

38 As they discussed who should be appointed for the job, Pharaoh said, "Who could do it better than Joseph? For he is a man who is obviously filled with the Spirit of God."

39 Turning to Joseph, Pharaoh said to him, "Since God has revealed the meaning of the dreams to you, you are the wisest man in the country!

40 I am hereby appointing you to be in charge of this entire project. What you say goes, throughout all the land of Egypt. I alone will outrank you."

41, 42 Then Pharaoh placed his own signet ring on Joseph's finger as a token of his authority, and dressed him in beautiful clothing and placed the royal golden chain about his neck and declared, "See, I have

[1]Or, "Let Pharaoh appoint officials to collect a fifth of all the crops . . ."

placed you in charge of all the land of Egypt."

43 Pharaoh also gave Joseph the chariot of his second-in-command, and wherever he went the shout arose, "Kneel down!"

44 And Pharaoh declared to Joseph, "I, the king of Egypt, swear that you shall have complete charge over all the land of Egypt."

45 Pharaoh gave him a name meaning "He has the god-like power of life and death!"[2] And he gave him a wife, a girl named Asenath, daughter of Poti-phera, priest of Heliopolis.[3] So Joseph became famous throughout the land of Egypt.

46 He was thirty years old as he entered the service of the king. Joseph went out from the presence of Pharaoh, and began traveling all across the land.

47 And sure enough, for the next seven years there were bumper crops everywhere.

48 During those years, Joseph requisitioned for the government a portion of all the crops grown throughout Egypt, storing them in nearby cities.

49 After seven years of this, the granaries were full to overflowing, and there was so much that no one kept track of the amount.

50 During this time before the arrival of the first of the famine years, two sons were born to Joseph by Asenath, the daughter of Potiphera, priest of the sun god Re of Heliopolis.

51 Joseph named his oldest son Manasseh (meaning "Made to Forget"—what he meant was that God had made up to him for all the anguish of his youth, and for the loss of his father's home).

---

[2]Or, "God (or Pharaoh) says 'He is living.' "
[3]Joseph thus married into a family of high nobility, his father-in-law being a major priest-politician of the time.

52 The second boy was named Ephraim (meaning "Fruitful"—"For God has made me fruitful in this land of my slavery," he said).

53 So at last the seven years of plenty came to an end.

54 Then the seven years of famine began, just as Joseph had predicted. There were crop failures in all the surrounding countries too, but in Egypt there was plenty of grain in the storehouses.

55 The people began to starve. They pleaded with Pharaoh for food, and he sent them to Joseph. "Do whatever he tells you to," he instructed them.

56, 57 So now, with severe famine all over the world, Joseph opened up the storehouses and sold grain to the Egyptians and to those from other lands who came to Egypt to buy grain from Joseph.

CHAPTER 42

When Jacob heard that there was grain available in Egypt he said to his sons, "Why are you standing around looking at one another?

2 I have heard that there is grain available in Egypt. Go down and buy some for us before we all starve to death."

3 So Joseph's ten older[1] brothers went down to Egypt to buy grain.

4 However, Jacob wouldn't let Joseph's younger brother Benjamin go with them, for fear some harm might happen to him [as it had to his brother Joseph[1]].

5 So it was that Israel's sons arrived in Egypt along with many others from many lands to buy food,

---
[1]Implied.

for the famine was as severe in Canaan as it was every-where else.

6 Since Joseph was governor of all Egypt, and in charge of the sale of the grain, it was to him that his brothers came, and bowed low before him, with their faces to the earth.

7 Joseph recognized them instantly, but pretended he didn't.

"Where are you from?" he demanded roughly.

"From the land of Canaan," they replied. "We have come to buy grain."

8, 9 Then Joseph remembered the dreams of long ago! But he said to them, "You are spies. You have come to see how destitute the famine has made our land."

10 "No, no," they exclaimed. "We have come to buy food.

11 We are all brothers and honest men, sir! We are not spies!"

12 "Yes, you are," he insisted. "You have come to see how weak we are."

13 "Sir," they said, "there are twelve of us brothers, and our father is in the land of Canaan. Our youngest brother is there with our father, and one of our brothers is dead."

14 "So?" Joseph asked. "What does that prove?[2] You are spies.

15 This is the way I will test your story: I swear by the life of Pharaoh that you are not going to leave Egypt until this youngest brother comes here.

16 One of you go and get your brother! I'll keep the rest of you here, bound in prison. Then we'll find

[2]Literally, "It is as I said: you are spies."

out whether your story is true or not. If it turns out that you don't have a younger brother, then I'll know you are spies."

17   So he threw them all into jail for three days.

18   The third day Joseph said to them, "I am a God-fearing man and I'm going to give you an opportunity to prove yourselves.

19   I'm going to take a chance that you are honorable:[3] only one of you shall remain in chains in jail, and the rest of you may go on home with grain for your families;

20   But bring your youngest brother back to me. In this way I will know whether you are telling me the truth; and if you are, I will spare you." To this they agreed.

21   Speaking among themselves, they said, "This has all happened because of what we did to Joseph long ago. We saw his terror and anguish and heard his pleadings, but we wouldn't listen."

22   "Didn't I tell you not to do it?" Reuben asked. "But you wouldn't listen. And now we are going to die because we murdered him."

23   Of course they didn't know that Joseph understood them as he was standing there, for he had been speaking to them through an interpreter.

24   Now he left the room and found a place where he could weep. Returning, he selected Simeon from among them and had him bound before their eyes.

25   Joseph then ordered his servants to fill the men's sacks with grain, but also gave secret instructions to put each brother's payment at the top of his sack! He also gave them provisions for their journey.

---

[3]Literally, "If you are forthright men."

26 So they loaded up their donkeys with the grain and started for home.

27 But when they stopped for the night and one of them opened his sack to get some grain to feed the donkeys, there was his money in the mouth of the sack!

28 "Look," he exclaimed to his brothers, "my money is here in my sack." They were filled with terror. Trembling, they exclaimed to each other, "What is this that God has done to us?"

29 So they came to their father Jacob in the land of Canaan and told him all that had happened.

30 "The king's chief assistant spoke very roughly to us," they told him, "and took us for spies.

31 'No, no,' we said, 'we are honest men, not spies.

32 We are twelve brothers, sons of one father; one is dead, and the youngest is with our father in the land of Canaan.'

33 Then the man told us, 'This is the way I will find out if you are what you claim to be. Leave one of your brothers here with me and take grain for your families and go on home,

34 But bring your youngest brother back to me. Then I shall know whether you are spies or honest men; if you prove to be what you say, then I will give you back your brother and you can come as often as you like to purchase grain.' "

35 As they emptied out the sacks, there at the top of each was the money paid for the grain!

Terror gripped them, as it did their father.

36 Then Jacob exclaimed, "You have bereaved me of my children—Joseph didn't come back, Simeon is gone, and now you want to take Benjamin too! Everything has been against me."

37 Then Reuben said to his father, "Kill my two sons if I don't bring Benjamin back to you. I'll be responsible for him."

38 But Jacob replied, "My son shall not go down with you, for his brother Joseph is dead and he alone is left of his mother's children. If anything should happen to him, I would die."

CHAPTER 43

But there was no relief from the terrible famine throughout the land.

2 When the grain they had brought from Egypt was almost gone, their father said to them, "Go again and buy us a little food."

3, 4, 5 But Judah told him, "The man wasn't fooling one bit when he said, 'Don't ever come back again unless your brother is with you.' We cannot go unless you let Benjamin go with us."

6 "Why did you ever tell him you had another brother?" Israel moaned. "Why did you have to treat me like that?"

7 "But the man specifically asked us about our family," they told him. "He wanted to know whether our father was still living and he asked us if we had another brother, so we told him. How could we know that he was going to say, 'Bring me your brother'?"

8 Judah said to his father, "Send the lad with me and we will be on our way; otherwise we will all die of starvation—and not only we, but you and all our little ones.

9 I guarantee his safety. If I don't bring him back to you, then let me bear the blame forever.

10 For we could have gone and returned by this

time if you had let him come."

11 So their father Israel finally said to them, "If if can't be avoided, then at least do this. Load your donkeys with the best products of the land. Take them to the man as gifts—balm, honey, spices, myrrh, pistachio nuts, and almonds.

12 Take double money so that you can pay back what was in the mouths of your sacks, as it was probably someone's mistake,

13 And take your brother and go.

14 May God Almighty give you mercy before the man, so that he will release Simeon and return Benjamin. And if I must bear the anguish of their deaths, then so be it."

15 So they took the gifts and double money and went to Egypt, and stood before Joseph.

16 When Joseph saw that Benjamin was with them he said to the manager of his household, "These men will eat with me this noon. Take them home and prepare a big feast."

17 So the man did as he was told and took them to Joseph's palace.

18 They were badly frightened when they saw where they were being taken. "It's because of the money returned to us in our sacks," they said. "He wants to pretend we stole it and seize us as slaves, with our donkeys."

19 As they arrived at the entrance to the palace, they went over to Joseph's household manager,

20 And said to him, "O sir, after our first trip to Egypt to buy food,

21 As we were returning home, we stopped for the night and opened our sacks, and the money was

there that we had paid for the grain. Here it is; we have brought it back again,

22 Along with additional money to buy more grain. We have no idea how the money got into our sacks."

23 "Don't worry about it," the household manager told them; "your God, even the God of your fathers, must have put it there, for we collected your money all right."

Then he released Simeon and brought him out to them.

24 They were then conducted into the palace and given water to refresh their feet; and their donkeys were fed.

25 Then they got their presents ready for Joseph's arrival at noon, for they were told that they would be eating there.

26 When Joseph came home they gave him their presents, bowing low before him.

27 He asked how they had been getting along. "And how is your father—the old man you spoke about? Is he still alive?"

28 "Yes," they replied. "He is alive and well."

Then again they bowed before him.

29 Looking at his brother[1] Benjamin, he asked, "Is this your youngest brother, the one you told me about? How are you, my son? God be gracious to you."

30 Then Joseph made a hasty exit, for he was overcome with love for his brother and had to go out and cry. Going into his bedroom, he wept there.

31 Then he washed his face and came out, keeping himself under control. "Let's eat," he said.

32 Joseph ate by himself, his brothers were served

---

[1] Literally, "his brother Benjamin, his mother's son."

at a separate table, and the Egyptians at still another; for Egyptians despise Hebrews and never eat with them.

33 He told each of them where to sit, and seated them in the order of their ages, from the oldest to the youngest, much to their amazement!

34 Their food was served to them from his own table. He gave the largest serving to Benjamin—five times as much as to any of the others! They had a wonderful time bantering back and forth, and the wine flowed freely!

CHAPTER 44

When his brothers were ready to leave,[1] Joseph ordered his household manager to fill each of their sacks with as much grain as they could carry—and to put into the mouth of each man's sack the money he had paid!

2 He was also told to put Joseph's own silver cup at the top of Benjamin's sack, along with the grain money. So the household manager did as he was told.

3 The brothers were up at dawn and on their way with their loaded donkeys.

4 But when they were barely out of the city Joseph said to his household manager, "Chase after them and stop them and ask them why they are acting like this when their benefactor has been so kind to them?

5 Ask them, 'What do you mean by stealing my lord's personal silver drinking cup, which he uses for fortune telling? What a wicked thing you have done!' "

6 So he caught up with them and spoke to them along the lines he had been instructed.

[1]Implied.

7 "What in the world are you talking about?" they demanded. "What kind of people do you think we are, that you accuse us of such a terrible thing as that?

8 Didn't we bring back the money we found in the mouth of our sacks? Why would we steal silver or gold from your master's house?

9 If you find his cup with any one of us, let that one die. And all the rest of us will be slaves forever to your master."

10 "Fair enough," the man replied, "except that only the one who stole it will be a slave, and the rest of you can go free."

11 They quickly took down their sacks from the backs of their donkeys and opened them.

12 He began searching the oldest brother's sack, going on down the line to the youngest. And the cup was found in Benjamin's!

13 They ripped their clothing in despair, loaded the donkeys again, and returned to the city.

14 Joseph was still home when Judah and his brothers arrived, and they fell to the ground before him.

15 "What were you trying to do?" Joseph demanded. "Didn't you know such a man as I would know who stole it?"

16 And Judah said, "Oh, what shall we say to my lord? How can we plead? How can we prove our innocence? God is punishing us for our sins. Sir, we have all returned to be your slaves, both we and he in whose sack the cup was found."

17 "No," Joseph said. "Only the man who stole the cup, he shall be my slave. The rest of you can go on home to your father."

18 Then Judah stepped forward and said, "O sir,

let me say just this one word to you. Be patient with me for a moment, for I know you can doom me in an instant, as though you were Pharaoh himself.

19   Sir, you asked us if we had a father or a brother,

20   And we said, 'Yes, we have a father, an old man, and a child of his old age, a little one. And his brother is dead, and he alone is left of his mother's children, and his father loves him very much.'

21   And you said to us, 'Bring him here so that I can see him.'

22   But we said to you, 'Sir, the lad cannot leave his father, for his father would die.'

23   But you told us, 'Don't come back here unless your youngest brother is with you.'

24   So we returned to our father and told him what you had said.

25   And when he said, 'Go back again and buy us a little food,'

26   We replied, 'We can't, unless you let our youngest brother go with us. Only then may we come.'

27   Then my father said to us, 'You know that my wife had two sons,

28   And that one of them went away and never returned—doubtless torn to pieces by some wild animal; I have never seen him since.

29   And if you take away his brother from me also, and any harm befalls him, I shall die with sorrow.'

30   And now, sir, if I go back to my father and the lad is not with us—seeing that our father's life is bound up in the lad's life—

31   When he sees that the boy is not with us, our father will die; and we will be responsible for bringing down his gray hairs with sorrow to the grave.

32   Sir, I pledged my father that I would take care of the lad. I told him, 'If I don't bring him back to you, I shall bear the blame forever.'

33   Please sir, let me stay here as a slave instead of the lad, and let the lad return with his brothers.

34   For how shall I return to my father if the lad is not with me? I cannot bear to see what this would do to him."

CHAPTER 45

Joseph could stand it no longer. "Out, all of you," he cried out to his attendants, and he was left alone with his brothers.

2   Then he wept aloud. His sobs could be heard throughout the palace, and the news was quickly carried to Pharaoh's palace.

3   "I am Joseph!" he said to his brothers. "Is my father still alive?" But his brothers couldn't say a word, they were so stunned with surprise.

4   "Come over here," he said. So they came closer. And he said again, "I am Joseph, your brother whom you sold into Egypt!

5   But don't be angry with yourselves that you did this to me, for God did it! He sent me here ahead of you to preserve your lives.

6   These two years of famine will grow to seven, during which there will be neither plowing nor harvest.

7   God has sent me here to keep you and your families alive, so that you will become a great nation.

8   Yes, it was God who sent me here, not you! And He has made me a counselor to Pharaoh, and manager of this entire nation, ruler of all the land of Egypt.

9   Hurry, return to my father and tell him, 'Your son Joseph says, "God has made me chief of all the land of Egypt. Come down to me right away!

10   You shall live in the land of Goshen so that you can be near me with all your children, your grandchildren, your flocks and herds, and all that you have.

11, 12   I will take care of you there" (you men are witnesses of my promise, and my brother Benjamin has heard me say it) "for there are still five years of famine ahead of us. Otherwise you will come to utter poverty along with all your household." '

13   Tell our father about all my power here in Egypt, and how everyone obeys me. And bring him to me quickly."

14   Then, weeping with joy, he embraced Benjamin and Benjamin began weeping too.

15   And he did the same with each of his brothers, who finally found their tongues!

16   The news soon reached Pharaoh—"Joseph's brothers have come"; and Pharaoh was very happy to hear it, as were his officials.

17   Then Pharaoh said to Joseph, "Tell your brothers to load their pack animals and return quickly to their homes in Canaan,

18   And to bring your father and all of your families and come here to Egypt to live. Tell them, 'Pharaoh will assign to you the very best territory in the land of Egypt. You shall live off the fat of the land!'

19   And tell your brothers to take wagons from Egypt to carry their wives and little ones, and to bring your father here.

20   Don't worry about your property, for the best of all the land of Egypt is yours."

21   So Joseph gave them wagons, as Pharaoh had commanded, and provisions for the journey,

22   And he gave each of them new clothes—but to Benjamin he gave five changes of clothes and three hundred pieces of silver!

23   He sent his father ten donkey-loads of the good things of Egypt, and ten donkeys loaded with grain and all kinds of other food, to eat on his journey.

24   So he sent his brothers off. "Don't quarrel along the way!" was his parting shot!

25   And leaving, they returned to the land of Canaan, to Jacob their father.

26   "Joseph is alive," they shouted to him. "And he is ruler over all the land of Egypt!" But Jacob's heart was like a stone; he couldn't take it in.

27   But when they had given him Joseph's messages, and when he saw the wagons filled with food that Joseph had sent him, his spirit revived.

28   And he said, "It must be true! Joseph my son is alive! I will go and see him before I die."

CHAPTER 46

So Israel set out with all his possessions, and came to Beer-sheba, and offered sacrifices there to the God of his father Isaac.

2   During the night God spoke to him in a vision. "Jacob! Jacob!" He called.

"Yes?" Jacob answered.

3, 4   "I am God," the voice replied, "the God of your father. Don't be afraid to go down to Egypt, for I will see to it that you become a great nation there. And I will go down with you into Egypt and I will bring your descendants back again; but you shall die in Egypt with Joseph at your side."

5 So Jacob left Beer-sheba, and his sons brought him to Egypt, along with their little ones and their wives, in the wagons Pharaoh had provided for them.

6 They brought their livestock too, and all their belongings accumulated in the land of Canaan, and came to Egypt—Jacob and all his children,

7 Sons and daughters, grandsons and granddaughters—all his loved ones.

8 Here are the names of his sons and grandchildren who went with him into Egypt:

Reuben, his oldest son;

9 Reuben's sons: Hanoch, Pallu, Hezron, and Carmi.

10 Simeon and his sons: Jemuel, Jamin, Ohad, Jachin, Zohar, and Shaul (Shaul's mother was a girl from Canaan).

11 Levi and his sons: Gershon, Kohath, Merari.

12 Judah and his sons: Er, Onan, Shelah, Perez, Zerah (however, Er and Onan died while still in Canaan, before Israel went to Egypt).
The sons of Perez were Hezron and Hamul.

13 Issachar and his sons: Tola, Puvah, Iob, Shimron.

14 Zebulun and his sons: Sered, Elon, Jahleel.

15 So these descendants of Jacob and Leah, not including their daughter Dinah, born to Jacob in

Paddam-aram, were thirty-three in all.

16 Also accompanying him were:

> Gad and his sons: Ziphion, Haggi, Shuni,
> Ezbon, Eri, Arodi, and Areli.

17 Asher and his sons: Imnah, Ishvah, Ishvi,
> Beriah, and a sister, Serah.
>
> Beriah's sons were Heber and Malchiel.

18 These sixteen persons were the sons of Jacob and Zilpah, the slave-girl given to Leah by her father, Laban.

19, 20, 21, 22 Also in the total of Jacob's household were these fourteen sons and descendants of Jacob and Rachel:

> Joseph and Benjamin;
>
> *Joseph's sons,* born in the land of Egypt,
> were Manasseh and Ephraim (their mother
> was Asenath, the daughter of Potiphera,
> priest of Heliopolis);
>
> *Benjamin's sons:* Bela, Becher, Ashbel,
> Gera, Naaman, Ehi, Rosh, Muppim, Hup-
> pim, and Ard.

23, 24, 25 Also in the group were these seven sons and descendants of Jacob and Bilhah, the slave-girl given to Rachel by her father, Laban:

> Dan and his son: Hushim.
>
> Naphtali and his sons: Jahzeel, Guni,
> Jezer, and Shillem.

26 So the total number of those going to Egypt, of his own descendants, not counting the wives of Jacob's sons, was sixty-six.

27 With Joseph's two sons included, this total of Jacob's household there in Egypt totaled seventy.

28　Jacob sent Judah on ahead to tell Joseph that they were on the way, and would soon arrive in Goshen —which they did.

29　Joseph jumped into his chariot and journeyed to Goshen to meet his father and they fell into each other's arms and wept a long while.

30　Then Israel said to Joseph, "Now let me die, for I have seen you again and know you are alive."

31　And Joseph said to his brothers and to all their households, "I'll go and tell Pharaoh that you are here, and that you have come from the land of Canaan to join me.

32　And I will tell him, 'These men are shepherds. They have brought with them their flocks and herds and everything they own.'

33　So when Pharaoh calls for you and asks you about your occupation,

34　Tell him, 'We have been shepherds from our youth, as our fathers have been for many generations.' When you tell him this, he will let you live here in the land of Goshen." For shepherds were despised and hated in other parts of Egypt.

CHAPTER 47

Upon their arrival, Joseph went in to see Pharaoh. "My father and my brothers are here from Canaan," he reported, "with all their flocks and herds and possessions. They wish to settle in the land of Goshen."

2　He took five of his brothers with him, and presented them to Pharaoh.

3　Pharaoh asked them, "What is your occupation?"

And they replied, "We are shepherds like our ancestors.

4 We have come to live here in Egypt, for there is no pasture for our flocks in Canaan—the famine is very bitter there. We request permission to live in the land of Goshen."

5, 6 And Pharaoh said to Joseph, "Choose anywhere you like for them to live. Give them the best land of Egypt. The land of Goshen will be fine. And if any of them are capable, put them in charge of my flocks, too."

7 Then Joseph brought his father Jacob to Pharaoh. And Jacob blessed Pharaoh.

8 "How old are you?" Pharaoh asked him.

9 Jacob replied, "I have lived 130 long, hard years, and I am not nearly as old as many of my forebears."

10 Then Jacob blessed Pharaoh again before he left.

11 So Joseph assigned the best land of Egypt— the land of Rameses—to his father and brothers, just as Pharaoh had commanded.

12 And Joseph furnished food to them in accordance with the number of their dependents.

13 The famine became worse and worse, so that all the land of Egypt and Canaan were starving.

14 Joseph collected all the money in Egypt and Canaan in exchange for grain, and he brought the money to Pharaoh's treasure-houses.

15 When the people were out of money, they came to Joseph crying again for food.

"Our money is gone," they said, "but give us bread; for why should we die?"

16 "Well then," Joseph replied, "give me your livestock. I will trade you food in exchange."

17 So they brought their cattle to Joseph in exchange for food. Soon all the horses, flocks, herds, and donkeys of Egypt were in Pharaoh's possession.

18 The next year they came again and said, "Our money is gone, and our cattle are yours, and there is nothing left but our bodies and land.

19 Why should we die? Buy us and our land and we will be serfs to Pharaoh. We will trade ourselves for food, then we will live, and the land won't be abandoned."

20 So Joseph bought all the land of Egypt for Pharaoh; all the Egyptians sold him their fields because the famine was so severe. And the land became Pharaoh's.

21 Thus all the people of Egypt became Pharaoh's serfs.

22 The only land he didn't buy was that belonging to the priests, for they were assigned food from Pharaoh and didn't need to sell.

23 Then Joseph said to the people, "See, I have bought you and your land for Pharaoh. Here is grain. Go and sow the land.

24 And when you harvest it, a fifth of everything you get belongs to Pharaoh. Keep four parts for yourselves to be used for next year's seed, and as food for yourselves and for your households and little ones."

25 "You have saved our lives," they said. "We will gladly be the serfs of Pharaoh."

26 So Joseph made it a law throughout the land of Egypt—and it is still the law—that Pharaoh should have as his tax twenty percent of all the crops except

those produced on the land owned by the temples.

27   So Israel lived in the land of Goshen in Egypt, and soon the people of Israel began to prosper, and there was a veritable population explosion among them.

28   Jacob lived seventeen years after his arrival, so that he was 147 years old at the time of his death.

29   As the time drew near for him to die, he called for his son Joseph and said to him, "Swear to me most solemnly that you will honor this, my last request: do not bury me in Egypt.

30   But when I am dead, take me out of Egypt and bury me beside my ancestors." And Joseph promised.

31   "Swear that you will do it," Jacob insisted. And Joseph did. Soon afterwards Jacob took to his bed.

CHAPTER 48

One day not long after this, word came to Joseph that his father was failing rapidly. So, taking with him his two sons, Manasseh and Ephraim, he went to visit him.

2   When Jacob heard that Joseph had arrived, he gathered his strength and sat up in the bed to greet him,

3   And said to him, "God Almighty appeared to me at Luz in the land of Canaan and blessed me,

4   And said to me, 'I will make you a great nation and I will give this land of Canaan to you and to your children's children, for an everlasting possession.'

5   And now, as to these two sons of yours, Ephraim and Manasseh, born here in the land of Egypt before I arrived, I am adopting them as my own, and they will inherit from me just as Reuben and Simeon will.

6 But any other children born to you shall be your own, and shall inherit Ephraim's and Manasseh's portion from you.

7 For your mother Rachel died after only two children[1] when I came from Paddan-aram, as we were just a short distance from Ephrath, and I buried her beside the road to Bethlehem."

8 Then Israel looked over at the two boys. "Are these the ones?" he asked.

9 "Yes," Joseph told him, "these are my sons whom God has given me here in Egypt." And Israel said, "Bring them over to me and I will bless them."

10 Israel was half blind with age, so that he could hardly see. So Joseph brought the boys close to him and he kissed and embraced them.

11 And Israel said to Joseph, "I never thought that I would see you again, but now God has let me see your children too."

12, 13 Joseph took the boys by the hand, bowed deeply to him, and led the boys to their grandfather's knees—Ephraim at Israel's left hand and Manasseh at his right.

14 But Israel crossed his arms as he stretched them out to lay his hands upon the boys' heads, so that his right hand was upon the head of Ephraim, the younger boy, and his left hand was upon the head of Manasseh, the older. He did this purposely.

15 Then he blessed Joseph with this blessing: "May God, the God of my fathers Abraham and Isaac, the God who has shepherded me all my life, wonderfully bless these boys.

16 He is the Angel who has kept me from all harm.

---

[1] Implied.

May these boys be an honor to my name and to the names of my fathers Abraham and Isaac; and may they become a mighty nation."

17 But Joseph was upset and displeased when he saw that his father had laid his right hand on Ephraim's head; so he lifted it to place it on Manasseh's head instead.

18 "No, father," he said. "You've got your right hand on the wrong head! This one over here is the older. Put your right hand on him!"

19 But his father refused. "I know what I'm doing, my son," he said. "Manasseh too shall become a great nation, but his younger brother shall be greater than he; he shall become many nations."

20 So Jacob blessed the boys that day with this blessing: "May the people of Israel bless each other by saying, 'God make you as prosperous as Ephraim and Manasseh.'" (Note that he put Ephraim before Manasseh.)

21 Then Israel said to Joseph, "I am about to die, but God will be with you and will bring you again to Canaan, the land of your fathers.

22 And I have given the choice land of Shekem to you instead of to your brothers, as your portion of that land which I took from the Amorites with my sword and with my bow."

CHAPTER 49

Then Jacob called together all his sons and said, "Gather around me and I will tell you what is going to happen to you in the days to come.

2 Listen to me, O sons of Jacob; listen to Israel your father.

3 Reuben, you are my oldest son, the child of my vigorous youth. You are the head of the list in rank and in honor.

4 But you are unruly as the wild waves of the sea, and you shall be first no longer. I am demoting you, for you slept with one of my wives and thus dishonored me.

5 Simeon and Levi are two of a kind. They are men of violence and injustice.

6 O my soul, stay away from them. May I never be a party to their wicked plans. For in their anger they murdered a man, and maimed oxen just for fun.

7 Cursed be their anger, for it is fierce and cruel. Therefore, I will scatter their descendants throughout Israel.[1]

8 Judah, your brothers shall praise you. You shall destroy your enemies. Your father's sons shall bow before you.

9 Judah is a young lion that has finished eating its prey. He has settled down as a lion—who will dare to rouse him?

10 The scepter shall not depart from Judah until Shiloh[2] comes, whom all the people shall obey.

11 He has chained his steed to the choicest vine, and washed his clothes in wine.[3]

12 His eyes are darker than wine and his teeth are whiter than milk.

13 Zebulun shall dwell on the shores of the sea and shall be a harbor for ships, with his borders extending to Sidon.

---

[1]That is, the tribes of Simeon and Levi were not given land holdings, as were their brother-tribes.
[2]Which means, "He to whom it belongs."
[3]Showing wealth and extravagance.

14 Issachar is a strong beast of burden resting among the saddle bags.

15 When he saw how good the countryside was, how pleasant the land, he willingly bent his shoulder to the task and served his masters with vigor.

16 Dan shall govern his people like any other tribe in Israel.

17 He shall be a serpent in the path that bites the horses' heels, so that the rider falls off.

18 I trust in Your salvation, Lord.

19 A marauding band shall stamp upon Gad, but he shall rob and pursue them!

20 Asher shall produce rich foods, fit for kings!

21 Naphtali is a deer let loose, producing lovely fawns.

22 Joseph is a fruitful tree beside a fountain. His branches shade the wall.

23 He has been severely injured by those who shot at him and persecuted him,

24 But their weapons were shattered by the Mighty One of Jacob, the Shepherd, the Rock of Israel.

25 May the God of your fathers, the Almighty, bless you with blessings of heaven above and of the earth beneath—blessings of the breasts and of the womb,

26 Blessings of the grain and flowers, blessings reaching to the utmost bounds of the everlasting hills. These shall be the blessings upon the head of Joseph who was exiled from his brothers.

27 Benjamin is a wolf that prowls. He devours his enemies in the morning, and in the evening divides the spoil."

28 So these are the blessings that Israel their father

blessed his twelve sons with.

29, 30   Then he told them, "Soon I will die. You must bury me with my fathers in the land of Canaan, in the cave in the field of Mach-pelah, facing Mamre— the field Abraham bought from Ephron the Hethite for a burial ground.

31   There they buried Abraham and Sarah his wife; there they buried Isaac and Rebekah his wife; and there I buried Leah.

32   It is the cave which my grandfather Abraham purchased from the sons of Heth."

33   Then, when Jacob had finished his prophecies to his sons, he lay back in the bed, breathed his last, and died.

CHAPTER 50

Joseph threw himself upon his father's body and wept over him and kissed him.

2   Afterwards he commanded his morticians to embalm the body.

3   The embalming process required forty days, with a period of national mourning of seventy days.

4   Then, when at last the mourning was over, Joseph approached Pharaoh's staff and requested them to speak to Pharaoh on his behalf.

5   "Tell his majesty," he requested them, "that Joseph's father made Joseph swear to take his body back to the land of Canaan, to bury him there. Ask his majesty to permit me to go and bury my father; assure him that I will return promptly."

6   Pharaoh agreed. "Go and bury your father, as you promised," he said.

7   So Joseph went, and a great number of Pha-

raoh's counselors and assistants—all the senior officers of the land,

8 As well as all of Joseph's people—his brothers and their families. But they left their little children and flocks and herds in the land of Goshen.

9 So a very great number of chariots, cavalry, and people accompanied Joseph.

10 When they arrived at Atad[1] (meaning "Threshing Place of Brambles"), beyond the Jordan River, they held a very great and solemn funeral service, with a seven-day period of lamentation for Joseph's father.

11 The local residents, the Canaanites, renamed the place Abel-mizraim (meaning "Egyptian Mourners") for they said, "It is a place of very deep mourning by these Egyptians."

12, 13 So his sons did as Israel commanded them, and carried his body into the land of Canaan and buried it there in the cave of Mach-pelah—the cave Abraham had bought in the field of Ephron the Hethite, close to Mamre.

14 Then Joseph returned to Egypt with his brothers and all who had accompanied him to the funeral of his father.

15 But now that their father was dead, Joseph's brothers were frightened.

"Now Joseph will pay us back for all the evil we did to him," they said.

16, 17 So they sent him this message: "Before he died, your father instructed us to tell you to forgive us for the great evil we did to you. We servants of the God of your father beg you to forgive us." When Joseph read the message, he broke down and cried.

---

[1]Located just west of the Jordan River, near Jericho.

18 Then his brothers came and fell down before him and said, "We are your slaves."

19 But Joseph told them, "Don't be afraid of me. Am I God, to judge and punish you?

20 As far as I am concerned, God turned into good what you meant for evil, for He brought me to this high position I have today so that I could save the lives of many people.

21 No, don't be afraid. Indeed, I myself will take care of you and your families." And he spoke very kindly to them, reassuring them.

22 So Joseph and his brothers and their families continued to live in Egypt. Joseph was 110 years old when he died.

23 He lived to see the birth of his son Ephraim's children, and the children of Machir, Manasseh's son, who played at his feet.

24 "Soon I will die," Joseph told his brothers, "but God will surely come and get you, and bring you out of this land of Egypt and take you back to the land He promised to the descendants of Abraham, Isaac, and Jacob."

25 Then Joseph made his brothers promise with an oath that they would take his body back with them when they returned to Canaan.

26 So Joseph died at the age of 110, and they embalmed him, and his body was placed in a coffin in Egypt.

Exodus

CHAPTER 1

This is the list of the sons of Jacob who accompanied him to Egypt, with their families:

2   Reuben,
           Simeon,
           Levi,
           Judah,
3   Issachar,
           Zebulun,
           Benjamin,
4   Dan,
           Naphtali,
           Gad,
           Asher.

5 So the total number who went with him was seventy (for Joseph was already there).

6 In due season Joseph and each of his brothers died, ending that generation.

7 Meanwhile, their descendants were very fertile, increasing rapidly in numbers; there was a veritable population explosion so that they soon became a large nation, and they filled the land of Goshen.

8 Then, eventually,[1] a new king came to the throne of Egypt who felt no obligation[2] to the descendants of Joseph.

---

[1]Implied. This incident occurred about four hundred years after Joseph's death.
[2]Literally, "who did not know Joseph."

9 He told his people, "These Israeli are becoming dangerous to us because there are so many of them.

10 Let's figure out a way to put an end to this. If we don't, and war breaks out, they will join our enemies and fight against us and escape out of the country."

11 So the Egyptians made slaves of them and put brutal taskmasters over them to wear them down under heavy burdens while building the store-cities Pithom and Ra-amses.

12 But the more the Egyptians mistreated and oppressed them, the more the Israeli seemed to multiply! The Egyptians became alarmed,

13, 14 And made the Hebrew slavery more bitter still, forcing them to toil long and hard in the fields and to carry heavy loads of mortar and brick.

15, 16 Then Pharaoh, the king of Egypt, instructed the Hebrew midwives (their names were Shiphrah and Puah) to kill all Hebrew boys as soon as they were born, but to let the girls live.

17 But the midwives feared God and didn't obey the king—they let the boys live too.

18 The king summoned them before him and demanded, "Why have you disobeyed my command and let the baby boys live?"

19 "Sir," they told him, "the Hebrew women have their babies so quickly that we can't get there in time! They are not slow like the Egyptian women!"

20 And God blessed the midwives. So the people of Israel continued to multiply and to become a mighty nation.

21 And because the midwives revered God, He gave them children of their own.

22 Then Pharaoh commanded all of his people to throw the newborn Hebrew boys into the Nile River. But the girls, he said, could live.

CHAPTER 2

There were at this time a Hebrew fellow and girl of the tribe of Levi who married and had a family, and a baby son was born to them. When the baby's mother saw that he was an unusually beautiful baby, she hid him at home for three months.

3 Then, when she could no longer hide him, she made a little boat from papyrus reeds, waterproofed it with tar, put the baby in it, and laid it among the reeds along the river's edge.

4 The baby's sister watched from a distance to see what would happen to him.

5 Well, this is what happened: a princess, one of Pharaoh's daughters, came down to bathe in the river, and as she and her maids were walking along the river bank, she spied the little boat among the reeds and sent one of the maids to bring it to her.

6 When she opened it, there was a baby! And he was crying. This touched her heart. "He must be one of the Hebrew children!" she said.

7 Then the baby's sister approached the princess and asked her, "Shall I go and find one of the Hebrew women to nurse the baby for you?"

8 "Yes, do!" the princess replied. So the little girl rushed home and called her mother!

9 "Take this child home and nurse him for me," the princess instructed the baby's mother, "and I will pay you well!" So she took him home and nursed him.

10 Later, when he was older, she brought him back

to the princess and he became her son. She named him Moses (meaning[1] "to draw out") because she had drawn him out of the water.

11   One day, many years later[2] when Moses had grown up and become a man, he went out to visit his fellow Hebrews and saw the terrible conditions they were under. During his visit he saw an Egyptian knock a Hebrew to the ground—one of his own Hebrew brothers!

12   Moses looked this way and that to be sure no one was watching, then killed the Egyptian and hid his body in the sand.

13   The next day as he was out visiting among the Hebrews again, he saw two of them fighting. "What are you doing, hitting your own Hebrew brother like that?" he said to the one in the wrong.

14   "And who are you?" the man demanded. "I suppose you think you are *our* prince and judge! And do you plan to kill me as you did that Egyptian yesterday?" When Moses realized that his deed was known, he was frightened.

15   And sure enough, when Pharaoh heard about it he ordered Moses arrested and executed. But Moses ran away into the land of Midian. As he was sitting there beside a well,

16   Seven girls who were daughters of the priest of Midian came to draw water and fill the water troughs for their father's flocks.

17   But the shepherds chased the girls away. Moses then came to their aid and rescued them from the shepherds and watered their flocks.

---

[1]The name Moses sounds like another Hebrew word meaning "to draw out."
[2]Implied.

18 When they returned to their father Reuel he asked, "How did you get the flocks watered so quickly today?"

19 "An Egyptian defended us against the shepherds," they told him; "he drew water for us and watered the flocks."

20 "Well, where is he?" their father demanded. "Did you just leave him there? Invite him home for supper."

21 Moses eventually decided to accept Reuel's invitation to live with them, and Reuel gave him one of the girls, Zipporah, as his wife.

22 They had a baby named Gershom (meaning "foreigner"), for he said "I am a stranger in a foreign land."

23 Several years later the king of Egypt died. The Israeli were groaning beneath their burdens, in deep trouble because of their slavery, and weeping bitterly before the Lord. He heard their cries from heaven,

24 And remembered His promise to Abraham, Isaac, and Jacob [to bring their descendants back into the land of Canaan³].

25 Looking down upon them, He knew that the time had come for their rescue.⁴

CHAPTER 3

One day as Moses was tending the flock of his father-in-law Jethro,¹ the priest of Midian, out at the edge of the desert near Horeb, the mountain of God.

2 Suddenly the Angel of Jehovah appeared to him

---

³Implied
⁴Literally, "knew their condition."
¹Moses' father-in-law goes under two names in these chapters, Jethro and Reuel.

as a flame of fire in a bush. When Moses saw that the bush was on fire and that it didn't burn up,

3, 4   He went over to investigate. Then God called out to him,

"Moses! Moses!"

"Who is it?" Moses asked.

5   "Don't come any closer," God told him. "Take off your shoes, for you are standing on holy ground.

6   I am the God of your fathers—the God of Abraham, Isaac, and Jacob." (Moses covered his face with his hands, for he was afraid to look at God.)

7   Then the Lord told him, "I have seen the deep sorrows of My people in Egypt, and have heard their pleas for freedom from their harsh taskmasters.

8   I have come to deliver them from the Egyptians and to take them out of Egypt into a good land, a large land, a land 'flowing with milk and honey'—the land where the Canaanites, Hittites, Amorites, Perizzites, Hivites, and Jebusites live.

9   Yes, the wail of the people of Israel has risen to Me in heaven, and I have seen the heavy tasks the Egyptians have oppressed them with.

10   Now I am going to send you to Pharaoh, to demand that he let you lead My people out of Egypt."

11   "But I'm not the person for a job like that!" Moses exclaimed.

12   Then God told him, "I will certainly be with you, and this is the proof that I am the one who is sending you: when you have led the people out of Egypt, you shall worship God here upon this mountain!"

13   But Moses asked, "If I go to the people of Israel and tell them that their fathers' God has sent

me, they will ask, 'Which God are you talking about?'
What shall I tell them?"

14 " 'The Sovereign God,' "[2] was the reply. "Just
say, 'I Am has sent me!'

15 Yes, tell them, 'Jehovah,[3] the God of your ancestors Abraham, Isaac, and Jacob, has sent me to you.'
(This is My eternal name, to be used throughout all
generations.)

16 Call together all the elders of Israel," God instructed him, "and tell them about Jehovah appearing
to you here in this burning bush and that He said to
you, 'I have visited my people, and have seen what is
happening to them there in Egypt.

17 I promise to rescue them from the drudgery
and humiliation they are undergoing, and to take them
to the land now occupied by the Canaanites, Hittites,
Amorites, Perizzites, Hivites, and Jebusites, a land
"flowing with milk and honey." '

18 The elders of the people of Israel will accept
your message. They must go with you to the king of
Egypt and tell him, 'Jehovah, the God of the Hebrews,
has met with us and instructed us to go three days'
journey into the desert to sacrifice to Him. Give us
your permission.'

19 But I know that the king of Egypt will not let
you go except under heavy pressure.

20 So I will give him all the pressure he needs!
I will destroy Egypt with My miracles, and then at last
he will let you go.

21 And I will see to it that the Egyptians load

---

[2] Or, "the Living God." Literally, "I am what I am," or, "I will be what
I will be."
[3] Properly the name should be pronounced "Yahweh," as it is spelled
in many modern versions. In this paraphrase "Yahweh" is translated
either "Jehovah" or "Lord."

you down with gifts when you leave, so that you will by no means go out empty-handed!

22 Every woman will ask for jewels, silver, gold, and the finest of clothes from her Egyptian master's wife and neighbors. You will clothe your sons and daughters with the best of Egypt!"

CHAPTER 4

But Moses said, "They won't believe me! They won't do what *I* tell them to. They'll say, 'Jehovah never appeared to you!' "

2 "What do you have there in your hand?" the Lord asked him.

And he replied, "A shepherd's rod."

3 "Throw it down on the ground," the Lord told him. So he threw it down—and it became a serpent, and Moses ran from it!

4 Then the Lord told him, "Grab it by the tail!" He did, and it became a rod in his hand again!

5 "Do that and they will believe you!" the Lord told him. "Then they will realize that Jehovah, the God of their ancestors Abraham, Isaac, and Jacob, has really appeared to you.

6 Now reach your hand inside your robe, next to your chest." And when he did, and took it out again, it was white with leprosy!

7 "Now put it in again," Jehovah said. And when he did, and took it out again, it was normal, just as before!

8 "If they don't believe the first miracle, they will the second," the Lord said,

9 "And if they don't accept you after these two signs, then take water from the Nile River and pour it upon the dry land, and it will turn to blood!"

10   But Moses pleaded, "O Lord, I'm just not a good speaker. I never have been, and I'm not now, even after You have spoken to me, for I have a speech impediment."[1]

11   "Who makes mouths?" Jehovah asked him. "Isn't it I, the Lord? Who makes a man so that he can speak or not speak, see or not see, hear or not hear?

12   Now go ahead and do as I tell you, for I will help you to speak well, and I will tell you what to say."

13   But Moses said, "Lord, please! Send someone else."

14   Then the Lord became angry, "All right," He said, "your brother Aaron[2] is a good speaker. And he is coming here to look for you, and will be very happy when he finds you.

15   So I will tell you what to tell him, and I will help both of you to speak well, and I will tell you what to do.

16   He will be your spokesman to the people. And you will be as God to him, telling him what to say.

17   And be sure to take your rod along so that you can perform the miracles I have shown you."

18   Moses returned home and talked it over with Jethro, his father-in-law. "With your permission," Moses said, "I will go back to Egypt and visit my relatives. I don't even know whether they are still alive!"

"Go with my blessing," Jethro replied.

19   Before Moses left Midian, Jehovah said to him, "Don't be afraid to return to Egypt, for all those who wanted to kill you are dead."

20   So Moses took his wife and sons and put them

---

[1]Literally, "my speech is slow and halting."
[2]Literally, "your brother the Levite."

on a donkey, and returned to the land of Egypt, holding tightly to the "rod of God"!

21   Jehovah told him, "When you arrive back in Egypt you are to go to Pharaoh and do the miracles I have shown you, but I will make him stubborn so that he will not let the people go.

22   Then you are to tell him, 'Jehovah says, "Israel is My eldest son,

23   And I have commanded you to let him go away and worship Me, but you have refused: and now, see, I will slay your eldest son." ' "

24   As Moses and his family were traveling along and had stopped for the night, Jehovah appeared to Moses and threatened to kill him.

25, 26   Then Zipporah his wife took a flint knife and cut off the foreskin of her young son's penis, and threw it against Moses' feet, remarking disgustedly, "What a blood-smeared husband you've turned out to be!"

Then God let him alone.

27   Now Jehovah said to Aaron, "Go into the wilderness to meet Moses!" So Aaron traveled to Mount Horeb, the mountain of God, and met Moses there, and they greeted each other warmly.

28   Moses told Aaron what God had said they must do, and what they were to say, and told him about the miracles they must do before Pharaoh.

29   So Moses and Aaron returned to Egypt and summoned the elders of the people of Israel to a council meeting.

30   Aaron told them what Jehovah had said to Moses, and Moses performed the miracles as they watched.

31   Then the elders believed that God had sent them, and when they heard that Jehovah had visited them and had seen their sorrows, and had decided to rescue them, they all rejoiced and bowed their heads and worshiped.

CHAPTER 5

After this presentation to the elders, Moses and Aaron went to see Pharaoh. They told him, "We bring you a message from Jehovah, the God of Israel. He says, 'Let My people go, for they must make a holy pilgrimage out into the wilderness, for a religious feast, to worship Me there.' "

2   "Is that so?" retorted Pharaoh. "And who is Jehovah, that I should listen to Him, and let Israel go? I don't know Jehovah and I will not let Israel go."

3   But Aaron and Moses persisted. "The God of the Hebrews has met with us," they declared. "We must take a three days' trip into the wilderness and sacrifice there to Jehovah our God: if we don't obey Him, we face death by plague or sword."

4, 5   "Who do you think you are," Pharaoh shouted, "distracting the people from their work? Get back to your jobs!"

6   That same day Pharaoh sent this order to the taskmasters and officers he had set over the people of Israel:

7, 8   "Don't give the people any more straw for making bricks! However, don't reduce their production quotas by a single brick, for they obviously don't have enough to do or else they wouldn't be talking about going out into the wilderness and sacrificing to their God.

9 Load them with work and make them sweat; that will teach them to listen to Moses' and Aaron's lies!"

10, 11 So the taskmasters and officers informed the people: "Pharaoh has given orders to furnish you with no more straw. Go and find it wherever you can; but you must produce just as many bricks as before!"

12 So the people scattered everywhere to gather straw.

13 The taskmasters were brutal. "Fulfill your daily quota just as before," they kept demanding.

14 Then they whipped the Israeli work-crew bosses. "Why haven't you fulfilled your quotas either yesterday or today?" they roared.

15 These foremen went to Pharaoh and pleaded with him. "Don't treat us like this," they begged.

16 "We are given no straw and told to make as many bricks as before, and we are beaten for something that isn't our fault—it is the fault of your taskmasters for making such unreasonable demands."

17 But Pharaoh replied, "You don't have enough work, or else you wouldn't be saying 'Let us go and sacrifice to Jehovah.'

18 Get back to work. No straw will be given you, and you must deliver the regular quota of bricks."

19 Then the foremen saw that they were indeed in a bad situation.

20 When they met Moses and Aaron waiting for them outside the palace, as they came out from their meeting with Pharaoh,

21 They swore at them. "May God judge you for making us stink before Pharaoh and his people," they said, "and for giving them an excuse to kill us."

22 Then Moses went back to the Lord. "Lord," he protested, "how can You mistreat Your own people like this? Why did You ever send me, if You were going to do this to them?

23 Ever since I gave Pharaoh Your message, he has only been more and more brutal to them, and You have not delivered them at all!"

CHAPTER 6

Now you will see what I shall do to Pharaoh," the Lord told Moses. "For he must be forced to let My people go; he will not only let them go, but will *drive them out of his land!*

2, 3 I am Jehovah, the Almighty God who appeared to Abraham, Isaac, and Jacob—though I did not reveal My name, Jehovah, to them.

4 And I entered into a solemn covenant with them; under its terms I promised to give them and their descendants the land of Canaan where they were living.

5 And now I have heard the groanings of the people of Israel, in slavery now to the Egyptians, and I remember My promise.

6 Therefore tell the descendants of Israel that I will use My mighty power and perform great miracles to deliver them from slavery, and make them free.

7 And I will accept them as My people and be their God. And they shall know that I am Jehovah their God who has rescued them from the Egyptians.

8, 9 I will bring them into the land I promised to give to Abraham, Isaac, and Jacob. It shall belong to My people." So Moses told the people what God had said, but they wouldn't listen any more because they were too dispirited after the tragic consequence of what he had said before.[1]

10   Now the Lord spoke to Moses again and told him,

11   "Go back again to Pharaoh and tell him that he *must* let the people of Israel go."

12   "But look," Moses objected, "my own people won't even listen to me any more; how can I expect Pharaoh to? I'm no orator!"

13   Then the Lord ordered Moses and Aaron to return to the people of Israel and to Pharaoh, king of Egypt, demanding that the people be permitted to leave.

*   *   *   *   *

14   These are the names of the heads of the clans of the various tribes of Israel:

> The sons of Reuben, Israel's oldest son:
>> Hanoch,
>> Pallu,
>> Hezron,
>> Carmi.

15   The heads of the clans of the tribe of Simeon:
>> Jemuel,
>> Jamin,
>> Ohad,
>> Jachin,
>> Zohar,
>> Shaul (whose mother was a Canaanite).

16   These are the names of the heads of the clans of the tribe of Levi, in the order of their ages:[2]
>> Gershon,

---

[1]Literally, "because of their broken spirit and the cruel bondage."
[2]Literally, "according to their generations."

Kohath,
Merari.
(Levi lived 137 years.)

17 The sons of Gershon were:
Libni,
Shime-i,
(and their clans).

18 The sons of Kohath:
Amram,
Izhar,
Hebron,
Uzziel.
(Kohath lived 133 years.)

19 The sons of Merari:
Mahli,
Mushi.

The above are the families of the Levites, listed according to their ages.[3]

20 And Amram[4] married Jochebed, his father's sister; and Aaron and Moses were their sons.

Amram lived to the age of 137.

21 The sons of Izhar:
Korah,
Nepheg,
Zichri.

22 The sons of Uzziel:
Misha-el,
Elzaphan,
Sithri.

23 Aaron married Elisheba, the daughter of Amminadab and sister of Nahshon. Their children were:

---

[3]Literally, "according to their generations."
[4]See verse 18.

Nadab,
Abihu,
Eleazar,
Ithamar.
24 The sons of Korah:
Assir,
Elkanah,
Abiasaph.

These are the families within the clan of Korah.

25 Aaron's son Eleazar married one of the daughters of Puti-el, and Phinehas was one of his children.

These are all the names of the heads of the clans of the Levites, and the families within the clans.

26 Aaron and Moses, included in that list, are the same Aaron and Moses to whom Jehovah said, "Lead all the people of Israel out of the land of Egypt,"

27 And who went to Pharaoh to ask permission to lead the people from the land,

28, 29 And to whom the Lord said, "I am Jehovah. Go in and give Pharaoh the message I have given you."

30 This is that Moses who argued with the Lord, "I can't do it; I'm no speaker—why should Pharaoh listen to *me*?"

CHAPTER 7

Then the Lord said to Moses, "See, I have appointed you as My ambassador to Pharaoh, and your brother Aaron shall be your spokesman.

2 Tell Aaron everything I say to you, and he will announce it to Pharaoh, demanding that the people of Israel be allowed to leave Egypt.

3 But I will cause Pharaoh to stubbornly refuse,

and I will multiply My miracles in the land of Egypt.

4   Yet even then Pharaoh won't listen to you; so I will crush Egypt with a final major disaster and then lead My people out.

5   The Egyptians will find out that I am indeed God when I show them My power and force them to let My people go."

6   So Moses and Aaron did as the Lord commanded them.

7   Moses was eighty years old and Aaron eighty-three at this time of their confrontation with Pharaoh.

8   Then the Lord said to Moses and Aaron,

9   "Pharaoh will demand that you show him a miracle to prove that God has sent you; when he does, Aaron is to throw down his rod, and it will become a serpent."

10   So Moses and Aaron went in to see Pharaoh, and performed the miracle, as Jehovah had instructed them—Aaron threw down his rod before Pharaoh and his court, and it became a serpent.

11   Then Pharaoh called in his sorcerers—the magicians of Egypt—and they were able to do the same thing with their magical arts!

12   Their rods became serpents, too! But Aaron's serpent swallowed their serpents!

13   Pharaoh's heart was still hard and stubborn, and he wouldn't listen, just as the Lord had predicted.

14   The Lord pointed this out to Moses, that Pharaoh's heart had been unmoved, and that he would continue to refuse to let the people go.

15   "Nevertheless," the Lord said, "go back to Pharaoh in the morning, to be there as he goes down to the river. Stand beside the river bank and meet him

there, holding in your hand the rod that turned into a serpent.

16 Say to him, 'Jehovah, the God of the Hebrews, has sent me back to demand that you let My people go to worship Me in the wilderness. You wouldn't listen before,

17 And now the Lord says this: "You are going to find out that I am God. For I have instructed Moses to hit the water of the Nile with his rod, and the river will turn to blood!

18 The fish will die and the river will stink, so that the Egyptians will be unwilling to drink it." ' "

19 Then the Lord instructed Moses: "Tell Aaron to point his rod toward the waters of Egypt: all its rivers, canals, marshes, and reservoirs, and even the water stored in bowls and pots in the homes will turn to blood."

20 So Moses and Aaron did as the Lord commanded them. As Pharaoh and all of his officials watched, Aaron hit the surface of the Nile with the rod, and the river turned to blood.

21 The fish died and the water became so foul that the Egyptians couldn't drink it; and there was blood throughout the land of Egypt.

22 But then the magicians of Egypt used their secret arts and they, too, turned water into blood; so Pharaoh's heart remained hard and stubborn, and he wouldn't listen to Moses and Aaron, just as the Lord had predicted,

23 And he returned to his palace, unimpressed.

24 Then the Egyptians dug wells along the river bank to get drinking water, for they couldn't drink from the river.

25   The following week
         (*continued in next chapter*)

CHAPTER 8

The Lord said to Moses, "Go in again to Pharaoh and tell him, 'Jehovah says, "Let My people go and worship Me.

2   If you refuse, I will send vast hordes of frogs across your land from one border to the other.

3, 4   The Nile River will swarm with them, and they will come out into your houses, even into your bedrooms and right into your beds! Every home in Egypt will be filled with them. They will fill your ovens and your kneading bowls; you and your people will be immersed in them!" ' "

5   Then the Lord said to Moses, "Instruct Aaron to point the rod toward all the rivers, streams, and pools of Egypt, so that there will be frogs in every corner of the land."

6   Aaron did, and frogs covered the nation.

7   But the magicians did the same with their secret arts, and they, too, caused frogs to come up upon the land.

8   Then Pharaoh summoned Moses and Aaron and begged, "Plead with God to take the frogs away, and I will let the people go and sacrifice to Him."

9   "Be so kind as to tell me when you want them to go," Moses said, "and I will pray that the frogs will die at the time you specify, everywhere except in the river."

10   "Do it tomorrow," Pharaoh said.

"All right," Moses replied, "it shall be as you have said; then you will know that there is no one like the Lord our God.

11   All the frogs will be destroyed, except those in the river."

12   So Moses and Aaron went out from the presence of Pharaoh, and Moses pleaded with the Lord concerning the frogs He had sent.

13   And the Lord did as Moses promised—dead frogs covered the countryside and filled the nation's homes.

14   They were piled into great heaps, making a terrible stench throughout the land.

15   But when Pharaoh saw that the frogs were gone, he hardened his heart and refused to let the people go, just as the Lord had predicted.

16   Then the Lord said to Moses, "Tell Aaron to strike the dust with his rod, and it will become lice, throughout all the land of Egypt."

17   So Moses and Aaron did as God commanded, and suddenly lice infested the entire nation, covering the Egyptians and their animals.

18   Then the magicians tried to do the same thing with their secret arts, but this time they failed.

19   "This is the finger of God," they exclaimed to Pharaoh. But Pharaoh's heart was hard and stubborn, and he wouldn't listen to them, just as the Lord had predicted.

20   Next the Lord told Moses, "Get up early in the morning and meet Pharaoh as he comes out to the river to bathe, and say to him, 'Jehovah says, "Let My people go and worship Me.

21   If you refuse I will send swarms of flies throughout Egypt. Your homes will be filled with them and the ground will be covered with them.

22 But it will be very different in the land of Goshen where the Israeli live. No flies will be there; thus you will know that I am the Lord God of all the earth,

23 For I will make a distinction between your people and My people. All this will happen tomorrow." ' "

24 And Jehovah did as He had said, so that there were terrible swarms of flies in Pharaoh's palace and in every home in Egypt.

25 Pharaoh hastily summoned Moses and Aaron and said, "All right, go ahead and sacrifice to your God, but do it here in the land. Don't go out into the wilderness."

26 But Moses replied, "That won't do! Our sacrifices to God are hated by the Egyptians, and if we do this right here before their eyes, they will kill us.

27 We must take a three-day trip into the wilderness and sacrifice there to Jehovah our God, as He commanded us."

28 "All right, go ahead," Pharaoh replied, "but don't go too far away. Now, hurry and plead with God for me."

29 "Yes," Moses said, "I will ask Him to cause the swarms of flies to disappear. But I am warning you that you must never again lie to us by promising to let the people go and then changing your mind."

30 So Moses went out from Pharaoh and asked the Lord to get rid of the flies.

31 And the Lord did as Moses asked and caused the swarms to disappear, so that not one remained. But Pharaoh hardened his heart again and did not let the people go!

CHAPTER 9

Go back to Pharaoh," the Lord commanded Moses, "and tell him, 'Jehovah, the God of the Hebrews, demands that you let His people go to sacrifice to Him.

2 If you refuse,

3 The power of God will send a deadly plague to destroy your cattle, horses, donkeys, camels, flocks, and herds.

4 But the plague will affect only the cattle of Egypt; none of the Israeli herds and flocks will even be touched!' "

5 The Lord announced that the plague would begin the very next day,

6 And it did. The next morning all the cattle of the Egyptians began dying, but not one of the Israeli herds was even sick.

7 Pharaoh sent to see whether it was true that none of the Israeli cattle were dead, yet when he found out that it was so, even then his mind remained unchanged and he refused to let the people go.

8 Then Jehovah said to Moses and Aaron, "Take ashes from the kiln. Moses, toss it into the sky as Pharaoh watches.

9 It will spread like fine dust over all the land of Egypt and cause boils to break out upon people and animals alike, throughout the land."

10 So they took ashes from the kiln and went to Pharaoh; as he watched, Moses tossed it toward the sky, and it became boils that broke out on men and animals alike throughout all Egypt.

11 And the magicians couldn't stand before Moses

because of the boils, for the boils appeared upon them too.

12 But Jehovah hardened Pharaoh in his stubbornness, so that he refused to listen, just as the Lord had predicted to Moses.

13 Then the Lord said to Moses, "Get up early in the morning and stand before Pharaoh and tell him, 'Jehovah the God of the Hebrews says, "Let My people go to worship Me.

14 This time I am going to send a plague that will really speak to you and to your servants and to all the Egyptian people, and prove to you there is no other God in all the earth.

15 I could have killed you all by now,

16 But I didn't, for I wanted to demonstrate My power to you and to all the earth.

17 So you still think you are so great, do you, and defy My power, and refuse to let My people go?

18 Well, tomorrow about this time I will send a hailstorm across the nation such as there has never been since Egypt was founded!

19 Quick! Bring in your cattle from the fields, for every man and animal left out in the fields will die beneath the hail!" ' "

20 Some of the Egyptians, terrified by this threat, brought their cattle and slaves in from the fields;

21 But those who had no regard for the word of Jehovah left them out in the storm.

22 Then Jehovah said to Moses, "Point your hand toward heaven and cause the hail to fall throughout all Egypt, upon the people, animals, and trees."

23 So Moses held out his hand, and the Lord sent

thunder and hail and lightning.

24   It was terrible beyond description. Never in all the history of Egypt had there been a storm like that.

25   All Egypt lay in ruins. Everything left in the fields, men and animals alike, was killed, and the trees were shattered and the crops were destroyed.

26   The only spot in all Egypt without hail that day was the land of Goshen where the people of Israel lived.

27   Then Pharaoh sent for Moses and Aaron. "I finally see my fault," he confessed. "Jehovah is right, and I and my people have been wrong all along.

28   Beg God to end this terrifying thunder and hail, and I will let you go at once."

29   "All right," Moses replied, "as soon as I have left the city I will spread out my hands to the Lord, and the thunder and hail will stop. This will prove to you that the earth is controlled by Jehovah.

30   But as for you and your officials, I know that even yet you will not obey Him."

31   All the flax and barley were knocked down and destroyed (for the barley was ripe, and the flax was in bloom),

32   But the wheat and the emmer were not destroyed, for they were not yet out of the ground.

33   So Moses left Pharaoh and went out of the city and lifted his hands to heaven to the Lord, and the thunder and hail stopped, and the rain ceased pouring down.

34   When Pharaoh saw this, he and his officials sinned yet more by their stubborn refusal to do what they had promised;

35   So Pharaoh refused to let the people leave, just

as the Lord had predicted to Moses.

CHAPTER 10

Then the Lord said to Moses, "Go back again and make your demand upon Pharaoh; but I have hardened him and his officials, so that I can do more miracles demonstrating My power.

2 What stories you can tell your children and grandchildren about the incredible things I am doing in Egypt! Tell them what fools I made of the Egyptians, and how I proved to you that I am Jehovah."

3 So Moses and Aaron requested another audience with Pharaoh and told him: "Jehovah, the God of the Hebrews, asks, 'How long will you refuse to submit to Me? Let My people go so they can worship Me.

4, 5 If you refuse, tomorrow I will cover the entire nation with a thick layer of locusts so that you won't even be able to see the ground, and they will finish destroying everything that escaped the hail.

6 They will fill your palace, and the homes of your officials, and all the houses of Egypt. Never in the history of Egypt has there been a plague like this will be!' " Then Moses stalked out.

7 The court officials now came to Pharaoh and asked him, "Are you going to destroy us completely? Don't you know even yet that all Egypt lies in ruins? Let the *men* go and serve Jehovah their God!"

8 So Moses and Aaron were brought back to Pharaoh. "All right, go and serve Jehovah your God!" he said, "but just who is it you want to go?"

9 "We will go with our sons and daughters, flocks and herds," Moses replied. "We will take everything with us; for we must all join in the holy pilgrimage."

10   "In the name of God I will not let you take your little ones!" Pharaoh retorted. "I can see your plot!

11   Never! You that are men, go and serve Jehovah, for that is what you asked for." And they were driven out from Pharaoh's presence.

12   Then the Lord said to Moses, "Hold out your hand over the land of Egypt to bring locusts—they will cover the land and eat everything the hail has left."

13   So Moses lifted his rod and Jehovah caused an east wind to blow all that day and night; and when it was morning, the east wind had brought the locusts.

14   And the locusts covered the land of Egypt from border to border; it was the worst locust plague in all Egyptian history; and there will never again be another like it.

15   For the locusts covered the face of the earth and blotted out the sun so that the land was darkened; and they ate every bit of vegetation the hail had left; there remained not one green thing—not a tree, not a plant throughout all the land of Egypt.

16   Then Pharaoh sent an urgent call for Moses and and Aaron and said to them, "I confess my sin against Jehovah your God and against you.

17   Forgive my sin only this once, and beg Jehovah your God to take away this death. I promise not to refuse afterwards to let you go."

18   So Moses went out from Pharaoh and entreated the Lord,

19   And He sent a very strong west wind that blew the locusts out into the Red Sea, so that there remained not one locust in all the land of Egypt!

20   But the Lord hardened Pharaoh's heart and he did not let the people go.

21   Then Jehovah said to Moses, "Lift your hands to heaven, and darkness without a ray of light will descend upon the land of Egypt."

22   So Moses did, and there was thick darkness over all the land for three days.

23   During all that time the people scarcely moved —but all the people of Israel had light as usual.

24   Then Pharaoh called for Moses and said, "Go and worship Jehovah—but let your flocks and herds stay here; you can even take your children with you."

25   "No," Moses said, "we must take our flocks and herds for sacrifices and burnt offerings to Jehovah our God.

26   Not a hoof shall be left behind; for we must have sacrifices for the Lord our God, and we do not know what He will choose until we get there."

27   So the Lord hardened Pharaoh's heart and he would not let them go.

28   "Get out of here and don't let me ever see you again," Pharaoh shouted at Moses. "The day you do, you shall die."

29   "Very well," Moses replied. "I will never see you again."

CHAPTER 11

Then the Lord said to Moses, "I will send just one more disaster on Pharaoh and his land, and after that he will let you go; in fact, he will be so anxious to get rid of you that he will practically throw you out of the country.

2   Tell all the men and women of Israel to pre-

pare to ask their Egyptian neighbors for costly gold and silver jewelry."

3 (For God caused the Egyptians to be very favorable to the people of Israel, and Moses was a very great man in the land of Egypt and was revered by Pharaoh's officials and the Egyptian people alike.)

4 Now Moses announced to Pharaoh,[1] "Jehovah says, 'About midnight I will pass through Egypt.

5 And all the oldest sons shall die in every family in Egypt, from the oldest child of Pharaoh, heir to his throne, to the oldest child of his lowliest slave; and even the firstborn of the animals.

6 The wail of death will resound throughout the entire land of Egypt; never before has there been such anguish, and it will never be again.

7 But not a dog shall move his tongue against any of the people of Israel, nor shall any of their animals die. Then you will know that Jehovah makes a distinction between Egyptians and Israeli.'

8 All these officials of yours will come running to me, bowing low and begging, 'Please leave at once, and take all your people with you.' Only then will I go!" Then, red-faced with anger, Moses stomped from the palace.[2]

9 The Lord had told Moses, "Pharaoh won't listen, and this will give Me the opportunity of doing mighty miracles to demonstrate My power."

10 So, although Moses and Aaron did these miracles right before Pharaoh's eyes, the Lord hardened his heart so that he wouldn't let the people leave the land.

---

[1]Implied.
[2]Literally, "he went out from Pharaoh."

CHAPTER 12

Then the Lord said to Moses and Aaron,

2　"From now on, this month will be the first and most important month of the Jewish calendar.

3, 4　Annually, on the tenth day of this month, (announce this to all the people of Israel), each family shall get a lamb[1] (or, if a family is small, let it share the lamb with another small family in the neighborhood; whether to share in this way depends on the size of the families).

5　This animal shall be a year-old male, either a sheep or a goat, without any defects.

6　On the evening of the fourteenth day of this month, all these lambs shall be killed,

7　And their blood shall be placed on the two side-frames of the door of every home and on the panel above the door. Use the blood of the lamb eaten in that home.

8　Everyone shall eat roast lamb that night, with unleavened bread and bitter herbs.

9　The meat must not be eaten raw or boiled, but roasted, including the head, legs, heart, and liver.[2]

10　Don't eat any of it the next day; if all is not eaten that night, burn what is left.

11　Eat it with your traveling clothes on, prepared for a long journey, wearing your walking shoes and carrying your walking sticks in your hands; eat it hurriedly. This observance shall be called the Lord's Passover.

12　For I will pass through the land of Egypt tonight

---

[1]The Hebrew word here translated "lamb" can also mean "kid"—a baby goat.
[2]Literally, "inner parts."

and kill all the oldest sons and firstborn male animals in all the land of Egypt, and execute judgment upon all the gods of Egypt—for I am Jehovah.

13 The blood you have placed on the doorposts will be proof that you obey Me, and when I see the blood I will pass over you and I will not destroy your firstborn children when I smite the land of Egypt.

14 You shall celebrate this event each year (this is a permanent law) to remind you of this fatal night.

15 The celebration shall last seven days. For that entire period you are to eat only bread made without yeast. Anyone who disobeys this rule at any time during the seven days of the celebration shall be excommunicated from Israel.

16 On the first day of the celebration, and again on the seventh day, there will be special religious services for the entire congregation, and no work of any kind may be done on those days except the preparation of food.

17 This annual 'Celebration with Unleavened Bread' will cause you always to remember today as the day when I brought you out of the land of Egypt; so it is a law that you must celebrate this day annually, generation after generation.

18 Only bread without yeast may be eaten from the evening of the fourteenth day of the month until the evening of the twenty-first day of the month.

19 For these seven days there must be no trace of yeast in your homes; during that time anyone who eats anything that has yeast in it shall be excommunicated from the congregation of Israel. These same rules apply to foreigners who are living among you just as much as to those born in the land.

20   Again I repeat, during those days you must not eat anything made with yeast; serve only yeastless bread."

21   Then Moses called for all the elders of Israel and said to them, "Go and get lambs from your flocks, a lamb for one or more families depending upon the number of persons in the families, and kill the lamb so that God will pass over you and not destroy you.

22   Drain the lamb's blood into a basin, and then take a cluster of hyssop branches and dip them into the lamb's blood, and strike the hyssop against the lintel above the door and against the two side panels, so that there will be blood upon them, and none of you shall go outside all night.

23   For Jehovah will pass through the land and kill the Egyptians; but when He sees the blood upon the panel at the top of the door and on the two side pieces, He will pass over[3] that home and not permit the Destroyer to enter and kill your firstborn.

24   And remember, this is a permanent law for you and your posterity.

25   And when you come into the land that the Lord will give you, just as He promised, and when you are celebrating the Passover,

26   And your children ask, 'What does all this mean? What is this ceremony about?'

27   You will reply, 'It is the celebration of Jehovah's passing over us, for He passed over the homes of the people of Israel, though He killed the Egyptians; He passed over our houses and did not come in to destroy us.' "

---

[3]Or, "He will pause at the door of that home and not permit the Destroyer to enter . . ."

And all the people bowed their heads and worshiped.

28 So the people of Israel did as Moses and Aaron had commanded.

29 And that night, at midnight, Jehovah killed all the firstborn sons in the land of Egypt, from Pharaoh's oldest son to the oldest son of the captive in the dungeon; also all the firstborn of the cattle.

30 Then Pharaoh and his officials and all the people of Egypt got up in the night; and there was bitter crying throughout all the land of Egypt, for there was not a house where there was not one dead.

31 And Pharaoh summoned Moses and Aaron during the night and said, "Leave us; please go away, all of you; go and serve Jehovah as you said.

32 Take your flocks and herds and be gone; and oh, give me a blessing[4] as you go."

33 And the Egyptians were urgent upon the people of Israel, to get them out of the land as quickly as possible. For they said, "We are as good as dead."

34 The Israeli took with them their bread dough without yeast, and bound their kneading troughs into their spare clothes, and carried them on their shoulders.

35 And the people of Israel did as Moses said and asked the Egyptians for silver and gold jewelry, and for clothing.

36 And the Lord gave the Israeli favor with the Egyptians, so that they gave them whatever they wanted. And the Egyptians were practically stripped of everything they owned!

37 That night the people of Israel left Rameses and started for Succoth; there were six hundred thousand

[4]Or, "say farewell to me forever!"

of them, besides all the women and children, going on foot.

38 People of various sorts[5] went with them; and there were flocks and herds—a vast exodus of cattle.

39 When they stopped to eat, they baked bread from the yeastless dough they had brought along. It was yeastless because the people were pushed out of Egypt and didn't have time to wait for bread to rise to take with them on the trip.

40, 41 The sons of Jacob and their descendants had lived in Egypt 430 years, and it was on the last day of the 430th year that all of Jehovah's people left the land.

42 This night was selected by the Lord to bring His people out from the land of Egypt; so the same night was selected as the date of the annual celebration of God's deliverance.

43 Then Jehovah said to Moses and Aaron, "These are the rules concerning the observance of the Passover. No foreigners shall eat the lamb,

44 But any slave who has been purchased may eat it if he has been circumcised.

45 A hired servant or a visiting foreigner may not eat of it.

46 You shall, all of you who eat each lamb, eat it together in one house, and not carry it outside; and you shall not break any of its bones.

47 All the congregation of Israel shall observe this memorial at the same time.

48 As to foreigners, if they are living with you and want to observe the Passover with you, let all the males be circumcised, and then they may come and celebrate

[5]Literally, "a mixed multitude." The meaning is not clear.

with you—then they shall be just as though they had been born among you; but no uncircumcised person shall ever eat the lamb.

49 The same law applies to those born in Israel and to foreigners living among you."

50 So the people of Israel followed all of Jehovah's instructions to Moses and Aaron.

51 That very day the Lord brought out the people of Israel from the land of Egypt, wave after wave of them crossing the border.[6]

CHAPTER 13

The Lord instructed Moses, "Dedicate to Me all of the firstborn sons[1] of Israel, and every firstborn male animal; they are Mine!"

3 Then Moses said to the people, "This is a day to remember forever—the day of leaving Egypt and your slavery; for the Lord has brought you out with mighty miracles. Now remember, during the annual celebration of this event you are to use no yeast; don't even have any in your homes.

4, 5 Mark this day of your exodus, at the end of March[2] each year, when Jehovah brings you into the land of the Canaanites, Hittites, Amorites, Hivites, and Jebusites—the land He promised your fathers, a land 'flowing with milk and honey.'

6, 7 For seven days you shall eat only bread without yeast, and there must be no yeast in your homes, or anywhere within the borders of your land! Then, on the seventh day, a great feast to the Lord shall be held.

[6]Or, ". . . from the land of Egypt, all of the communities of them."
[1]Literally, "all the firstborn."
[2]Literally, "the tenth day of Abib."

8   During those celebration days each year you must explain to your children why you are celebrating —it is a celebration of what the Lord did for you when you left Egypt.

9   This annual memorial week will brand you as My own unique people, just as though I had branded My mark of ownership upon your hands or your forehead.

10   So celebrate the event annually in late March.[3]

11   And remember, when the Lord brings you into the land He promised to your ancestors long ago, where the Canaanites are now living,

12   All firstborn sons and firstborn male animals belong to the Lord, and you shall give them to Him.

13   A firstborn donkey may be purchased back from the Lord in exchange for a lamb or baby goat; but if you decide not to trade, the donkey shall be killed. However, you *must* buy back your firstborn sons.

14   And in the future, when your children ask you, 'What is this all about?' you shall tell them, 'With mighty miracles Jehovah brought us out of Egypt from our slavery.

15   Pharaoh wouldn't let us go, so Jehovah killed all the firstborn males throughout the land of Egypt, both of men and animals; that is why we now give all the firstborn males to the Lord—except that all the eldest sons are always brought back.'

16   Again I say, this celebration shall identify you as God's people, just as much as if His brand of ownership were placed upon your foreheads. It is a reminder that the Lord brought us out of Egypt with great power."

[3]Literally, "in its season from year to year."

* * * * *

17, 18   So at last Pharaoh let the people go.

God did not lead them through the land of the Philistines, although that was the most direct route from Egypt to the Promised Land. The reason was that God felt the people might become discouraged by having to fight their way through, even though they had left Egypt armed; He thought they might return to Egypt.

Instead, God led them along a route through the Red Sea wilderness.

19   Moses took the bones of Joseph with them, for Joseph had made the sons of Israel vow before God that they would take his bones with them when God led them out of Egypt—as he was sure God would.

20   Leaving Succoth, they camped in Etham at the edge of the wilderness.

21   The Lord guided them by a pillar of cloud during the daytime, and by a pillar of fire at night. So they could travel either by day or night.

22   The cloud and fire were never out of sight.

CHAPTER 14

J ehovah now instructed Moses,

2   "Tell the people to turn toward Piha-hiroth between Migdol and the sea, opposite Baal-zephon, and to camp there along the shore.

3   For Pharaoh will think, 'Those Israelites are trapped now, between the desert and the sea!'

4   And once again I will harden Pharaoh's heart and he will chase after you. I have planned this to gain great honor and glory over Pharaoh and all his armies,

and the Egyptians shall know that I am the Lord."

So they camped where they were told.

5   When word reached the king of Egypt that the Israeli were not planning to return to Egypt after three days, but to keep on going, Pharaoh and his staff became bold again. "What is this we have done, letting all these slaves get away?" they asked.

6   So Pharaoh led the chase in his chariot,

7   Followed by the pick of Egypt's chariot corps —600 chariots in all—and other chariots driven by Egyptian officers.

8   He pursued the people of Israel, for they had taken much of the wealth of Egypt with them.

9   Pharaoh's entire cavalry—horses, chariots, and charioteers—was used in the chase; and the Egyptian army overtook the people of Israel as they were camped beside the shore near Piha-hiroth, across from Baal-zephon.

10   As the Egyptian army approached, the people of Israel saw them far in the distance, speeding after them, and they were terribly frightened, and cried out to the Lord to help them.

11   And they turned against Moses, whining, "Have you brought us out here to die in the desert because there were not enough graves for us in Egypt? Why did you make us leave Egypt?

12   Isn't this what we told you, while we were slaves, to leave us alone? We said it would be better to be slaves to the Egyptians than dead in the wilderness."

13   But Moses told the people, "Don't be afraid. Just stand where you are and watch, and you will see the wonderful way the Lord will rescue you today. The

Egyptians you are looking at—you will never see them again.

14　The Lord will fight for you, and you won't need to lift a finger!"[1]

15　Then the Lord said to Moses, "Quit praying and get the people moving! Forward, march!

16　Use your rod—hold it out over the water, and the sea will open up a path before you, and all the people of Israel shall walk through on dry ground!

17　I will harden the hearts of the Egyptians and they will go in after you and you will see the honor I will get in defeating Pharaoh and all his armies, chariots, and horsemen.

18　And all Egypt shall know that I am Jehovah."

19　Then the Angel of God, who was leading the people of Israel, moved the cloud around behind them,

20　And it stood between the people of Israel and the Egyptians. And that night, as it changed to a pillar of fire, it gave darkness to the Egyptians but light to the people of Israel! So the Egyptians couldn't find the Israeli!

21　Meanwhile, Moses stretched his rod over the sea, and the Lord opened up a path through the sea, with walls of water on each side; and a strong east wind blew all that night, drying the sea bottom.

22　So the people of Israel walked through the sea on dry ground!

23　Then the Egyptians followed them between the walls of water along the bottom of the sea—all of Pharaoh's horses, chariots, and horsemen.

24　But in the early morning Jehovah looked down from the cloud of fire upon the array of the Egyptians,

---

[1]Or, "you will be speechless with amazement!"

and began to harrass them.

25   Their chariot wheels began coming off, so that their chariots scraped along the dry ground. "Let's get out of here," the Egyptians yelled. "Jehovah is fighting for them and against us."

26   When all the Israelites were on the other side,[2] the Lord said to Moses, "Stretch out your hand again over the sea, so that the waters will come back over the Egyptians and their chariots and horsemen."

27   Moses did, and the sea returned to normal beneath the morning light. The Egyptians tried to flee, but the Lord drowned them in the sea.

28   The water covered the path and the chariots and horsemen. And of all the army of Pharaoh that chased after Israel through the sea, not one remained alive.

29   The people of Israel had walked through on dry land, and the waters had been walled up on either side of them.

30   Thus Jehovah saved Israel that day from the Egyptians; and the people of Israel saw the Egyptians dead, washed up on the seashore.

31   When the people of Israel saw the mighty miracle the Lord had done for them against the Egyptians, they were afraid and revered the Lord, and believed in Him and in His servant Moses.

CHAPTER 15

Then Moses and the people of Israel sang this song to the Lord:

> I will sing to the Lord, for He has triumphed gloriously;

---

[2]Implied.

He has thrown both horse and rider into
the sea.

2 The Lord is my strength, my song, and my
salvation.

He is my God, and I will praise Him.

He is my father's God—I will exalt Him.

3 The Lord is a warrior—

Yes, Jehovah is His name.

4 He has overthrown Pharaoh's chariots and
armies,

Drowning them in the sea.

The famous Egyptian captains are dead
beneath the waves.

5 The water covers them.

They went down into the depths like a
stone.

6 Your right hand, O Lord, is glorious in
power;

It dashes the enemy to pieces.

7 In the greatness of Your majesty

You overthrew all those who rose against
You.

You sent forth your anger, and it consumed them as fire consumes straw.

8 At the blast of Your breath

The waters divided!

They stood as solid walls to hold the seas
apart.

9 The enemy said, "I will chase after them,

Catch up with them, destroy them.

I will cut them apart with my sword

And divide the captured booty."

10   But God blew with His wind, and the sea covered them.

      They sank as lead in the mighty waters.

11   Who else is like the Lord among the gods?

      Who is glorious in holiness like Him?

      Who is so awesome in splendor,

      A wonder-working God?

12   You reached out Your hand and the earth swallowed them.

13   You have led the people You redeemed.

      But in Your lovingkindness

      You have guided them wonderfully

      To Your holy land.

14   The nations heard what happened, and they trembled.

      Fear has gripped the people of Philistia.

15   The leaders of Edom are appalled,

      The mighty men of Moab tremble;

      All the people of Canaan melt with fear.

16   Terror and dread have overcome them.

      O Lord, because of Your great power they won't attack us!

      Your people whom You purchased

      Will pass by them in safety.

17   You will bring them in and plant them on Your mountain,

      Your own homeland, Lord—

      The sanctuary You made for them to live in.

18   Jehovah shall reign forever and forever.

19   The horses of Pharaoh, his horsemen, and his chariots

      Tried to follow through the sea;

> But the Lord let down the walls of water
>> on them
> While the people of Israel walked through
>> on dry land.

20 Then Miriam the prophetess, the sister of Aaron, took a timbrel and led the women in dances.

21 And Miriam sang this song:

> Sing to the Lord, for He has triumphed
>> gloriously.
> The horse and rider have been drowned in
>> the sea.

22 Then Moses led the people of Israel on from the Red Sea, and they moved out into the wilderness of Shur and were there three days without water.

23 Arriving at Marah, they couldn't drink the water because it was bitter (that is why the place was called Marah, meaning "bitter").

24 Then the people turned against Moses. "Must we die of thirst?" they demanded.

25 Moses pleaded with the Lord to help them, and the Lord showed him a tree to throw into the water, and the water became sweet.

It was there at Marah that the Lord laid before them the following conditions, to test their commitment to Him:

26 "If you will listen to the voice of the Lord your God, and obey it, and do what is right, then I will not make you suffer the diseases I send on the Egyptians, for I am the Lord who heals you."

27 And they came to Elim where there were twelve springs and seventy palm trees; and they camped there beside the springs.

CHAPTER 16

Now they left Elim and journeyed on into the Sihn Wilderness, between Elim and Mt. Sinai, arriving there on the fifteenth day of the second month after leaving Egypt.

2   There too, the people spoke bitterly against Moses and Aaron.

3   "Oh, that we were back in Egypt," they moaned, "and that the Lord had killed us there! For there we had plenty to eat. But now you have brought us into this wilderness to kill us with starvation."

4   Then the Lord said to Moses, "Look, I'm going to rain down food from heaven for them. Everyone can go out each day and gather as much food as he wishes. And I will test them in this, to see whether they will follow My instructions or not.

5   Tell them to gather twice as much as usual on the sixth day of each week."

6   Then Moses and Aaron called a meeting of all the people of Israel and told them, "This evening you will realize that it was the Lord who brought you out of the land of Egypt.

7, 8, 9   In the morning you will see more of His glory; for He has heard your complaints against Him (for you aren't really complaining against *us*—who are *we*?). The Lord will give you meat to eat each evening, and bread each morning. Come now before Jehovah, and hear His reply to your complaints."

10   So Aaron called them together and suddenly, out toward the wilderness, from within the guiding cloud, there appeared the awesome glory of Jehovah.

11, 12   And Jehovah said to Moses, "I have heard

their complaints. Tell them, 'In the evening you will
have meat and in the morning you will be stuffed with
bread, and you shall know that I am Jehovah your
God.' "

13　That evening vast numbers of quail arrived
and covered the camp, and in the morning the desert
all around the camp was wet with dew;

14　And when the dew disappeared later in the
morning it left tiny flakes of something as small as
hoarfrost on the ground.

15　When the people of Israel saw it they asked
each other, "What is it?" And Moses told them, "It
is the food Jehovah has given you to eat.

16　Jehovah has said for everyone to gather as
much as is needed for his household—about three
quarts[1] for each person in his home."

17　So the people of Israel went out and gathered it.

18　And when they poured it into a three-quart
measure, there was just enough for everyone—three
quarts apiece; those who gathered a lot had nothing
left over and those who gathered little had no lack!
Each home had just enough.

19　And Moses told them, "Don't leave it overnight."

20　But of course some of them wouldn't listen,
and left it until morning; and when they looked, it was
full of maggots and had a terrible odor; and Moses
was very angry with them.

21　So they gathered the food morning by morning, each home according to its need; and when the
sun became hot upon the ground, the food melted and
disappeared.

---

[1]Literally, "an omer." The exact measure is not known.

22   On the sixth day they gathered twice as much as usual, six quarts instead of three; then the leaders of the people came and asked Moses why this had been commanded them.

23   And he told them, "Because the Lord has appointed tomorrow as a day of seriousness and rest, a holy Sabbath to the Lord when we must refrain from doing our daily tasks. So cook as much as you want to today, and keep what is left overnight."

24   And the next morning the food was wholesome and good, without maggots or odor.

25   Moses said, "This is your food for today, for today is the Sabbath to Jehovah and there will be no food on the ground today.

26   Gather the food for six days, but the seventh is a Sabbath, and there will be none there for you on that day."

27   But some of the people went out anyway to gather food, even though it was the Sabbath, but there wasn't any.

28, 29   "How long will these people refuse to obey?" the Lord asked Moses. "Don't they realize that I am giving them twice as much on the sixth day, so that there will be enough for two days? For the Lord has given you the seventh day as a day of Sabbath rest; stay in your tents and don't go out to pick up food from the ground that day."

30   So the people rested on the seventh day.

31   And the food became known as "manna" (meaning "What is it?"); it was white, like coriander seed, and flat, and tasted like honey bread.

32   Then Moses gave them this further instruction from the Lord: they were to take three quarts of it to

be kept as a museum specimen forever, so that later generations could see the bread the Lord had fed them with in the wilderness, when He brought them from Egypt.

33 Moses told Aaron to get a container and put three quarts of manna in it and to keep it in a sacred place from generation to generation.

34 Aaron did this, just as the Lord had instructed Moses, and eventually it was kept in the Ark in the Tabernacle.

35 So the people of Israel ate the manna forty years until they arrived in the land of Canaan, where there were crops to eat.

36 The omer—the container used to measure the manna—held about three quarts; it is approximately a tenth of a bushel.

CHAPTER 17

Now, at God's command, the people of Israel left the Sihn desert, going by easy stages to Rephidim. But upon arrival, there was no water!

2 So once more the people growled and complained to Moses. "Give us water!" they wailed.

"Quiet!" Moses commanded, "are you trying to test God's patience with you?"

3 But, tormented by thirst, they cried out, "Why did you ever take us out of Egypt? Why did you bring us here to die, with our children and cattle too?"

4 Then Moses pleaded with Jehovah. "What shall I do? For they are almost ready to stone me."

5, 6 Then Jehovah said to Moses, "Take the elders of Israel with you and lead the people out to

Mt. Horeb. I will meet you there at the rock. Strike it with your rod[1]—the same one you struck the Nile with—and water will come pouring out, enough for everyone!" Moses did as he was told, and the water gushed out!

7 Moses named the place Massah (meaning "tempting Jehovah to slay us"), and sometimes they referred to it as Meribah (meaning "argument" and "strife!")—for it was there that the people of Israel argued against God and tempted Him to slay[1] them by saying, "Is Jehovah going to take care of us or not?"

8 But now the warriors of Amalek came to fight against the people of Israel at Rephidim.

9 Moses instructed Joshua to issue a call to arms to the Israelites, to fight the army of Amalek. "Tomorrow," Moses told him, "I will stand at the top of the hill, with the rod of God in my hand!"

10 So Joshua and his men went out to fight the army of Amalek. Meanwhile Moses, Aaron, and Hur[2] went to the top of the hill.

11 And as long as Moses held up the rod in his hands, Israel was winning; but whenever he rested his arms at his sides, the soldiers of Amalek were winning.

12 Moses' arms finally became too tired to hold up the rod any longer; so Aaron and Hur rolled a stone for him to sit on, and they stood on each side, holding up his hands until sunset.

13 As a result, Joshua and his troops crushed the army of Amalek, putting them to the sword.

14 Then the Lord instructed Moses, "Write this into a permanent record, to be remembered forever,

---

[1]Implied.
[2]Hur was a man of Judah, of the family of Hezron, house of Caleb (I Chronicles 2:18,19). He was the grandfather of Bezalel (Exodus 31:1,2).

and announce to Joshua that I will utterly blot out every trace of Amalek."

15, 16   Moses built an altar there and called it "Jehovah-nissi" (meaning "Jehovah is my flag"). "Raise the banner of the Lord!" Moses said, "for the Lord will be at war with Amalek generation after generation."

CHAPTER 18

W ord soon reached Jethro, Moses' father-in-law, the priest of Midian, about all the wonderful things God had done for His people and for Moses, and how the Lord had brought them out of Egypt.

2   Then Jethro took Moses' wife, Zipporah, to him (for he had sent her home),

3   Along with Moses' two sons, Gershom (meaning "foreigner," for Moses said when he was born, "I have been wandering in a foreign land")

4   And Eliezer (meaning "God is my help," for Moses said at his birth, "The God of my fathers was my helper, and delivered me from the sword of Pharaoh").

5, 6   They arrived while Moses and the people were camped at Mt. Sinai.[1] "Jethro, your father-in-law, has come to visit you," Moses was told, "and he has brought your wife and your two sons."

7   Moses went out to meet his father-in-law and greeted him warmly; they asked about each other's health and then went into Moses' tent to talk further.

8   Moses related to his father-in-law all that had been happening and what the Lord had done to Pha-

---

[1] Or, "Mt. Horeb." Literally, "the mountain of God."

raoh and the Egyptians in order to deliver Israel, and all the problems there had been along the way, and how the Lord had delivered His people from all of them.

9　Jethro was very happy about everything the Lord had done for Israel, and about His bringing them out of Egypt.

10　"Bless the Lord," Jethro said, "for He has saved you from the Egyptians and from Pharaoh, and has rescued Israel.

11　I know now that the Lord is greater than any other god because He delivered His people from the proud and cruel Egyptians."

12　Jethro offered sacrifices[2] to God, and afterwards Aaron and the leaders of Israel came to meet Jethro, and they all ate the sacrificial meal together before the Lord.

13　The next day Moses sat as usual to hear the people's complaints against each other, from morning to evening.

14　When Moses' father-in-law saw how much time this was taking, he said, "Why are you trying to do all this alone, with people standing here all day long to get your help?"

15, 16　"Well, because the people come to me with their disputes, to ask for God's decisions," Moses told him. "I am their judge, deciding who is right and who is wrong, and instructing them in God's ways. I apply the laws of God to their particular disputes."

17　"It's not right!" his father-in-law exclaimed.

18　"You're going to wear yourself out—and if you do, what will happen to the people? Moses, this

---

[2]Literally, "a burnt offering and sacrifices for God."

job is too heavy a burden for you to try to handle all by yourself.

19, 20 Now listen, and let me give you a word of advice, and God will bless you: Be these people's lawyer—their representative before God—bringing Him their questions to decide; you will tell them His decisions, teaching them God's laws, and showing them the principles of godly living.

21 Find some capable, godly, honest men who hate bribes, and appoint them as judges, one judge for each 1000 people; he in turn will have ten judges under him, each in charge of a hundred; and under each of them will be two judges, each responsible for the affairs of fifty people; and each of these will have five judges beneath him, each counseling ten persons.

22 Let these men be responsible to serve the people with justice at all times. Anything that is too important or complicated can be brought to you. But the smaller matters they can take care of themselves. That way it will be easier for you because you will share the burden with them.

23 If you follow this advice, and if the Lord agrees, you will be able to endure the pressures, and there will be peace and harmony in the camp."

24 Moses listened to his father-in-law's advice, and followed this suggestion.

25 He chose able men from all over Israel and made them judges over the people—thousands, hundreds, fifties, and tens.

26 They were constantly available to administer justice. They brought the hard cases to Moses but judged the smaller matters themselves.

27 Soon afterwards Moses let his father-in-law return to his own land.

CHAPTER 19

The Israeli arrived in the Sinai peninsula three months after the night of their departure from Egypt.

2, 3 After breaking camp at Rephidim, they came to the base of Mt. Sinai and set up camp there. Moses climbed the rugged mountain to meet with God, and from somewhere in the mountain God called to him and said, "Give these instructions to the people of Israel. Tell them,

4 'You have seen what I did to the Egyptians, and how I brought you to Myself as though on eagle's wings.

5 Now if you will obey Me and keep your part of My contract with you, you shall be My own little flock from among all the nations of the earth; for all the earth is Mine.

6 And you shall be a kingdom of priests to God, a holy nation.' "

7 Moses returned from the mountain and called together the leaders of the people and told them what the Lord had said.

8 They all responded in unison, "We will certainly do everything He asks of us." Moses reported the words of the people to the Lord.

9 Then He said to Moses, "I am going to come to you in the form of a dark cloud, so that the people themselves can hear Me when I talk with you, and then they will always believe you.

10 Go down now and see that the people are ready

for My visit. Sanctify them today and tomorrow, and have them wash their clothes.

11 Then, the day after tomorrow, I will come down upon Mt. Sinai as all the people watch.

12 Set boundary lines the people may not pass, and tell them, 'Beware! Do not go up into the mountain, or even touch its boundaries; whoever does shall die—

13 No hand shall touch him, but he shall be stoned or shot to death with arrows, whether man or animal.' Stay away from the mountain entirely until you hear a ram's horn sounding one long blast; then gather at the foot of the mountain!"

14 So Moses went down to the people and sanctified them and they washed their clothing.

15 He told them, "Get ready for God's appearance two days from now, and do not have sexual intercourse with your wives."

16 On the morning of the third day there was a terrific thunder and lightning storm, and a huge cloud came down upon the mountain, and there was a long, loud blast as from a ram's horn; and all the people trembled.

17 Moses led them out from the camp to meet God, and they stood at the foot of the mountain.

18 All Mt. Sinai was covered with smoke because Jehovah descended upon it in the form of fire; the smoke billowed into the sky as from a furnace, and the whole mountain shook with a violent earthquake.

19 As the trumpet blast grew louder and louder, Moses spoke and God thundered His reply.

20 So the Lord came down upon the top of Mt. Sinai and called Moses up to the top of the mountain,

and Moses ascended to God.

21   But the Lord told Moses, "Go back down and warn the people not to cross the boundaries. They must not come up here to try to see God, for they will die.

22   Even the priests on duty[1] must sanctify themselves, lest Jehovah destroy them."

23   "But the people won't come up into the mountain!" Moses protested. "You told them not to! You told me to set boundaries around the mountain, and to declare it off limits because it is reserved for God."

24   But Jehovah said, "Go on down, and bring Aaron back with you, and don't let the priests and the people break across the boundaries to try to come up here, or I will destroy them."

25   So Moses went down to the people and told them what God had said.

CHAPTER 20

Then God issued this edict:

2   "I am Jehovah your God who liberated you from your slavery in Egypt.

3   You may worship no other god than Me.

4   You shall not make yourselves any idols: any images resembling animals, birds, or fish.[1]

5   You must never bow to an image or worship it in any way; for I, the Lord your God, am very possessive. I will not share your affection with any other god!

And when I punish people for their sins, the punishment continues upon the children, grandchildren, and great-grandchildren of those who hate Me;

---

[1]Literally, "The priests who come near to Jehovah."
[1]Literally, "of anything in heaven or earth or in the sea."

6 But I lavish My love upon thousands of those who love Me and obey My commandments.

7 You shall not use the name of Jehovah your God irreverently,[2] nor use it to swear to a falsehood. You will not escape punishment if you do.

8 Remember to observe the Sabbath as a holy day.

9 Six days a week are for your daily duties and your regular work,

10 But the seventh day is a day of Sabbath rest before the Lord your God. On that day you are to do no work of any kind, nor shall your son, daughter, or slaves—whether men or women—or your cattle or your house guests.

11 For in six days the Lord made the heaven, earth, and sea, and everything in them, and rested the seventh day; so He blessed the Sabbath day and set it aside for rest.[3]

12 Honor your father and mother, that you may have a long, good life in the land the Lord your God will give you.

13 You must not murder.

14 You must not commit adultery.

15 You must not steal.

16 You must not lie.[4]

17 You must not be envious of your neighbor's house, or want to sleep with his wife, or want to own his slaves, oxen, donkeys, or anything else he has."

18 All the people saw the lightning and the smoke billowing from the mountain, and heard the thunder and the long, frightening trumpet blast; and they stood at a

---

[2]Or, "use the name of the Lord your God to swear falsely."
[3]Or, "hallowed it."
[4]Or, "you must not give false testimony in court."

distance, shaking with fear.

19 They said to Moses, "You tell us what God says and we will obey, but don't let God speak directly to us, or it will kill us."

20 "Don't be afraid," Moses told them, "for God has come in this way to show you His awesome power, so that from now on you will be afraid to sin against Him!"

21 As the people stood in the distance, Moses entered into the deep darkness where God was.

22 And the Lord told him: "Tell the people of Israel, 'You are witnesses to the fact that I have made known My will to you from heaven.

23 Remember, you must not make or worship idols made of silver or gold or of anything else!

24 The altars you make for Me must be simple altars of earth. Offer upon them your sacrifices to Me —your burnt offerings and peace offerings of sheep and oxen. Build altars only where I tell you to, and I will come and bless you there.

25 You may also build altars from stone, but if you do, then use only uncut stones and boulders. Don't chip or shape the stones with a tool, for that would make them unfit for My altar.

26 And don't make steps for the altar, or someone might look up beneath the skirts of your clothing and see your nakedness.'

CHAPTER 21

Here are other laws you must obey:

2 If you buy[1] a Hebrew slave, he shall serve

---

[1]That is, "If he owes you money and defaults on the payment, and thus becomes your slave."

only six years and be freed in the seventh year, and need pay nothing to regain his freedom.

3   If he sold himself as a slave before he married, then if he married afterwards, only he shall be freed; but if he was married before he became a slave, then his wife shall be freed with him at the same time.

4   But if his master gave him a wife while he was a slave, and they have sons or daughters, the wife and children shall still belong to the master, and he shall go out by himself free.

5   But if the man shall plainly declare, 'I prefer my master, my wife, and my children, and I would rather not go free,'

6   Then his master shall bring him before the judges and shall publicly bore his ear with an awl, and after that he will be a slave forever.

7   If a man sells his daughter as a slave, she shall not be freed at the end of six years as the men are.

8   If she does not please the man who bought her, then he shall let her be bought back again; but he has no power to sell her to foreigners, since he has wronged her by no longer wanting her after marrying her.

9   And if he arranges an engagement between a Hebrew slave-girl and his son, then he may no longer treat her as a slave-girl, but must treat her as a daughter.

10   If he himself marries her and then takes another wife, he may not reduce her food or clothing, or fail to sleep with her as his wife.

11   If he fails in any of these three things, then she may leave freely without any payment.

12 Anyone who hits a man so hard that he dies shall surely be put to death.

13 But if it is accidental—an act of God—and not intentional, then I will appoint a place where he can run and get protection.

14 However, if a man deliberately attacks another, intending to kill him, drag him even from My altar, and kill him.

15 Anyone who strikes his father or mother shall surely be put to death.

16 A kidnapper must be killed, whether he is caught in possession of his victim or has already sold him as a slave.

17 Anyone who reviles or curses his mother or father shall surely be put to death.

18 If two men are fighting, and one hits the other with a stone or with his fist and injures him so that he must be confined to bed, but doesn't die,

19 If later he is able to walk again, even with a limp,[2] the man who hit him will be innocent except that he must pay for the loss of his time until he is thoroughly healed, and pay any medical expenses.

20 If a man beats his slave to death—whether the slave is male or female—that man shall surely be punished.

21 However, if the slave does not die for a couple of days, then the man shall not be punished—for the slave is his property.

22 If two men are fighting, and in the process hurt a pregnant woman so that she has a miscarriage, but she lives, then the man who injured her shall be fined

---

[2]Literally, "if he walks abroad with his staff."

whatever amount the woman's husband shall demand, and as the judges approve.

23 But if any harm comes to the woman and she dies, he shall be executed.

24 If her eye is injured, injure his; if her tooth is knocked out, knock out his; and so on—hand for hand, foot for foot,

25 Burn for burn, wound for wound, lash for lash.

26 If a man hits his slave in the eye, whether man or woman, and the eye is blinded, then the slave shall go free because of his eye.

27 And if a master knocks out his slave's tooth, he shall let him go free to pay for the tooth.

28 If an ox gores a man or woman to death, the ox shall be stoned and its flesh not eaten, but the owner shall not be held—

29 Unless the ox was known to gore people in the past, and the owner had been notified and still the ox was not kept under control; in that case, if it kills someone, the ox shall be stoned and the owner also shall be killed.

30 But the dead man's relatives may accept a fine instead, if they wish. The judges will determine the amount.[3]

31 The same law holds if the ox gores a boy or a girl.

32 But if the ox gores a slave, whether male or female, the slave's master shall be given thirty pieces of silver, and the ox shall be stoned.

33 If a man digs a well and doesn't cover it, and an ox or a donkey falls into it,

---

[3]Literally, verse 30 reads: "But if a ransom is laid upon him, then he shall give for the redemption of his life whatever is laid upon him."

34 The owner of the well shall pay full damages to the owner of the animal, and the dead animal shall belong to him.

35 If a man's ox injures another, and it dies, then the two owners shall sell the live ox and divide the price between them—and each shall also own half of the dead ox.

36 But if the ox was known from past experience to gore, and its owner has not kept it under control, then there will not be a division of the income; but the owner of the living ox shall pay in full for the dead ox, and the dead one shall be his.

CHAPTER 22

If a man steals an ox or sheep and then kills or sells it, he shall pay a fine of five to one—five oxen shall be returned for each stolen ox. For sheep, the fine shall be four to one—four sheep returned for each sheep stolen.

2 If a thief is caught in the act of breaking into a house and is killed, the one who killed him is not guilty.

3 But if it happens in the daylight, it must be presumed to be murder and the man who kills him is guilty.

If a thief is captured, he must make full restitution; if he can't, then he must be sold as a slave for his debt.

4 If he is caught in the act of stealing a live ox or donkey or sheep or whatever it is, he shall pay double value as his fine.

5 If someone deliberately lets his animal loose and it gets into another man's vineyard; or if he turns it

into another man's field to graze, he must pay for all damages by giving the owner of the field or vineyard an equal amount of the best of his own crop.

6   If the field is being burned off and the fire gets out of control and goes into another field so that the shocks of grain, or the standing grain, are destroyed, the one who started the fire shall make full restitution.

7   If someone gives money or goods to anyone to keep for him, and it is stolen, the thief shall pay double if he is found.

8   But if no thief is found, then the man to whom the valuables were entrusted shall be brought before God to determine whether or not he himself has stolen his neighbor's property.

9   In every case in which an ox, donkey, sheep, clothing, or anything else is lost, and the owner believes he has found it in the possession of someone else who denies it, both parties to the dispute shall come before God for a decision, and the one whom God declares guilty shall pay double to the other.

10   If a man asks his neighbor to keep a donkey, ox, sheep, or any other animal for him, and it dies, or is hurt, or gets away, and there is no eyewitness to report just what happened to it,

11   Then the neighbor must take an oath that he has not stolen it, and the owner must accept his word, and no restitution shall be made for it.

12   But if the animal or property has been stolen, the neighbor caring for it must repay the owner.

13   If it was attacked by some wild animal, he shall bring the torn carcass to confirm the fact, and shall not be required to make restitution.

14   If a man borrows an animal (or anything else)

from a neighbor, and it is injured or killed, and the owner is not there at the time, then the man who borrowed it must pay for it.

15 But if the owner is there, he need not pay; and if it was rented, then he need not pay, because this possibility was included in the original rental fee.

16 If a man seduces a girl[1] who is not engaged to anyone, and sleeps with her, he must pay the usual dowry[2] and accept her as his wife.

17 But if her father utterly refuses to let her marry him, then he shall pay the money anyway.

18 A sorceress shall be put to death.

19 Anyone having sexual relations with an animal shall certainly be executed.

20 Anyone sacrificing to any other god than Jehovah shall be executed.[3]

21 You must not oppress a stranger in any way; remember, you yourselves were foreigners in the land of Egypt.

22 You must not exploit widows or orphans;

23 If you do so in any way, and they cry to me for My help, I will surely give it.

24 And My anger shall flame out against you, and I will kill you with enemy armies, so that your wives will be widows and your children fatherless.

25 If you lend money to a needy fellow-Hebrew, you are not to handle the transaction in an ordinary way, with interest.

26 If you take his clothing as a pledge of his repayment, you must let him have it back at night.

---

[1]Literally, "a virgin."
[2]More literally, "customary marriage present from a bridegroom to the bride's parents."
[3]Literally, "shall be utterly destroyed."

27 For it is probably his only warmth; how can he sleep without it? If you don't return it, and he cries to Me for help, I will hear and be very gracious to him [at your expense],[4] for I am very compassionate.

28 You shall not blaspheme God, nor curse government officials—your judges and your rulers.

29 You must be prompt in givng Me the tithe of your crops and your wine, and the redemption payment for your oldest son.

30 As to the firstborn of the oxen and the sheep, give it to Me on the eighth day, after leaving it with its mother for seven days.

31 And since you yourselves are holy—My special people—do not eat any animal that has been attacked and killed by a wild animal. Leave its carcass for the dogs to eat.

CHAPTER 23

Do not pass along untrue reports. Do not cooperate with an evil man by affirming on the witness stand something you know is false.

2, 3 Don't join mobs intent on evil. When on the witness stand, don't be swayed in your testimony by the mood of the majority present, and do not slant your testimony in favor of a man just because he is poor.

4 If you come upon an enemy's ox or donkey that has strayed away, you must take it back to its owner.

5 If you see your enemy trying to get his donkey onto its feet beneath a heavy load, you must not go on by, but must help him.

6 A man's poverty is no excuse for twisting justice against him.

---

[4]Implied.

7 Keep far away from falsely charging anyone with evil; never let an innocent person be put to death. I will not stand for this.[1]

8 Take no bribes, for a bribe makes you unaware of what you clearly see! A bribe hurts the cause of the person who is right.

9 Do not oppress foreigners; you know what it's like to be a foreigner; remember your own experience in the land of Egypt.

10 Sow and reap your crops for six years,

11 But let the land rest and lie fallow during the seventh year, and let the poor among the people harvest any volunteer crop that may come up; leave the rest for the animals to enjoy. The same rule applies to your vineyards and your olive groves.

12 Work six days only, and rest the seventh; this is to give your oxen and donkeys a rest, as well as the people of your household—your slaves and visitors.

13 Be sure to obey all of these instructions; and remember—never mention the name of any other god.[2]

14 There are three annual religious pilgrimages you must make.[3]

15 The first is the Pilgrimage of Unleavened Bread, when for seven days you are not to eat bread with yeast, just as I commanded you before. This celebration is to be an annual event at the regular time in March, the month you left Egypt; everyone must bring Me a sacrifice at that time.

16 Then there is the Harvest Pilgrimage, when you must bring to Me the first of your crops. And,

[1]Literally, "I will not acquit the wicked."
[2]In prayer, or in taking an oath.
[3]Or, "feasts you must celebrate."

finally, the Pilgrimage of In-gathering at the end of the harvest season.

17   At these three times each year, every man in Israel shall appear before the Lord God.

18   No sacrificial blood shall be offered with leavened bread; no sacrificial fat shall be left unoffered until the next morning.

19   As you reap each of your crops, bring Me the choicest sample of the first day's harvest; it shall be offered[4] to the Lord your God.

Do not boil a young goat in its mother's milk.

20   See, I am sending an Angel before you to lead you safely to the land I have prepared for you.

21   Reverence Him and obey all of His instructions; do not rebel against Him, for He will not pardon your transgression; He is My representative[5]—He bears My name.

22   But if you are careful to obey Him, following all My instructions, then I will be an enemy to your enemies.

23   For My Angel shall go before you and bring you into the land of the Amorites, Hittites, Perizzites, Canaanites, Hivites, and Jebusites, to live there. And I will destroy those people before you.

24   You must not worship the gods of these other nations, nor sacrifice to them in any way, and you must not follow the evil example of these heathen people; you must utterly conquer them and break down their shameful idols.

25   You shall serve the Lord your God only; then I will bless you with food and with water, and I will

---

[4]Literally, "you shall bring [it] into the house of Jehovah thy God."
[5]Literally, "my name is in Him."

take away sickness from among you.

26 There will be no miscarriages nor barrenness throughout your land, and you will live out the full quota of the days of your life.

27 The terror of the Lord shall fall upon all the people whose land you invade, and they will flee before you;

28 And I will send hornets to drive out the Hivites, Canaanites, and Hittites from before you.

29 I will not do it all in one year, for the land would become a wilderness, and the wild animals would become too many to control.

30 But I will drive them out a little at a time, until your population has increased enough to fill the land.

31 And I will set your enlarged boundaries from the Red Sea to the Philistine coast, and from the southern deserts as far as the Euphrates River; and I will cause you to defeat the people now living in the land, and you will drive them out ahead of you.

32 You must make no covenant with them, nor have anything to do with their gods.

33 Don't let them live among you! For I know that they will infect you with their sin of worshiping false gods, and that would be an utter disaster to you."

CHAPTER 24

The Lord now instructed Moses, "Come up here with Aaron, Nadab, Abihu, and seventy of the elders of Israel. All of you except Moses are to worship at a distance.

2 Moses alone shall come near to the Lord; and remember, none of the ordinary people are permitted to come up into the mountain at all."

3 Then Moses announced to the people all the laws and regulations God had given him; and the people answered in unison, "We will obey them all."

4 Moses wrote down the laws; and early the next morning he built an altar at the foot of the mountain, with twelve pillars around the altar because there were twelve tribes of Israel.

5 Then he sent some of the young men to sacrifice the burnt offerings and peace offerings to the Lord.

6 Moses took half of the blood of these animals, and drew it off into basins. The other half he splashed against the altar.

7 And he read to the people the Book he had written—the Book of the Covenant—containing God's directions and laws. And the people said again, "We solemnly promise to obey every one of these rules."

8 Then Moses threw the blood from the basins towards the people and said, "This blood confirms and seals the covenant the Lord has made with you in giving you these laws."

9 Then Moses, Aaron, Nadab, Abihu, and seventy of the elders of Israel went up into the mountain.

10 And they saw the God of Israel; under His feet there seemed to be a pavement of brilliant sapphire stones, as clear as the heavens.

11 Yet, even though the elders saw God, He did not destroy them; and they had a meal together before the Lord.

12 And the Lord said to Moses, "Come up to Me into the mountain, and remain until I give you the laws and commandments I have written on tablets of stone, so that you can teach the people from them."

13 So Moses and Joshua, his assistant, went up into the mountain of God.

14 He told the elders, "Stay here and wait for us until we come back; if there are any problems while I am gone, consult with Aaron and Hur."

15 Then Moses went up the mountain and disappeared into the cloud at the top.

16 And the glory of the Lord rested upon Mt. Sinai and the cloud covered it six days; the seventh day He called to Moses from the cloud.

17 Those at the bottom of the mountain saw the awesome sight: the glory of the Lord on the mountain top looked like a raging fire.

18 And Moses disappeared into the cloud-covered mountain top, and was there for forty days and forty nights.

CHAPTER 25

Jehovah said to Moses, "Tell the people of Israel that everyone who wants to may bring Me an offering from this list:

         Gold,

         Silver,

         Bronze,

4   Blue cloth,

         Purple cloth,

         Scarlet cloth,

         Fine-twined linen,

         Goat's hair,

5   Red-dyed ram's skins,

         Goat's skins,

         Acacia wood,

6   Olive oil for the lamps,

Spices for the anointing oil and for the fragrant incense,

7   Onyx stones,

Stones to be set in the ephod and in the breastplate.

8   For I want the people of Israel to make Me a sacred Temple where I can live among them.

9   This home of Mine shall be a tent pavilion— a Tabernacle. I will give you a drawing of the construction plan, and the details of each furnishing.

10   Using acacia wood, make an Ark 3¾ feet long, 2¼ feet wide, and 2¼ feet high.

11   Overlay it inside and outside with pure gold, with a molding of gold all around it.

12   Cast four rings of gold for it and attach them to the four lower corners, two rings on each side.

13, 14   Make poles from acacia wood overlaid with gold, and fit the poles into the rings at the sides of the Ark, to carry it.

15   These carrying poles shall never be taken from the rings, but are to be left there permanently.

16   When the Ark is finished, place inside it the tablets of stone I will give you, with the Ten Commandments engraved on them.[1]

17   And make a lid of pure gold, 3¾ feet long and 2¼ feet wide. This is the place of mercy for your sins.[2]

18   Then make images of angels,[3] using beaten gold, and place them at the two ends of the lid of the Ark.

[1]Implied. Literally, "Put into the ark the Testimony which I shall give you.
[2]Literally, "mercy seat" or "place of making propitiation."
[3]Literally, "cherubim." We are not told what they looked like.

19 They shall be one piece with the mercy place, one at each end.

20 The cherubim—the angels—shall be facing each other, looking down upon the place of mercy, and shall have wings spread out above the gold lid.

21 Install the lid upon the Ark, and place within the Ark the tablets of stone I shall give you.

22 And I will meet with you there and talk with you from above the place of mercy between the cherubim; and the Ark will contain the laws of My covenant. There I will tell you My commandments for the people of Israel.

23 Then make a table of acacia wood three feet long, 1½ feet wide, and 2¼ feet high.

24 Overlay it with pure gold, and run a rib of gold around it.

25 Put a molding four inches wide around the edge of the top, and a gold ridge along the molding, all around.

26, 27 Make four golden rings and put the rings at the outside corner of the four legs, close to the top; these are rings for the poles that will be used to carry the table.

28 Make the poles from acacia wood overlaid with gold.

29 And make golden dishes, spoons, pitchers, and flagons;

30 And always keep the special Bread of the Presence on the table before Me.

31 Make a lampstand of pure, beaten gold. The entire lampstand and its decorations shall be one piece —the base, shaft, lamps, and blossoms.

32, 33 It will have three branches going out from

each side of the center shaft, each branch decorated with three almond flowers.

34, 35   The central shaft itself will be decorated with four almond flowers—one placed between each set of branches; also, there will be one flower above the top set of branches and one below the bottom set.

36   These decorations and branches and the shaft are all to be one piece of pure, beaten gold.

37   Then make seven lamps for the lampstand, and set them so that they reflect their light forward.

38   The snuffers and trays are to be made of pure gold.

39   You will need about 107[4] pounds of pure gold for the lampstand and its accessories.

40   Be sure that everything you make follows the pattern I am showing you here on the mountain.

CHAPTER 26

Make the Tabernacle-tent from ten colored sheets of fine-twined linen, forty-two feet long and six feet wide, dyed blue, purple, and scarlet, with cherubim embroidered on them.

3   Join five sheets end to end for each side of the tent, forming two long pieces, one for each side.

4, 5   Use loops at the edges to join these two long pieces together side by side. There are to be fifty loops on each side, opposite each other.

6   Then make fifty golden clasps to fasten the loops together, so that the Tabernacle, the dwelling place of God, becomes a single unit.

7, 8   The roof of the Tabernacle is made of goat's hair tarpaulins. There are to be eleven of these tar-

---

[4]Literally, "a [gold] talent." The exact weight is not known.

paulins, each forty-five feet across and six feet wide.

9 Connect five of these tarpaulins into one wide section; and use the other six for another wide section. (The sixth tarpaulin will hang down to form a curtain across the front of the sacred tent.)

10, 11 Use fifty loops along the edges of each of these two wide pieces, to join them together with fifty bronze clasps. Thus the two widths become one.

12 There will be a 1½ foot length of this roof-covering hanging down from the back of the tent,

13 And a 1½ foot length at the front.

14 On top of these blankets are placed a layer of rams' skins, dyed red, and over them a top layer of goat skins. This completes the roof-covering.

15, 16 The framework of the sacred tent shall be made from acacia wood, each frame-piece being fifteen feet high and 2¼ feet wide, standing upright,

17 With grooves on each side to mortise into the next upright piece.

18, 19 Twenty of these frames will form the south side of the sacred tent, with forty silver bases for the frames to fit into—two bases under each piece of the frame.

20 On the north side there will also be twenty of these frames,

21 With their forty silver bases, two bases for each frame, one under each edge.

22 On the west side there will be six frames,

23 And two frames at each corner.

24 These corner frames will be connected at the bottom and top with clasps.

25 So, in all, there will be eight frames on that end of the building with sixteen silver bases for the

frames—two bases under each frame.

26, 27 Make bars of acacia wood to run across the frames, five bars on each side of the Tabernacle. Also five bars for the rear of the building, facing westward.

28 The middle bar, halfway up the frames, runs all the way from end to end of the Tabernacle.

29 Overlay the frames with gold, and make gold rings to hold the bars; and also overlay the bars with gold.

30 Set up this Tabernacle-tent in the manner I showed you in the mountain.

31 [Inside the Tabernacle[1]], make a veil from blue, purple, and scarlet cloth, the fine-twined linen, with cherubim embroidered into the cloth.

32 Hang this upon four acacia pillars overlaid with gold, with four golden hooks. The pillars are to rest in four silver bases.

33 Hang the curtain from the hooks. Behind this curtain place the Ark containing the stone tablets engraved with God's laws. The curtain will separate the Holy Place and the Most Holy Place.

34 Now install the mercy place—the golden lid of the ark—in the Most Holy Place.

35 Place the table and lampstand across the room from each other on the outer side of the veil. The lampstand will be on the south side of the Holy Place and the table on the north side.

36 As a screen for the door of the sacred tent, make another curtain from skillfully embroidered blue, purple, and scarlet fine-twined linen.

37 Hang up this curtain on five acacia wood posts,

---

[1]Implied.

overlaid with gold, with hooks of gold, and a bronze socket for each pillar.

CHAPTER 27

Using acacia wood, make a square altar 7½ feet wide, and three feet high.

2   Make horns for the four corners of the altar, attach them firmly, and overlay everything with bronze.

3   The ash buckets, shovels, basins, carcass-hooks, and fire pans are all to be made of bronze.

4   Make a bronze grating, with a metal ring at each corner,

5   And fit the grating halfway down into the fire box, resting it upon the ledge built there.

6   For moving the altar, make poles from acacia wood overlaid with bronze.

7   To carry it, put the poles into the rings at each side of the altar.

8   The altar is to be hollow, made from planks, just as was shown you on the mountain.

9, 10   Then make a courtyard for the Tabernacle, enclosed with curtains made from fine-twined linen. On the south side the curtains will stretch for 150 feet, and be held up by twenty posts, fitting into twenty bronze post holders. The curtains will be held up with silver hooks attached to silver rods, attached to the posts.

11   It will be the same on the north side of the court—150 feet of curtains held up by twenty posts fitted into bronze sockets, with silver hooks and rods.

12   The west side of the court will be seventy-five feet wide, with ten posts and ten sockets.

13   The east side will also be seventy-five feet.

14, 15   On each side of the entrance there will be 22½ feet of curtain, held up by three posts imbedded in three sockets.

16   The entrance to the court will be a thirty-foot-wide curtain, made of beautifully embroidered blue, purple, and scarlet fine-twined linen, and attached to four posts imbedded in their four sockets.

17   All the posts around the court are to be connected by silver rods, using silver hooks, the posts being imbedded in solid bronze bases.

18   So the entire court will be 150 feet long, and 75 feet wide, with curtain walls 7½ feet high, made from fine-twined linen.

19   All utensils used in the work of the Tabernacle, including all the pins and pegs for hanging the utensils on the walls, will be made of bronze.

20   Instruct the people of Israel to bring you pure olive oil to use in the lamps of the Tabernacle, to burn there continually.

21   Aaron and his sons shall place this eternal flame in the outer holy room, tending it day and night before the Lord, so that it never goes out. This is a permanent rule for the people of Israel.

CHAPTER 28

Consecrate Aaron your brother, and his sons Nadab, Abihu, Eleazer, and Ithamar, to be priests, to minister to Me.

2   Make special clothes for Aaron, to indicate his separation to God—beautiful garments that will lend dignity to his work.

3   Instruct those to whom I have given special skill as tailors to make the garments that will set him

apart from others, so that he may minister to Me in the priest's office.

4   This is the wardrobe they shall make: a chestpiece, an ephod,[1] a robe, a checkered tunic, a turban, and a sash. They shall also make special garments for Aaron's sons.

5, 6   The ephod shall be made by the most skilled of the workmen, using blue, purple, and scarlet threads of fine-twined linen.

7   It will consist of two pieces, front and back, joined at the shoulders.

8   And the sash shall be made of the same material—threads of gold, blue, purple, and scarlet finetwined linen.

9   Take two onyx stones, and engrave on them the names of the tribes of Israel.

10   Six names shall be on each stone, so that all the tribes are named in the order of their births.

11   When engraving these names, use the same technique as in making a seal; and mount the stones in gold settings.

12   Fasten the two stones upon the shoulders of the ephod, as memorial stones for the people of Israel: Aaron will carry their names before the Lord as a constant reminder.

13, 14   Two chains of pure, twisted gold shall be made and attached to golden clasps on the shoulder of the ephod.

15   Then, using the most careful workmanship, make a chestpiece to be used as God's oracle; use the same gold, blue, purple, and scarlet threads of finetwined linen as you did in the ephod.

---

[1]Apparently a sort of sleeveless tunic reaching from the shoulders to below the knees.

16 This chestpiece is to be of two folds of cloth, forming a pouch.

17 Attach to it four rows of stones: A ruby, a topaz, and an emerald shall be in the first row;

18 The second row will be an emerald, a sapphire, and a diamond.

19 The third row will be an amber, an agate, and an amethyst.

20 The fourth row will be an onyx, a beryl, and a jasper—all set in gold settings.

21 Each stone will represent one of the tribes of Israel and the name of that tribe will be engraved upon it like a seal.

22, 23, 24 Attach the top of the chestpiece to the ephod by means of two twisted cords of pure gold. One end of each cord is attached to golden rings placed at the outer top edge of the chestpiece.

25 The other ends of the two cords are attached to the front edges of the two settings of the onyx stones on the shoulder of the ephod.

26 Then make two more golden rings and place them on the two lower, inside edges of the chestpiece;

27 Also make two other golden rings for the bottom front edge of the ephod at the sash.

28 Now attach the bottom of the chestpiece to the bottom rings of the ephod by means of blue ribbons; this will prevent the chestpiece from coming loose from the ephod.

29 In this way Aaron shall carry the names of the tribes of Israel on the chestpiece over his heart (it is God's oracle) when he goes in to the Holy Place; thus Jehovah will be reminded of them continually.

30, 31 Insert into the pocket of the chestpiece

the Urim and Thummim,[2] to be carried over Aaron's heart when he goes in before Jehovah. Thus Aaron shall always be carrying the oracle over his heart when he goes in before the Lord. The ephod shall be made of blue cloth,

32   With an opening for Aaron's head. It shall have a woven band around this opening, just as on the neck of a coat of mail, so that it will not fray.

33, 34   The bottom edge of the ephod shall be embroidered with blue, purple, and scarlet pomegranates, alternated with gold bells.

35   Aaron shall wear the ephod whenever he goes in to minister to the Lord: the bells will tinkle as he goes in and out of the presence of the Lord in the Holy Place, so that he will not die.

36   Next, make a plate of pure gold and engrave on it, just as you would upon a seal, 'Consecrated to Jehovah.'

37, 38   This plate is to be attached by means of a blue ribbon to the front of Aaron's turban.

In this way Aaron will be wearing it upon his forehead, and thus bear the guilt connected with any errors regarding the offerings of the people of Israel. It shall always be worn when he goes into the presence of the Lord, so that the people will be accepted and forgiven.

39   Weave Aaron's tunic from fine-twined linen, using a checkerboard pattern; make the turban, too, of this linen; and make him an embroidered sash.

40   Then, for Aaron's sons, make robes, sashes, and turbans to give them honor and respect.

---

[2]What these looked like has been lost in antiquity. Possibly they were two stones that were marked in some way and used by the High Priest to determine God's "yes" or "no" on urgent matters.

41   Clothe Aaron and his sons with these garments, and then dedicate these men to their ministry by anointing their heads with olive oil, thus sanctifying them as the priests, My ministers.

42   Also make linen undershorts for them, to be worn beneath their robes next to their bodies, reaching from hips to knees.

43   These are to be worn whenever Aaron and his sons go into the Tabernacle or to the altar in the Holy Place, lest they be guilty and die. This is a permanent ordinance for Aaron and his sons.

CHAPTER 29

This is the ceremony for the dedication of Aaron and his sons as priests: get a young bull and two rams with no defects,

2   And bread made without yeast, and thin sheets of sweetened bread mingled with oil, and unleavened wafers with oil poured over them. (The various kinds of bread shall be made with finely ground wheat flour.)

3, 4   Place the bread in a basket and bring it to the entrance of the Tabernacle, along with the young bull and the two rams. Bathe Aaron and his sons there at the entrance.

5   Then put Aaron's robe on him, and the tunic, ephod, chestpiece, and sash,

6   And place on his head the turban with the golden plate.

7   Then take the anointing oil and pour it upon his head.

8   Next, dress his sons in their robes,

9   With their woven sashes, and place caps on

their heads. They will then be priests forever; thus you shall consecrate Aaron and his sons.

10 Then bring the young bull to the Tabernacle, and Aaron and his sons shall lay their hands upon its head;

11 And you shall kill it before the Lord, at the entrance of the Tabernacle.

12 Place its blood upon the horns of the altar, smearing it on with your finger, and pour the rest at the base of the altar.

13 Then take all the fat that covers the inner parts, also the gall bladder and two kidneys, and the fat on them, and burn them upon the altar.

14 Then take the body, including the skin and the dung, outside the camp and burn it as a sin offering.

15, 16 Next, Aaron and his sons shall lay their hands upon the head of one of the rams as it is killed. Its blood shall also be collected and sprinkled upon the altar.

17 Cut up the ram and wash off the entrails and the legs; place them with the head and the other pieces of the body,

18 And burn it all upon the altar; it is a burnt offering to the Lord, and very pleasant to Him.

19, 20 Now take the other ram, and Aaron and his sons shall lay their hands upon its head as it is killed. Collect the blood and place some of it upon the tip of the right ear of Aaron and his sons, and upon their right thumbs and the big toes of their right feet; sprinkle the rest of the blood over the altar.

21 Then scrape off some of the blood from the altar and mix it with some of the anointing oil and sprinkle it upon Aaron and his sons and upon their

clothes; and they and their clothing shall be sanctified to the Lord.

22 Then take the fat of the ram, including the fat tail and the fat that covers the insides, also the gall bladder and the two kidneys and the fat surrounding them, and the right thigh—for this is the ram for ordination of Aaron and his sons—

23 And one loaf of bread, one cake of shortening bread, and one wafer from the basket of unleavened bread that was placed before the Lord:

24 Place these in the hands of Aaron and his sons, to wave them in a gesture of offering to the Lord.

25 Afterwards, take them from their hands and burn them on the altar as a fragrant burnt offering to Him.

26 Then take the breast of Aaron's ordination ram and wave it before the Lord in a gesture of offering; afterwards, keep it for yourself.

27 Give the breast and thigh of the consecration ram

28 To Aaron and his sons. The people of Israel must always contribute this portion of their sacrifices —whether peace offerings or thanksgiving offerings— as their contribution to the Lord.

29 These sacred garments of Aaron shall be preserved for the consecration of his son who succeeds him, from generation to generation, for his anointing ceremony.

30 Whoever is the next High Priest after Aaron shall wear these clothes for seven days before beginning to minister in the Tabernacle and the Holy Place.

31 Take the ram of consecration—the ram used

in the ordination ceremony—and boil its meat in a sacred area.

32   Aaron and his sons shall eat the meat, also the bread in the basket, at the door of the Tabernacle.

33   They alone shall eat those items used in their atonement (that is, in their consecration ceremony). The ordinary people shall not eat them, for these things are set apart and holy.

34   If any of the meat or bread remains until the morning, burn it; it shall not be eaten, for it is holy.

35   This, then, is the way you shall ordain Aaron and his sons to their offices. This ordination shall go on for seven days.

36   Every day you shall sacrifice a young bull as a sin offering for atonement; afterwards,[3] purge the altar by making atonement for it; pour olive oil upon it to sanctify it.

37   Make atonement for the altar and consecrate it to God every day for seven days. After this the altar shall be exceedingly holy, so that whatever touches it shall be set apart for God.[4]

38   Each day offer two yearling lambs upon the altar,

39   One in the morning and the other in the evening.

40   With one of them offer three quarts of finely ground flour mixed with 2½ pints of oil, pressed from olives; also 2½ pints of wine, as a libation.

41   Offer the other lamb in the evening, along with flour and the wine libation as in the morning, for a

---

[3]Implied.
[4]Or, "shall become holy," or, "only those who are holy may touch it."

fragrant burnt offering to the Lord.

42 This shall be a perpetual daily offering at the door of the Tabernacle before the Lord, where I will meet with you and speak with you.

43 And I will meet with the people of Israel there, and the Tabernacle shall be sanctified by My glory.

44 Yes, I will sanctify the Tabernacle and the altar and Aaron and his sons who are My ministers, the priests.

45 And I will live among the people of Israel and be their God,

46 And they shall know that I am the Lord their God. I brought them out of Egypt so that I could live among them. I am Jehovah their God.

CHAPTER 30

Then make a small altar for burning incense. It shall be made from acacia wood.

2 It is to be eighteen inches square and three feet high, with horns carved from the wood of the altar—they are not to be merely separate parts that are attached.

3 Overlay the top, sides, and horns of the altar with pure gold, and run a gold molding around the entire altar.

4 Beneath the molding, on each of two sides, construct two gold rings to hold the carrying poles.

5 The poles are to be made of acacia wood overlaid with gold.

6 Place the altar just outside the veil, near the place of mercy that is above the Ark containing the Ten Commandments. I will meet with you there.

7 Every morning when Aaron trims the lamps,

he shall burn sweet spices on the altar,

8 And each evening when he lights the lamps he shall burn the incense before the Lord, and this shall go on from generation to generation.

9 Offer no unauthorized incense, burnt offerings, meal offerings, or drink offerings.

10 Once a year Aaron must sanctify[1] the altar, smearing[2] upon its horns the blood of the sin offering for atonement. This shall be a regular, annual event from generation to generation, for this is the Lord's supremely holy altar."

11, 12 And Jehovah said to Moses, "Whenever you take a census of the people of Israel, each man who is numbered shall give a ransom to the Lord for his soul, so that there will be no plague among the people when you number them.

13 His payment shall be half a dollar.[3]

14 All who have reached their twentieth birthday shall give this offering.

15 The rich shall not give more and the poor shall not give less, for it is an offering to the Lord to make atonement for yourselves.

16 Use this money for the care of the Tabernacle; it is to bring you, the people of Israel, to the Lord's attention, and to make atonement for you."

17, 18 And the Lord said to Moses, "Make a bronze basin with a bronze pedestal. Put it between the Tabernacle and the altar, and fill it with water.

19 Aaron and his sons shall wash their hands and feet there,

---

[1]Literally, "shall make an atonement for the altar."
[2]Implied.
[3]Literally, "half a shekel after the shekel of the sanctuary [the shekel is twenty gerahs], half a shekel for an offering to Jehovah."

20 When they go into the Tabernacle to appear before the Lord, or when they approach the altar to burn offerings to the Lord. They must always wash before doing so, or they will die.

21 These are instructions to Aaron and his sons from generation to generation."

22, 23 Then the Lord told Moses to collect the choicest of spices—eighteen pounds[4] of pure myrrh; half as much of cinnamon and of sweet cane;

24 The same amount of cassia as of myrrh; and 1½ gallons of olive oil.

25 The Lord instructed skilled perfume-makers to compound all this into a holy anointing oil.

26, 27 "Use this," He said, "to anoint the Tabernacle, the Ark, the table and all its instruments, the lampstand and all its utensils, the incense altar,

28 The burnt offering altar with all its instruments, and the washbasin and its pedestal.

29 Sanctify them, to make them holy; whatever touches them shall become holy.[5]

30 Use it to anoint Aaron and his sons, sanctifying them so that they can minister to Me as priests.

31 And say to the people of Israel, 'This shall always be My holy anointing oil.

32 It must never be poured upon an ordinary person, and you shall never make any of it yourselves, for it is holy, and it shall be treated by you as holy.

33 Anyone who compounds any incense like it or puts any of it upon someone who is not a priest shall be excommunicated.' "

34 These were the Lord's directions to Moses con-

---

[4] Literally, "five hundred shekels." The exact weight can not be ascertained.
[5] Or, "shall be set apart for God," or, "only what is holy may touch them."

cerning the incense: "Use sweet spices—stacte, onycha, galbanum, and pure frankincense, weighing out the same amounts of each,

35 Using the usual techniques of the incense-maker, and seasoning it with salt; it shall be a pure and holy incense.

36 Beat some of it very fine and put some of it in front of the Ark where I meet with you in the Tabernacle; this incense is most holy.

37 Never make it for yourselves, for it is reserved for the Lord and you must treat it as holy.

38 Anyone making it for himself shall be excommunicated."

CHAPTER 31

The Lord also said to Moses, "See, I have appointed Bezalel (son of Uri, and grandson of Hur, of the tribe of Judah),

3 And have filled him with the spirit of God, giving him great wisdom, ability, and skill in constructing the Tabernacle and everything it contains.

4 He is highly capable as an artistic designer of objects made of gold, silver, and bronze.

5 He is skilled, too, as a jeweler and in carving wood.

6 And I have appointed Oholiab (son of Ahisamach of the tribe of Dan) to be his assistant; moreover, I have given special skill to all who are known as experts, so that they can make all the things I have instructed you to make:

7 The Tabernacle; the Ark with the place of mercy upon it; all the furnishings of the Tabernacle;

8 The table and its instruments; the pure gold

lampstand with its instruments; the altar of incense;

9 The burnt offering altar with its instruments; the laver and its pedestal;

10 The beautifully made, holy garments for Aaron the priest, and the garments for his sons, so that they can minister as priests;

11 The anointing oil; and the sweet-spice incense for the holy place. They are to follow exactly the directions I gave you."

12, 13 The Lord then gave these further instructions to Moses: "Tell the people of Israel to rest on My Sabbath day, for the Sabbath is a reminder of the covenant between Me and you forever; it helps you to remember that I am Jehovah who makes you holy.

14, 15 Yes, rest on the Sabbath, for it is holy. Anyone who does not obey this command must die: anyone who does any work on that day shall be killed.

16 Work six days only, for the seventh day is a special day of solemn rest, holy to the Lord. This law is a perpetual covenant and obligation for the people of Israel.

17 It is an eternal symbol of the covenant between Me and the people of Israel. For in six days the Lord made heaven and earth, and rested on the seventh day, and was refreshed."

18 Then, as God finished speaking with Moses on Mount Sinai, He gave him the two tablets of stone on which the Ten Commandments were written with the finger of God.

CHAPTER 32

When Moses didn't come back down the mountain right away, the people went to Aaron. "Look," they said, "make us a god to lead us, for this fellow Moses who brought us here from Egypt has disappeared; something must have happened to him."

2, 3 "Give me your golden earrings," Aaron replied.

So they all did—men and women, boys and girls.

4 Aaron melted the gold, then molded and tooled it into the form of a calf.

The people exclaimed, "O Israel, this is the god that brought you out of Egypt!"

5 When Aaron saw how happy the people were about it, he built an altar before the calf and announced, "Tomorrow there will be a feast to Jehovah!"

6 So they were up early the next morning and began offering burnt offerings and peace offerings to the calf-idol; afterwards they sat down to feast and drink at a wild party, followed by sexual immorality.

7 Then the Lord told Moses, "Quick! Go on down, for your people that you brought from Egypt have defiled themselves,

8 And have quickly abandoned all My laws. They have molded themselves a calf, and worshiped it, and sacrificed to it, and said, 'This is your god, O Israel, that brought you out of Egypt.' "

9 Then the Lord said, "I have seen what a stubborn, rebellious lot these people are.

10 Now let Me alone and My anger shall blaze out against them and destroy them all; and I will make you, Moses, into a great nation instead of them."

11 But Moses begged God not to do it. "Lord," he pleaded, "why is Your anger so hot against Your own people whom You brought from the land of Egypt

with such great power and mighty miracles?

12 Do You want the Egyptians to say, 'God tricked them into coming to the mountains so that He could slay them, destroying them from off the face of the earth'? Turn back from Your fierce wrath. Turn away from this terrible evil You are planning against Your people!

13 Remember Your promise to Your servants—to Abraham, Isaac, and Israel. For You swore by Your own self, 'I will multiply your posterity as the stars of heaven, and I will give them all of this land I have promised to your descendants, and they shall inherit it forever.' "

14 So the Lord changed His mind and spared them.

15 Then Moses went down the mountain, holding in his hands the Ten Commandments written on both sides of two stone tablets.

16 (God Himself had written the commandments on the tablets.)

17 When Joshua heard the noise below them, of all the people shouting, he exclaimed to Moses, "It sounds as if they are preparing for war!"

18 But Moses replied, "No, it's not a cry of victory or defeat, but singing."

19 When they came near the camp, Moses saw the calf and the dancing, and in terrible anger he threw the tablets to the ground and they lay broken at the foot of the mountain.

20 He took the calf and melted it in the fire, and when the metal cooled, he ground it into powder and spread it upon the water and made the people drink it.

21 Then he turned to Aaron. "What in the world did the people do to you," he demanded, "to make you bring such a terrible sin upon them?"

22 "Don't get so upset," Aaron replied. "You know these people and what a wicked bunch they are.

23 They said to me, 'Make us a god to lead us, for something has happened to this fellow Moses who led us out of Egypt.'

24 Well, I told them, 'Bring me your gold earrings.' So they brought them to me and I threw them into the fire, and . . . well . . . this calf came out!"

25 When Moses saw that the people had been committing adultery—at Aaron's encouragement, and much to the amusement of their enemies—

26 He stood at the camp entrance and shouted, "All of you who are on the Lord's side, come over here and join me." And all the Levites came.

27 He told them, "Jehovah the God of Israel says, 'Get your swords and go back and forth from one end of the camp to the other and kill even your brothers, friends, and neighbors.'"

28 So they did, and about three thousand men died that day.

29 Then Moses told the Levites, "Today you have ordained yourselves for the service of the Lord, for you obeyed Him even though it meant killing your own sons and brothers; now He will give you a great blessing."

30 The next day Moses said to the people, "You have sinned a great sin, but I will return to the Lord on the mountain—perhaps I will be able to obtain His forgiveness for you."

31 So Moses returned to the Lord and said, "Oh, these people have sinned a great sin, and have made themselves gods of gold.

32 Yet now if You will only forgive their sin—;

and if not, then blot *me* out of the book You have written."[1]

33 And the Lord replied to Moses, "Whoever has sinned against Me will be blotted out of My book.

34 And now go, lead the people to the place I told you about, and I assure you that My Angel shall travel on ahead of you; however, when I come to visit these people, I will punish them for their sins."

35 And the Lord sent a great plague upon the people because they had worshiped Aaron's calf.

CHAPTER 33

The Lord said to Moses, "Lead these people you brought from Egypt to the land I promised Abraham, Isaac, and Jacob; for I said, 'I will give this land to your descendants.'

2 I will send an Angel before you to drive out the Canaanites, Amorites, Hittites, Perizzites, Hivites, and Jebusites.

3 It is a land 'flowing with milk and honey'; but I will not travel among you, for you are a stubborn, unruly people, and I would be tempted to destroy you along the way."

4 When the people heard these stern words, they went into mourning and stripped themselves of their jewelry and ornaments.

5 For the Lord had told Moses to tell them, "You are an unruly, stubborn people. If I were there among you for even a moment, I would exterminate you. Remove your jewelry and ornaments until I decide what to do with you."

6 So, after that, they wore no jewelry.

---

[1]Or, "then kill me instead of them."

7   Moses always erected the sacred tent (the "Tent for Meeting with God," he called it) far outside the camp, and everyone who wanted to consult with Jehovah went out there.

8   Whenever Moses went to the Tabernacle, all the people would rise and stand in their tent doors watching until he reached its entrance.

9   As he entered, the pillar of cloud would come down and stand at the door while the Lord spoke with Moses.

10   Then all the people worshiped from their tent doors, bowing low to the pillar of cloud.

11   Inside the tent the Lord spoke to Moses face to face, as a man speaks to his friend. Afterwards Moses would return to the camp, but the young man who assisted him, Joshua (son of Nun), stayed behind in the Tabernacle.

12   Moses talked there with the Lord and said to Him, "You have been telling me, 'Take these people to the Promised Land,' but You haven't told me whom You will send with me. You say You are my friend,[1] and that I have found favor before You;

13   Please, if this is really so, guide me clearly along the way You want me to travel[2] so that I will understand You and walk acceptably before You. For don't forget that this nation is Your people."

14   And the Lord replied, "I Myself will go with you and give you success."

15   For Moses had said, "If You aren't going with us, don't let us move a step from this place.

16   If You don't go with us, who will ever know

---

[1] Literally, "You have said You know me by name."
[2] Or, "show me Your ways," or, "show me Your majesty."

that I and my people have found favor with You, and that we are different from any other people upon the face of the earth?"

17   And the Lord had replied to Moses, "Yes, I will do what you have asked, for you have certainly found favor with Me, and you are my friend."[3]

18   Then Moses asked to see God's glory.

19   The Lord replied, "I will make My goodness pass before you, and I will announce to you the meaning of My name[4] Jehovah, the Lord. I show kindness and mercy to anyone I want to.

20   But you may not see the glory of My face, for man may not see Me and live.

21   However, stand here on this rock beside Me.

22   And when My glory goes by, I will put you in the cleft of the rock and cover you with My hand until I have passed.

23   Then I will remove My hand and you shall see My back, but not My face."

CHAPTER 34

The Lord told Moses, "Prepare two stone tablets like the first ones and I will write upon them the same commands that were on the tablets you broke.

2   Be ready in the morning to come up into Mount Sinai and present yourself to Me on the top of the mountain.

3   No one shall come with you and no one must be anywhere on the mountain. Do not let the flocks or herds feed close to the mountain."

4   So Moses took two tablets of stone like the first

---

[3]Literally, "I know you by name."
[4]Literally, "I will proclaim before you My name." His name, Jehovah, means "I will be what I will be." See Exodus 3:14.

ones, and was up early and climbed Mount Sinai, as the Lord had told him to, taking the two stone tablets in his hands.

5, 6   Then the Lord descended in the form of a pillar of cloud and stood there with him, and passed in front of him and announced the meaning of His name.[1] "I am Jehovah, the merciful and gracious God," He said, "slow to anger and rich in steadfast love and truth.

7   I, Jehovah, show this steadfast love to many thousands by forgiving their sins;[2] or else[3] I refuse to clear the guilty, and require that a father's sins be punished in the sons and grandsons, and even later generations."

8   Moses fell down before the Lord and worshiped.

9   And he said, "If it is true that I have found favor in Your sight, O Lord, then please go with us to the Promised Land; yes, it is an unruly, stubborn people, but pardon our iniquity and our sins, and accept us as Your own."

10   The Lord replied, "All right, this is the contract I am going to make with you. I will do miracles such as have never been done before anywhere in all the earth, and all the people of Israel shall see the power of the Lord—the terrible power I will display through you.

11   Your part of the agreement is to obey all of My commandments; then I will drive out from before you the Amorites, Canaanites, Hittites, Perizzites, Hivites, and Jebusites.

12   Be very, very careful never to compromise with

---

[1] Literally, "proclaimed the name of Jehovah."
[2] Literally, "forgiving iniquity and transgression and sin."
[3] Implied.

the people there in the land where you are going, for if you do, you will soon be following their evil ways.

13   Instead, you must break down their heathen altars, smash the obelisks they worship, and cut down their shameful idols.[4]

14   For you must worship no other gods, but only Jehovah, for He is a God who claims absolute loyalty and exclusive devotion.

15   No, do not make a peace treaty of any kind with the people living in the land, for they are spiritual prostitutes, committing adultery against Me[5] by sacrificing to their gods. If you become friendly with them and one of them invites you to go with him and worship his idol, you are apt to do it.

16   And you would accept their daughters, who worship other gods, as wives for your sons—and then your sons would commit adultery against Me by worshiping their wives' gods.

17   You must have nothing to do with idols.

18   Be sure to celebrate the Feast of Unleavened Bread for seven days, just as I instructed you, at the dates appointed each year in March; that was the month you left Egypt.

19   Every firstborn male[6] is Mine—cattle, sheep, and goats.

20   The firstborn colt of a donkey may be redeemed by giving a lamb in its place. If you decide not to redeem it, then its neck must be broken. But your sons must all be redeemed. And no one shall appear before Me without a gift.

---

[4]Literally, "Asherim." These were carved statues of male and female genital organs.
[5]Literally, "they play the harlot worshiping their gods."
[6]Literally, "all that opens the womb."

21   Even during plowing and harvest times, work only six days, and rest on the seventh.

22   And you must remember to celebrate these three annual religious festivals: the Festival of Weeks, the Festival of the First Wheat, and the Harvest Festival.

23   On each of these three occasions all the men and boys of Israel shall appear before the Lord.

24   No one will attack and conquer your land when you go up to appear before the Lord your God those three times each year. For I will drive out the nations from before you and enlarge your boundaries.

25   You must not use leavened bread with your sacrifices to Me, and none of the meat of the Passover lamb may be kept over until the following morning.

26   And you must bring the best of the first of each year's crop to the Tabernacle of the Lord your God. You must not cook a young goat in its mother's milk."

27   And the Lord said to Moses, "Write down these[7] laws that I have given you, for they represent the terms of My covenant with you and with Israel."

28   Moses was up on the mountain with the Lord for forty days and forty nights, and in all that time he neither ate nor drank. At that time God[8] wrote out the Covenant—the Ten Commandments—on the stone tablets.

29   Moses didn't realize as he came back down the mountain with the tablets that his face glowed from being in the presence of God.

30   Because of this radiance upon his face, Aaron and the people of Israel were afraid to come near him.

---

[7]That is, the preceding laws in verses 12-26.
[8]Implied. See Exodus 34:1, Deuteronomy 10:1-4.

31   But Moses called them over to him, and Aaron and the leaders of the congregation came and talked with him.

32   Afterwards, all the people came to him, and he gave them the commandments the Lord had given him upon the mountain.

33   When Moses had finished speaking with them, he put a veil over his face;[9]

34   But whenever he went into the Tabernacle to speak with the Lord, he removed the veil until he came out again; then he would pass on to the people whatever instructions God had give him,

35   And the people would see his face aglow. Afterwards he would put the veil on again until he returned to speak with God.

CHAPTER 35

Now Moses called a meeting of all the people and told them, "These are the laws of Jehovah you must obey.

2   Work six days only; the seventh day is a day of solemn rest, a holy day to be used to worship Jehovah; anyone working on that day must die.

3   Don't even light the fires in your homes that day."

4   Then Moses said to all the people, "This is what the Lord has commanded:

5   All of you who wish to, all those with generous hearts, may bring these offerings to Jehovah:

        Gold, silver, and bronze;

6   Blue, purple, and scarlet cloth, made of

---

[9]So that the people would not see the glory fade. See II Corinthians 3:13.

fine-twined linen or of goat's hair;

7   Tanned rams' skins and specially treated goatskins;

Acacia wood;

8   Olive oil for the lamps;

Spices for the anointing oil and for the incense;

9   Onyx stones and stones to be used for the ephod and chestpiece.

10   Come, all of you who are skilled craftsmen having special talents, and construct what God has commanded us:

11   The Tabernacle tent, and its coverings, clasps, frames, bars, pillars, and bases;

12   The Ark and its poles;

The place of mercy;

The veil to enclose the Holy Place;

13   The table, its carrying poles, and all of its utensils;

The Bread of the Presence;

14   Lamp holders, with lamps and oil;

15   The incense altar and its carrying poles;

The anointing oil and sweet incense;

The curtain for the door of the Tabernacle;

16   The altar for the burnt offerings;

The bronze grating of the altar, and its carrying poles and utensils;

The basin with its pedestal;

17   The drapes for the walls of the court;

The pillars and their bases;

Drapes for the entrance to the court;

18   The posts of the Tabernacle court, and their cords;

19   The beautiful clothing for the priests, to

be used when ministering in the Holy Place;

The holy garments for Aaron the priest, and for his sons.

20 So all the people went to their tents to prepare their gifts.

21 Those whose hearts were stirred by God's Spirit returned with their offerings of materials for the Tabernacle, its equipment, and for the holy garments.

22 Both men and women came, all who were willing-hearted. They brought to the Lord their offerings of gold, jewelry—earrings, rings from their fingers, necklaces—and gold objects of every kind.

23 Others brought blue, purple, and scarlet cloth made from fine-twined linen or goats' hair; and ram skins dyed red, and specially treated goatskins.

24 Others brought silver and bronze as their offering to the Lord; and some brought the acacia wood needed in the construction.

25 The women skilled in sewing and spinning prepared blue, purple, and scarlet thread and cloth, and fine-twined linen, and brought them in.

26 Some other women gladly used their special skill to spin the goats' hair into cloth.

27 The leaders brought onyx stones to be used for the ephod and the chestpiece;

28 And spices, and oil—for the light, and for compounding the anointing oil and the sweet incense.

29 So the people of Israel—every man and woman who wanted to assist in the work given to them by the Lord's command to Moses—brought their freewill offerings to Him.

30, 31 And Moses told them, "Jehovah has specifically appointed Bezalel (the son of Uri and grandson of Hur of the tribe of Judah) as general superintendent of the project.

32 He will be able to create beautiful workmanship from gold, silver, and bronze;

33 He can cut and set stones like a jeweler, and can do beautiful carving; in fact, he has every needed skill.

34 And God has made him and Oholiab gifted teachers of their skills to others. (Oholiab is the son of Ahisamach, of the tribe of Dan.)

35 God has filled them both with unusual skills as jewelers, carpenters, embroidery designers in blue, purple, and scarlet on linen backgrounds, and as weavers —they excel in all the crafts we will be needing in the work.

CHAPTER 36

All the other craftsmen with God-given abilities are to assist Bezalel and Oholiab in constructing and furnishing the Tabernacle." So Moses told Bezalel and Oholiab and all others who felt called to the work to begin.

3 Moses gave them the materials donated by the people and additional gifts were received each morning.

4, 5, 6, 7 But finally the workmen all left their task to meet with Moses and told him, "We have more than enough materials on hand now to complete the job!" So Moses sent a message throughout the camp announcing that no more donations were needed. Then at last the people were restrained from bringing more!

8, 9 The skilled weavers first made ten sheets from finely-twined blue, purple, and scarlet linen, with cherubim skillfully embroidered upon them.

10   Five of these sheets were attached end to end, then five others similarly attached, forming two long roof-sheets.

11, 12   Fifty blue ribbons were looped along the edges of these two long sheets, each loop being opposite its mate on the other long sheet.

13   Then fifty clasps of gold were made to connect the loops, thus tying the two long sheets together to form the ceiling of the Tabernacle.

14, 15   Above the ceiling was a second layer formed by eleven draperies made of goats' hair (uniformly forty-five feet long and six feet wide).

16   Bezalel coupled five of these draperies together to make one long piece, and six others to make another long piece.

17   Then he made fifty loops along the end of each,

18   And fifty small bronze clasps to couple the loops so that the draperies were firmly attached to each other.

19   The top layer of the roof was made of rams' skins, dyed red, and tanned goat skins.

20   For the sides of the Tabernacle he used frames of acacia wood standing on end.

21   The height of each frame was fifteen feet and the width 2¼ feet.

22   Each frame had two clasps joining it to the next.

23   There were twenty frames on the south side,

24   With the bottoms fitting into forty silver bases. Each frame was connected to its base by two clasps.

25, 26   There were also twenty frames on the north

side of the Tabernacle, with forty silver bases, two for each frame.

27   The west side of the Tabernacle, which was its rear, was made from six frames,

28   Plus another at each corner.

29   These frames, including those at the corners, were linked to each other at both top and bottom by rings.

30   So, on the west side, there were a total of eight frames with sixteen silver bases beneath them, two for each frame.

31, 32   Then he made five sets of bars from acacia wood to tie the frames together along the sides, five for each side of the Tabernacle.

33   The middle bar of the five was halfway up the frames, along each side, running from one end to the other.

34   The frames and bars were all overlaid with gold, and the rings were pure gold.

35   The blue, purple, and scarlet inner[1] veil was made from woven linen, with cherubim skillfully embroidered into it.

36   The veil was then attached to four gold hooks set into four posts of acacia wood, overlaid with gold and set into four silver bases.

37   Then he made a drapery for the entrance to the Tabernacle; it was woven from fine-twined linen, embroidered with blue, purple, and scarlet.

38   This drapery was connected by five hooks to five posts. The posts and their capitals and rods were overlaid with gold; their five bases were molded from bronze.

---

[1]Implied.

CHAPTER 37

Next Bezalel made the Ark. This was constructed of acacia wood and was 3¾ feet long, 2¼ feet wide, and 2¼ feet high.

2 It was plated with pure gold inside and out, and had a molding of gold all the way around the sides.

3 There were four golden rings fastened into its four feet, two rings at each end.

4 Then he made poles from acacia wood, and overlaid them with gold,

5 And put the poles into the rings at the sides of the Ark, to carry it.

6 Then, from pure gold, he made a lid called "the place of mercy"; it was 3¾ feet long and 2¼ feet wide.

7 He made two cherubim of beaten gold and placed them at the two ends of the golden lid.

8 They were molded so that they were actually a part of the golden lid—it was all one piece.

9 The cherubim faced each other, with outstretched wings that overshadowed the place of mercy, looking down upon it.

10 Then he made a table, using acacia wood, three feet long, 1½ feet wide and 2¼ feet high.

11 It was overlaid with pure gold, with a golden molding all around the edge.

12 A rim four inches high was constructed around the edges of the table, with a gold molding along the rim.

13 Then he cast four rings of gold and placed them into the four table legs,

14 Close to the molding, to hold the carrying poles in place.

15, 16 Next, using pure gold, he made the bowls, flagons, dishes, and spoons to be placed upon this table.

17 Then he made the lampstand, again using pure, beaten gold. Its base, shaft, lamp-holders, and decorations of almond flowers were all of one piece.

18 The lampstand had six branches, three from each side.

19 Each of the branches was decorated with identical carvings of blossoms.

20, 21 The main stem of the lampstand was similarly decorated with almond blossoms, a flower on the stem beneath each pair of branches; also a flower below the bottom pair and above the top pair, four in all.

22 The decorations and branches were all one piece of pure, beaten gold.

23, 24 Then he made the seven lamps at the ends of the branches, the snuffers, and the ashtrays, all of pure gold. The entire lampstand weighed 107 pounds, all pure gold.

25 The incense altar was made of acacia wood. It was eighteen inches square and three feet high, with its corner-horns made as part of the altar so that it was all one piece.

26 He overlaid it all with pure gold and ran a gold molding around the edge.

27 Two gold rings were placed on each side, beneath this molding, to hold the carrying poles.

28 The carrying poles were gold-plated acacia wood.

29　Then, from sweet spices, he made the sacred oil for anointing the priests, and the pure incense, using the techniques of the most skilled perfumers.

CHAPTER 38

The burnt-offering altar was also constructed of acacia wood; it was 7½ feet square at the top, and 4½ feet high.

2　There were four horns at the four corners, all of one piece with the rest. This altar was overlaid with bronze.

3　Then he made bronze utensils to be used with the altar—the pots, shovels, basins, meat hooks, and fire pans.

4　Next he made a bronze grating that rested upon a ledge about halfway up [in the fire box[1]].

5　Four rings were cast for each side of the grating, to insert the carrying poles.

6　The carrying poles themselves were made of acacia wood, overlaid with bronze.

7　The carrying poles were inserted into the rings at the side of the altar. The altar was hollow, with plank siding.

8　The bronze washbasin and its bronze pedestal were cast from the solid bronze mirrors donated by the women who assembled at the entrance to the Tabernacle.

9　Then he constructed the courtyard. The south wall was 150 feet long; it consisted of drapes woven from fine-twined linen thread.

10　There were twenty posts to hold drapes, with bases of bronze and with silver hooks and rods.

---

[1]Implied.

11　The north wall was also 150 feet long, with twenty bronze posts and bases and with silver hooks and rods.

12　The west side was seventy-five feet wide; the walls were made from drapes supported by ten posts and bases, and with silver hooks and rods.

13　The east side was also seventy-five feet wide.

14, 15　The drapes at either side of the entrance were 22½ feet wide, each with three posts and three bases.

16　All the drapes making up the walls of the court were woven of fine-twined linen.

17　Each post had a bronze base, and all the hooks and rods were silver; the tops of the posts were overlaid with silver, and the rods to hold up the drapes were solid silver.

18　The drapery covering the entrance to the court was made of fine-twined linen, beautifully embroidered with blue, purple, and scarlet thread. It was thirty feet long and 7½ feet wide, just the same as the drapes composing the walls of the court.

19　It was supported by four posts, with four bronze bases, and with silver hooks and rods; the tops of the posts were also silver.

20　All the nails used in constructing the Tabernacle and court were bronze.

21　This summarizes the various steps in building the Tabernacle to house the Ark, so that the Levites could carry on their ministry. All was done in the order designated by Moses and was supervised by Ithamar, son of Aaron the priest.

22　Bezalel (son of Uri and grandson of Hur, of the tribe of Judah) was the master craftsman,

23   Assisted by Oholiab (son of Ahisamach of the tribe of Dan); he too was a skilled craftsman and also an expert at engraving, weaving, and at embroidering blue, purple, and scarlet threads into fine linen cloth.

24   The people brought gifts of 3,140 pounds of gold, all of which was used throughout the Tabernacle.

25, 26   The amount of silver used was 9,575 pounds, which came from the fifty-cent head tax collected from all those registered in the census who were twenty years old or older, a total of 603,550 men.

27   The bases for the frames of the sanctuary walls and for the posts supporting the veil required 9,500 pounds of silver, ninety-five pounds[2] for each socket.

28   The silver left over was used for the posts and to overlay their tops, and for the rods and hooks.

29   The people brought 7,540 pounds of bronze, which was used for casting the bases for the posts at the entrance to the Tabernacle, and for the bronze altar, the bronze grating, the altar utensils, the bases for the posts supporting the drapes enclosing the court, and for all the nails used in the construction of the Tabernacle and the court.

CHAPTER 39

Then, for the priests, the people made beautiful garments of blue, purple, and scarlet cloth—garments to be used while ministering in the Holy Place. This same cloth was used for Aaron's sacred garments, in accordance with the Lord's instructions to Moses.

2   The ephod was made from this cloth too, woven from fine-twined linen thread.

3   Bezalel beat gold into thin plates and cut it into

---

[2]Literally, "a [silver] talent." The exact weight cannot be ascertained.

wire threads, to work into the blue, purple, and scarlet linen; it was a skillful and beautiful piece of workmanship when finished.

4, 5   The ephod was held together by shoulder straps at the top, and was tied down by an elaborate one-piece woven sash made of the same gold, blue, purple, and scarlet cloth cut from fine-twined linen thread, just as God had directed Moses.

6, 7   The [two[1]] onyx stones, attached to the [two[1]] shoulder straps of the ephod, were set in gold, and the stones were engraved with the names of the tribes of Israel, just as initials are engraved upon a ring. These stones were reminders to Jehovah concerning the people of Israel;[2] all this was done in accordance with the Lord's instructions to Moses.

8   The chestpiece was a beautiful piece of work, just like the ephod, made from the finest gold, blue, purple, and scarlet linen.

9   It was a piece nine inches square, doubled over to form a pouch;

10   There were four rows of stones across it. In the first row were a sardius, a topaz, and a carbuncle;

11   In the second row were an emerald, a sapphire, and a diamond.

12   In the third row were a jacinth, an agate, and an amethyst.

13   In the fourth row, a beryl, an onyx, and a jasper —all set in gold filigree.

14   The stones were engraved like a seal, with the names of the twelve tribes of Israel.

15, 16, 17, 18   [To attach the chestpiece to the

---

[1]Implied.
[2]Literally, "to be stones of memorial for the children of Israel."

ephod[3]], a gold ring was placed at the top of each shoulder strap of the ephod, and from these gold rings, two strands of twined gold attached to gold clasps on the top corners of the chestpiece.

19　Two gold rings were also set at the lower edge of the chestpiece, on the under side, next to the ephod.

20　Two other gold rings were placed low on the shoulder straps of the ephod, close to where the ephod joined its beautifully woven sash.

21　The chestpiece was held securely above the beautifully woven sash of the ephod by tying the rings of the chestpiece to the rings of the ephod, with a blue ribbon.

All this was commanded to Moses by the Lord.

22　The main part of the ephod was woven, all of blue,

23　And there was a hole at the center just as in a coat of mail, for the head to go through, reinforced around the edge so that it would not tear.

24　Pomegranates were attached to the bottom edge of the robe; these were made of linen cloth, embroidered[4] with blue, purple, and scarlet.

25, 26　Bells of pure gold were placed between the pomegranates along the bottom edge of the skirt, with bells and pomegranates alternating all around the edge. This robe was worn when Aaron ministered to the Lord, just as the Lord had commanded Moses.

27　Robes were now made for Aaron and his sons from fine-twined linen thread.

28, 29　The chestpiece, the beautiful turbans, and the caps and the underclothes were all made of this linen, and the linen belt was beautifully embroidered

[3]Implied.
[4]Implied.

with blue, purple, and scarlet threads, just as Jehovah had commanded Moses.

30 Finally they made the holy plate of pure gold to wear on the front of the turban, engraved with the words, "Consecrated to Jehovah."

31 It was tied to the turban with a blue cord, just as the Lord had instructed.

32 And so at last the Tabernacle was finished, following all of the Lord's instructions to Moses.

33 Then they brought the entire Tabernacle to Moses:

Furniture;

Clasps;

Frames;

Bars;

Posts;

Bases;

34 Layers of covering for the roof and sides— the rams' skins dyed red, the specially tanned goat skins, and the entrance drape;

35 The Ark with the Ten Commandments in it;

The carrying poles;

The place of mercy;

36 The table and all its utensils;

The Bread of the Presence;

37 The pure [gold[5]] lampstand with its lamps, utensils, and oil;

38 The golden altar;

The anointing oil;

The sweet incense;

The curtain-door of the Tabernacle;

39 The bronze altar;

[5]Implied.

The bronze grating;

The poles and the utensils;

The washbasin and its base;

40   The drapes for the walls of the court and the posts holding them up;

The bases and the drapes at the gate of the court;

The cords and nails;

All the utensils used there in the work of the Tabernacle.

41   They also brought for his inspection the beautifully tailored garments to be worn while ministering in the Holy Place, and the holy garments for Aaron the priest and those for his sons, to be worn when on duty.

42   So the people of Israel followed all the Lord's instructions to Moses.

43   And Moses inspected all their work and blessed them because it was all as the Lord had instructed him.

CHAPTER 40

The Lord now said to Moses,

2   "Put together the Tabernacle on the first day of the first month.

3   In it, place the Ark containing the Ten Commandments; and install the veil to enclose the Ark within the Holy of Holies.

4   Then bring in the table and place the utensils on it, and bring in the lampstand and light the lamps.

5   Place the golden altar for the incense in front of the Ark. Set up the drapes at the entrance of the Tabernacle,

6   And place the altar for burnt offerings in front of the entrance.

7 Set the washbasin between the Tabernacle-tent and the altar, and fill it with water.

8 Then make the courtyard around the outside of the tent, and hang the curtain-door at the entrance to the courtyard.

9 Take the anointing oil and sprinkle it here and there upon the Tabernacle and everything in it, upon all of its utensils and parts, and all the furniture, to hallow it; and it shall become holy.

10 Sprinkle the anointing oil upon the altar of burnt offering and its utensils, sanctifying it; for the altar shall then become most holy.

11 Then anoint the washbasin and its pedestal, sanctifying it.

12 Now bring Aaron and his sons to the entrance of the Tabernacle and wash them with water;

13 And clothe Aaron with the holy garments and anoint him, sanctifying him to minister to Me as a priest.

14 Then bring his sons and put their robes upon them,

15 And anoint them as you did their father, that they may minister to Me as priests; their anointing shall be permanent from generation to generation: all their children and children's children shall forever be My priests."

16 So Moses proceeded to do all as the Lord had commanded him.

17 On the first day of the first month, in the second year, the Tabernacle was put together.

18 Moses erected it by setting its frames into their bases and attaching the bars.

19 Then he spread the coverings over the frame-

work, and put on the top layers, just as the Lord had commanded him.

20 Inside the Ark he placed the stones with the Ten Commandments engraved on them, and attached the carrying poles to the Ark and installed the golden lid, the place of mercy.

21 Then he brought the Ark into the Tabernacle and set up the veil to screen it, just as the Lord had commanded.

22 Next he placed the table at the north side of the room outside the veil,

23 And set the Bread of the Presence upon the table before the Lord, just as the Lord had commanded.

24 And he placed the lampstand next to the table, on the south side of the Tabernacle.

25 Then he lighted the lamps before the Lord, following all the instructions,

26 And placed the golden altar in the Tabernacle next to the veil,

27 And burned upon it the incense made from sweet spices, just as the Lord had commanded.

28 He attached the curtain at the entrance of the Tabernacle,

29 And placed the outside altar for the burnt offerings near the entrance, and offered upon it a burnt offering and a meal offering, just as the Lord had commanded him.

30 Next he placed the washbasin between the tent and the altar, and filled it with water so that the priests could use it for washing.

31 Moses and Aaron and Aaron's sons washed their hands and feet there.

32 Whenever they walked past the altar to enter

the Tabernacle, they stopped and washed, just as the Lord had commanded Moses.

33 Then he erected the enclosure surrounding the tent and the altar, and set up the curtain-door at the entrance of the enclosure. So at last Moses finished the work.

34 Then the cloud covered the Tabernacle and the glory of the Lord filled it.

35 Moses was not able to enter because the cloud was standing there, and the glory of the Lord filled the Tabernacle.

36 Whenever the cloud lifted and moved, the people of Israel journeyed onward, following it.

37 But if the cloud stayed, they stayed until it moved.

38 The cloud rested upon the Tabernacle during the daytime, and at night there was fire in the cloud so that all the people of Israel could see it.

This continued throughout all their journeys.

Leviticus

CHAPTER 1

The Lord now spoke to Moses from the Tabernacle, 2, 3 And commanded him to give the following instructions to the people of Israel: "When you sacrifice to the Lord, use animals from your herds and flocks. If your sacrifice is to be an ox given as a burnt offering, use only a bull with no physical defects. Bring the animal to the entrance of the Tabernacle where the priests will accept your gift for the Lord.

4 The person bringing it is to lay his hand upon its head, and it then becomes his substitute: the death of the animal will be accepted by God instead of the death of the man who brings it, as the penalty for his sins.[1]

5 The man shall then kill the animal there before the Lord, and Aaron's sons, the priests, will present the blood before the Lord, sprinkling it upon all sides of the altar at the entrance of the Tabernacle.

6, 7 Then the priests will skin the animal[2] and quarter it, and build a wood fire upon the altar,

8 And put the sections of the animal and its head and fat upon the wood.

9 The internal organs and the legs are to be washed, then the priests will burn them upon the

---

[1]Literally, "to make atonement for him."
[2]Literally, "he . . . shall skin . . ."

altar, and they will be an acceptable burnt offering with which the Lord is pleased.[3]

10   If the animal used as a burnt offering is a sheep or a goat, it too must be a male, and without any blemishes.

11   The man who brings it will kill it before the Lord on the north side of the altar, and Aaron's sons, the priests, will sprinkle its blood back and forth upon the altar.

12   Then the man will quarter it, and the priests will lay the pieces, with the head and the fat, on top of the wood on the altar.

13   But the internal organs and the legs shall first be washed with water. Then the priests shall burn it all upon the altar as an offering to the Lord; for burnt offerings give much pleasure to the Lord.

14   If anyone wishes to use a bird as his burnt offering, he may choose either turtle doves or young pigeons.

15, 16, 17   A priest will take the bird to the altar and wring off its head, and the blood shall be drained out at the side of the altar. Then the priest will remove the crop and the feathers and throw them on the east side of the altar with the ashes. Then, grasping it by the wings, he shall tear it apart, but not completely. And the priest shall burn it upon the altar, and the Lord will have pleasure in this sacrifice.[3]

CHAPTER 2

Anyone who wishes to sacrifice a grain offering to the Lord is to bring fine flour and is to pour olive oil and incense upon it.

---

[3]Literally, "it will be a sweet savor unto the Lord."

2   Then he is to take a handful, representing the entire amount,[1] to one of the priests to burn, and the Lord will be fully pleased.

3   The remainder of the flour is to be given to Aaron and his sons as their food; but all of it is counted as a holy burnt offering to the Lord.

4   If bread baked in the oven is brought as an offering to the Lord, it must be made from finely-ground flour, baked with olive oil but without yeast. Wafers made without yeast and spread with olive oil may also be used as an offering.

5   If the offering is something from the griddle, it shall be made of finely ground flour without yeast, and mingled with olive oil.

6   Break it into pieces and pour oil upon it—it is a form of grain offering.

7   If your offering is cooked in a pan, it too shall be made of fine flour mixed with olive oil.

8   However it is prepared—whether baked, fried, or grilled—you are to bring this grain offering to the priest and he shall take it to the altar to present it to the Lord.

9   The priests are to burn only a representative portion[2] of the offering, but all of it will be fully appreciated by the Lord.

10   The remainder belongs to the priests for their own use, but it is all counted as a holy burnt offering to the Lord.

11   Use no yeast with your offerings of flour; for no yeast or honey is permitted in burnt offerings to the Lord.

---

[1]Literally, "shall burn the memorial portion thereof upon the altar, an offering made by fire."
[2]Literally, "the memorial."

12　You may offer yeast bread and honey as thanksgiving offerings at harvest time, but not as burnt offerings.[3]

13　Every offering must be seasoned with salt,[4] because the salt is a reminder of God's covenant.

14　If you are offering from the first of your harvest, remove the kernels from a fresh ear, crush and roast them, then offer them to the Lord.

15　Put olive oil and incense on the offering, for it is a grain offering.

16　Then the priests shall burn part of the bruised grain mixed with oil and all of the incense as a representative portion before the Lord.

CHAPTER 3

When anyone wants to give an offering of thanksgiving to the Lord, he may use either a bull or a cow, but the animal must be entirely without defect if it is to be offered to the Lord!

2　The man who brings the animal shall lay his hand upon its head and kill it at the door of the Tabernacle. Then Aaron's sons shall throw the blood against the sides of the altar,

3, 4, 5　And shall burn before the Lord the fat that covers the inward parts, the two kidneys and the loin-fat on them, and the gall bladder. And it will give the Lord much pleasure.

6　If a goat or sheep is used as a thank-offering to the Lord, it must have no defect and may be either

---

[3]Literally, "but not for a sweet savor on the altar."
[4]In many of the languages of the ancient Near East, the word "salt" is a homonym of the word "good." It was used symbolically for "goodness" in making covenants.

a male or female—ram or ewe, billy goat or nanny goat.

7, 8 If it is a lamb, the man who brings it shall lay his hand upon its head and kill it at the entrance of the Tabernacle; the priests shall throw the blood against the sides of the altar,

9, 10, 11 And shall offer upon the altar the fat, the tail removed close to the backbone, the fat covering the internal organs, the two kidneys with the loin-fat on them, and the gall bladder, as a burnt offering to the Lord.

12 If anyone brings a goat as his offering to the Lord,

13 He shall lay his hand upon its head and kill it at the entrance of the Tabernacle. The priest shall throw its blood against the sides of the altar,

14 And shall offer upon the altar, as a burnt offering to the Lord, the fat which covers the insides,

15, 16 The two kidneys and the loin-fat on them, and the gall bladder. This burnt offering is very pleasing to the Lord. All the fat is Jehovah's.

17 This is a permanent law throughout your land, that you shall eat neither fat nor blood."

CHAPTER 4

Then the Lord gave these further instructions to Moses:

2 "Tell the people of Israel that these are the laws concerning anyone who unintentionally breaks any of My commandments.

3 If a priest sins unintentionally, and so brings guilt upon the people, he must offer a young bull with-

out defect as a sin offering to the Lord.

4 He shall bring it to the door of the Tabernacle, and shall lay his hand upon its head and kill it there before Jehovah.

5 Then the priest shall take the animal's blood into the Tabernacle,

6 And shall dip his finger in the blood and sprinkle it seven times before the Lord in front of the veil that bars the way to the Holy of Holies.

7 Then the priest shall put some of the blood upon the horns of the incense altar before the Lord in the Tabernacle; the remainder of the blood shall be poured out at the base of the altar for burnt offerings, at the entrance to the Tabernacle.

8 Then he shall take all the fat on the entrails,

9 The two kidneys and the loin-fat on them, and the gall bladder,

10 And shall burn them on the altar of burnt offering, just as in the case of a bull or cow sacrificed as a thank-offering.

11, 12 But the remainder of the young bull—the skin, meat, head, legs, internal organs, and intestines —shall be carried to a ceremonially clean place outside the camp—a place where the ashes are brought from the altar—and burned there on a wood fire.

13 If the entire nation of Israel sins without realizing it, and does something that Jehovah has said not to do, all the people are guilty.

14 When they realize it, they shall offer a young bull for a sin offering, bringing it to the Tabernacle

15 Where the leaders[1] of the nation shall lay their

---
[1]Literally, "elders."

hands upon the animal's head and kill it before the Lord.

16 Then the priest shall bring its blood into the Tabernacle,

17 And shall dip his finger in the blood and sprinkle it seven times before the Lord, in front of the veil.

18 Then he shall put blood upon the horns of the altar there in the Tabernacle before the Lord, and all the remainder of the blood shall be poured out at the base of the burnt offering altar, at the entrance to the Tabernacle.

19 All the fat shall be removed and burned upon the altar.

20 He shall follow the same procedure as for a sin offering; in this way the priest shall make atonement for the nation, and everyone will be forgiven.

21 The priest shall then cart the young bull outside the camp and burn it there, just as though it were a sin offering for an individual, only this time it is a sin offering for the entire nation.

22 If one of the leaders sins without realizing it and is guilty of disobeying one of God's laws,

23 As soon as it is called to his attention he must bring as his sacrifice a billy goat without any physical defect.

24 He shall lay his hand upon its head and kill it at the place where the burnt offerings are killed, and present it to the Lord. This is his sin offering.

25 Then the priest shall take some of the blood of this sin offering and place it with his finger upon the horns of the altar of burnt offerings, and the rest of the blood shall be poured out at the base of the altar.

26　All the fat shall be burned upon the altar, just as if it were the fat of the sacrifice of a thank-offering;[2] thus the priest shall make atonement for the leader concerning his sin, and he shall be forgiven.

27　If any one of the common people sins and doesn't realize it, he is guilty.

28　But as soon as he does realize it, he is to bring as his sacrifice a nanny goat without defect to atone for his sin.

29　He shall bring it to the place where the animals for burnt offerings are killed, and there lay his hand upon the head of the sin offering and kill it.

30　And the priest shall take some of the blood with his finger and smear it upon the horns of the burnt offering altar. Then the priest shall pour out the remainder of the blood at the base of the altar.

31　All the fat shall be taken off, just as in the procedure for the thank-offering[2] sacrifice, and the priest shall burn it upon the altar; and the Lord will appreciate it. Thus the priest shall make atonement for that man, and he shall be forgiven.

32　However, if he chooses to bring a lamb as his sin offering, it must be a female without physical defect.

33　He shall bring it to the place where the burnt offerings are killed, and lay his hand upon its head and kill it there as a sin offering.

34　The priest shall take some of the blood with his finger and smear it upon the horns of the burnt offering altar, and all the rest of the blood shall be poured out at the base of the altar.

35　The fat shall be used just as in the case of a

---

[2]Literally, "peace offering."

thank-offering[3] lamb—the priest shall burn the fat on the altar as in any other sacrifice made to Jehovah by fire; and the priest shall make atonement for the man, and his sin shall be forgiven.

CHAPTER 5

A nyone refusing to give testimony concerning what he knows about a crime is guilty.

2 Anyone touching anything ceremonially unclean—such as the dead body of an animal forbidden for food, wild or domesticated, or the dead body of some forbidden insect—is guilty, even though he wasn't aware of touching it.

3 Or if he touches human discharge of any kind, he becomes guilty as soon as he realizes that he has touched it.

4 If anyone makes a rash vow, whether the vow is good or bad, when he realizes what a foolish vow he has taken, he is guilty.

5 In any of these cases, he shall confess his sin

6 And bring his guilt offering to the Lord, a female lamb or goat, and the priest shall make atonement for him, and he shall be freed from his sin, and need not fulfill the vow.[1]

7 If he is too poor to bring a lamb to the Lord, then he shall bring two turtle doves or two young pigeons as his guilt offering; one of the birds shall be his sin offering and the other his burnt offering.

8 The priest shall offer as the sin sacrifice whichever bird is handed to him first, wringing its neck, but not severing its head from its body.

---

[3]Literally, "peace offering."
[1]Implied.

9 Then he shall sprinkle some of the blood at the side of the altar and the rest shall be drained out at the base of the altar; this is the sin offering.

10 He shall offer the second bird as a burnt offering, following the customary procedures that have been set forth; so the priest shall make atonement for him concerning his sin and he shall be forgiven.

11 If he is too poor to bring turtle doves or young pigeons as his sin offering, then he shall bring a tenth of a bushel of fine flour. He must not mix it with olive oil or put any incense on it, because it is a sin offering.

12 He shall bring it to the priest and the priest shall take out a handful as a representative portion, and burn it on the altar just as any other offering to Jehovah made by fire; this shall be his sin offering.

13 In this way the priest shall make atonement for him for any sin of this kind, and he shall be forgiven. The rest of the flour shall belong to the priest, just as was the case with the grain offering."

14 And the Lord said to Moses,

15 "If anyone sins by unintentionally defiling what is holy, then he shall bring a ram without defect, worth whatever fine[2] you charge against him, as his guilt offering to the Lord.

16 And he shall make restitution for the holy thing he has spoiled, or the tithe omitted,[3] by paying for the loss, plus a twenty percent penalty; he shall bring it to the priest, and the priest shall make atonement for him with the ram of the guilt offering, and he shall be forgiven.

17, 18 Anyone who disobeys some law of God

---

[2]Literally, "using the standard of the shekel of the sanctuary."
[3]Implied in remainder of the verse.

without realizing it is guilty anyway, and must bring his sacrifice of a value determined by Moses. This sacrifice shall be a ram without blemish taken to the priest as a guilt offering; with it the priest shall make atonement for him, so that he will be forgiven for whatever it is he has done without realizing it.

19   It must be offered as a guilt offering, for he is certainly guilty before the Lord."

CHAPTER 6

A nd the Lord said to Moses,

2   "If anyone sins against Me by refusing to return a deposit on something borrowed or rented, or by refusing to return something entrusted to him, or by robbery, or by oppressing his neighbor,

3   Or by finding a lost article and lying about it, swearing that he doesn't have it—

4, 5   On the day he is found guilty of any such sin, he shall restore what he took, adding a twenty percent fine, and give it to the one he has harmed; and on the same day he shall bring his guilt offering to the Tabernacle.

6   His guilt offering shall be a ram without defect, and must be worth whatever value you demand. He shall bring it to the priest,

7   And the priest shall make atonement for him before the Lord, and he shall be forgiven."

8   Then the Lord said to Moses,

9   *"Give Aaron and his sons these regulations con-cerning the burnt offering:*

The burnt offering shall be left upon the hearth of the altar all night, with the altar fire kept burning.

10   (The next morning) the priest shall put on his

linen undergarments and his linen outer garments and clean out the ashes of the burnt offering and put them beside the altar.

11 Then he shall change his clothes and carry the ashes outside the camp to a place that is ceremonially clean.

12 Meanwhile, the fire on the altar must be kept burning—it must not go out. The priest shall put on fresh wood each morning, and lay the daily burnt offering on it, and burn the fat of the daily peace offering.

13 The fire must be kept burning upon the altar continually. It must never go out.

14. *These are the regulations concerning the grain offering:* Aaron's sons shall stand in front of the altar to offer it before the Lord.

15 The priest shall then take out a handful of the finely ground flour with the olive oil and the incense mixed into it, and burn it upon the altar as a representative portion for the Lord; and it will be received with pleasure by the Lord.

16 After taking out this handful, the remainder of the flour will belong to Aaron and his sons for their food; it shall be eaten without yeast in the courtyard of the Tabernacle.

17 (Stress this instruction, that if it is baked it must be without yeast.) I have given to the priests this part of the burnt offerings made to Me. However, all of it is most holy, just as is the entire sin offering and the entire guilt offering.

18 It may be eaten by any male descendant of Aaron, any priest, generation after generation. But

only[1] the priests may eat these offerings made by fire to the Lord."

19, 20   And Jehovah said to Moses,

"On the day Aaron and his sons are anointed and inducted into the priesthood, they shall bring to the Lord a regular grain offering—a tenth of a bushel of fine flour, half to be offered in the morning and half in the evening.

21   It shall be cooked on a griddle, using olive oil, and should be well cooked, then brought to the Lord as an offering that pleases Him very much.

22, 23   As the sons of the priests replace their fathers, they shall be inducted into office by offering this same sacrifice on the day of their anointing. This is a perpetual law. These offerings shall be entirely burned up before the Lord; none of it shall be eaten."

24   Then the Lord said to Moses,

25   *Tell Aaron and his sons that these are the instructions concerning the sin offering:*

This sacrifice is most holy, and shall be killed before the Lord at the place where the burnt offerings are killed.

26   The priest who performs the ceremony shall eat it in the courtyard of the Tabernacle.

27   Only those who are sanctified—the priests— may touch this meat; if any blood sprinkles onto their clothing, it must be washed in a holy place.

28   Then the clay pot in which the clothing is boiled shall be broken; or if a bronze kettle is used, it must be scoured and rinsed out thoroughly.

29   Every male among the priests may eat this

---

[1]Literally, "(only) whoever is holy may touch them," or "whoever touches them shall become holy."

offering, but only they, for it is most holy.

30 No sin offering may be eaten by the priests if any of its blood is taken into the Tabernacle, to make atonement in the Holy Place. That carcass must be entirely burned with fire before the Lord.

CHAPTER 7

H*ere are the instructions concerning the most holy offering for guilt:*

2 The sacrificial animal shall be killed at the place where the burnt offering sacrifices are slain, and its blood shall be sprinkled back and forth upon the altar.

3 The priest will offer upon the altar all its fat, including the tail, the fat that covers the insides,

4 The two kidneys and the loin-fat, and the gall bladder—all shall be set aside for sacrificing.

5 The priests will burn them upon the altar as a guilt offering to the Lord.

6 Only males among the priests may then eat the carcass, and it must be eaten in a holy place, for this is a most holy sacrifice.

7 The same instructions apply to both the sin offering and the guilt offering—the carcass shall be given to the priest who is in charge of the atonement ceremony, for his food.

8 (When the offering is a burnt sacrifice, the priest who is in charge shall also be given the animal's hide.)

9 The priests who present the people's grain offerings to the Lord shall be given whatever remains of the sacrifice after the ceremony is completed. This rule applies whether the sacrifice is baked, fried, or grilled.

10 All other grain offerings, whether mixed with

olive oil or dry, are the common property of all sons of Aaron.

11 *Here are the instructions concerning the sacrifices given to the Lord as special peace offerings:*

12 If it is an offering of thanksgiving, unleavened short bread[1] shall be included with the sacrifice, along with unleavened wafers spread with olive oil and loaves from a batter of flour mixed with olive oil.

13 This thanksgiving peace offering shall be accompanied with loaves of leavened bread.

14 Part of this sacrifice shall be presented to the Lord by a gesture of waving it before the altar, then it shall be given to the assisting priest, the one who sprinkles the blood of the animal presented for the sacrifice.

15 After the animal has been sacrificed and presented to the Lord as a peace offering to show special appreciation and thanksgiving to Him, its meat is to be eaten that same day, and none left to be eaten the next day.

16 However, if someone brings a sacrifice that is not for thanksgiving, but is because of a vow or is simply a voluntary offering to the Lord, any portion of the sacrifice that is not eaten the day it is sacrificed may be eaten the next day.

17, 18 But anything left over until the third day shall be burned. For if any of it is eaten on the third day, the Lord will not accept it; it will have no value as a sacrifice, and there will be no credit to the one who brought it to be offered; and the priest who eats it shall be guilty, for it is detestable to the Lord, and the person who eats it must answer for his sin.

---

[1]Literally, "unleavened loaves mingled with oil."

19   Any meat that comes into contact with anything that is ceremonially unclean shall not be eaten, but burned; and as for the meat that may be eaten, it may be eaten only by a person who is ceremonially clean.

20   Any priest who is ceremonially unclean but eats the thanksgiving offering anyway, shall be cut off from his people, for he has defiled what is sacred.[2]

21   Anyone who touches anything that is ceremonially unclean, whether it is uncleanness from man or beast, and then eats the peace offering, shall be cut off from his people, for he has defiled what is holy."

22   Then the Lord said to Moses,

23   "Tell the people of Israel never to eat fat, whether from oxen, sheep, or goats.

24   The fat of an animal that dies of disease, or is attacked and killed by wild animals, may be used for other purposes, but never eaten.

25   Anyone who eats fat from an offering sacrificed by fire to the Lord shall be outlawed from his people.

26, 27   Never eat blood, whether of birds or animals. Anyone who does shall be excommunicated from his people."

28   And the Lord said to Moses,

29   "Tell the people of Israel that anyone bringing a thanksgiving offering to the Lord must bring it personally with his own hands.

30   He shall bring the offering of the fat and breast, which is to be presented to the Lord by waving it before the altar.

31   Then the priest shall burn the fat upon the altar, but the breast shall belong to Aaron and his sons,

---

[2]Literally, "it pertains unto Jehovah."

32, 33   While the right thigh shall be given to the officiating priest.

34   For I have designated the breast and thigh as donations from the people of Israel to the sons of Aaron. Aaron and his sons must always be given this portion of the sacrifice.

35   This is their pay! It is to be set apart from the burnt offerings, and given to all who have been appointed to minister to the Lord as priests—to Aaron and to his sons.

36   For on the day the Lord anointed them, He commanded that the people of Israel give these portions to them; it is their right forever throughout all their generations."

37   These were the instructions concerning the burnt offering, grain offering, sin offering, and guilt offering, and concerning the consecration offering and the peace offering;

38   These instructions were given to Moses by the Lord on Mount Sinai, to be passed on to the people of Israel so that they would know how to offer their sacrifices to God in the Sinai desert.

CHAPTER 8

The Lord said to Moses, "Now bring Aaron and his sons to the entrance of the Tabernacle, together with their garments, the anointing oil, the young bull for the sin offering, the two rams, and the basket of bread made without yeast; and summon all Israel to a meeting there."

4   So all the people assembled,

5   And Moses said to them, "What I am now going to do has been commanded by Jehovah."

6   Then he took Aaron and his sons and washed them with water,

7   And he clothed Aaron with the special coat, sash, robe, and the ephod-jacket with its beautifully woven belt.

8   Then he put on him the chestpiece and deposited the Urim and the Thummim[1] inside its pouch;

9   And placed on Aaron's head the turban with the sacred golden plate at its front—the holy crown—as the Lord had commanded Moses.

10   Then Moses took the anointing oil and sprinkled it upon the Tabernacle itself and on each item in it, sanctifying them.

11   When he came to the altar he sprinkled it seven times, and also sprinkled the utensils of the altar and the washbasin and its pedestal, to sanctify them.

12   Then he poured the anointing oil upon Aaron's head, thus setting him apart for his work.

13   Next Moses placed the robes on Aaron's sons, with the belts and caps, as the Lord had commanded him.

14   Then he took the young bull for the sin offering, and Aaron and his sons laid their hands upon its head

15, 16   As Moses killed it. He smeared some of the blood with his finger upon the four horns of the altar, and upon the altar itself, to sanctify it, and poured out the rest of the blood at the base of the altar; thus he sanctified the altar, making atonement for it. He took all the fat covering the entrails, the fatty mass above the liver, and the two kidneys and

---

[1]Apparently a kind of sacred lot used to determine the Lord's will by simple "Yes" or "No" alternatives.

their fat, and burned them all on the altar.

17   The carcass of the young bull, with its hide and dung, was burned outside the camp, as the Lord had commanded Moses.

18   Then he presented to the Lord the ram for the burnt offering. Aaron and his sons laid their hands upon its head,

19   And Moses killed it and sprinkled the blood back and forth upon the altar.

20   Next he quartered the ram and burned the pieces, the head and the fat.

21   He then washed the insides and the legs with water, and burned them upon the altar, so that the entire ram was consumed before the Lord; it was a burnt offering that pleased the Lord very much, for Jehovah's directions to Moses were followed in every detail.

22   Then Moses presented the other ram, the ram of consecration; Aaron and his sons laid their hands upon its head.

23   Moses killed it and took some of its blood and smeared it upon the lobes of Aaron's right ear and the thumb of his right hand and upon the big toe of his right foot.

24   Next he smeared some of the blood upon Aaron's sons—upon the lobes of their right ears, upon their right thumbs, and upon the big toes of their right feet. The rest of the blood he sprinkled back and forth upon the altar.[2]

25   Then he took the fat, the tail, the fat upon the inner organs, the gall bladder, the two kidneys with their fat, and the right shoulder,

---

[2]Literally, "Moses threw the blood upon the altar round about."

26 And placed on top of these one unleavened wafer, one wafer spread with olive oil, and a slice of bread, all taken from the basket which had been placed there before the Lord.

27 All this was placed in the hands of Aaron and his sons to present to the Lord by a gesture of waving them before the altar.

28 Moses then took it all back from them and burned it upon the altar, along with the burnt offering[3] to the Lord; and Jehovah was pleased by the offering.

29 Now Moses took the breast and presented it to the Lord by waving it before the altar; this was Moses' portion of the ram of consecration, just as the Lord had instructed him.

30 Next he took some of the anointing oil and some of the blood that had been sprinkled upon the altar, and sprinkled it upon Aaron and upon his clothes and upon his sons and upon their clothes, thus consecrating to the Lord's use Aaron and his sons and their clothes.

31 Then Moses said to Aaron and his sons, "Boil the meat at the entrance of the Tabernacle, and eat it along with the bread that is in the basket of consecration, just as I instructed you to do.

32 Anything left of the meat and bread must be burned."

33 Next he told them not to leave the Tabernacle entrance for seven days, after which time their consecration would be completed—for it takes seven days.

34 Then Moses stated again that all he had done that day had been commanded by the Lord in order to make atonement for them.

---

[3]Literally, "upon the burnt offering."

35   And again he warned Aaron and his sons to stay at the entrance of the Tabernacle day and night for seven days. "If you leave," he told them, "you will die—this is what the Lord has said."

36   So Aaron and his sons did all that the Lord had commanded Moses.

CHAPTER 9

On the eighth day (of the consecration ceremonies), Moses summoned Aaron and Aaron's sons and the elders of Israel,

2   And told Aaron to take a bull calf from the herd for a sin offering, and a ram without bodily defect for a burnt offering, and to offer them before the Lord.

3   "And tell the people of Israel," Moses instructed, "to select a male goat for their sin offering, also a yearling calf and a yearling lamb, all without bodily defect, for their burnt offering.

4   In addition, the people are to bring to the Lord a peace offering sacrifice—an ox and a ram, and a grain offering—flour mingled with olive oil. For today," Moses said, "Jehovah will appear to them."

5   So they brought all these things to the entrance of the Tabernacle, as Moses had commanded, and the people came and stood there before the Lord.

6   Moses told them, "When you have followed the Lord's instructions, His glory will appear to you."

7   Moses then told Aaron to proceed to the altar and to offer the sin offering and the burnt offering, making atonement for himself first, and then for the people, as the Lord had commanded.

8   So Aaron went up to the altar and killed the

calf as a sacrifice for his own sin;

9 His sons caught the blood for him, and he dipped his finger in it and smeared it upon the horns of the altar, and poured out the rest at the base of the altar.

10 Then he burned upon the altar the fat, kidneys, and gall bladder from this sin offering, as the Lord had commanded Moses,

11 But he burned the meat and hide outside the camp.

12 Next he killed the burnt offering animal, and his sons caught the blood and he sprinkled it back and forth upon the altar;

13 They brought the animal to him piece by piece, including the head, and he burned each part upon the altar.

14 Then he washed the insides and the legs, and offered these also upon the altar as a burnt offering.

15 Next he sacrificed the people's offering; he killed the goat and offered it in just the same way as he had the sin offering for himself.[1]

16 Thus he sacrificed their burnt offering to the Lord, in accordance with the instructions God had given.

17 Then he presented the grain offering, taking a handful and burning it upon the altar in addition to the regular morning offering.

18 Next he killed the ox and ram—the people's peace offering sacrifice; and Aaron's sons brought the blood to him and he sprinkled it back and forth upon the altar.

19 Then he collected the fat of the ox and the

---

[1] See verses 8-11.

ram—the fat from their tails and the fat covering the inner organs—and the kidneys and gall bladders.

20   The fat was placed upon the breasts of these animals, and Aaron burned it upon the altar;

21   But he waved the breasts and right shoulders slowly before the Lord as a gesture of offering it to Him, just as Moses had commanded.

22   Then, with hands spread out towards the people, Aaron blessed them and came down from the altar.

23   Moses and Aaron went into the Tabernacle, and when they came out again they blessed the people; and the glory of the Lord appeared to the whole assembly.

24   Then fire came from the Lord and consumed the burnt offering and fat on the altar; and when the people saw it, they all shouted and fell flat upon the ground before the Lord.

CHAPTER 10

But Nadab and Abihu, the sons of Aaron, placed unholy fire in their censers, laid incense on the fire, and offered the incense before the Lord[1]—contrary to what the Lord had just commanded them!

2   So fire blazed forth from the presence of the Lord and destroyed them.

3   Then Moses said to Aaron, "This is what the Lord meant when He said, 'I will show Myself holy among those who approach Me, and I will be glorified before all the people.' " And Aaron was speechless.

4   Then Moses called for Misha-el and Elzaphon,

---

[1]Or, "placed fire in their censers . . . and offered unholy fire . . ." Their fatal error is not clearly identified.

Aaron's cousins, the sons of Uzziel, and told them, "Go and get the charred bodies from before the Tabernacle, and carry them outside the camp."

5   So they went over and got them, and carried them out in their coats as Moses had told them to.

6   Then Moses said to Aaron and his sons Eleazar and Ithamar, "Do not mourn—do not let your hair hang loose as a sign of your mourning, and do not tear your clothes. If you do, God will strike you dead too, and His wrath will come upon all the people of Israel. But the rest of the people of Israel may lament the death of Nadab and Abihu, and mourn because of the terrible fire the Lord has sent.

7   But you are not to leave the Tabernacle under penalty of death, for the anointing oil of Jehovah is upon you." And they did as Moses commanded.

8, 9   Now the Lord instructed Aaron, "Never drink wine or strong drink when you go into the Tabernacle, lest you die; and this rule applies to your sons and to all your descendants from generation to generation.

10   Your duties will be to arbitrate for the people, to teach them the difference between what is holy and what is ordinary, what is pure and what is impure;

11   And to teach them all the laws Jehovah has given through Moses."

12   Then Moses said to Aaron and to his sons who were left, Eleazar and Ithamar, "Take the grain offering—the food that remains after the handful has been offered to the Lord by burning it on the altar—make sure there is no leaven in it, and eat it beside the altar. The offering is most holy;

13   Therefore you must eat it in the sanctuary, in a

holy place. It belongs to you and to your sons, from the offerings to Jehovah made by fire; for so I am commanded.

14 But the breast and the thigh, which have been offered to the Lord by the gesture of waving it before Him, may be eaten in any holy place. It belongs to you and to your sons and daughters for your food. It is your portion of the peace offering sacrifices of the people of Israel.

15 The people are to bring the thigh that was set aside, along with the breast that was offered when the fat was burned, and they shall be presented before the Lord by the gesture of waving them. And afterwards they shall belong to you and your family, for the Lord has commanded this."

16 Then Moses searched everywhere for the goat of the sin offering and discovered that it had been burned! He was very angry about this with Eleazar and Ithamar, the remaining sons of Aaron.

17 "Why haven't you eaten the sin offering in the sanctuary, since it is most holy, and God has given it to you to take away the iniquity and guilt of the people, to make atonement for them before the Lord?" he demanded.

18 "Since its blood was not taken inside the sanctuary, you should certainly have eaten it there, as I ordered you."

19 But Aaron interceded with Moses. "They offered their sin offering and burnt offering before the Lord," he said, "but if I had eaten the sin offering on such a day as this, would it have pleased the Lord?"

20 And when Moses heard that, he was satisfied.

CHAPTER 11

Then the Lord said to Moses and Aaron,
    2, 3   "Tell the people of Israel that the animals which may be used for food include any animal with cloven hooves which chews its cud.

    4, 5, 6   This means that the following may *not* be eaten:

> The camel (it chews the cud but does not have cloven hooves);

> The coney, or, rock badger (because although it chews the cud, it does not have cloven hooves);

> The hare (because although it chews the cud, it does not have cloven hooves);

    7   The swine (because although it has cloven hooves, it does not chew the cud).

    8   You may not eat their meat or even touch their dead bodies; they are forbidden foods for you.

    9   As to fish, you may eat whatever has fins and scales, whether taken from rivers or from the sea;

    10   But all other water creatures are strictly forbidden to you.

    11   You mustn't eat their meat or even touch their dead bodies.

    12   I'll repeat it again—any water creature that does not have fins or scales is forbidden to you.

    13   Among the birds, these are the ones you may *not* eat:

> The eagle,
> The metire,
> The osprey,

    14   The falcon (all kinds),

	The kite,
15	The raven (all kinds),
16	The ostrich,
	The nighthawk,
	The seagull,
	The hawk (all kinds),
17	The owl,
	The cormorant,
	The ibis,
18	The marsh hen,
	The pelican,
	The vulture,
19	The stork,
	The heron (all kinds),
	The hoopoe,
	The bat.

20   Flying insects with four legs must not be eaten,

21, 22   With the exception of those that jump; locusts of all varieties—ordinary locusts, bald locusts, crickets, and grasshoppers—may be eaten.

23   All other things that fly and have four feet are forbidden to you.

24   Anyone touching their dead bodies shall be defiled until the evening,

25   And must wash his clothes immediately. He must also quarantine himself until nightfall, as being ceremonially defiled.

26   You are also defiled by touching any animal with only semi-parted hoofs, or any animal that does not chew the cud.

27   Any animal that walks on paws is forbidden to you as food. Anyone touching the dead body of such an animal shall be defiled until evening.

28   Anyone carrying away the carcass shall wash his clothes and be ceremonially defiled until evening; for it is forbidden to you.

29   These are the forbidden small animals which scurry about your feet or crawl upon the ground:

> The mole,
> The rat,
> The great lizard,

30   The gecko,
> The mouse,
> The lizard,
> The snail,
> The chameleon.

31   Anyone touching their dead bodies shall be defiled until evening,

32   And anything upon which the carcass falls shall be defiled—any article of wood, or of clothing, a rug, or a sack; anything it touches must be put into water, and is defiled until evening. After that it may be used again.

33   If it falls into a pottery bowl, anything in the bowl is defiled, and you shall smash the bowl.

34   If the water used to cleanse the defiled article touches any food, all of it is defiled. Any drink which is in the defiled bowl is also contaminated.

35   If the dead body of such an animal touches any clay oven, it is defiled and must be smashed.

36   If the body falls into a spring or cistern where there is water, that water is not defiled; yet anyone who pulls out the carcass is defiled.

37   And if the carcass touches grain to be sown in the field, it is not contaminated;

38   But if the seeds are wet and the carcass falls upon it, the seed is defiled.

39   If an animal which you are permitted to eat dies of disease, anyone touching the carcass shall be defiled until evening.

40   Also, anyone eating its meat or carrying away its carcass shall wash his clothes and be defiled until evening.

41, 42   Animals that crawl shall not be eaten. This includes all reptiles that slither along upon their bellies as well as those that have legs. No crawling thing with many feet may be eaten, for it is defiled.

43   Do not defile yourselves by touching it.

44   I am the Lord your God. Keep yourselves pure concerning these things, and be holy, for I am holy; therefore do not defile yourselves by touching any of these things that crawl upon the earth.

45   For I am the Lord who brought you out of the land of Egypt to be your God. You must therefore be holy, for I am holy."

46   These are the laws concerning animals, birds, and whatever swims in the water or crawls upon the ground.

47   These are the distinctions between what is ceremonially clean and may be eaten, and what is ceremonially defiled and may not be eaten, among all animal life upon the earth.

CHAPTER 12

The Lord told Moses to give these instructions to the people of Israel:

2   "When a baby boy is born, the mother shall be ceremonially defiled for seven days, and under the same restrictions as during her monthly periods.

3   On the eighth day, her son must be circumcised.

4   Then, for the next thirty-three days, while she is recovering from her ceremonial impurity, she must not touch anything sacred, nor enter the Tabernacle.

5   When a baby girl is born, the mother's ceremonial impurity shall last two weeks, during which time she will be under the same restrictions as during menstruation. Then for a further sixty-six days she shall continue her recovery.[1]

6   When these days of purification are ended (the following instructions are applicable whether her baby is a boy or girl), she must bring a yearling lamb as a burnt offering, and a young pigeon or a turtledove for a sin offering. She must take them to the door of the Tabernacle to the priest;

7   And the priest will offer them before the Lord and make atonement for her; then she will be ceremonially clean again after her bleeding at childbirth.

These then, are the procedures after childbirth.

8   But if she is too poor to bring a lamb, then she must bring two turtledoves or two young pigeons. One will be for a burnt offering and the other for a sin offering. The priest will make atonement for her with these, so that she will be ceremonially pure again."

CHAPTER 13

The Lord said to Moses and Aaron, "If anyone notices a swelling in his skin, or a scab or boil or pimple with transparent skin, leprosy is to be suspected. He must be brought to Aaron the priest or to one of his sons

3   For the spot to be examined. If the hair in this spot turns white, and if the spot looks to be more than

---

[1]Literally, "shall continue in her blood of purification."

skin-deep, it is leprosy, and the priest must declare him a leper.[1]

4 But if the white spot in the skin does not seem to be deeper than the skin and the hair in the spot has not turned white, the priest shall quarantine him for seven days.

5 At the end of that time, on the seventh day, the priest will examine him again, and if the spot has not changed and has not spread in the skin, then the priest must quarantine him seven days more.

6 Again on the seventh day the priest will examine him, and if the marks of the disease have become fainter and have not spread, then the priest shall pronounce him cured; it was only a scab, and the man need only wash his clothes and everything will be normal again.

7 But if the spot spreads in the skin after he has come to the priest to be examined, he must come back to the priest again,

8 And the priest shall look again, and if the spot has spread, then the priest must pronounce him a leper.

9, 10 When anyone suspected of having leprosy is brought to the priest, the priest is to look to see if there is a white swelling in the skin with white hairs in the spot, and an ulcer developing.

11 If he finds these symptoms, it is an established case of leprosy, and the priest must pronounce him defiled. The man is not to be quarantined for further observation, for he is definitely diseased.

12 But if the priest sees that the leprosy has erupted and spread all over his body from head to foot wherever he looks,

---

[1]Literally, "shall declare him unclean."

13 Then the priest shall pronounce him cured of leprosy, for it has all turned white; he is cured.

14, 15 But if there is raw flesh anywhere, the man shall be declared a leper. It is proved by the raw flesh.

16, 17 But if the raw flesh later changes to white, the leper will return to the priest to be examined again. If the spot has indeed turned completely white, then the priest will pronounce him cured.

18 In the case of a man who has a boil in his skin which heals,

19 But which leaves a white swelling or a bright spot, sort of reddish white, the man must go to the priest for examination.

20 If the priest sees that the trouble seems to be down under the skin, and if the hair at the spot has turned white, then the priest shall declare him defiled, for leprosy has broken out from the boil.

21 But if the priest sees that there are no white hairs in this spot, and the spot does not appear to be deeper than the skin, and if the color is gray, then the priest shall quarantine him for seven days.

22 If during that time the spot spreads, the priest must declare him a leper.

23 But if the bright spot grows no larger and does not spread, it is merely the scar from the boil, and the priest shall declare that all is well.

24 If a man is burned in some way, and the burned place becomes bright reddish-white or white,

25 Then the priest must examine the spot. If the hair in the bright spot turns white, and the problem seems to be more than skin-deep, it is leprosy that has broken out from the burn, and the priest must pro-

nounce him a leper.[2]

26   But if the priest sees that there are no white hairs in the bright spot, and the brightness appears to be no deeper than the skin and is fading, the priest shall quarantine him for seven days,

27   And examine him again the seventh day. If the spot spreads in the skin, the priest must pronounce him a leper.[2]

28   But if the bright spot does not move or spread in the skin, and is fading, it is simply a scar from the burn, and the priest shall declare that he does not have leprosy.

29, 30   If a man or woman has a sore on the head or chin, the priest must examine him; if the infection seems to be below the skin and yellow hair is found in the sore, the priest must pronounce him a leper.

31   But if the priest's examination reveals that the spot seems to be only in the skin and that there is black hair in it, then he shall be quarantined for seven days,

32   And examined again on the seventh day. If the spot has not spread and no yellow hair has appeared, and if the infection does not seem to be deeper than the skin,

33   He shall shave off all the hair around the spot (but not on the spot itself) and the priest shall quarantine him for another seven days.

34   He shall be examined again on the seventh day, and if the spot has not spread, and it appears to be no deeper than the skin, the priest shall pronounce him well, and after washing his clothes, he is free.[3]

35   But if, later on, this spot begins to spread,

---

[2]Literally, "pronounce him unclean."
[3]Literally, "he is clean."

36   Then the priest must examine him again and, without waiting to see if any yellow hair develops, declare him a leper.

37   But if it appears that the spreading has stopped and black hairs are found in the spot, then he is healed and is not a leper, and the priest shall declare him healed.

38   If a man or a woman has white, transparent areas in the skin,

39   But these spots are growing dimmer, this is not leprosy, but an ordinary infection that has broken out in the skin.

40   If a man's hair is gone, this does not make him a leper even though he is bald!

41   If the hair is gone from the front part of his head, he simply has a bald forehead, but this is not leprosy.

42   However, if in the baldness there is a reddish white spot, it may be leprosy breaking out.

43   In that case the priest shall examine him, and if there is a reddish white lump that looks like leprosy,

44   Then he is a leper, and the priest must pronounce him such.

45   Anyone who is discovered to have leprosy must tear his clothes and let his hair grow in wild disarray, and cover his upper lip and call out as he goes, "I am a leper, I am a leper."[4]

46   As long as the disease lasts, he is defiled and must live outside the camp.

47, 48   If leprosy is suspected in a woolen or linen garment or fabric, or in a piece of leather or leatherwork,

---

[4]Literally, "Unclean, unclean."

49   And there is a greenish or a reddish spot in it, it is probably leprosy, and must be taken to the priest to be examined.

50   The priest will put it away for seven days

51   And look at it again on the seventh day. If the spot has spread, it is a contagious leprosy,

52   And he must burn the clothing, fabric, linen or woolen covering, or leather article, for it is contagious and must be destroyed by fire.

53   But if when he examines it again on the seventh day the spot has not spread,

54   The priest shall order the suspected article to be washed, then isolated for seven more days.

55   If after that time the spot has not changed its color, even though it has not spread, it is leprosy and shall be burned, for the article is infected through and through.[5]

56   But if the priest sees that the spot has faded after the washing, then he shall cut it out from the garment or leather goods or whatever it is in.

57   However, if it then reappears, it is leprosy and he must burn it.

58   But if after washing it there is no further trouble, it can be put back into service after another washing."

59   These are the regulations concerning leprosy in a garment or anything made of skin or leather, indicating whether to pronounce it leprous or not.

CHAPTER 14

A nd the Lord gave Moses these regulations concerning a person whose leprosy disappears:

---

[5]Literally, "whether the bareness be within or without" or, "whether it be bald in the head thereof or in the forehead thereof."

3 "The priest shall go out of the camp to examine him. If the priest sees that the leprosy is gone,

4 He shall require two living birds of a kind permitted for food, and shall take some cedar wood, a scarlet string, and some hyssop branches, to be used for the purification ceremony of the one who is healed.

5 The priest shall then order one of the birds killed in an earthenware pot held above running water.

6 The other bird, still living, shall be dipped in the blood, along with the cedar wood, the scarlet thread, and the hyssop branch.

7 Then the priest shall sprinkle the blood seven times upon the man cured of his leprosy, and the priest shall pronounce him cured, and shall let the living bird fly into the open field.

8 Then the man who is cured shall wash his clothes, shave off all his hair, and bathe himself, and return to live inside the camp; however, he must stay outside his tent for seven days.

9 The seventh day he shall again shave all the hair from his head, beard, and eyebrows, and wash his clothes and bathe, and shall then be declared fully cured of his leprosy.

10 The next day, the eighth day, he shall take two male lambs without physical defect, one yearling ewe-lamb without physical defect, ten quarts of finely ground flour mixed with olive oil, and a pint of olive oil;

11 Then the priest who examines him shall place the man and his offerings before the Lord at the entrance of the Tabernacle.

12 The priest shall take one of the lambs and the pint of olive oil and offer them to the Lord as a guilt

offering by the gesture of waving them before the altar.

13　Then he shall kill the lamb at the place where sin offerings and burnt offerings are killed, there at the Tabernacle; this guilt offering shall then be given to the priest for food, as in the case of a sin offering. It is a most holy offering.

14　The priest shall take the blood from this guilt offering and smear some of it upon the tip of the right ear of the man being cleansed, and upon the thumb of his right hand, and upon the big toe of his right foot.

15　Then the priest shall take the olive oil and pour it into the palm of his left hand,

16　And dip his right finger into it, and sprinkle it with his finger seven times before the Lord.

17　Some of the oil remaining in his left hand shall then be placed by the priest upon the tip of the man's right ear and the thumb of his right hand and the big toe of his right foot—just as he did with the blood of the guilt offering.

18　The remainder of the oil in his hand shall be used to anoint the man's head. Thus the priest shall make atonement for him before the Lord.

19　Then the priest must offer the sin offering and again[1] perform the rite of atonement for the person being cleansed from his leprosy; and afterwards the priest shall kill the burnt offering,

20　And offer it along with the grain offering upon the altar, making atonement for the man, who shall then be pronounced finally cleansed.

21　If he is so poor that he cannot afford two lambs, then he shall bring only one, a male lamb for the guilt offering, to be presented to the Lord in the rite of

[1]Implied.

atonement by waving it before the altar; and only three quarts of fine white flour, mixed with olive oil, for a grain offering, and a pint of olive oil.

22 He shall also bring two turtledoves or two young pigeons—whichever he is able to afford—and use one of the pair for a sin offering and the other for a burnt offering.

23 He shall bring them to the priest at the entrance of the Tabernacle on the eighth day, for his ceremony of cleansing before the Lord.

24 The priest shall take the lamb for the guilt offering, and the pint of oil, and wave them before the altar as a gesture of offering to the Lord.

25 Then he shall kill the lamb for the guilt offering and smear some of its blood upon the tip of the man's right ear—the man on whose behalf the ceremony is being performed—and upon the thumb of his right hand and on the big toe of his right foot.

26 The priest shall then pour the olive oil into the palm of his own left hand,

27 And with his right finger he is to sprinkle some of it seven times before the Lord.

28 Then he must put some of the olive oil from his hand upon the tip of the man's right ear, and upon the thumb of his right hand, and upon the big toe of his right foot, just as he did with the blood of the guilt offering.

29 The remaining oil in his hand shall be placed upon the head of the man being cleansed, to make atonement for him before the Lord.

30 Then he must offer the two turtledoves or two young pigeons (whichever pair he is able to afford).

31 One of the pair is for a sin offering and the

other for a burnt offering, to be sacrificed along with the grain offering; and the priest shall make atonement for the man before the Lord."

32   These, then, are the laws concerning those who are cleansed of leprosy but are not able to bring the sacrifices normally required for the ceremony of cleansing.

33, 34   Then the Lord said to Moses and Aaron, "When you arrive in the land of Canaan which I have given you, and I place leprosy in some house there,

35   Then the owner of the house shall come and report to the priest, 'It seems to me that there may be leprosy in my house!'

36   The priest shall order the house to be emptied before he examines it, so that everything in the house will not be declared contaminated if he decides that there is leprosy there.

37   If he finds greenish or reddish streaks in the walls of the house which seem to be beneath the surface of the wall,

38   He shall close up the house for seven days,

39   And return the seventh day to look at it again. If the spots have spread in the wall,

40   Then the priest shall order the removal of the spotted section of wall, and the material must be thrown into a defiled place outside the city.

41   Then he shall order the inside walls of the house scraped thoroughly, and the scrapings dumped in a defiled place outside the city.

42   Other stones shall be brought to replace those that have been removed, new mortar used, and the house replastered.

43   But if the spots appear again,

44 The priest shall come again and look, and if he sees that the spots have spread, it is leprosy, and the house is defiled.

45 Then he shall order the destruction of the house —all its stones, timbers, and mortar shall be carried out of the city to a defiled place.

46 Anyone entering the house while it is closed shall be defiled until evening.

47 Anyone who lies down or eats in the house shall wash his clothing.

48 But if, when the priest comes again to look, the spots have not reappeared after the fresh plastering, then he will pronounce the house cleansed, and declare the leprosy gone.

49 He shall also perform the ceremony of cleansing, using two birds, cedar wood, scarlet thread, and hyssop branches.

50 He shall kill one of the birds over fresh water in an earthenware bowl,

51, 52 And dip the cedar wood, hyssop branch, and scarlet thread, as well as the living bird, into the blood of the bird that was killed over the fresh water, and shall sprinkle the house seven times.

In this way the house shall be cleansed.

53 Then he shall let the live bird fly away into an open field outside the city. This is the method for making atonement for the house and cleansing it."

54 These, then, are the laws concerning the various places where leprosy may appear:

55 In a garment or in a house,

56 Or in any swelling in one's skin, or a scab from a burn, or a bright spot.

57 In this way you will know whether or not it is actually leprosy. That is why these laws are given.

CHAPTER 15

The Lord told Moses and Aaron to give the people of Israel these further instructions: "Any man who has a genital discharge[1] is ceremonially defiled.

3   This applies not only while the discharge is active, but also for a time after it heals.

4   Any bed he lies on and anything he sits on is contaminated;

5   So anyone touching the man's bed is ceremonially defiled until evening, and must wash his clothes and bathe himself.

6   Anyone sitting on a seat the man has sat upon while defiled is himself ceremonially unclean until evening, and must wash his clothes and bathe himself.

7   The same instructions apply to anyone touching him.

8   Anyone he spits on is ceremonially unclean until evening, and must wash his clothes and bathe himself.

9   Any saddle he rides on is defiled.

10   Anyone touching or carrying anything else that was beneath him shall be defiled until evening, and must wash his clothes and bathe himself.

11   If the defiled man touches anyone without first rinsing his hands, that person must wash his clothes and bathe himself and be defiled until evening.

12   Any earthen pot touched by the defiled man must be broken, and every wooden utensil must be rinsed in water.

13   When the discharge stops, he shall begin a seven-day cleansing ceremony by washing his clothes and bathing in running water.

14   On the eighth day he shall take two turtledoves

---

[1]Literally, "an issue out of his flesh."

or two young pigeons and come before the Lord at the entrance of the Tabernacle, and give them to the priest.

15 The priest shall sacrifice them there, one for a sin offering and the other for a burnt offering; thus the priest shall make atonement before the Lord for the man because of his discharge.

16 Whenever a man's semen goes out from him, he shall take a complete bath and be unclean until the evening.

17 Any clothing or bedding the semen spills on must be washed and remain ceremonially defiled until evening.

18 After sexual intercourse, the woman as well as the man must bathe, and they are ceremonially defiled until the next evening.

19 Whenever a woman menstruates, she shall be in a state of ceremonial defilement for seven days afterwards, and during that time anyone touching her shall be defiled until evening.

20 Anything she lies on or sits on during that time shall be defiled.

21, 22, 23 Anyone touching her bed or anything she sits upon shall wash his clothes and bathe himself and be ceremonially defiled until evening.

24 A man having sexual intercourse with her during this time is ceremonially defiled for seven days, and every bed he lies upon shall be defiled.

25 If the menstrual flow continues after the normal time, or at some irregular time during the month, the same rules apply as indicated above,

26 So that anything she lies upon during that time is defiled, just as it would be during her normal menstrual period, and everything she sits on is in a

similar state of defilement.

27 Anyone touching her bed or anything she sits on shall be defiled, and shall wash his clothes and bathe and be defiled until evening.

28 Seven days after the menstruating stops, she is no longer ceremonially defiled.

29 On the eighth day, she shall take two turtle-doves or two young pigeons and bring them to the priest at the entrance of the Tabernacle,

30 And the priest shall offer one for a sin offering and the other for a burnt offering, and make atonement for her before the Lord, for her menstrual defilement.

31 In this way you shall cleanse the people of Israel from their defilement, lest they die because of defiling My Tabernacle that is among them."

32 This, then, is the law for the man who is defiled by a genital disease[2] or by a seminal emission;

33 And for a woman's menstrual period; and for anyone who has sexual intercourse with her while she is in her period of defilement afterwards.

CHAPTER 16

After Aaron's two sons died before the Lord, the Lord said to Moses, "Warn your brother Aaron not to enter into the Holy Place behind the veil, where the Ark and the place of mercy are, just whenever he chooses. The penalty for intrusion is death. For I Myself am present in the cloud above the place of mercy.

3 Here are the conditions for his entering there: he must bring a young bull for a sin offering, and a ram for a burnt offering.

---

[2]Literally, "has an issue."

4   He must bathe himself and put on the sacred linen coat, shorts, belt, and turban.

5   The people of Israel shall then bring him two male goats for their sin offering, and a ram for their burnt offering.

6   First he shall present to the Lord the young bull as a sin offering for himself, making atonement for himself and his family.

7   Then he shall bring the two goats before the Lord at the entrance of the Tabernacle,

8   And cast lots to determine which is the Lord's and which is to be sent away.[1]

9   The goat allotted to the Lord shall then be sacrified by Aaron as a sin offering.

10   The other goat shall be kept alive and placed before the Lord. The rite of atonement shall be performed over it, and it shall then be sent out into the desert as a scapegoat.[1]

11   After Aaron has sacrificed the young bull as a sin offering for himself and his family,

12   He shall take a censer full of live coals from the altar of the Lord, and fill his hands with sweet incense beaten into fine powder, and bring it inside the veil.

13   There before the Lord he shall put the incense upon the coals, so that a cloud of incense will cover the mercy place above the Ark (containing the stone tablets of the Ten Commandments); thus he will not die.

14   And he shall bring some of the blood of the young bull and sprinkle it with his finger upon the east side of the mercy place, and then seven times in front of it.

---

[1]Literally, "for Azazel" or "for removal."

15 Then he must go out[2] and sacrifice the people's sin offering goat, and bring its blood within the veil, and sprinkle it upon the place of mercy and in front of it, just as he did with the blood of the young bull.

16 Thus he shall make atonement for the holy place because it is defiled by the sins of the people of Israel, and for the Tabernacle, located right among them and surrounded by their defilement.

17 Not another soul shall be inside the Tabernacle when Aaron enters to make atonement in the Holy Place—not until after he comes out again and has made atonement for himself and his household and for all the people of Israel.

18 Then he shall go out to the altar before the Lord and make atonement for it. He must smear the blood of the young bull and the goat on the horns of the altar,

19 And sprinkle blood upon the altar seven times with his finger, thus cleansing it from the sinfulness of Israel, and making it holy.[3]

20 When he has completed the rite of atonement for the Holy Place, the entire Tabernacle, and the altar, he shall bring the live goat and,

21 Laying both hands upon its head, confess over it all the sins of the people of Israel. He shall lay all their sins upon the head of the goat and send it into the desert, led by a man appointed for the task.

22 So the goat shall carry all the sins of the people into a land where no one lives,[4] and the man shall let it loose in the wilderness.

23 Then Aaron shall go into the Tabernacle again

---

[2]Implied.
[3]Literally, "hallowing it."
[4]Literally, "a solitary land."

and take off the linen garments he wore when he went behind the veil, and leave them there in the Tabernacle.

24 Then he shall bathe in a sacred place, put on his clothes again, and go out and sacrifice his own burnt offering and the burnt offering for the people, making atonement for himself and for them.

25 He shall also burn upon the altar the fat for the sin offering.

26 (The man who took the goat out into the desert[5] shall afterwards wash his clothes and bathe himself and then come back into the camp.)

27 And the young bull and the goat used for the sin offering (their blood was taken into the Holy Place by Aaron, to make atonement) shall be carried outside the camp and burned, including the hides and internal organs.

28 Afterwards, the person doing the burning shall wash his clothes and bathe himself and then return to camp.

29, 30 This is a permanent law: You must do no work on the twenty-fifth day of September[6], but must spend the day in self-examination and humility. This applies whether you are born in the land or are a foreigner living among the people of Israel; for this is the day commemorating the atonement, cleansing you in the Lord's eyes from all of your sins.

31 It is a Sabbath of solemn rest for you, and you shall spend the day in quiet humility;[7] this is a permanent law.

32 This ceremony, in later generations, shall be

---

[5]Literally, "for Azazel" or "for removal."
[6]Literally, "on the tenth day of the seventh month" of the Hebrew calendar.
[7]Or, "in fasting."

performed by the anointed High Priest, consecrated in place of his ancestor Aaron; he shall be the one to put on the holy linen garments.

33　　And make atonement for the holy sanctuary, the Tabernacle, the altar, the priests, and the people.

34　　This shall be an everlasting law for you, to make atonement for the people of Israel once each year, because of their sins."

35　　And Aaron followed all these instructions that the Lord gave to Moses.

CHAPTER 17

The Lord gave to Moses these additional instructions for Aaron and the priests and for all the people of Israel:

3, 4　　"Any Israelite who sacrifices[1] an ox, lamb, or goat anywhere except at the Tabernacle is guilty of murder and shall be excommunicated from his nation.

5　　The purpose of this law is to stop the people of Israel from sacrificing in the open fields, and to cause them to bring their sacrifices to the priest at the entrance of the Tabernacle, and to burn the fat as a savor the Lord will appreciate and enjoy—

6　　For in this way the priest will be able to sprinkle the blood upon the altar of the Lord at the entrance of the Tabernacle, and to burn the fat as a savor the Lord will appreciate and enjoy—

7　　Instead of the people's sacrificing to evil spirits[2] out in the fields. This shall be a permanent law for you, from generation to generation.

8, 9　　I repeat: Anyone, whether an Israelite or a

---

[1]Literally, "slaughters."
[2]Literally, "hairy ones."

foreigner living among you who offers a burnt offering or a sacrifice anywhere other than at the entrance of the Tabernacle, where it will be sacrificed to the Lord, shall be excommunicated.

10   And I will turn My face against anyone, whether an Israelite or a foreigner living among you, who eats blood in any form. I will excommunicate him from his people.

11   For the life of the flesh is in the blood, and I have given you the blood to sprinkle upon the altar as an atonement for your souls; it is the blood that makes atonement, because it is the life.[3]

12   That is the reasoning behind My decree to the people of Israel, that neither they, nor any foreigner living among them, may eat blood.

13   Anyone, whether an Israelite or a foreigner living among you, who goes hunting and kills an animal or bird of a kind permitted for food, must pour out the blood and cover it with dust,

14   For the blood is the life. That is why I told the people of Israel never to eat it, for the life of every bird and animal[4] is its blood. Therefore, anyone who eats blood must be excommunicated.

15   And anyone—native born or foreigner—who eats the dead body of an animal that dies of itself, or is torn by wild animals, must wash his clothes and bathe himself and be defiled until evening; after that he shall be declared cleansed.

16   But if he does not wash his clothes and bathe, he shall suffer the consequence."

---

[3]Implied.
[4]Literally, "every creature."

CHAPTER 18

The Lord then told Moses to tell the people of Israel, "I am Jehovah your God,

3 So don't act like heathen—like the people of Egypt where you lived so long, or the people of Canaan where I am going to take you.

4, 5 You must obey only My laws, and you must carry them out in detail, for I am the Lord your God. If you obey them you shall live.[1] I am the Lord.

6 None of you shall marry[2] a near relative, for I am the Lord.

7 A girl may not marry her father; nor a son his mother,

8 Nor any other of his father's wives,

9 Nor his sister or half-sister, whether the daughter of his father or his mother, whether born in the same house or elsewhere.

10 You shall not marry your granddaughter—the daughter of either your son or your daughter—for she is a close relative.[3]

11 You may not marry a half-sister—your father's wife's daughter;

12 Nor your aunt—your father's sister—because she is so closely related to your father;

13 Nor your aunt—your mother's sister—because she is a close relative of your mother;

14 Nor your aunt—the wife of your father's brother.[4]

---

[1]Literally, "shall live in them" or "shall live by them."
[2]Literally, "uncover the nakedness of," that is, "have sexual intercourse with."
[3]Literally, "for their's is your own nakedness."
[4]This prohibition applied not only while her husband lived, but also after his death.

15   You may not marry your daughter-in-law—your son's wife;

16   Nor your brother's wife, for she is your brother's.[5]

17   You may not marry both a woman and her daughter or granddaughter, for they are near relatives, and to do so is horrible wickedness.

18   You shall not marry two sisters, for they will be rivals. However, if your wife dies, then it is all right to marry her sister.

19   There must be no sexual relationship with a woman who is menstruating;

20   Nor with anyone else's wife, to defile yourself with her.

21   You shall not give any of your children to Molech, burning them upon his altar; never profane the name of your God, for I am Jehovah.

22   Homosexuality is absolutely forbidden, for it is an enormous sin.

23   A man shall have no sexual intercourse with any female animal, thus defiling himself; and a woman must never give herself to a male animal, to mate with it; this is a terrible perversion.

24   Do not defile yourselves in any of these ways, for these are the things the heathen do; and because they do them I am going to cast them out from the land into which you are going.

25   That entire country is defiled with this kind of activity; that is why I am punishing the people living there, and will throw them out of the land.[6]

---

[5]Except when the brother died and left no heir, in which case his wife was left to a brother to beget children from her to carry on the name and inheritance of the deceased. See Deut. 25:5.
[6]Literally, "the land vomits out her inhabitants."

26   You must strictly obey all of My laws and ordinances, and you must not do any of these abominable things; these laws apply both to you who are born in the nation of Israel and to foreigners living among you.

27   Yes, all these abominations have been done continually by the people of the land where I am taking you, and the land is defiled.

28   Do not do these things or I will throw you out of the land, just as I will throw out[7] the nations that live there now.

29, 30   Whoever does any of these terrible deeds shall be excommunicated from this nation. So be very sure to obey My laws, and do not practice any of these horrible customs. Do not defile yourselves with the evil deeds of those living in the land where you are going. For I am Jehovah your God."

CHAPTER 19

The Lord also told Moses to tell the people of Israel, "You must be holy because I, the Lord your God, am holy. You must respect your mothers and fathers, and obey My Sabbath law, for I am the Lord your God.

3, 4   Do not make or worship idols, for I am Jehovah your God.

5   When you sacrifice a peace offering to the Lord, offer it correctly so that it will be accepted:

6   Eat it the same day you offer it, or the next day at the latest; any remaining until the third day must be burned.

7   For any of it eaten on the third day is repulsive to Me, and will not be accepted.

---

[7]Literally, "that the land vomit not you out also . . . as it vomited out . . ."

8   If you eat it on the third day you are guilty,
for you profane the holiness of Jehovah, and you shall
be excommunicated from Jehovah's people.

9   When you harvest your crops, don't reap the
corners of your fields, and don't pick up stray grains
of wheat from the ground.

10   It is the same with your grape crop—don't strip
every last piece of fruit from the vines, and don't pick
up the grapes that fall to the ground. Leave them for
the poor and for those traveling through, for I am
Jehovah your God.

11   You must not steal nor lie nor defraud.

12   You must not swear to a falsehood, thus bringing reproach upon the name of your God, for I am
Jehovah.

13   You shall not rob nor oppress anyone, and you
shall pay your hired workers promptly. If something
is due them, don't even keep it overnight.

14   You must not curse the deaf nor trip up a blind
man as he walks. Fear your God; I am Jehovah!

15   Judges must always be just in their sentences,
not noticing whether a person is poor or rich; they
must always be perfectly fair.

16   Don't gossip. Don't falsely accuse your neighbor
of some crime,[1] for I am Jehovah.

17   Don't hate your brother. Rebuke anyone who
sins; don't let him get away with it, or you will be
equally guilty.

18   Don't seek vengeance. Don't bear a grudge; but
love your neighbor as yourself, for I am Jehovah.

19   Obey My laws: do not mate your cattle with a
different kind; don't sow your field with two kinds of

---

[1]Literally, "neither shall you stand against the blood of your neighbor."

seed; don't wear clothes made of half wool and half linen.

20   If a man seduces a slave[2] girl who is engaged to be married, they shall be tried in a court but not put to death, because she is not free.

21   The man involved shall bring his guilt offering to the Lord at the entrance of the Tabernacle; the offering shall be a ram.

22   The priest shall make atonement with the ram for the sin the man has committed, and it shall be forgiven him.

23   When you enter the land and have planted all kinds of fruit trees, do not eat the first three crops, for they are considered ceremonially defiled.[3]

24   And the fourth year the entire crop shall be devoted to the Lord, and shall be given to the Lord in praise to Him.

25   Finally, in the fifth year, the crop is yours.

26   I am Jehovah your God! You must not eat meat with undrained blood; nor use fortune telling or witchcraft.

27   You must not trim off your hair on your temples or clip the edges of your beard, as the heathen do.[4]

28   You shall not cut yourselves nor put tattoo marks upon yourselves in connection with funeral rites; I am the Lord.

29   Do not violate your daughter's sanctity by making her a prostitute, lest the land become full of enormous wickedness.

30   Keep My Sabbath laws and reverence My Tabernacle, for I am the Lord.

---

[2]Literally, "not yet redeemed, nor given her freedom."
[3]Literally, "you shall count the fruit thereof as their uncircumcision."
[4]Implied.

31   Do not defile yourselves by consulting mediums and wizards, for I am Jehovah your God.

32   You shall give due honor and respect to the elderly, in the fear of God. I am Jehovah.

33   Do not take advantage of foreigners in your land; do not wrong them.

34   They must be treated like any other citizen; love them as yourself, for remember that you too were foreigners in the land of Egypt. I am Jehovah your God.

35, 36   You must be impartial in judgment. Use accurate measurements—lengths, weights, and volumes —and give full measure, for I am Jehovah your God who brought you from the land of Egypt.

37   You must heed all of My commandments and ordinances, carefully obeying them, for I am Jehovah."

CHAPTER 20

The Lord gave Moses these further instructions for the people of Israel:

"Anyone—whether an Israelite or a foreigner living among you—who sacrifices his child as a burnt offering to Molech shall without fail be stoned by his peers.

3   And I Myself will turn against that man and cut him off from all his people, because he has given his child to Molech, thus making My Tabernacle[1] unfit for Me to live in, and insulting My holy name.

4   And if the people of the land pretend they do not know what the man has done, and refuse to put him to death,

5   Then I Myself will set My face against that man and his family and cut him off, along with all others

---
[1] Literally, "My sanctuary . . ."

who turn to other gods than Me.

6   I will set my face against anyone who consults mediums and wizards instead of Me and I will cut that person off from his people.

7   So sanctify yourselves and be holy, for I am the Lord your God.

8   You must obey all of My commandments, for I am the Lord who sanctifies you.

9   Anyone who curses his father or mother shall surely be put to death—for he has cursed his own flesh and blood.

10   If a man commits adultery with another man's wife, both the man and woman shall be put to death.

11   If a man sleeps with his father's wife, he has defiled what is his father's; both the man and the woman must die, for it is their own fault.

12   And if a man has sexual intercourse with his daughter-in-law, both shall be executed: they have brought it upon themselves by defiling each other.

13   The penalty for homosexual acts is death to both parties. They have brought it upon themselves.

14   If a man has sexual intercourse with a woman and with her mother, it is a great evil. All three shall be burned alive to wipe out wickedness from among you.

15   If a man has sexual intercourse with an animal, he shall be executed and the animal killed.

16   If a woman has sexual intercourse with an animal, kill the woman and the animal, for they deserve their punishment.[2]

17   If a man has sexual intercourse with his sister, whether the daughter of his father or of his mother,

[2]Literally, "their blood shall be upon them."

it is a shameful thing, and they shall publicly be cut off from the people of Israel. He shall bear his guilt.

18   If a man has sexual intercourse with a woman during her period of menstruation, both shall be excommunicated, for he has uncovered her uncleanness.

19   Sexual intercourse is outlawed between a man and his maiden aunt—whether the sister of his mother or of his father—for they are near of kin; they shall bear their guilt.

20   If a man has intercourse with his uncle's widow,[3] he has taken what belongs to his uncle; their punishment is that they shall bear their sin and die childless.

21   If a man marries his brother's widow,[4] this is impurity; for he has taken what belongs to his brother, and they shall be childless.

22   You must obey all of My laws and ordinances so that I will not throw you out of your new land.[5]

23   You must not follow the customs of the nations I cast out before you, for they do all these things I have warned you against; that is the reason I abhor them.

24   I have promised you their land; I will give it to you to possess it. It is a land 'flowing with milk and honey.' I am the Lord your God who has made a distinction between you and the people of other nations.

25   You shall therefore make a distinction between the birds and animals I have given you permission to eat and those you may not eat. You shall not contaminate yourselves and make yourselves hateful to Me by eating any animal or bird which I have forbidden, though the land teem with them.

---

[3]Literally, "his uncle's wife."
[4]Literally, "his brother's wife." However such a marriage was required if she had no children. See Deut. 25:5.
[5]Literally, "that the land I give you will not vomit you out again."

26 You shall be holy to Me, for I the Lord am holy, and I have set you apart from all other peoples, to be Mine.

27 A medium or a wizard—whether man or woman—shall surely be stoned to death. They have caused their own doom."

CHAPTER 21

The Lord said to Moses: "Tell the priests never to defile themselves by touching a dead person,

2, 3 Unless it is a near relative—a mother, father, son, daughter, brother, or unmarried[1] sister for whom he has special responsibility since she has no husband.

4 For the priest is a leader among his people and he may not ceremonially defile himself as an ordinary person can.

5 The priests shall not clip bald spots in their hair or beards, nor cut their flesh.

6 They shall be holy unto their God, and shall not dishonor and profane His name; otherwise they will be unfit to make food offerings by fire to the Lord their God.

7 A priest shall not marry a prostitute, nor a woman of another tribe, and he shall not marry a divorced woman, for he is a holy man of God.

8 The priest is set apart to offer the sacrifices of your God; he is holy, for I, the Lord who sanctifies you, am holy.

9 The daughter of any priest who becomes a prostitute, thus violating her father's holiness as well as her own, shall be burned alive.

10 The High Priest—anointed with the special

---

[1] Literally, "a virgin."

anointing oil and wearing the special garments—must not let his hair hang loose in mourning, nor tear his clothing,

11 Nor be in the presence of any dead person—not even his father or mother.[2]

12 He shall not leave the sanctuary [when on duty[3]], nor treat My Tabernacle like an ordinary house, for the consecration of the anointing oil of his God is upon him; I am Jehovah.

13 He must marry a virgin.

14, 15 He may not marry a widow, nor a woman who is divorced, nor a prostitute. She must be a virgin from his own tribe, for he must not be the father of children of mixed blood—half priestly and half ordinary."[4]

16, 17 And the Lord said to Moses, "Tell Aaron that any of his descendants from generation to generation who have any bodily defect may not offer the sacrifices to God.

18 For instance, if a man is blind or lame, or has a broken nose or any extra fingers or toes,

19 Or has a broken foot or hand,

20 Or has a humped back, or is a dwarf, or has a defect in his eye, or has pimples or scabby skin, or has imperfect testicles—

21 Although he is a descendant of Aaron—he is not permitted to offer the fire sacrifices to the Lord because of his physical defect.

22 However, he shall be fed with the food of the priests from the offerings sacrificed to God, both from the holy and most holy offerings.

---

[2]Note that this rule applied to the High Priest, while the contrary instructions in verse 1 applied to ordinary priests.
[3]Implied.
[4]Literally, "he must not profane his offspring among his people."

23   But he shall not go in behind the veil, nor come near the altar, because of the physical defect; this would defile My sanctuary, for it is Jehovah who sanctifies it."

24   So Moses gave these instructions to Aaron and his sons and to all the people of Israel.

CHAPTER 22

The Lord said to Moses, "Instruct Aaron and his sons to be very careful not to defile My holy name by desecrating the peoples' sacred gifts; for I am Jehovah.

3   From now on and forever, if a priest who is ceremonially defiled sacrifices the animals brought by the people or handles the gifts dedicated to Jehovah, he shall be discharged from the priesthood. For I am Jehovah!

4   No priest who is a leper or who has a running sore may eat the holy sacrifices until healed. And any priest who touches a dead person, or who is defiled by a seminal emission,

5   Or who touches any reptile or other forbidden thing, or who touches anyone who is ceremonially defiled for any reason—

6   That priest shall be defiled until evening, and shall not eat of the holy sacrifices until after he has bathed that evening.

7   When the sun is down, then he shall be purified again and may eat the holy food, for it is his source of life.

8   He may not eat any animal that dies of itself or is torn by wild animals, for this will defile him. I am Jehovah.

9 Warn the priests to follow these instructions carefully, lest they be declared guilty and die for violating these rules. I am the Lord who sanctifies them.

10 No one may eat of the holy sacrifices unless he is a priest; no one visiting the priest, for instance, nor a hired servant, may eat this food.

11 However, there is one exception—if the priest buys a slave with his own money, that slave may eat it, and any slave children born in his household may eat it.

12 If a priest's daughter is married outside the tribe, she may not eat the sacred offerings.[1]

13 But if she is a widow or divorced and has no son to support her, and has returned home to her father's household, she may eat of her father's food again. But otherwise, no one who is not in the priestly families may eat this food.

14 If someone should eat of the holy sacrifices without realizing it, he shall return to the priest the amount he has used, with twenty per cent added;

15 For the holy sacrifices brought by the people of Israel must not be defiled by being eaten by unauthorized persons, for these sacrifices have been offered to the Lord.

16 Anyone who violates this law is guilty and is in great danger because he has eaten the sacred offerings; for I am Jehovah who sanctifies the offerings."

17, 18 And the Lord said to Moses, "Tell Aaron and his sons and all the people of Israel that if an Israelite or other person living among you offers a burnt offering sacrifice to the Lord—whether it is to fulfill a promise or is a spontaneous free will offering—

19 It will only be acceptable to the Lord if it is a

---

[1] Literally, "the elevation of the holy things."

male animal without defect; it must be a young bull or a sheep or a goat.

20 Anything that has a defect must not be offered, for it will not be accepted.

21 Anyone sacrificing a peace offering to the Lord from the herd or flock, whether to fulfill a vow or as a voluntary offering, must sacrifice an animal that has no defect, or it will not be accepted:

22 An animal that is blind or disabled or mutilated, or which has sores or itch or any other skin disease, must not be offered to the Lord; it is not a fit burnt offering for the altar of the Lord.

23 If the young bull or lamb presented to the Lord has anything superfluous or lacking in its body parts, it may be offered as a free will offering, but not for a vow.

24 An animal that has injured genitals—crushed or castrated—shall not be offered to the Lord at any time.

25 This restriction applies to the sacrifices made by foreigners among you as well as those made by yourselves, for no defective animal is acceptable for this sacrifice."

26, 27 And the Lord said to Moses, "When a bullock, sheep, or goat is born, it shall be left with its mother for seven days, but from the eighth day onward it is acceptable as a sacrifice by fire to the Lord.

28 You shall not slaughter a mother animal and her offspring the same day, whether she is a cow or ewe.

29, 30 When you offer the Lord a sacrifice of thanksgiving, you must do it in the right way, eating the sacrificial animal the same day it is slain. Leave none of it for the following day. I am the Lord.

31　You must keep all of My commandments, for I am the Lord.

32, 33　You must not treat Me as common and ordinary. Revere Me and hallow Me, for I, the Lord, made you holy to Myself and rescued you from Egypt to be My own people! I am the Lord!"

CHAPTER 23

The Lord said to Moses, "Announce to the people of Israel that they are to celebrate several annual festivals of the Lord—times when all Israel will assemble and worship Me.

3　(These are in addition to your Sabbaths[1]—the seventh day of every week—which are always days of solemn rest in every home, times for assembling to worship, and for resting from the normal business of the week.)

4　These are the holy festivals which are to be observed each year:

5　*The Passover of the Lord:* This is to be celebrated at the end of March.[2]

6　*The Festival of Unleavened Bread:* This is to be celebrated beginning the day following the Passover.

7　On the first day of this festival, you shall gather the people for worship, and all ordinary work shall cease.[3]

8　You shall do the same on the seventh day of the festival. On each of the intervening days you shall make an offering by fire to the Lord.

9, 10, 11　*The Festival of First Fruits:* When you

---

[1]Implied.
[2]Literally, "on the fourteenth day of the first month" (of the Hebrew calendar).
[3]Literally, "you shall do no hard work."

arrive in the land I will give you and reap your first harvest, bring the first sheaf of the harvest to the priest on the day after the Sabbath. He shall wave it before the Lord in a gesture of offering, and it will be accepted by the Lord as your gift.

12   That same day you shall sacrifice to the Lord a male yearling lamb without defect as a burnt offering.

13   A grain offering shall accompany it, consisting of a fifth of a bushel of finely ground flour mixed with olive oil, to be offered by fire to the Lord; this will be very pleasant to Him. Also offer a drink offering consisting of three pints of wine.

14   Until this is done you must not eat any of the harvest for yourselves—neither fresh kernels nor bread nor parched grain. This is a permanent law throughout your nation.

15, 16   *The Festival of Pentecost:* Fifty days later you shall bring to the Lord an offering of a sample of the new grain of your later crops.

17   This shall consist of two loaves of bread from your homes to be waved before the Lord in a gesture of offering. Bake this bread from a fifth of a bushel of fine flour containing yeast. It is an offering to the Lord of the first sampling of your later crops.[4]

18   Along with the bread and the wine, you shall sacrifice as burnt offerings to the Lord seven yearling lambs without defects, one young bull, and two rams. All are fire offerings, very acceptable to Jehovah.[5]

19   And you shall offer one male goat for a sin offering, and two male yearling lambs for a peace offering.

---

[4]Literally, "as first fruits to the Lord."
[5]Literally, "of a sweet odor to the Lord."

20 The priests shall wave these offerings before the Lord along with the loaves representing the first sampling of your later crops. They are holy to the Lord, and will be given to the priests as food.

21 That day shall be announced as a time of sacred convocation of all the people; don't do any work that day. This is a law to be honored from generation to generation.

22 (When you reap your harvests, you must not thoroughly reap all the corners of the fields, nor pick up the fallen grain; leave it for the poor and for foreigners living among you who have no land of their own; I am Jehovah your God!)

23, 24 *The Festival of Trumpets:* Mid-September[6] is a solemn time for all the people to meet together for worship; it is a time of remembrance, and is to be announced by loud blowing of trumpets.

25 Don't do any work on the day of the celebration, but offer a sacrifice by fire to the Lord.

26, 27 *The Day of Atonement* follows nine days later:[7] all the people are to come together before the Lord, saddened by their sin; and they shall offer sacrifices by fire to the Lord.

28 Don't do any work that day, for it is a special day for making atonement before the Lord your God.

29 Anyone who does not spend the day in repentance and sorrow for sin shall be excommunicated from his people.

30, 31 And I will put to death anyone who does any kind of work that day. This is a law of Israel from generation to generation.

---

[6]Literally, "the first day of the seventh month" (of the Hebrew calendar).
[7]Literally, "on the tenth day of the seventh month" (of the Hebrew calendar).

32 For this is a Sabbath of solemn rest, and in it you shall humble your souls and be filled with remorse; this time for atonement begins on the previous evening and goes on until the next evening.

33, 34 *The Festival of Tabernacles:* Five days later, on the last day of September,[8] is the Festival of Shelters[9] to be celebrated before the Lord for seven days.

35 On the first day there will be a sacred assembly of all the people; don't do any hard work that day.

36 On each of the seven days of the festival you are to sacrifice an offering by fire to the Lord. The eighth day requires another sacred convocation of all the people, at which time there will again be an offering by fire to the Lord. It is a joyous celebration, and no heavy work is permitted.

37 (These, then, are the regular annual festivals— sacred convocations of all people—when offerings to the Lord are to be made by fire.

38 These annual festivals are in addition to your regular weekly days of holy rest. The sacrifices made during the festivals are to be in addition to your regular giving and normal fulfillment of your vows.)

39 This last day of September, at the end of your harvesting, is the time to celebrate this seven-day festival before the Lord. Remember that the first and last days of the festival are days of solemn rest.

40 On the first day, take boughs of fruit trees laden with fruit, and palm fronds, and the boughs of leafy trees—such as willows that grow by the brooks—and

---

[8]Literally, "on the fifteenth day of the seventh month" (of the Hebrew calendar).
[9]Or, "Feast of Tabernacles."

[build shelters with them[10]], rejoicing before the Lord your God for seven days.

41 This seven-day annual feast is a law from generation to generation.

42 During those seven days, all of you who are native Israelites are to live in these shelters.

43 The purpose of this is to remind the people of Israel, generation after generation, that I rescued you from Egypt, and caused you to live in shelters. I am Jehovah your God."

44 So Moses announced these annual festivals of the Lord to the people of Israel.

CHAPTER 24

The Lord said to Moses, "Tell the people of Israel to bring you pure olive oil for an eternal flame

3, 4 In the lampstand of pure gold which stands outside the veil that secludes the Holy of Holies. Each morning and evening Aaron shall supply it with fresh oil and trim the wicks. It will be an eternal flame before the Lord from generation to generation.

5-8 Every Sabbath day the High Priest shall place twelve loaves of bread in two rows upon the golden table that stands before the Lord. These loaves shall be baked from finely ground flour, using a fifth of a bushel for each. Pure frankincense shall be sprinkled along each row. This will be a memorial offering made by fire to the Lord, in memory of His everlasting covenant with the people of Israel.

9 The bread shall be eaten by Aaron and his sons, in a place set apart for the purpose. For these are offerings made by fire to the Lord under a perma-

---

[10]Implied.

nent law of God, and are most holy."

10   Out in the camp one day, a young man whose mother was an Israelite and whose father was an Egyptian, got into a fight with one of the men of Israel.

11   During the fight the Egyptian man's son[1] cursed God,[2] and was brought to Moses for judgment. (His mother's name was Shelomith, daughter of Dibri of the tribe of Dan.)

12   He was put in jail until the Lord would indicate what to do with him.

13, 14   And the Lord said to Moses, "Take him outside the camp and tell all who heard him to lay their hands upon his head; then all the people are to execute him by stoning.

15, 16   And tell the people of Israel that anyone who curses his God must pay the penalty: he must die. All the congregation shall stone him; this law applies to the foreigner as well as to the Israelite who blasphemes the name of Jehovah. He must die.

17   Also, all murderers must be executed.

18   Anyone who kills an animal [that isn't his[3]] shall replace it.[4]

19   The penalty for injuring anyone is to be injured in exactly the same way:

20   Fracture for fracture, eye for eye, tooth for tooth. Whatever anyone does to another shall be done to him.

21   To repeat, whoever kills an animal must replace it, and whoever kills a man must die.

22   You shall have the same law for the foreigner as

---

[1]Literally, "the Israelite woman's son."
[2]Literally, "blasphemed the Name."
[3]Implied.
[4]Literally, "shall make it good life for life."

for the home-born citizen, for I am Jehovah your God."

23   So they took the youth out of the camp and stoned him until he died, as Jehovah had commanded Moses.

CHAPTER 25

While Moses was on Mount Sinai, the Lord gave him these instructions for the people of Israel: "When you come into the land I am going to give you, you must let the land rest before the Lord every seventh year.

3   For six years you may sow your field and prune your vineyards and harvest your crops,

4   But during the seventh year the land is to lie fallow before the Lord, uncultivated. Don't sow your crops and don't prune your vineyards during that entire year.

5   Don't even reap for yourself the volunteer crops that come up, and don't gather the grapes for yourself; for it is a year of rest for the land.

6, 7   Any crops that do grow that year shall be free to all—for you, your servants, your slaves, and any foreigners living among you. Cattle and wild animals alike shall be allowed to graze there.

8   Every fiftieth year,

9   On the Day of Atonement,[1] let the trumpets blow loud and long throughout the land.

10   For the fiftieth year shall be holy, a time to proclaim liberty throughout the land to all enslaved debtors, and a time for the canceling of all public and private debts. It shall be a year when all the family

---

[1]Literally, "the tenth day of the seventh month" (of the Hebrew calendar).

estates sold to others shall be returned to the original owners or their heirs.

11   What a happy year it will be! In it you shall not sow, nor gather crops nor grapes;

12   For it is a holy Year of Jubilee for you. That year your food shall be the volunteer crops that grow wild in the fields.

13   Yes, during the Year of Jubilee everyone shall return home to his original family possession; if he has sold it, it shall be his again!

14, 15, 16   Because of this, if the land is sold or bought during the preceding forty-nine years, a fair price shall be arrived at by counting the number of years until the Jubilee. If the Jubilee is many years away, the price will be high; if few years, the price will be low; for what you are really doing is selling the number of crops the new owner will get from the land before it is returned to you.

17, 18   You must fear your God and not over-charge! For I am Jehovah. Obey My laws if you want to live safely in the land.

19   When you obey, the land will yield bumper crops and you can eat your fill in safety.

20   But you will ask, 'What shall we eat the seventh year, since we are not allowed to plant or harvest crops that year?'

21, 22   The answer is, 'I will bless you with bumper crops the sixth year that will last you until the crops of the eighth year are harvested!'

23   And remember, the land is Mine, so you may not sell it permanently. You are merely My tenants and sharecroppers!

24   In every contract of sale there must be a stipu-

lation that the land can be redeemed at any time by the seller.

25 If anyone becomes poor and sells some of his land, then his nearest relatives may redeem it.

26 If there is no one else to redeem it, and he himself gets together enough money,

27 Then he may always buy it back at a price proportionate to the number of harvests until the Jubilee, and the owner must accept the money and return the land to him.

28 But if the original owner is not able to redeem it, then it shall belong to the new owner until the Year of Jubilee; but at the Jubilee year it must be returned again.

29 If a man sells a house in the city,[2] he has up to one year to redeem it, with full right of redemption during that time.

30 But if it is not redeemed within the year, then it will belong permanently to the new owner—it does not return to the original owner in the Year of Jubilee.

31 But village houses—a village is a settlement without fortifying walls around it—are like farmland, redeemable at any time, and are always returned to the original owner in the Year of Jubilee.

32 There is one exception: the homes of the Levites, even though in walled cities, may be redeemed at any time,

33 And must be returned to the original owners in the Year of Jubilee; for the Levites will not be given farmland like the other tribes, but will receive only houses in their cities, and the surrounding fields.[3]

---

[2]Literally, "in a walled city."
[3]Implied.

34   The Levites are not permitted to sell the fields of common land surrounding their cities, for these are their permanent possession, and they must belong to no one else.

35   If your brother becomes poor, you are responsible to help him; invite him to live with you as a guest in your home.

36   Fear your God and let your brother live with you; and don't charge him interest on the money you lend him.

37   Remember—no interest; and give him what he needs, at your cost: don't try to make a profit!

38   For I, the Lord your God, brought you out of the land of Egypt to *give* you the land of Canaan, and to be your God.

39   If a fellow Israelite becomes poor and sells himself to you, you must not treat him as an ordinary slave,

40   But rather as a hired servant or as a guest; and he shall serve you only until the Year of Jubilee.

41   At that time he can leave with his children, and return to his own family and possessions.

42   For I brought you from the land of Egypt, and you are My servants; so you may not be sold as ordinary slaves,

43   Or treated harshly; fear your God.

44   However, you may purchase slaves from the foreign nations living around you,

45   And you may purchase the children of the foreigners living among you, even though they have been born in your land.

46   They will be permanent slaves for you to pass on to your children after you; but your brothers, the

people of Israel, shall not be treated so.

47 If a foreigner living among you becomes rich, and an Israelite becomes poor and sells himself to the foreigner or to the foreigner's family,

48 He may be redeemed by one of his brothers,

49 His uncle, nephew, or anyone else who is a near relative. He may also redeem himself if he can find the money.

50 The price of his freedom shall be in proportion to the number of years left before the Year of Jubilee— whatever it would cost to hire a servant for that number of years.

51 If there are still many years until the Jubilee, he shall pay almost the amount he received when he sold himself;

52 If the years have passed and only a few remain until the Jubilee, then he will repay only a small part of the amount he received when he sold himself.

53 If he sells himself to a foreigner, the foreigner must treat him as a hired servant rather than as a slave or as property.

54 If he has not been redeemed by the time the Year of Jubilee arrives, then he and his children shall be freed at that time.

55 For the people of Israel are *My* servants; I brought them from the land of Egypt; I am the Lord your God.

CHAPTER 26

You must have no idols: you must never worship carved images, obelisks, or shaped stones, for I am the Lord your God.

2 You must obey My Sabbath laws of rest, and

reverence My Tabernacle, for I am the Lord.

3   If you obey all of My commandments,

4, 5   I will give you regular rains, and the land will yield bumper crops, and the trees will be loaded with fruit long after the normal time![1] And grapes will still be ripening when sowing time comes again. You shall eat your fill, and live safely in the land,

6   For I will give you peace, and you will go to sleep without fear. I will chase away the dangerous animals.

7   You will chase your enemies; they will die beneath your swords.

8   Five of you will chase a hundred, and a hundred of you, ten thousand! You will defeat all of your enemies.

9   I will look after you, and multiply you, and fulfill My covenant with you.

10   You will have such a surplus of crops that you won't know what to do with them when the new harvest is ready!

11   And I will live among you, and not despise you.

12   I will walk among you and be your God, and you shall be My people.

13   For I am the Lord your God who brought you out of the land of Egypt, with the intention that you be slaves no longer; I have broken your chains and will make you walk with dignity.[2]

14   But if you will not listen to Me or obey Me,

15   But reject My laws,

16   This is what I will do to you: I will punish you with sudden terrors and panic, and with tuberculosis

---

[1]Literally, "until the grape harvest."
[2]Literally, "and made you go upright."

and burning fever; your eyes shall be consumed and your life shall ebb away; you will sow your crops in vain, for your enemies will eat them.

17   I will set My face against you and you will flee before your attackers; those who hate you will rule you; you will even run when no one is chasing you!

18   And if you still disobey Me, I will punish you seven times more severely for your sins.

19   I will break your proud power and make your heavens as iron, and your earth as bronze.

20   Your strength shall be spent in vain; for your land shall not yield its crops, nor your trees their fruit.

21   And if even then you will not obey Me and listen to Me, I will send you seven times more plagues because of your sins.

22   I will send wild animals to kill your children and destroy your cattle and reduce your numbers so that your roads will be deserted.

23   And if even this will not reform you, but you continue to walk against My wishes,

24   Then I will walk against your wishes, and I, even I, will personally smite you seven times for your sin.

25   I will revenge the breaking of My covenant by bringing war against you. You will flee to your cities, and I will send a plague among you there; and you will be conquered by your enemies.

26   I will destroy your food supply so that one oven will be large enough to bake all the bread available for ten entire families; and you will still be hungry after your pittance has been doled out to you.

27   And if you still won't listen to Me or obey Me,

28   Then I will let loose My great anger and send

you seven times greater punishment for your sins.

29   You shall eat your own sons and daughters,

30   And I will destroy the altars on the hills where you worship your idols, and I will cut down your incense altars, leaving your dead bodies to rot among your idols; and I will abhor you.

31   I will make your cities desolate, and destroy your places of worship, and will not respond to your incense offerings.

32   Yes, I will desolate your land; your enemies shall live in it, utterly amazed at what I have done to you.

33   I will scatter you out among the nations, destroying you with war as you go. Your land shall be desolate and your cities destroyed.

34, 35   Then at last the land will rest and make up for the many years you refused to let it lie idle; for it will lie desolate all the years that you are captives in enemy lands. Yes, then the land will rest and enjoy its Sabbaths! It will make up for the rest you didn't give it every seventh year when you lived upon it.

36   And for those who are left alive, I will cause them to be dragged away to distant lands as prisoners of war, and slaves. There they will live in constant fear. The sound of a leaf driven in the wind will send them fleeing as though chased by a man with a sword; they shall fall when no one is pursuing them.

37   Yes, though none pursue they shall stumble over each other in flight, as though fleeing in battle, with no power to stand before their enemies.

38   You shall perish among the nations and be destroyed among your enemies.

39   Those left shall pine away in enemy lands be-

cause of their sins, the same sins as those of their fathers.

40, 41 But at last they shall confess their sins and their fathers' sins of treachery against Me. (Because they were against Me, I was against them, and brought them into the land of their enemies.) When at last their evil hearts are humbled and they accept the punishment I send them for their sins,

42 Then I will remember again My promises to Abraham, Isaac, and Jacob, and I will remember the land (and its desolation).

43 For the land shall enjoy its Sabbaths as it lies desolate. But then at last they shall accept their punishment for rejecting My laws and for despising My rule.

44 But despite all they have done, I will not utterly destroy them and My covenant with them, for I am Jehovah their God.

45 For their sakes I will remember My promises to their ancestors, to be their God. For I brought their forefathers out of Egypt as all the nations watched in wonder. I am Jehovah."

46 These were the laws, ordinances, and instructions that Jehovah gave to the people of Israel, through Moses, on Mount Sinai.

CHAPTER 27

The Lord said to Moses, "Tell the people of Israel that when a person makes a special vow to give himself to the Lord, he shall give these payments instead:

3 A man from the age of twenty to sixty shall pay twenty-five dollars;[1]

4 A woman from the age of twenty to sixty shall pay fifteen dollars;

5 A boy from five to twenty shall pay ten dollars; a girl, five dollars.

6 A boy one month to five years old shall have paid for him two and a half dollars; a girl, one and a half dollars.

7 A man over sixty shall pay seven and a half dollars; a woman, five dollars.

8 But if the person is too poor to pay this amount, he shall be brought to the priest and the priest shall talk it over with him, and he shall pay as the priest shall decide.

9 But if it is an animal that is vowed to be given to the Lord as a sacrifice, it must be given.

10 The vow may not be changed; the donor may neither change his mind about giving it to the Lord, nor substitute good for bad or bad for good; if he does, both the first and the second shall belong to the Lord!

11, 12 But if the animal given to the Lord is not a kind that is permitted as a sacrifice, the owner shall bring it to the priest to value it, and he shall be told how much to pay instead.

13 If the animal is a kind that may be offered as a sacrifice,[2] but the man wants to redeem it, then he shall pay twenty per cent more than the value set by the priest.

14, 15 If someone donates his home to the Lord

---

[1]Note: The actual value by today's standards is uncertain. The above figures are approximate.
[2]Implied.

and then wishes to redeem it, the priest will decide its value and the man shall pay that amount plus twenty per cent, and the house will be his again.

16 If a man dedicates any part of his field to the Lord, value it in proportion to its size, as indicated by the amount of seed required to sow it. A section of land that requires ten bushels of barley seed for sowing is valued at twenty-five dollars.

17 If a man dedicates his field in the Year of Jubilee, then the whole estimate shall stand;

18 But if it is after the Year of Jubilee, then the value shall be in proportion to the number of years remaining until the next Year of Jubilee.

19 If the man decides to redeem the field, he shall pay twenty per cent in addition to the priest's valuation, and the field will be his again.

20 But if he decides not to redeem the field, or if he has sold the field to someone else [and has given to the Lord his rights to it at the Year of Jubilee[3]], it shall not be returned to him again.

21 When it is freed in the Year of Jubilee, it shall belong to the Lord as a field devoted to Him, and it shall be given to the priests.

22 If a man dedicates to the Lord a field he has bought, but which is not part of his family possession,

23 The priest shall estimate the value until the Year of Jubilee, and he shall immediately give that estimated value to the Lord,

24 And in the Year of Jubilee the field shall return to the original owner from whom it was bought.

---

[3]Implied.

25 All the valuations shall be stated in standard money.[4]

26 You may not dedicate to the Lord the firstborn of any ox or sheep, for it is already His.

27 But if it is the firstborn of an animal that cannot be sacrificed because it is not on the list of those acceptable to the Lord, then the owner shall pay the priest's estimate of its worth, plus twenty per cent; or if the owner does not redeem it, the priest may sell it to someone else.

28 However, anything utterly devoted to the Lord —people, animals, or inherited fields—shall not be sold or redeemed, for they are most holy to the Lord.

29 No one sentenced by the courts to die may pay a fine instead; he shall surely be put to death.[5]

30 A tenth of the produce of the land, whether grain or fruit, is the Lord's, and is holy.

31 If anyone wants to buy back this fruit or grain, he must add a fifth to its value.

32 And the Lord owns every tenth animal of your herds and flocks and other domestic animals, as they pass by for counting.

33 The tenth given to the Lord shall not be selected on the basis of whether it is good or bad, and there shall be no substitutions; for if there is any change made, then both the original and the substitution shall belong to the Lord, and may not be bought back!"

34 These are the commandments the Lord gave to Moses for the people of Israel on Mount Sinai.

---

[4]Literally, "and all your estimations shall be according to the shekel of the sanctuary: twenty gerahs shall be the shekel."
[5]Literally, "no one who is under the ban of God to be put to death, may be ransomed."

Numbers

CHAPTER 1

I t was on the fifteenth day of April[1] of the second year after the Israeli left Egypt that the Lord issued the following instructions to Moses. (He was in the Tabernacle at the camp of Israel on the Sinai peninsula at the time.)

2, 3, 4 "Take a census of all the men twenty years old and older who are able to go to war, indicating their tribe and family. You and Aaron are to direct the project, assisted by leaders from each tribe:"

	TRIBE	LEADER
5	Reuben	Elizur (son of Shedeur)
6	Simeon	Shelumi-el (son of Zuri-shaddai)
7	Judah	Nahshon (son of Amminadab)
8	Issachar	Nethanel (son of Zuar)
9	Zebulun	Eliab (son of Helon)
10	Ephraim (son of Joseph)	Elishama (son of Ammihud)

---

[1]Literally, "on the first day of the second month" (of the Jewish calendar).

	TRIBE	LEADER
	Manasseh (son of Joseph)	Gamaliel (son of Pedahzur)
11	Benjamin	Abidan (son of Gideoni)
12	Dan	Ahiezer (son of Ammishaddai)
13	Asher	Pagiel (son of Ochran)
14	Gad	Eliasaph (son of Deuel)
15	Naphtali	Ahira (son of Enan)

16 These were the tribal leaders elected from among the people.

17, 18, 19 On that same day[2] Moses and Aaron and the above-named leaders summoned all the men of Israel who were twenty years old or older to come and register, each man indicating his tribe and family, as the Lord had commanded Moses.[3]

20, 21 Here is the final tabulation:

	TRIBE	TOTAL
	Reuben (the oldest son of Jacob)	46,500
22, 23	Simeon	59,300
24, 25	Gad	45,650
26, 27	Judah	74,600
28, 29	Issachar	54,400
30, 31	Zebulun	57,400

---

[2]Literally, "on the first day of the second month" (of the Jewish calendar).
[3]Added in the Hebrew text is this sentence: "So he numbered them in the wilderness of Sinai."

32, 33	Joseph: Ephraim (son of Joseph)	40,500
34, 35	Joseph: Manasseh (son of Joseph)	32,200
36, 37	Benjamin	35,400
38, 39	Dan	62,700
40, 41	Asher	41,500
42, 43	Naphtali	53,400

44, 45, 46   Grand Total: 603,550

47, 48, 49   This total does not include the Levites, for the Lord had said to Moses, "Exempt the entire tribe of Levi from the draft, and do not include their number in the census.

50   For the Levites are assigned for the work connected with the Tabernacle and its transportation. They are to live near the Tabernacle,

51   And whenever the Tabernacle is moved, the Levites are to take it down and set it up again; anyone else touching it shall be executed.

52   Each tribe of Israel shall have a separate camping area with its own flag.

53   The Levites' tents shall be clustered around the Tabernacle as a wall between the people of Israel and God's wrath—to protect them from His fierce anger against their sins."

54   So all these instructions of the Lord to Moses were put into effect.

CHAPTER 2

The Lord gave these further instructions to Moses and Aaron: "Each tribe will have its own tent area, with its flagpole and tribal banner; and at the center of these tribal compounds will be the Tabernacle."

3, 4   Here are the tribal locations:[1]

TRIBE:	LEADER:	LOCATION:	CENSUS:
Judah	Nahshon (son of Amminadab)	East side of the Tabernacle	74,600
5, 6 Issachar	Nethanel (son of Zuar)	Next to Judah	54,400
7, 8 Zebulun	Eliab (son of Helon)	Next to Issachar	57,400

9   So the total of all those on Judah's side of the camp was 186,400. These three tribes led the way whenever the Israelites traveled to a new campsite.

10, 11	Reuben	Elizur (son of Shedeur)	South side of the Tabernacle	46,500
12, 13	Simeon	Shelumi-el (son of Zurishaddai)	Next to Reuben	59,300
14, 15	Gad	Eliasaph (son of Reuel[2])	Next to Simeon	45,650

16   So the total of the Reuben side of the camp was 151,450. These three tribes were next in line whenever the Israeli traveled.

---

[1] Implied.
[2] Deuel in chapter 1.

17 Next in the line of march was the Tabernacle, with the Levites. When traveling, each tribe stayed together under its own flag, just as each was separate from the others in camp.

18, 19	Ephraim	Elishama (son of Ammihud)	West side of Tabernacle	40,500
20, 21	Manasseh	Gamaliel (son of Pedahzur)	Next to Ephraim	32,200
22, 23	Benjamin	Abidan (son of Gideoni)	Next to Manasseh	35,400

24 So the total on the Ephraim side of the camp was 108,100, and they were next in the line of march.

25, 26	Dan	Ahiezer (son of Ammi-shaddai)	North side of Tabernacle	62,700
27, 28	Asher	Pagiel (son of Ochran)	Next to Dan	41,500
29, 30	Naphtali	Ahira (son of Enan)	Next to Asher	53,400

31 So the total on Dan's side of the camp was 157,600. They brought up the rear whenever Israel traveled.

32, 33 In summary, the armies of Israel totalled 603,550 (not including the Levites, who were exempted by Jehovah's commandment to Moses).

34　So the people of Israel set up their camps, each tribe under its own banner, in the locations indicated by the Lord to Moses.

CHAPTER 3

A t the time when the Lord spoke to Moses on Mount Sinai,

2　Aaron's[1] sons were:

> Nadab (his oldest),
> Abihu,
> Eleazar,
> Ithamar.

3　All were anointed as priests and set apart to minister at the Tabernacle.

4　But Nadab and Abihu died before the Lord in the wilderness of Sinai when they used unholy fire. And since they had no children, this left only Eleazar and Ithamar to assist their father Aaron.

5　Then the Lord said to Moses,

6　"Summon the tribe of Levi and present them to Aaron as his assistants.

7, 8, 9　They will follow his instructions and perform the sacred duties at the Tabernacle on behalf of all the people of Israel. For they are assigned to him as representatives of all the people of Israel. They are in charge of all the furnishings and maintenance of the Tabernacle.

10　However, only Aaron and his sons may carry out the duties of the priesthood; anyone else who presumes to assume this office shall be executed."

11, 12　And the Lord said to Moses, "I have accepted the Levites in substitution for all the oldest sons

[1] Literally, "these are the generations of Aaron and Moses."

of the people of Israel. The Levites are Mine

13   In exchange for all the oldest sons. From the day I killed all the oldest sons of the Egyptians, I took for Myself all the firstborn in Israel of both men and animals! They are Mine, for I am Jehovah."

14, 15   The Lord now spoke again to Moses at the Sinai peninsula, telling him, "Take a census of the tribe of Levi, indicating each person's clan; count every male down to one month old."

16   So Moses did:

	Levi's sons	*Levi's*	*Census*	*Leader*	*Camp*
17-24	GERSHON	*grand-sons*	7,500	Elisaph	*Location*
		(clan names)		(son of Lael)	West side of the Tabernacle
		Libni			
		Shime-i			

25, 26   *Responsibilities:*
    The responsibility of these two clans of Levites was the care of the Tabernacle: its coverings, its entry drapes, the drapes covering the fence surrounding the courtyard, the screen at the entrance of the courtyard surrounding the Tabernacle, the altar, and all the ropes used in tying the Tabernacle together.

27-30	KOHATH	Amram	8,600	Eliza-phan	South side of the Tabernacle
		Izhar		(son of Uzziel)	
		Hebron			
		Uzziel			

31   *Responsibilities:*
    The responsibility of these four clans of Levites was the care of the Ark, the table, the lampstand, the altars, the various utensils used in the Tabernacle, the

veil, and any repairs needed on any of these items.

32 (Note: Eleazar, Aaron's son, shall be the chief administrator over the leaders of the Levites, with special responsibility for the oversight of the sanctuary.)

33-35	MERARI	Mahli	6,200	Zuriel	North side
		Mushi		(son of	of the
				Abihail)	Tabernacle

36, 37 *Responsibilities:*

The responsibility of these two clans was the care of the frames of the Tabernacle building; the posts; the bases for the posts, and all of the equipment needed for their use; the posts around the courtyard and their bases, pegs, and ropes.

38 The area east of the Tabernacle was reserved for the tents of Moses and of Aaron and his sons, who had the final responsibility for the Tabernacle on behalf of the people of Israel. (Anyone who was not a priest or Levite, but came into the Tabernacle, was to be executed.)

39 So all the Levites, as numbered by Moses and Aaron at the command of the Lord, were 22,000 males a month old and older.

40 Then the Lord said to Moses, "Now take a census of all the eldest sons in Israel who are a month old and older, and register each name.

41 The Levites shall be Mine (I am Jehovah) as substitutes for the eldest sons of Israel; and the Levites' cattle are Mine as substitutes for the firstborn cattle of the whole nation."

42 So Moses took a census of the eldest sons of the people of Israel, as the Lord had commanded,

43   And found the total number of eldest sons a month old and older to be 22,273.

44   Now the Lord said to Moses,

45   "Give Me the Levites instead of the eldest sons of the people of Israel; and give Me the cattle of the Levites instead of the firstborn cattle of the people of Israel; yes, the Levites shall be Mine; I am Jehovah.

46   To redeem the 273 eldest sons in excess of the number of Levites,

47, 48   Pay five dollars[2] for each one to Aaron and his sons."

49   So Moses received redemption money for the 273 eldest sons of Israel who were in excess of the number of Levites. (All the others were redeemed because the Levites had been given to the Lord in their place.)

50   The money collected came to a total of $1,365.[3]

51   And Moses gave it to Aaron and his sons as the Lord had commanded.

CHAPTER 4

Then the Lord said to Moses and Aaron, "Take a census of the Kohath division of the Levite tribe.

3   This census will be of all males from ages thirty to fifty who are able to work in the Tabernacle.

4   These are their sacred duties:

5   When the camp moves, Aaron and his sons will enter the Tabernacle first and take down the veil and cover the Ark with it.

6   Then they will cover the veil with goatskin leather, cover the goatskins with a blue cloth, and

---

[2]Literally, "five shekels apiece by the polls; after the shekel of the sanctuary shalt thou take them. (The shekel is twenty gerahs.)"
[3]Literally, "1,365 shekels after the shekel of the sanctuary."

place the carrying poles of the Ark in their rings.

7 Next they must spread a blue cloth over the table where the Bread of the Presence is displayed, and place the dishes, spoons, bowls, cups, and the Bread upon the cloth.

8 They will spread a scarlet cloth over that, and finally a covering of goatskin leather on top of the scarlet cloth. Then they shall insert the carrying poles into the table.

9 Next they must cover with a blue cloth the lampstand, the lamps, snuffers, trays, and the reservoir of olive oil.

10 This entire group of objects shall then be covered with goatskin leather, and the bundle shall be placed upon a carrying frame.

11 They must then spread a blue cloth over the gold altar, cover it with a covering of goatskin leather, and insert the carrying poles into the altar.

12 All of the remaining utensils of the Tabernacle are to be wrapped in a blue cloth, covered with goatskin leather, and placed on the carrying frame.

13 The ashes are to be removed from the altar, and the altar shall be covered with a purple cloth.

14 All of the altar utensils are to be placed upon the cloth—the firepans, hooks, shovels, basins, and other containers—and a cover of goatskin leather will be spread over them. Finally, the carrying poles are to be put in place.

15 When Aaron and his sons have finished packing the sanctuary and all the utensils, the clan of Kohath shall come and carry the units to wherever the camp is traveling; but they must not touch the holy items,

lest they die. This, then, is the sacred work of the sons of Kohath.

16 Aaron's son Eleazar shall be responsible for the oil for the light, the sweet incense, the daily grain offering, and the anointing oil—in fact, the supervision of the entire Tabernacle and everything in it will be his responsibility."

17, 18, 19 Then the Lord said to Moses and Aaron, "Don't let the families of Kohath destroy themselves! This is what you must do so that they will not die when they carry the most holy things: Aaron and his sons shall go in with them and point out what each is to carry.

20 Otherwise they must never enter the sanctuary for even a moment, lest they look at the sacred objects there and die."

21, 22, 23 And the Lord said to Moses, "Take a census of the Gershonite division of the tribe of Levi, all of the men between the ages of thirty and fifty who are eligible for the sacred work of the Tabernacle.

24 These will be their duties:

25 They will carry the curtains of the Tabernacle, the Tabernacle itself with its coverings, the goatskin leather roof, and the curtain for the Tabernacle entrance.

26 They are also to carry the drapes covering the courtyard fence, and the curtain across the entrance to the courtyard that surrounds the altar and the Tabernacle. They will also carry the altar, the ropes, and all of the accessories. They are fully responsible for the transportation of these items.

27 Aaron or any of his sons may assign the Gershonites' tasks to them,

28 But the Gershonites will be directly responsible to Aaron's son Ithamar.

29 Now take a census of the Merari division of the Levite tribe, all of the men from thirty to fifty who are eligible for the Tabernacle service.

30, 31 When the Tabernacle is moved, they are to carry the frames of the Tabernacle, the bars, the bases,

32 The frames for the courtyard fence with their bases, pegs, cords, and everything else connected with their use and repair.

Assign duties to each man by name.

33 The Merari division will also report to Aaron's son Ithamar."

34 So Moses and Aaron and the other leaders took a census of the Kohath division,

35 Including all of the men thirty to fifty years of age who were eligible for the Tabernacle service,

36 And found that the total number was 2,750.

37 All this was done to carry out the Lord's instructions to Moses.

38-41 A similar census of the Gershon division totaled 2,630.

42-45 And of the Merari division, 3,200.

46, 47, 48 Thus Moses and Aaron and the leaders of Israel found that the total of all the Levites who were thirty to fifty years old and who were eligible for the Tabernacle service and transportation, was 8,580.

49 This census was taken in response to the Lord's instructions to Moses.

CHAPTER 5

These are further instructions from the Lord to Moses: "Inform the people of Israel that they must expel all lepers from the camp, and all who have open sores, or who have been defiled by touching a dead person.

3 This applies to men and women alike. Remove them so that they will not defile the camp where I live among you."

4 These instructions were put into effect.

5, 6 Then the Lord said to Moses, "Tell the people of Israel that when anyone, man or woman, betrays the Lord by betraying a trust, it is sin.

7 He must confess his sin and make full repayment for what he has stolen,[1] adding twenty per cent and returning it to the person he took it from.

8 But if the person he wronged is dead,[2] and there is no near relative to whom the payment can be made, it must be given to the priest, along with a lamb for atonement.

9, 10 When the people of Israel bring a gift to the Lord it shall go to the priests."

11, 12 And the Lord said to Moses, "Tell the people of Israel that if a man's wife commits adultery,

13 But there is no proof, there being no witness,

14 And he is jealous and suspicious,

15 The man shall bring his wife to the priest with an offering for her of a tenth of a bushel of barley meal without oil or frankincense mingled with it—for it is a suspicion offering—to bring out the truth[3] as to

---

[1] Literally, "for his wrong."
[2] Implied.
[3] Literally, "an offering for remembrance."

whether or not she is guilty.

16 The priest shall bring her before the Lord,

17 And take holy water in a clay jar and mix into it dust from the floor of the Tabernacle.

18 He shall unbind her hair and place the suspicion offering in her hands to determine whether or not her husband's suspicions are justified. The priest shall stand before her holding the jar of bitter water that brings a curse.

19 He shall require her to swear that she is innocent, and then he shall say to her, 'If no man has slept with you except your husband, be free from the effects of this bitter water that causes the curse.

20 But if you have committed adultery,

21, 22 Then Jehovah shall make you a curse among your people, for He will make your thigh rot away and your body swell.' And the woman shall be required to say, 'Yes, let it be so.'

23 Then the priest shall write these curses in a book and wash them off into the bitter water.

24 (When he requires the woman to drink the water, it becomes bitter within her [if she is guilty[4]].)

25 Then the priest shall take the suspicion offering from the woman's hand and wave it before Jehovah, and carry it to the altar.

26 He shall take a handful, representing all of it, and burn the handful upon the altar, and then require the woman to drink the water.

27 If she has been defiled, having committed adultery against her husband, the water will become bitter within her, and her body will swell and her thigh will rot, and she shall be a curse among her people.

---

[4]Implied.

28 But if she is pure and has not committed adultery, she shall be unharmed and will soon become pregnant.

29 This, then, is the law concerning a wayward wife—or a husband's suspicions against his wife—

30 To determine whether or not she has been unfaithful to him. He shall bring her before the Lord and the priest shall handle the situation as outlined above.

31 Her husband shall not be brought to trial for causing her horrible disease, for she is responsible."

CHAPTER 6

The Lord gave Moses these further instructions for the people of Israel: "When either a man or a woman takes the special vow of a Nazirite, consecrating himself to the Lord in a special way,

3, 4 He must not thereafter, during the entire period of his special consecration to the Lord, taste strong drink or wine or even fresh wine, grape juice, grapes, or raisins! He may eat nothing that comes from grape vines, not even the seeds or skins!

5 Throughout that time he must never cut his hair, for he is holy and consecrated to the Lord; that is why he must let his hair grow.

6, 7 And he may not go near any dead body during the entire period of his vow, even if it is the body of his father, mother, brother, or sister; for his vow of consecration remains in effect,

8 And he is consecrated to the Lord throughout the entire period.

9 If he is defiled by having someone fall dead beside him, then seven days later he shall shave his

defiled head; he will then be cleansed from the contamination of being in the presence of death.

10 The next day, the eighth day, he must bring two turtledoves or two young pigeons to the priest at the entrance of the Tabernacle.

11 The priest shall offer one of the birds for a sin offering, and the other for a burnt offering, and make atonement for his defilement. And he must renew his vows that day and let his hair begin to grow again.

12 The days of his vow that were fulfilled before his defilement no longer count. He must begin all over again with a new vow, and must bring a male lamb a year old for a guilt offering.

13 At the conclusion of the period of his vow of separation to the Lord, he must go to the entrance of the Tabernacle

14 And offer a burnt sacrifice to the Lord, a year-old lamb without defect. He must also offer a sin offering, a yearling ewe lamb without defect; a peace offering, a ram without defect;

15 A basket of bread made without yeast; pancakes made of fine flour mixed with olive oil; unleavened wafers spread with oil; and the accompanying grain offering and drink offerings.

16 The priest shall present these offerings before the Lord: first the sin offering and the burnt offering;

17 Then the ram for a peace offering, along with the basket of bread made without yeast; and finally the grain offering along with the drink offering.

18 Then the Nazirite shall shave his long hair—the sign of his vow of separation. This shall be done at the entrance of the Tabernacle, after which the hair shall be put in the fire under the peace offering sacrifice.

19 After the man's head has been shaved, the priest shall take the roasted shoulder of the lamb, one of the pancakes (made without yeast), and one of the wafers (also made without yeast), and put them all into the man's hands.

20 The priest shall then wave it all back and forth before the Lord in a gesture of offering; all of it is a holy portion for the priest, as are the rib piece and shoulder that were waved before the Lord. After that the Nazirite may again drink wine, for he is freed from his vow.

21 These are the regulations concerning a Nazirite and his sacrifices at the conclusion of his period of special dedication. In addition to these sacrifices he must bring any further offering he promised at the time he took his vow to become a Nazirite."

22, 23 Now the Lord said to Moses, "Tell Aaron and his sons that they are to give this special blessing to the people of Israel:

24 'May the Lord bless and protect you;

25 May the Lord's face radiate with joy because of you;

    May He be gracious to you,

26 Show you His favor,

    And give you His peace.'

27 This is how Aaron and his sons shall call down My blessings[1] upon the people of Israel; and I Myself will personally bless them."

CHAPTER 7

Moses anointed and sanctified each part of the Tabernacle, including the altar and its utensils, on the day he finished setting it up.

---

[1]Literally, "shall put My name upon the people of Israel."

2   Then the leaders of Israel—the chiefs of the tribes, the men who had organized the census—brought their offerings.

3   They brought six covered wagons, each drawn by two oxen—a wagon for every two leaders and an ox for each one; and they presented them to the Lord in front of the Tabernacle.

4, 5   "Accept their gifts," the Lord told Moses, "and use these wagons for the work of the Tabernacle. Give them to the Levites for whatever needs they may have."

6   So Moses presented the wagons and the oxen to the Levites.

7   Two wagons and four oxen were given to the Gershon division for their use,

8   And four wagons and eight oxen were given to the Merari division, which was under the leadership of Ithamar, Aaron's son.

9   None of the wagons or teams was given to the Kohath division, for they were required to carry their portion of the Tabernacle upon their shoulders.

10   The leaders also presented dedication gifts on the day the altar was anointed, placing them before the altar.

11   The Lord said to Moses, "Let each of them bring his gift on a different day for the dedication of the altar."

12   So Nahshon, the son of Amminadab of the tribe of Judah, brought his gift the first day.

13   It consisted of a silver platter weighing two pounds and a silver bowl of about one pound, both filled with grain offerings of fine flour mixed with oil.

14 He also brought a tiny[1] gold box of incense which weighed only about six ounces.

15 He brought a young bull, a ram, and a male yearling lamb as burnt offerings;

16 A male goat for a sin offering;

17 And for the peace offerings two oxen, five rams, five male goats, and five male yearling lambs.

18-23 The next day Nethanel, the son of Zuar, chief of the tribe of Issachar, brought his gifts and offerings. They were exactly the same as Nahshon had presented on the previous day.[2]

24-29 On the third day Eliab, the son of Helon, chief of the tribe of Zebulun, came with his offerings—the same as those presented on the previous days.[2]

30-35 On the fourth day the gifts were presented by Elizur, son of Shedeur, chief of the tribe of Reuben; his gifts and offerings were the same as those given on the previous days.[2]

36-41 On the fifth day came Shelumi-el, the son of Zuri-shaddai, chief of the tribe of Simeon, with the same gifts.[2]

42-47 The next day it was Eliasaph's turn, son of Deuel, chief of the tribe of Gad. He, too, offered the same gifts and sacrifices.[2]

48-53 On the seventh day, Elishama, the son of Ammihud, chief of the tribe of Ephraim, brought his gifts, the same as those presented on the previous days.[2]

54-59 Gamaliel, son of Pedahzur, prince of the tribe of Manasseh, came the eighth day with the same offerings.[2]

60-65 On the ninth day it was Abidan the son of

[1]Implied.
[2]The original text repeats the lists of the offerings recorded in verses 13 to 17.

Gideoni, chief of the tribe of Benjamin, with his gifts, the same as those offered by the others.[3]

66-71 Ahiezer, the son of Ammishaddai, brought his gifts on the tenth day. He was the chief of the tribe of Dan and his offerings were the same as those on the previous days.[3]

72-77 Pagiel, son of Ochran, chief of the tribe of Asher, brought his gifts on the eleventh day—the same gifts and offerings as the others.[3]

78-83 On the twelfth day came Ahira, son of Enan, chief of the tribe of Naphtali, with his offerings; they were identical to those brought by the others.[3]

84, 85, 86 So, beginning the day the altar was anointed, it was dedicated by these gifts from the chiefs of the tribes of Israel. Their combined offerings were as follows:

> 12 silver platters (each weighing about two pounds);
> 12 silver bowls (each weighing about one pound); (so the total weight of the silver was about thirty-six pounds);
> 12 golden trays (the trays weighing about four ounces apiece); (so the total weight of gold was about three pounds).

87 For the burnt offerings they brought:
> 12 bulls,
> 12 rams,
> 12 yearling male goats (with the grain offerings that accompanied them).

For sin offerings they brought:
> 12 male goats.

---

[3]The original text repeats the lists of the offerings recorded in verses 13 to 17.

88   For the peace offerings they brought:
      24 young bulls,
      60 rams,
      60 male goats,
      60 male lambs a year old.

89   When Moses went into the Tabernacle to speak with God, he heard the Voice speaking to him from above the place of mercy over the Ark, the spot between the two cherubim.

CHAPTER 8

The Lord said to Moses,
2   "Tell Aaron that when he lights the seven lamps in the lampstand, he is to set them so that they will throw their light forward."

3   So Aaron did this.

4   The lampstand, including the floral decorations on the base and branches, was made entirely of beaten gold. It was constructed according to the exact design the Lord had shown Moses.

5, 6   Then the Lord said to Moses, "Now set apart the Levites from the other people of Israel.

7   Do this by sprinkling water of purification upon them, then having them shave their entire bodies and wash their clothing and themselves.

8   Have them bring a young bull and a grain offering of fine flour mingled with oil, along with another young bull for a sin offering.

9   Then bring the Levites to the door of the Tabernacle as all the people watch.

10   There the leaders[1] of the tribes shall lay their hands upon them,

11   And Aaron, with a gesture of offering, shall

[1]Implied.

present them to the Lord as a gift from the entire nation of Israel. The Levites will represent all the people in serving the Lord.

12   Next, the Levite leaders[1] shall lay their hands upon the heads of the young bulls and offer them before the Lord; one for a sin offering and the other for a burnt offering, to make atonement for the Levites.

13   Then the Levites are to be presented to Aaron and his sons, just as any other gift to the Lord is given to the priests!

14   In this way you will dedicate the Levites from among the rest of the people of Israel, and the Levites shall be Mine.

15   After you have sanctified them and presented them in this way, they shall go in and out of the Tabernacle to do their work.

16   They are Mine from among all the people of Israel, and I have accepted them in place of all the firstborn children of the Israelites: I have taken the Levites as their substitutes.

17   For all the firstborn among the people of Israel are Mine, both men and animals; I claimed them for Myself the night I killed all the firstborn Egyptians.

18   Yes, I have accepted the Levites in place of all the eldest sons of Israel.

19   And I will give the Levites as a gift to Aaron and his sons. The Levites will carry out the sacred duties required of the people of Israel in the Tabernacle, and will offer the people's sacrifices, making atonement for them. There will be no plague among the Israelites—as there would be if the ordinary people entered the Tabernacle."

---

[1]Implied.

20 So Moses and Aaron and all the people of Israel dedicated the Levites, carefully following Jehovah's instructions to Moses.

21 The Levites purified themselves and washed their clothes, and Aaron presented them to the Lord in a gesture of offering. He then performed the rite of atonement over them to purify them.

22 After that they went into the Tabernacle as assistants to Aaron and his sons; everything was done just as the Lord had commanded Moses.

23, 24 The Lord also instructed Moses, "The Levites are to begin serving in the Tabernacle at the age of twenty-five, and are to retire at the age of fifty.

25, 26 After retirement they can assist with various light duties in the Tabernacle, but will have no regular responsibilities."

CHAPTER 9

Jehovah gave these instructions to Moses while he and the rest of the Israeli were on the Sinai peninsula, during the first month of the second year after leaving Egypt:

2, 3 "The people of Israel must celebrate the Passover annually on the fourteenth day of this first month,[1] beginning in the evening. Be sure to follow all of My instructions concerning this celebration."

4, 5 So Moses announced that the Passover celebration would begin on the evening of the fourteenth, there in the Sinai peninsula, just as the Lord had commanded.

6, 7 But as it happened, some of the men had

---

[1]Note: The 14th day of the first month of the Hebrew calendar corresponds approximately to our 1st day of April.

just attended a funeral, and were ceremonially defiled by having touched the dead, so they couldn't eat the Passover lamb that night. They came to Moses and Aaron and explained their problem and protested at being forbidden from offering their sacrifice to the Lord at the time He had appointed.

8 Moses said he would ask the Lord about it,

9 And this was God's reply:

10 "If any of the people of Israel, now or in the generations to come, are defiled at Passover time because of touching a dead body, or if they are on a journey and cannot be present, they may still celebrate the Passover, but one month later,

11 On the fourteenth day of the *second* month, beginning in the evening. They are to eat the lamb at that time, with unleavened bread and bitter herbs.

12 They must not leave any of it until the next morning, and must not break a bone of it, and must follow all the regular instructions concerning the Passover.

13 But anyone who is not defiled, and anyone who is not away on a trip, and yet refuses to celebrate the Passover at the regular time, shall be excommunicated from the people of Israel for refusing to sacrifice to Jehovah at the proper time; he must bear his guilt.

14 And if a foreigner is living among you and wants to celebrate the Passover to the Lord, he shall follow all these same instructions. There is one law for all."

15 On the day the Tabernacle was raised, the Cloud covered it; and that evening the Cloud changed to the appearance of fire, and stayed that way throughout the night.

16   It was always so—the daytime Cloud changing to the appearance of fire at night.

17   When the Cloud lifted, the people of Israel moved on to wherever it stopped, and camped there.

18   In this way they journeyed at the command of the Lord and stopped where He told them to, then remained there as long as the Cloud stayed.

19   If it stayed a long time, then they stayed a long time. But if it stayed only a few days, then they remained only a few days; for so the Lord had instructed them.

20, 21   Sometimes the fire-cloud stayed only during the night and moved on the next morning. But day or night, when it moved, the people broke camp and followed.

22   If the Cloud stayed above the Tabernacle two days, a month, or a year, that is how long the people of Israel stayed; but as soon as it moved, they moved.

23   So it was that they camped or traveled at the commandment of the Lord; and whatever the Lord told Moses they should do, they did.

CHAPTER 10

Now the Lord said to Moses, "Make two trumpets of beaten silver to be used for summoning the people to assemble and for signaling the breaking of camp.

3   When both trumpets are blown, the people will know that they are to gather at the entrance of the Tabernacle.

4   But if only one is blown, then only the chiefs of the tribes of Israel shall come to you.

5, 6, 7   Different trumpet blasts will be necessary

to distinguish between the summons to assemble and the signal to break camp and move onward.[1] When the travel signal is blown, the tribes camped on the east side of the Tabernacle shall leave first; at the second signal, the tribes on the south shall go.

8 Only the priests are permitted to blow the trumpets. This is a permanent instruction to be followed from generation to generation.

9 When you arrive in the Promised Land and go to war against your enemies, God will hear you and save you from your enemies when you sound the alarm with these trumpets.

10 Use the trumpets in times of gladness, too, blowing them at your annual festivals and at the beginning of each month to rejoice over your burnt offerings and peace offerings. And God will be reminded of His covenant with you. For I am Jehovah, your God."

11 The Cloud lifted from the Tabernacle on the twentieth day of the second month[2] of the second year of Israel's leaving Egypt;

12 So the Israelites left the Sinai wilderness, and followed the Cloud until it stopped in the wilderness of Paran.

13 This was their first journey after having received the Lord's travel instructions to Moses.

14 At the head of the march was the tribe of Judah grouped behind its flag, and led by Nahshon, the son of Amminadab.

15 Next came the tribe of Issachar, led by Nethanel, the son of Zuar,

---

[1]More literally, verse 7 reads: "But when the Assembly is to be gathered together, you shall blow but you shall not sound the alarm."
[2]Note: This was approximately May 5.

16 And the tribe of Zebulun, led by Eliab, the son of Helon.

17 The Tabernacle was taken down and the men of the Gershon and Merari divisions of the tribe of Levi were next in the line of march, carrying the Tabernacle upon their shoulders.

18 Then came the flag of the camp of Reuben, with Elizur the son of Shedeur leading his people.

19 Next was the tribe of Simeon headed by Shelumi-el, the son of Zuri-shaddai;

20 And the tribe of Gad led by Eliasaph, the son of Deuel.

21 Next came the Kohathites carrying the items from the inner sanctuary. (The Tabernacle was already erected in its new location by the time they arrived.)

22 Next in line was the tribe of Ephraim behind its flag, led by Elishama, the son of Ammihud;

23 And the tribe of Manasseh led by Gamaliel the son of Pedahzur;

24 And the tribe of Benjamin, led by Abidan the son of Gideoni.

25 Last of all were the tribes headed by the flag of the tribe of Dan under the leadership of Ahiezer, the son of Ammishaddai;

26 The tribe of Asher, led by Pagiel, the son of Ochran;

27 And the tribe of Naphtali, led by Ahira, the son of Enan.

28 That was the order in which the tribes traveled.

29 One day Moses said to his brother-in-law Hobab (son of Reuel, the Midianite), "At last we are on our way to the Promised Land. Come with us and

we will do you good; for the Lord has given wonderful promises to Israel!"

30 But his brother-in-law replied, "No, I must return to my own land and kinfolk."

31 "Stay with us," Moses pleaded, "for you know the ways of the wilderness and will be a great help to us.[3]

32 If you come, you will share in all the good things the Lord does for us."

33 They traveled for three days after leaving Mount Sinai,[4] with the Ark at the front of the column to choose a place for them to stop.

34 It was daytime when they left, with the Cloud moving along ahead of them as they began their march.

35 As the Ark was carried forward, Moses cried out, "Arise, O Lord, and scatter Your enemies; let them flee before You."

36 And when the Ark was set down he said, "Return, O Lord, to the millions of Israel."

CHAPTER 11

The people were soon complaining about all their misfortunes, and the Lord heard them. His anger flared out against them because of their complaints, so the fire of the Lord began destroying those at the far end of the camp.

2 They screamed to Moses for help, and when he prayed for them the fire stopped.

3 Ever after, the area was known as "The Place

---

[3]Literally, "you know how we are to encamp in the wilderness, and you will serve as eyes for us."
[4]Literally, "the mount of Jehovah."

of Burning,"[1] because the fire from the Lord burned among them there.

4, 5　Then the Egyptians who had come with them began to long for the good things of Egypt. This added to the discontent of the people of Israel and they wept, "Oh, for a few bites of meat! Oh, that we had some of the delicious fish we enjoyed so much in Egypt, and the wonderful cucumbers and melons, leeks, onions, and garlic!

6　But now our strength is gone, and day after day we have to face this manna!"

7　The manna was about the size of coriander seed, and looked like droplets of gum from the bark of a tree.

8　The people gathered it from the ground and crushed it into flour or pounded it in mortars, boiled it, and then made pancakes from it—they tasted like pancakes fried in vegetable oil.[2]

9　The manna fell with the dew during the night.

10　Moses heard all the families standing around their tent doors weeping, and the anger of the Lord grew hot; Moses too was highly displeased.

11　Moses said to the Lord, "Why pick on me, to give me the burden of a people like this?

12　Are they *my* children? Am I their father? Is that why You have given me the job of nursing them along like babies until we get to the land You promised their ancestors?

13　Where am I supposed to get meat for all these people? For they weep to me saying, 'Give us meat!'

---

[1] Literally, "Taberah."
[2] Literally, "olive oil."

14 I can't carry this nation by myself! The load is far too heavy!

15 If You are going to treat me like this, please kill me right now; it will be a kindness! Let me out of this impossible situation!"

16 Then the Lord said to Moses, "Summon before Me seventy of the leaders of Israel; bring them to the Tabernacle, to stand there with you.

17 I will come down and talk with you there and I will take of the Spirit which is on you and will put it upon them also; they shall bear the burden of the people along with you, so that you will not have the task alone.

18 And tell the people to purify themselves, for tomorrow they shall have meat to eat. Tell them, 'The Lord has heard your tearful complaints about all you left behind in Egypt, and He is going to give you meat. You shall eat it,

19, 20 Not for just a day or two, or five or ten or even twenty! For one whole month you will have meat until you vomit it from your noses; for you have rejected the Lord who is here among you, and you have wept for Egypt.' "

21 But Moses said, "There are 600,000 men alone, [besides all the women and children[3]], and yet You promise them meat for a whole month!

22 If we butcher all our flocks and herds it won't be enough! We would have to catch every fish in the ocean to fulfill Your promise!"

23 Then the Lord said to Moses, "When did I become weak? Now you shall see whether My word comes true or not!"

---

[3]Implied.

24 So Moses left the Tabernacle and reported Jehovah's words to the people; and he gathered the seventy elders and placed them around the Tabernacle.

25 And the Lord came down in the Cloud and talked with Moses, and the Lord took of the Spirit that was upon Moses and put it upon the seventy elders; and when the Spirit rested upon them, they prophesied for some time.

26 But two of the seventy—Eldad and Medad—were still in the camp, and when the Spirit rested upon them, they prophesied there.

27 Some young men ran and told Moses what was happening,

28 And Joshua (the son of Nun), one of Moses' personally chosen assistants, protested, "Sir, make them stop!"

29 But Moses replied, "Are you jealous for my sake? I only wish that all of the Lord's people were prophets, and that the Lord would put His Spirit upon them all!"

30 Then Moses returned to the camp with the elders of Israel.

31 The Lord sent a wind that brought quail from the sea, and let them fall into the camp and all around it! As far as one could walk in a day in any direction, there were quail flying three or four feet above the ground.[4]

32 So the people caught and killed quail all that day and through the night and all the next day too! The least anyone gathered was 100 bushels! Quail were spread out all around[5] the camp.

---

[4]Or, "The ground was covered with them, three feet thick!"
[5]To cure them by drying.

33 But as everyone began eating the meat, the anger of the Lord rose against the people and He killed large numbers of them with a plague.

34 So the name of that place was called, "The Place of the Graves Caused by Lust,"[6] because they buried the people there who had lusted for meat and for Egypt.

35 And from that place they journeyed to Hazeroth, where they stayed awhile.

CHAPTER 12

One day Miriam and Aaron were criticizing Moses because his wife was a Cushite[1] woman,

2 And they said, "Has the Lord spoken only through Moses? Hasn't He spoken through us, too?" But the Lord heard them.

3, 4 Immediately He summoned Moses, Aaron, and Miriam to the Tabernacle: "Come here, you three," He commanded. So they stood before the Lord. (Now Moses was the humblest man on earth.)

5 Then the Lord descended in the Cloud and stood at the entrance of the Tabernacle. "Aaron and Miriam, step forward," He commanded; and they did.

6 And the Lord said to them, "Even with a prophet, I would communicate by visions and dreams;

7, 8 But that is not how I communicate with My servant Moses. He is completely at home in My house! With him I speak face to face! And he shall see the

---

[6]Literally, "Kibroth-hattaavah."
[1]Literally, "because of the Cushite woman he had married." Apparently they were referring to his wife Zipporah, the Midianite daughter of Reuel (Exodus 2:21); for the land of Midian from which she came was sometimes called Cush. But areas of Ethiopia and Babylon were also known as Cush, so it is possible that the reference is to a second wife of Moses. It is indeterminate from the text as to whether the criticism was because she was a Gentile or (if she was a Cushite from Ethiopia) because of her color.

very form of God! Why then were you not afraid to criticize him?"

9 Then the anger of the Lord grew hot against them, and He departed.

10 As the Cloud moved from above the Tabernacle, Miriam suddenly became white with leprosy. When Aaron saw what had happened,

11 He cried out to Moses, "Oh, sir, do not punish us for this sin; we were fools to do such a thing.

12 Don't let her be as one dead, whose body is half rotted away at birth."

13 And Moses cried out to the Lord, "Heal her, O God, I beg You!"

14 And the Lord said to Moses, "If her father had but spit in her face she would be defiled seven days. Let her be confined outside the camp for seven days, and after that she can come back again."

15 So Miriam was excluded from the camp for seven days, and the people waited until she was brought back in before they traveled again.

16 Afterwards they left Hazeroth and camped in the wilderness of Paran.

CHAPTER 13

Jehovah now instructed Moses,

2 "Send spies into the land of Canaan—the land I am giving to Israel; send one leader from each tribe.

3 (The Israeli were camped in the wilderness of Paran at the time.) Moses did as the Lord had commanded and sent these twelve tribal leaders:

4   Shammu-a, son of Zaccur, from the tribe of Reuben;

5   Shaphat, son of Hori, from the tribe of Simeon;

6   Caleb, son of Jephunneh, from the tribe of Judah;

7   Igal, son of Joseph, from the tribe of Issachar;

8   Hoshea,[1] son of Nun, from the half tribe of Ephraim;

9   Palti, son of Raphu, from the tribe of Benjamin;

10   Gaddiel, son of Sodi, from the tribe of Zebulun;

11   Gaddi, son of Susi, from the tribe of Joseph (actually, the half tribe of Manasseh);

12   Ammiel, son of Gemalli, from the tribe of Dan;

13   Sethur, son of Michael, from the tribe of Asher;

14   Nahbi, son of Vophsi, from the tribe of Naphtali;

15   Geuel, son of Machi, from the tribe of Gad.

16   It was at this time that Moses changed Hoshea's name to Joshua.[2]

17   Moses sent them out with these instructions: "Go northward into the hill country of the Negeb,

18   And see what the land is like; see also what the people are like who live there, whether they are strong or weak, many or few;

19   And whether the land is fertile or not; and what cities there are, and whether they are villages or are fortified;

---

[1]Or, "Joshua." See verse 16.
[2]"Hoshea" means "salvation"; "Joshua" means, "Jehovah is salvation." Joshua is the same name in Hebrew as the Greek name "Jesus."

20 Whether the land is rich or poor, and whether there are many trees. Don't be afraid, and bring back some samples of the crops you see." (The first of the grapes were being harvested at that time.)

21 So they spied out the land all the way from the Wilderness of Zin to Rehob near Hamath.

22 Going northward, they passed first through the Negeb and arrived at Hebron. There they saw the Ahimanites, Sheshites, and Talmites, all families descended from Anak. (By the way, Hebron was very ancient, having been founded seven years before Tanis[3] in Egypt).

23 Then they came to what is now known as the Valley of Eshcol where they cut down a single cluster of grapes so large that it took two of them to carry it on a pole between them! They also took some samples of the pomegranates and figs.

24 The Israeli named the valley "Eshcol" at that time (meaning "Cluster") because of the cluster of grapes they found!

25 Forty days later they returned from their tour.

26 They made their report to Moses, Aaron, and all the people of Israel in the Wilderness of Paran at Kadesh, and they showed the fruit they had brought with them.

27 This was their report: "We arrived in the land you sent us to see, and it is indeed a magnificent country —a land 'flowing with milk and honey.' Here is some fruit we have brought as proof.

28 But the people living there are powerful, and

[3]Tanis (or Zoan, as it was pronounced in ancient times) was founded about 1720 B.C.

their cities are fortified and very large; and what's more, we saw Anakim giants there!

29 The Amalekites live in the south, while in the hill country there are the Hittites, Jebusites, and Amorites; down along the coast of the Mediterranean Sea and in the Jordan River valley are the Canaanites."

30 But Caleb reassured the people as they stood before Moses. "Let us go up at once and possess it," he said, "for we are well able to conquer it!"

31 "Not against people as strong as they are!" the other spies said. "They would crush us!"

32 So the majority report of the spies was negative: "The land is full of warriors, the people are powerfully built,

33 And we saw some of the Anakim there, descendants of the ancient race of giants. We felt like grasshoppers before them, they were so tall!"

CHAPTER 14

Then all the people began weeping aloud, and they carried on all night.

2 Their voices rose in a great chorus of complaint against Moses and Aaron. "We wish we had died in Egypt," they wailed, "or even here in the wilderness,

3 Rather than be taken into this country ahead of us. Jehovah will kill us there, and our wives and little ones will become slaves. Let's get out of here and return to Egypt!"

4 The idea swept the camp. "Let's elect a leader to take us back to Egypt!" they shouted.

5 Then Moses and Aaron fell face downward on the ground before the people of Israel;

6 Two of the spies, Joshua (the son of Nun), and

Caleb (the son of Jephunneh), ripped their clothing

7 And said to all the people, "It is a wonderful country ahead,

8 And the Lord loves us. He will bring us safely into the land and give it to us. It is *very* fertile, a land 'flowing with milk and honey'!

9 Oh, do not rebel against the Lord, and do not fear the people of the land. For they are but bread for us to eat! The Lord is with us and He has removed His protection from them! Don't be afraid of them!"

10, 11 But the only response of the people was to talk of stoning them. Then the glory of the Lord appeared, and the Lord said to Moses, "How long will these people despise Me? Will they *never* believe Me, even after all the miracles I have done among them?

12 I will disinherit them and destroy them with a plague, and I will make you into a nation far greater and mightier than they are!"

13 "But what will the Egyptians think when they hear about it?" Moses pleaded with the Lord. "They know full well the power You displayed in rescuing Your people.

14 They have told this to the inhabitants of this land, who are well aware that You are with Israel and that You talk with her face to face. They see the pillar of cloud and fire standing above us, and they know that You lead and protect us day and night.

15 Now if You kill all Your people, the nations that have heard Your fame will say,

16 'The Lord had to kill them because He wasn't able to take care of them in the wilderness. He wasn't strong enough to bring them into the land He swore He would give them.'

17, 18　Oh, please, show the great power [of Your patience[1]] by forgiving our sins and showing us Your steadfast love. Forgive us, even though You have said that You don't let sin go unpunished, and that you punish the father's fault in the children to the third and fourth generation.

19　Oh, I plead with You, pardon the sins of this people because of Your magnificent, steadfast love, just as You have forgiven them all the time from when we left Egypt until now."

20, 21　Then the Lord said, "All right, I will pardon them as you have requested. But I vow by My own name that just as it is true that all the earth shall be filled with the glory of the Lord,

22　So it is true that not one of the men who has seen My glory and the miracles I did both in Egypt and in the wilderness—and ten times refused to trust Me and obey Me—

23　Shall even see the land I promised to this people's ancestors.

24　But My servant Caleb is a different kind of man—he has obeyed Me fully. I will bring him into the land he entered as a spy, and his descendants shall have their full share in it.

25　But now, since the people of Israel are so afraid of the Amalekites and the Canaanites living in the valleys, tomorrow you must turn back into the wilderness in the direction of the Red Sea."

26, 27　Then the Lord added to Moses and to Aaron, "How long will these wicked people complain about Me? For I have heard all that they have been saying.

---

[1]Implied.

28   Tell them, 'The Lord vows to do to you what you feared:

29   You will all die here in this wilderness! Not a single one of you twenty years old and older, who has complained against me,

30   Shall enter the Promised Land. Only Caleb (son of Jephunneh) and Joshua (son of Nun) are permitted to enter it.

31   You said your children would become slaves of the people of the land. Well, instead I will bring *them* safely into the land and they shall inherit what you have despised.

32   But as for you, your dead bodies shall fall in this wilderness.

33   You must wander in the desert like nomads for forty years. In this way you will pay for your faithlessness, until the last of you lies dead in the desert.

34, 35   Since the spies were in the land for forty days, you must wander in the wilderness for forty years—a year for each day, bearing the burden of your sins. I will teach you what it means to reject Me. I, Jehovah, have spoken. Every one of you who has conspired against Me shall die here in this wilderness.' "

36, 37, 38   Then the ten spies who had incited the rebellion against Jehovah by striking fear into the hearts of the people were struck dead before the Lord. Of all the spies, only Joshua and Caleb remained alive.

39   What sorrow there was throughout the camp when Moses reported God's words to the people!

40   They were up early the next morning, and started towards the Promised Land. "Here we are!" they said. "We realize that we have sinned, but now

we are ready to go on into the land the Lord has promised us."

41 But Moses said, "It's too late. Now you are disobeying the Lord's orders to return to the wilderness.

42 Don't go ahead with your plan or you will be crushed by your enemies, for the Lord is not with you.

43 Don't you remember? The Amalekites and the Canaanites are there! You have deserted the Lord, and now He will desert you."

44 But they went ahead into the hill country, despite the fact that neither the Ark nor Moses left the camp.

45 Then the Amalekites and the Canaanites who lived in the hills came down and attacked them and chased them to Hormah.

CHAPTER 15

The Lord told Moses to give these instructions to the people of Israel: "When your children finally live in the land I am going to give them,

3, 4 And they want to please the Lord with a burnt offering or any other offering by fire, their sacrifice must be an animal from their flocks of sheep and goats, or from their herds of cattle. Each sacrifice—whether an ordinary one, or a sacrifice to fulfill a vow, or a free-will offering, or a special sacrifice at any of the annual festivals—must be accompanied by a grain offering. If a lamb is being sacrificed, use three quarts of fine flour mixed with three pints of oil,

5 Accompanied by three pints of wine for a drink offering.

6 If the sacrifice is a ram, use six quarts of fine flour mixed with four pints of oil,

7   And four pints of wine for a drink offering. This will be a sacrifice that is a pleasing fragrance to the Lord.

8, 9   If the sacrifice is a young bull, then the grain offering accompanying it must consist of nine quarts of fine flour mixed with three quarts of oil,

10   Plus three quarts of wine for the drink offering. This shall be offered by fire as a pleasing fragrance to the Lord.

11, 12   These are the instructions for what is to accompany each sacrificial bull, ram, lamb, or young goat.

13, 14   These instructions apply both to native-born Israeli and to foreigners living among you who want to please the Lord with sacrifices offered by fire;

15, 16   For there is the same law for all, native-born or foreigner, and this shall be true forever from generation to generation; all are equal before the Lord.[1] Yes, one law for all!"

17, 18   The Lord also said to Moses at this time, "Instruct the people of Israel that when they arrive in the land that I am going to give them,

19, 20, 21   They must present to the Lord a sample of each year's new crops by making a loaf, using coarse flour from the first grain that is cut each year. This loaf must be waved back and forth before the altar in a gesture of offering to the Lord. It is an annual offering from your threshing floor, and must be observed from generation to generation.

22   If by mistake you or future generations fail to carry out all of these regulations which the Lord has given you over the years through Moses,

---

[1]Literally, "as you are, so shall the foreigner be before Jehovah."

23, 24 Then when the people realize their error, they must offer one young bull for a burnt offering. It will be a pleasant odor before the Lord, and must be offered along with the usual grain offering and drink offering, and one male goat for a sin offering.

25 And the priest shall make atonement for all of the people of Israel and they shall be forgiven; for it was an error, and they have corrected it with their sacrifice made by fire before the Lord, and by their sin offering.

26 All the people shall be forgiven, including the foreigners living among them, for the entire population is involved in such error and forgiveness.

27 If the error is made by a single individual, then he shall sacrifice a one-year-old female goat for a sin offering,

28 And the priest shall make atonement for him before the Lord, and he shall be forgiven.

29 This same law applies to individual foreigners who are living among you.

30 But anyone who deliberately makes the 'mistake,' whether he is a native Israeli or a foreigner, is blaspheming Jehovah, and shall be cut off from among his people.

31 For he has despised the commandment of the Lord and deliberately failed to obey His law; he must be executed,[2] and die in his sin."

32 One day while the people of Israel were in the wilderness, one of them was caught gathering wood on the Sabbath day.

---

[2]Literally, "that soul shall be utterly cut off; his iniquity shall be upon him."

33　He was arrested and taken before Moses and Aaron and the other judges.[3]

34　They jailed him until they could find out the Lord's mind concerning him.

35　Then the Lord said to Moses, "The man must die—all the people shall stone him to death outside the camp."

36　So they took him outside the camp and killed him as the Lord had commanded.

37, 38　The Lord said to Moses, "Tell the people of Israel to make tassels for the hems of their clothes (this is a permanent regulation from generation to generation) and to attach the tassels to their clothes with a blue cord.

39　The purpose of this regulation is to remind you, whenever you notice the tassels, of the commandments of the Lord, and that you are to obey His laws instead of following your own desires and going your own ways, as you used to do in serving other gods.

40　It will remind you to be holy to your God.

41　For I am Jehovah your God who brought you out of the land of Egypt; yes, I am the Lord, your God."

CHAPTER 16

One day Korah (son of Izhar, grandson of Kohath, and a descendent of Levi) conspired with Dathan and Abiram (the sons of Eliab) and On (the son of Peleth; these three were from the tribe of Reuben),

2　To incite a rebellion against Moses. Two hundred and fifty popular leaders, all members of the Assembly, were involved.

---

[3]Literally, "to all the congregation."

3 They went to Moses and Aaron and said, "We have had enough of your presumption; you are no better than anyone else; everyone in Israel has been chosen of the Lord, and He is with all of us. What right do you have to put yourselves forward, claiming that we must obey you, and acting as though you were greater than anyone else among all these people of the Lord?"

4 When Moses heard what they were saying he fell face downward to the ground.

5 Then he said to Korah and to those who were with him, "In the morning the Lord will show you who are His, and who is holy, and whom He has chosen as His priest.

6, 7 Do this: You, Korah, and all those with you, take censers tomorrow and light them, and put incense upon them before the Lord, and we will find out whom the Lord has chosen.[1] You are the presumptuous ones, you sons of Levi."

8, 9 Then Moses spoke again to Korah: "Does it seem a small thing to you that the God of Israel has chosen you from among all the people of Israel to be near to Himself as you work in the Tabernacle of Jehovah, and to stand before the people to minister to them?

10 Is it nothing to you that He has given this task to only you Levites? And now are you demanding the priesthood also?

11, 12 That is what you are really after! That is why you are revolting against Jehovah. And what has Aaron done, that you are dissatisfied with him?" Then

---

[1] Literally, "whom Jehovah chooses to be the holy one."

Moses summoned Dathan and Abiram (the sons of Eliab), but they refused to come.

13   "Is it a small thing," they mimicked,[2] "that you brought us out of lovely Egypt to kill us here in this terrible wilderness, and that now you want to make yourself our king?

14   What's more, you haven't brought us into the wonderful country you promised, nor given us fields and vineyards. Whom are you trying to fool? We refuse to come."

15   Then Moses was very angry and said to the Lord, "Do not accept their sacrifices! I have never stolen so much as a donkey from them, and have not hurt one of them."

16   And Moses said to Korah, "Come here tomorrow before the Lord with all your friends; Aaron will be here too.

17   Be sure to bring your censers with incense on them; a censer for each man, 250 in all; and Aaron will also be here with his."

18   So they did. They came with their censers and lit them and placed the incense on them, and stood at the entrance of the Tabernacle with Moses and Aaron.

19   Meanwhile, Korah had stirred up the entire nation against Moses and Aaron, and they all assembled to watch. Then the glory of Jehovah appeared to all the people,

20   And Jehovah said to Moses and Aaron,

21   "Get away from these people so that I may instantly destroy them."

22   But Moses and Aaron fell face downward to

---

[2]Literally, "said."

the ground before the Lord. "O God, the God of all mankind," they pleaded, "must You be angry with all the people when one man sins?"

23 And the Lord said to Moses, "Then tell the people to get away from the tents of Korah, Dathan, and Abiram."

24, 25 So Moses rushed over to the tents of Dathan and Abiram, followed closely by the 250 Israeli leaders.

26 "Quick!" he told the people, "get away from the tents of these wicked men, and don't touch anything that belongs to them, lest you be included in their sins [and be destroyed with them[3]]."

27 So all the people stood back from the tents of Korah, Dathan, and Abiram. And Dathan and Abiram came out and stood at the entrances of their tents with their wives and sons and little ones.

28 And Moses said, "By this you shall know that Jehovah has sent me to do all these things that I have done—for I have not done them on my own.

29 If these men die a natural death or from some ordinary accident or disease, then Jehovah has not sent me.

30 But if the Lord does a miracle and the ground opens up and swallows them and everything that belongs to them, and they go down alive into Sheol, then you will know that these men have despised the Lord."

31 He had hardly finished speaking the words when the ground suddenly split open beneath them,

32 And a great fissure swallowed them up, along with their tents and families and the friends who were standing with them, and everything they owned.

---

[3]Implied.

33   So they went down alive into Sheol and the earth closed upon them, and they perished.

34   All of the people of Israel fled at their screams, fearing that the earth would swallow them too.

35   Then fire came forth from Jehovah and burned up the 250 men who were offering incense.

36, 37   And the Lord said to Moses, "Tell Eleazar the son of Aaron the priest to pull those censers from the fire; for they are holy, dedicated to the Lord. He must also scatter the burning incense

38   From the censers of these men who have sinned at the cost of their lives. He shall then beat the metal into a sheet as a covering for the altar, for these censers are holy because they were used before the Lord; and the altar sheet shall be a reminder to the people of Israel."

39   So Eleazar the priest took the 250 bronze censers and beat them out into a sheet of metal to cover the altar,

40   To be a reminder to the people of Israel that no unauthorized person—no one who is not a descendant of Aaron—may come before the Lord to burn incense, lest the same thing happen to him as happened to Korah and his associates. Thus the Lord's directions to Moses were carried out.

41   But the very next morning all the people began muttering again against Moses and Aaron, saying, "You have killed the Lord's people."

42   Soon a great, sullen mob formed; suddenly, as they looked toward the Tabernacle, the Cloud appeared and the awesome glory of the Lord was seen.

43, 44   Moses and Aaron came and stood at the entrance of the Tabernacle, and the Lord said to Moses,

45 "Get away from these people so that I can instantly destroy them." But Moses and Aaron fell face downward to the earth before the Lord.

46 And Moses said to Aaron, "Quick, take a censer and place fire in it from the altar; lay incense on it, and carry it quickly among the people and make atonement for them; for God's anger has gone out among them—the plague has already begun."

47 Aaron did as Moses had told him to, and ran among the people, for the plague had indeed already begun; and he put on the incense and made atonement for them.

48 And he stood between the living and the dead, and the plague was stopped,

49 But not before 14,700 people had died (in addition to those who had died the previous day with Korah).

50 Then Aaron returned to Moses at the entrance of the Tabernacle; and so the plague was stopped.

CHAPTER 17

Then the Lord said to Moses, "Tell the people of Israel that each of their tribal chiefs is to bring you a wooden rod with his name inscribed upon it. Aaron's name is to be on the rod of the tribe of Levi.

4 Put these rods in the inner room of the Tabernacle where I meet with you, in front of the Ark.

5 I will use these rods to identify the man I have chosen: for buds will grow on his rod! Then at last this murmuring and complaining against you will stop!"

6 So Moses gave the instructions to the people,

and each of the twelve chiefs (including Aaron) brought him a rod.

7 He put them before the Lord in the inner room of the Tabernacle,

8 And when he went in the next day, he found that Aaron's rod, representing the tribe of Levi, had budded and was blossoming, and had ripe almonds hanging from it!

9 When Moses brought them out to show the others, they stared in disbelief! Then each man except Aaron claimed his rod.

10 The Lord told Moses to place Aaron's rod permanently beside the Ark as a reminder of this rebellion. He was to [bring it out and show it to the people again[1]] if there were any further complaints about Aaron's authority; this would ward off further catastrophe to the people.

11 So Moses did as the Lord commanded him.

12, 13 But the people of Israel only grumbled the more. "We are as good as dead," they whined. "Everyone who even comes close to the Tabernacle dies. Must we all perish?"

CHAPTER 18

The Lord now spoke to Aaron: "You and your sons and your family are responsible for any desecration of the sanctuary," He said, "and will be held liable for any impropriety in your priestly work.

2, 3 Your kinsmen, the tribe of Levi, are your assistants; but only you and your sons may perform the sacred duties in the Tabernacle itself. The Levites must be careful not to touch any of the sacred articles

[1]Implied.

or the altar, lest I destroy both them and you.

4 No one who is not a member of the tribe of Levi shall assist you in any way.

5 Remember, only the priests are to perform the sacred duties within the sanctuary and at the altar. If you follow these instructions the wrath of God will never again fall upon any of the people of Israel for violating this law.

6 I say it again—your kinsmen the Levites are your assistants for the work of the Tabernacle. They are a gift to you from the Lord.

7 But you and your sons, the priests, shall personally handle all the sacred service, including the altar and all that is within the veil, for the priesthood is your special gift of service. Anyone else who attempts to perform these duties shall die."

8 The Lord gave these further instructions to Aaron: "I have given the priests all the gifts which are brought to the Lord by the people; all these offerings presented to the Lord by the gesture of waving them before the altar belong to you and your sons, by permanent law.

9 The grain offerings, the sin offerings, and the guilt offerings are yours, except for the sample presented to the Lord by burning upon the altar. All these are most holy offerings.

10 They are to be eaten only in a most holy place, and only by males.

11 All other gifts presented to Me by the gesture of waving them before the altar are for you and your families, sons and daughters alike. For all the members of your families may eat these unless anyone is ceremonially impure at the time.

12 Yours also are the first-of-the-harvest gifts the people bring as offerings to the Lord—the best of the olive oil, wine, grain,

13 And every other crop. Your families may eat these unless they are ceremonially defiled at the time.

14, 15 So everything that is dedicated to the Lord shall be yours, including the firstborn sons of the people of Israel, and the firstborn of their animals.

16 However, you may never accept the firstborn sons, nor the firstborn of any animals that I do not permit for food. Instead, there must be a payment of two and a half dollars made for each firstborn child. It is to be brought when he is one month old.

17 However, the firstborn of cows, sheep, or goats may not be bought back; they must be sacrificed to the Lord.[1] Their blood is to be sprinkled upon the altar, and their fat shall be burned as a fire offering; it is very pleasant to the Lord.

18 The meat of these animals shall be yours, including the breast and right thigh that are presented to the Lord by the gesture of waving before the altar.

19 Yes, I have given to you all of these 'wave offerings' brought by the people of Israel to the Lord; they are for you and your families as food; this is a permanent contract[2] between the Lord and you and your descendants.

20 You priests may own no property, nor have any other income, for I am all that you need.

21 As for the tribe of Levi, your relatives, they shall be paid for their service with the tithes from the entire land of Israel.

---

[1]Literally, "they are holy."
[2]Literally, "a covenant of salt."

22 From now on Israelites other than the priests and Levites shall not enter the sanctuary, lest they be judged guilty and die.

23 Only the Levites shall do the work there, and they shall be guilty if they fail. This is a permanent law among you, that the Levites shall own no property in Israel,

24 For the people's tithes, offered to the Lord by the gesture of waving before the altar, shall belong to the Levites; these are their inheritance, and so they have no need for property."

25, 26 The Lord also said to Moses, "Tell the Levites to give to the Lord a tenth of the tithes they receive—a tithe of the tithe, to be presented to the Lord by the gesture of waving before the altar.

27 The Lord will consider this as your first-of-the-harvest offering to Him of grain and wine, as though it were from your own property.

28, 29 This tithe of the tithe shall be selected from the choicest part of the tithes you receive as the Lord's portion, and shall be given to Aaron the priest.

30 It shall be credited to you just as though it were from your own threshing floor and wine press.

31 Aaron and his sons and their families may eat it in their homes or anywhere they wish, for it is their compensation for their service in the Tabernacle.

32 You Levites will not be held guilty for accepting the Lord's tithes if you then give the best tenth to the priests. But beware that you do not treat the holy gifts of the people of Israel as though they were common, lest you die."

CHAPTER 19

The Lord said to Moses and Aaron, "Here is another of My laws:

Tell the people of Israel to bring you a red heifer without defect, one that has never been yoked. Give her to Eleazar the priest and he shall take her outside the camp and someone shall kill her as he watches.

4 Eleazar shall take some of her blood upon his finger and sprinkle it seven times towards the front of the Tabernacle.

5 Then someone shall burn the heifer as he watches—her hide, meat, blood, and dung.

6 Eleazar shall take cedar wood and hyssop branches and scarlet thread, and throw them into the burning pile.

7 Then he must wash his clothes, and bathe, and afterwards return to the camp and be ceremonially defiled until the evening.

8 And the one who burns the animal must wash his clothes, and bathe, and he too shall be defiled until evening.

9 Then someone who is not ceremonially defiled shall gather up the ashes of the heifer and place them in some purified place outside the camp, where they shall be kept for the people of Israel as a source of water for the purification ceremonies, for removal of sin.

10 And the one who gathers up the ashes of the heifer must wash his clothes and be defiled until evening; this is a permanent law for the benefit of the

people of Israel and any foreigners living among them.

11 Anyone who touches a dead human body shall be defiled for seven days,

12 And must purify himself the third and seventh days with water [run through the ashes of the red heifer[1]]; then he will be purified; but if he does not do this on the third day, he will continue to be defiled even after the seventh day.

13 Anyone who touches a dead person and does not purify himself in the manner specified, has defiled the Tabernacle of the Lord, and shall be excommunicated from Israel. The cleansing water was not sprinkled upon him, so the defilement continues.

14 When a man dies in a tent, these are the various regulations: everyone who enters the tent, and those who are in it at the time, shall be defiled seven days.

15 Any container in the tent without a lid over it is defiled.

16 If someone out in a field touches the corpse of someone who has been killed in battle, or who has died in any other way, or if he even touches a bone or a grave, he shall be defiled seven days.

17 To become purified again, ashes from the red heifer sin offering[2] are to be added to spring water in a kettle.

18 Then a person who is not defiled shall take hyssop branches and dip them into the water and sprinkle the water upon the tent and upon all the pots and pans in the tent, and upon anyone who has been defiled by being in the tent, or by touching a bone,

---

[1]Implied. See verse 17.
[2]Literally, "ashes of the burnt sin offering."

or touching someone who has been killed or is otherwise dead, or has touched a grave.

19 This shall take place on the third and seventh days; then the defiled person must wash his clothes and bathe himself, and that evening he will be out from under the defilement.

20 But anyone who is defiled and doesn't purify himself shall be excommunicated, for he has defiled the sanctuary of the Lord, and the water to cleanse him has not been sprinkled upon him; so he remains defiled.

21 This is a permanent law. The man who sprinkles the water must afterwards wash his clothes; and anyone touching the water shall be defiled until evening.

22 And anything a defiled person touches shall be defiled until evening."

CHAPTER 20

The people of Israel arrived in the wilderness of Zin in April[1] and camped at Kadesh, where Miriam died and was buried.

2 There was not enough water to drink at that place, so the people again rebelled against Moses and Aaron. A great mob formed,

3 And they held a protest meeting. "Would that we too had died with our dear brothers the Lord killed!" they shouted at Moses.

4 "You have deliberately brought us into this wilderness to get rid of us, along with our flocks and herds.

5 Why did you ever make us leave Egypt and bring us here to this evil place? Where is the fertile land

---
[1]Literally, "the first month."

of wonderful crops—the figs, vines, and pomegranates you told us about? Why, there isn't even water enough to drink!"

6   Moses and Aaron turned away and went to the entrance of the Tabernacle, where they fell face downward before the Lord; and the glory of Jehovah appeared to them.

7   And He said to Moses,

8   "Get Aaron's[2] rod; then you and Aaron must summon the people. As they watch, speak to that rock over there and tell it to pour out its water! You will give them water from a rock, enough for all the people and all their cattle!"

9   So Moses did as instructed. He took the rod from the place where it was kept before the Lord;

10   Then Moses and Aaron summoned the people to come and gather at the rock; and he said to them, "Listen, you rebels! Must we bring you water from this rock?"

11   Then Moses lifted the rod and struck the rock twice, and water gushed out; and the people and their cattle drank.

12   But the Lord said to Moses and Aaron, "Because you did not believe Me[3] and did not sanctify Me in the eyes of the people of Israel, you shall not bring them into the land I have promised them!"

13   This place was named Meribah (meaning "Rebel Waters"), because it was where the people of Israel fought against Jehovah, and where He showed Himself to be holy before them.

14   While Moses was at Kadesh he sent messengers

---

[2]Literally, "Get the rod."
[3]Literally, "did not sanctify Me." The Lord had said to *speak* to the rock. Moses *struck* it, not once, but *twice*.

to the King of Edom: "We are the descendants of your brother[4] Israel," he declared. "You know our sad history,

15　How our ancestors went down to visit Egypt and stayed there so long, and became slaves of the Egyptians.

16　But when we cried to the Lord He heard us and sent an Angel who brought us out of Egypt, and now we are here at Kadesh, encamped on the borders of your land.

17　Please let us pass through your country. We will be careful not to go through your planted fields, nor through your vineyards; we won't even drink water from your wells, but will stay on the main road and not leave it until we have crossed your border on the other side."

18　But the king of Edom said, "Stay out! If you attempt to enter my land I will meet you with an army!"

19　"But sir," protested the Israeli ambassadors, "we will stay on the main road and will not even drink your water unless we pay whatever you demand for it. We only want to pass through, and nothing else."

20　But the king of Moab was adamant. "Stay out!" he warned, and, mobilizing his army, he marched to the frontier with a great force.

21, 22　Because Edom refused to allow Israel to pass through their country, Israel turned back and journeyed from Kadesh to Mount Hor.

23　Then the Lord said to Moses and Aaron at the border of the land of Edom,

24　"The time has come for Aaron to die—for he shall not enter the land I have given the people of

---

[4]The people of Edom were descended from Esau, while the people of Israel were descended from his brother Jacob, whose name was later changed to Israel.

Israel, for the two of you rebelled against My instructions concerning the water at Meribah.

25 Now summon Aaron and his son Eleazar and take them up onto Mount Hor.

26 There you shall remove Aaron's priestly garments from him and put them on Eleazer his son; and Aaron shall die there."

27 So Moses did as the Lord commanded him. The three[5] of them went up together into Mount Hor as all the people watched.

28 When they reached the summit, Moses removed the priestly garments from Aaron and put them on his son Eleazar; and Aaron died on the top of the mountain. Moses and Eleazar returned,

29 And when the people were informed of Aaron's death, they mourned for him for thirty days.

CHAPTER 21

When the king of Arad heard that the Israeli were approaching (for they were traveling the same route as the spies), he mobilized his army and attacked Israel, taking some of the men as prisoners.

2 Then the people of Israel vowed to the Lord that if He would help them conquer the king of Arad and his people, they would completely annihilate all the cities of that area.

3 The Lord heeded their request and defeated the Canaanites; and the Israeli completely destroyed them and their cities. The name of the region was thereafter called Hormah (meaning "Utterly Destroyed").

4 Then the people of Israel returned to Mount Hor, and from there continued southward along the

---

[5]Implied.

road to the Red Sea in order to go around the land of
Edom. The people were very discouraged;

5   They began to murmur against God and to complain against Moses. "Why have you brought us out of
Egypt to die here in the wilderness?" they whined.
"There is nothing to eat here, and nothing to drink, and
we hate this insipid manna."

6   So the Lord sent poisonous snakes among them
to punish them, and many of them were bitten and
died.

7   Then the people came to Moses and cried out,
"We have sinned, for we have spoken against Jehovah
and against you. Pray to Him to take away the snakes."
Moses prayed for the people.

8   Then the Lord told him, "Make a bronze
replica[1] of one of these snakes and attach it to the top
of a pole; anyone who is bitten shall live if he simply
looks at it!"

9   So Moses made the replica, and whenever anyone who had been bitten looked at the bronze snake, he
recovered!

10   Israel journeyed next to Oboth and camped
there.

11   Then they went on to Iye-abarim, in the wilderness, a short distance east of Moab,

12   And from there they traveled to the valley of
the brook Zared and set up camp.

13   Then they moved to the far side of the Arnon
River, near the borders of the Amorites. (The Arnon
River is the boundary line between the Moabites and
the Amorites.

14   This fact is mentioned in *The Book of the Wars*

---

[1]Literally, "Make a fiery serpent."

of Jehovah, where it is stated that the valley of the Arnon River, and the city of Waheb,

15 Lie between the Amorites and the people of Moab.)

16 Then Israel traveled to Beer (meaning "A Well"). This is the place where the Lord told Moses, "Summon the people, and I will give them water."

17 What happened is described in this song that the people sang:

> Spring up, O well!
> Sing of the water!

18   This is a well
> The leaders dug.
> It was hollowed
> With their staves
> And shovels.

Then they left the desert and proceeded on through Mattanah,

19 Nahaliel, and Bamoth;

20 Then to the valley in the plateau of Moab, which overlooks the desert with Mount Pisgah in the distance.

21 Israel now sent ambassadors to King Sihon of the Amorites.

22 "Let us travel through your land," they requested. "We will not leave the road until we have passed beyond your borders. We won't trample your fields or touch your vineyards or drink your water."

23 But King Sihon refused. Instead he mobilized his army and attacked Israel in the wilderness, battling them at Jahaz.

24 But Israel slaughtered them and occupied their land from the Arnon River to the Jabbok River, as

far as the borders of the Ammonites; but they were stopped there by the rugged terrain.[2]

25, 26   So Israel captured all the cities of the Amorites and lived in them, including the city of Heshbon, which had been King Sihon's capital.

27   The ancient poets had referred to King Sihon in this poem:

> Come to Heshbon,
> King Sihon's capital,

28
> For a fire has flamed forth
> And devoured
> The city of Ar in Moab,
> On the heights of the Arnon River.

29
> Woe to Moab!
> You are finished,
> O people of Chemosh;
> His sons have fled,
> And his daughters are captured
> By King Sihon of the Amorites.

30
> He has destroyed
> The little children
> And the men and women
> As far as Dibon, Nophah, and Medeba.

31, 32   While Israel was there in the Amorite country, Moses sent spies to look over the Jazer area; he followed up with an armed attack, capturing all of the towns and driving out the Amorites.

33   They next turned their attention to the city of Bashan, but King Og of Bashan met them with his army at Edre-i.

34   The Lord told Moses not to fear—that the

---

[2]Literally, "For the border of the children of Ammon was strong." Deut. 2:19 indicates that God had promised the land of the Ammonites to the descendants of Lot.

enemy was already conquered! "The same thing will happen to King Og as happened to King Sihon at Heshbon," the Lord assured him.

35   And sure enough, Israel was victorious and killed King Og, his sons, and his subjects, so that not a single survivor remained; and Israel occupied the land.

CHAPTER 22

The people of Israel now traveled to the plains of Moab and camped east of the Jordan River opposite Jericho.

2, 3   When King Balak of Moab (the son of Zippor) realized how many of them there were, and when he learned what they had done to the Amorites, he and his people were terrified.

4   They quickly consulted with the leaders of Midian. "This mob will eat us like an ox eats grass," they exclaimed. So King Balak

5, 6   Sent messengers to Balaam (son of Beor) who was living in his native land of Pethor, near the Euphrates River. He begged Balaam to come and help him. "A vast horde of people has arrived from Egypt, and they cover the face of the earth and are headed toward me," he frantically explained. "Please come and curse them for me, so that I can drive them out of my land; for I know what fantastic blessings fall on those whom you bless, and I also know that those whom you curse are doomed."

7   The messengers he sent were some of the top leaders of Moab and Midian. They went to Balaam with money in hand, and urgently explained to him what Balak wanted.

8   "Stay here overnight," Balaam said, "and I'll

tell you in the morning whatever the Lord directs me to say." So they did.

9   That night God came to Balaam and asked him, "Who are these men?"

10   "They have come from King Balak of Moab," he replied.

11   "The king says that a vast horde of people from Egypt has arrived at his border, and he wants me to go at once and curse them, in the hope that he can battle them successfully."

12   "Don't do it!" God told him. "You are not to curse them, for I have blessed them!"

13   The next morning Balaam told the men, "Go on home! The Lord won't let me do it."

14   So King Balak's ambassadors returned without him and reported his refusal.

15   Balak tried again. This time he sent a larger number of even more distinguished ambassadors than the former group.

16, 17   They came to Balaam with this message: "King Balak pleads with you to come. He promises you great honors plus any payment you ask. Name your own figure! Only come and curse these people for us."

18   But Balaam replied, "If he were to give me a palace filled with silver and gold, I could do nothing contrary to the command of the Lord my God.

19   However, stay here tonight so that I can find out whether the Lord will add anything to what He said before."

20   That night God told Balaam, "Get up and go with these men, but be sure to say only what I tell you to."

21   So the next morning he saddled his donkey and started off with them.

22, 23   But God was angry about Balaam's eager attitude,[1] so He sent an angel to stand in the road to kill him. As Balaam and two servants were riding along, Balaam's donkey suddenly saw the angel of the Lord standing in the road with a drawn sword. She bolted off the road into a field, but Balaam beat her back onto the road.

24   Now the angel of the Lord stood at a place where the road went between two vineyard walls.

25   When the donkey saw him standing there, she squirmed past by pressing against the wall, crushing Balaam's foot in the process. So he beat her again.

26   Then the angel of the Lord moved farther down the road and stood in a place so narrow that the donkey couldn't get by at all.

27   So she lay down in the road! In a great fit of temper Balaam beat her again with his staff.

28   Then the Lord caused the donkey to speak! "What have I done that deserves your beating me these three times?" she asked.

29   "Because you have made me look like a fool!" Balaam shouted. "I wish I had a sword with me, for I would kill you."

30   "Have I ever done anything like this before in my entire life?" the donkey asked.

"No," he admitted.

31   Then the Lord opened Balaam's eyes and he saw the angel standing in the roadway with drawn sword, and he fell flat on the ground before him.

32   "Why did you beat your donkey those three

---

[1]Literally, "God was angry because he went."

times?" the angel demanded. "I have come to stop you because you are headed for destruction.

33 Three times the donkey saw me and shied away from me; otherwise I would certainly have killed you by now, and spared her."

34 Then Balaam confessed, "I have sinned. I didn't realize you were there. I will go back home if you don't want me to go on."

35 But the angel told him, "Go with the men, but say only what I tell you to say." So Balaam went on with them.

36 When King Balak heard that Balaam was on the way, he left the capital and went out to meet him at the Arnon River, at the border of his land.

37 "Why did you delay so long?" he asked Balaam. "Didn't you believe me when I said I would give you great honors?"

38 Balaam replied, "I have come, but I have no power to say anything except what God tells me to say; and that is what I shall speak."

39 Balaam accompanied the king to Kiriathhuzoth,

40 Where King Balak sacrificed oxen and sheep, and gave animals to Balaam and the ambassadors for their sacrifices.

41 The next morning Balak took Balaam to the top of Mount Bamoth-baal, from which he could see the people of Israel spread out before him.

CHAPTER 23

Balaam said to the king, "Build seven altars here, and prepare seven young bulls and seven rams for sacrifice."

2 Balak followed his instructions, and a young

bull and a ram were sacrificed on each altar.

3, 4   Then Balaam said to the king, "Stand here by your burnt offerings and I will see if the Lord will meet me; and I will tell you what He says to me." So he went up to a barren height, and God met him there. Balaam told the Lord, "I have prepared seven altars, and have sacrificed a young bull and a ram on each."

5   Then the Lord gave Balaam a message for King Balak.

6   When Balaam returned, the king was standing beside the burnt offerings with all the princes of Moab.

7   This was Balaam's message:

> King Balak, king of Moab, has brought me
> From the land of Aram,
> From the eastern mountains.
> 'Come,' he told me, 'curse Jacob for me!
> Let your anger rise on Israel.'

8   But how can I curse
> What God has not cursed?
> How can I denounce
> A people God has not denounced?

9   I see them from the cliff tops,
> I watch them from the hills.
> They live alone,
> And prefer to remain distinct
> From every other nation.

10   They are as numerous as dust!
> They are beyond numbering.
> If only I could die as happy as an Israelite!
> Oh, that my end might be like theirs!

11   "What have you done to me?" demanded King Balak. "I told you to curse my enemies, and now you have blessed them!"

12   But Balaam replied, "Can I say anything except what Jehovah tells me to?"

13   Then Balak told him, "Come with me to another place; there you will see only a portion of the nation of Israel. Curse at least that many!"

14   So King Balak took Balaam into the fields of Zophim at the top of Mount Pisgah, and built seven altars there; and he offered up a young bull and a ram on each altar.

15   Then Balaam said to the king, "Stand here by your burnt offering while I go to meet the Lord."

16   And the Lord met Balaam and told him what to say.

17   So he returned to where the king and the princes of Moab were standing beside their burnt offerings.

"What has Jehovah said?" the king eagerly inquired.

18   And he replied,

        Rise up, Balak, and hear:
        Listen to me, you son of Zippor.

19   God is not a man, that He should lie;
        He doesn't change His mind like humans
            do.
        Has He ever promised,
        Without doing what He said?

20   Look! I have received a command to bless
            them,
        For God has blessed them,
        And I cannot reverse it!

21   He has not seen sin in Jacob.
        He will not trouble Israel!
        Jehovah their God is with them.

He is their king!

22 God has brought them out of Egypt.
Israel has the strength of a wild ox.

23 No curse can be placed on Jacob,
And no magic shall be done against him.
For now it shall be said of Israel,
'What wonders God has done for them!'

24 These people rise up as a lion;
They shall not lie down
Until they have eaten what they capture
And have drunk the blood of the slain!

25 "If you aren't going to curse them, at least don't *bless* them!" the king exclaimed to Balaam.

26 But Balaam replied, "Didn't I tell you that I must say whatever Jehovah tells me to?"

27 Then the king said to Balaam, "I will take you to yet another place. Perhaps it will please God to let you curse them from there."

28 So King Balak took Balaam to the top of Mount Peor, overlooking the desert.

29 Balaam again told the king to build seven altars, and to prepare seven young bulls and seven rams for the sacrifice.

30 The king did as Balaam said, and offered a young bull and ram on every altar.

CHAPTER 24

Balaam realized by now that Jehovah planned to bless Israel, so he didn't even go to meet the Lord as he had earlier. Instead, he went at once and looked out toward the camp of Israel

2 Which stretched away across the plains, divided by tribal areas. Then the Spirit of God came upon him,

3 And he prophesied concerning them,
   Balaam the son of Beor says that
   The man whose eyes are open says,

4   "I have listened to the word of God,
   I have seen what God Almighty showed
    me;
   I fell, and my eyes were opened:

5   Oh, the joys awaiting Israel,
   Joys in the homes of Jacob.

6   I see them spread before me as green
    valleys,
   And fruitful gardens by the riverside;
   As aloes planted by the Lord Himself;
   As cedar trees beside the waters.

7   They shall be blessed with an abundance
    of water,
   And they shall live in many places.
   Their king will be greater than Agag;
   Their kingdom is exalted.

8   God has brought them from Egypt.
   Israel has the strength of a wild ox,
   And shall eat up the nations that oppose
    him;
   He shall break their bones in pieces,
   And shall shoot them with many arrows.

9   Israel sleeps as a lion or a lioness—
   Who dares arouse him?
   Blessed is everyone who blesses you, O
    Israel,
   And curses shall fall upon everyone who
    curses you."

10 King Balak was livid with rage by now. Striking his hands together in anger and disgust he shouted,

"I called you to curse my enemies and instead you have blessed them three times.

11 Get out of here! Go back home! I had planned to promote you to great honor, but Jehovah has kept you from it!"

12 Balaam replied, "Didn't I tell your messengers

13 That even if you gave me a palace filled with silver and gold, I could not go beyond the words of Jehovah, and could not say a word of my own? I said that I would say only what Jehovah says!

14 Yes, I shall return now to my own people. But first, let me tell you what the Israelites are going to do to your people!"

15 So he spoke this prophecy to him:

Balaam the son of Beor is the man
Whose eyes are open!

16 He hears the words of God
And has knowledge from the Most High;
He sees what Almighty God has shown him;
He fell, and his eyes were opened:

17 I see in the future of Israel,
Far down the distant trail,
That there shall come a star from Jacob!
This ruler of Israel
Shall smite the people of Moab,
And destroy the sons of Sheth.

18 Israel shall possess all Edom and Seir.
They shall overcome their enemies.

19 Jacob shall arise in power
And shall destroy many cities.

20 Then Balaam looked over at the tents of the people of Amalek and prophesied:

Amalek was the first of the nations,
But its destiny is destruction!

21   Then he looked over at the Kenites:
Yes, you are strongly situated,
Your nest is set in the rocks!

22   But the Kenites shall be destroyed,
And the mighty army of the king of
Assyria shall deport you from this land!

23   He concluded his prophecies by saying:
Alas, who can live when God does this?

24   Ships shall come from the coasts of
Cyprus,
And shall oppress both Eber and Assyria.
They too must be destroyed.

25   So Balaam and Balak returned to their homes.[1]

CHAPTER 25

While Israel was camped at Acacia, some of the young men began going to wild parties with the local Moabite girls.

2   These girls also invited them to attend the sacrifices to their gods, and soon the men were not only attending the feasts, but also bowing down and worshiping the idols.

3   Before long all Israel was joining freely in the worship of Baal, the god of Moab; and the anger of the Lord was hot against His people.

4   He issued the following command to Moses: "Execute all the tribal leaders of Israel. Hang them up before the Lord in broad daylight, so that His fierce anger will turn away from the people."

[1]But not before Balaam gave insidious advice that brought about the situation described in Numbers 25:1-3. See Numbers 31:16.

5   So Moses ordered the judges to execute all who had worshiped Baal.

6   But one of the Israeli men insolently brought a Midianite girl into the camp, right before the eyes of Moses and all the people, as they were weeping at the door of the Tabernacle.

7   When Phinehas (son of Eleazar and grandson of Aaron the priest) saw this, he jumped up, grabbed a spear,

8   And rushed after the man into his tent, where he had taken the girl. He thrust the spear all the way through the man's body and into her stomach. So the plague was stopped,

9   But only after 24,000 people had already died.

10, 11   Then the Lord said to Moses, "Phinehas (son of Eleazar and grandson of Aaron the priest) has turned away My anger, for he was as angry as I, concerning My honor; so I have stopped destroying all Israel as I had intended.

12, 13   Now because of what he has done—because of his zeal for his God, and because he has made atonement for the people of Israel by what he did—I promise that he and his descendants shall be priests forever."

14   The name of the man who was killed with the Midianite girl was Zimri, son of Salu, a leader of the tribe of Simeon.

15   The girl's name was Cozbi, daughter of Zur, a Midianite prince.

16, 17   Then the Lord said to Moses, "Destroy the Midianites,

18   For they are destroying you with their wiles. They are causing you to worship Baal, and they are

leading you astray, as you have just seen by the death of Cozbi."

CHAPTER 26

A fter the plague had ended, Jehovah said to Moses and to Eleazar (son of Aaron the priest),

2 "Take a census of all the men of Israel who are twenty years old or older, to find out how many of each tribe and clan are able to go to war."

3, 4 So Moses and Eleazar issued census instructions to the leaders of Israel. (The entire nation was camped in the plains of Moab beside the Jordan River, opposite Jericho.)

Here are the results of the census:

5-11 *The tribe of Reuben:* 43,730.

(Reuben was Israel's eldest son.) In this tribe were the following clans, named after Reuben's sons:

The Hanochites, named after their ancestor Hanoch.

The Palluites, named after their ancestor Pallu.

(In the sub-clan of Eliab—who was one of the sons of Palu—were the families of Nemu-el, Abiram, and Dathan. This Dathan and Abiram were the two leaders who conspired with Korah against Moses and Aaron, and in fact challenged the very authority of God! But the earth opened and swallowed them; and 250 men were destroyed by fire from the Lord that day, as a warning to the entire nation.)

The Hezronites, named after their ancestor Hezron.

The Carmites, named after their ancestor Carmi.

12-14   *The tribe of Simeon: 22,200.*

In this tribe were the following clans, founded by Simeon's sons:

The Nemu-elites, named after their ancestor Nemu-el.

The Jaminites, named after their ancestor Jamin.

The Jachinites, named after their ancestor Jachin.

The Zerahites, named after their ancestor Zerah.

The Shaulites, named after their ancestor Shaul.

15-18   *The tribe of Gad: 40,500.*

In this tribe were the following clans founded by the sons of Gad:

The Zephonites, named after their ancestor Zephon.

The Haggites, named after their ancestor Haggi.

The Shunites, named after their ancestor Shuni.

The Oznites, named after their ancestor Ozni.

The Erites, named after their ancestor Eri.

The Arodites, named after their ancestor Arod.

The Arelites, named after their ancestor Areli.

19-22   *The tribe of Judah:* 76,500.

In this tribe were the following clans named after the sons of Judah—but not including Er and Onan who died in the land of Canaan:

> The Shelanites, named after their ancestor Shelah.

> The Perezites, named after their ancestor Perez.

> The Zerahites, named after their ancestor Zerah.

> This census also included the sub-clans of Perez:

>> The Hezronites, named after their ancestor Hezron.

>> The Hamulites, named after their ancestor Hamul.

23-25   *The tribe of Issachar:* 64,300.

In this tribe were the following clans named after the sons of Issachar:

> The Tolaites, named after their ancestor Tola.

> The Punites, named after their ancestor Puvah.

> The Jashubites, named after their ancestor Jashub.

> The Shimronites, named after their ancestor Shimron.

26, 27   *The tribe of Zebulun:* 60,500.

In this tribe were the following clans named after the sons of Zebulun:

> The Seredites, named after their ancestor Sered.

> The Elonites, named after their ancestor Elon.

The Jahleelites, named after their ancestor Jahleel.

28-37 *The tribe of Joseph: 32,500 in the half-tribe of Ephraim; and 52,750 in the half-tribe of Manasseh.*

In the half-tribe of Manasseh was the following clan of Machirites, named after their ancestor Machir.

The sub-clan of the Machirites was the Gileadites, named after their ancestor Gilead.

The tribes of the Gileadites:

The Jezerites, named after their ancestor Jezer.

The Helekites, named after their ancestor Helek.

The Asrielites, named after their ancestor Asriel.

The Shechemites, named after their ancestor Shechem.

The Shemidaites, named after their ancestor Shemida.

The Hepherites, named after their ancestor Hepher. (Hepher's son, Zelophehad, had no sons. Here are the names of his daughters:

Mahlah,

Noah,

Hoglah,

Milcah,

Tirzah.)

The 32,500 registered in the half-tribe of Ephraim included the following clans, named after the sons of Ephraim:

The Shuthelahites, named after their ancestor Shuthelah. (A sub-clan of the Shuthelahites was the Eranites, named after their ancestor Eran, a son of Shuthelah.)

The Becherites, named after their ancestor Becher.

The Tahanites, named after their ancestor Tahan.

38-41 *The tribe of Benjamin:* 45,600.

In this tribe were the following clans named after the sons of Benjamin:

The Bela-ites, named after their ancestor Bela.

Sub-clans named after sons of Bela were:

The Ardites, named after their ancestor Ard.

The Naamites, named after their ancestor Naaman.

The Ashbelites, named after their ancestor Ashbel.

The Ahiramites, named after their ancestor Ahiram.

The Shuphamites, named after their ancestor Shephupham.

The Huphamites, named after their ancestor Hupham.

42, 43 *The tribe of Dan:* 64,400.

In this tribe was the clan of the Shuhamites, named after Shuham, the son of Dan.

44-47 *The tribe of Asher:* 53,400.

In this tribe were the following clans named after the sons of Asher:

The Imnites, named after their ancestor Imnah.

The Ishvites, named after their ancestor Ishvi.

The Beriites, named after their ancestor Beriah.

Sub-clans named after the sons of Beriah were:

The Heberites, named after their ancestor Heber.

The Malchi-elites, named after their ancestor Malchi-el.

Asher also had a daughter named Serah.

48-50   *The tribe of Naphtali:* 45,400.

In this tribe were the following clans, named after the sons of Naphtali:

The Jahzeelites, named after their ancestor Jahzeel.

The Gunites, named after their ancestor Guni.

The Jezerites, named after their ancestor Jezer.

The Shillemites, named after their ancestor Shillem.

51   So the total number of the draftable men throughout Israel was 601,730.

52, 53   Then the Lord told Moses to divide the land among the tribes in proportion to their population, as indicated by the census—

54   The larger tribes to be given more land, the smaller tribes less land.

55, 56   "Let the representatives of the larger tribes have a lottery, drawing for the larger section," the Lord instructed, "and let the smaller tribes draw for the smaller sections."

57   These are the clans of the Levites numbered in the census:

> The Gershonites, named after their ancestor Gershon.
>
> The Kohathites, named after their ancestor Kohath.
>
> The Merarites, named after their ancestor Merari.

58, 59   These are the families of the tribe of Levi:

> The Libnites,
> The Hebronites,
> The Mahlites,
> The Mushites,
> The Korahites.

While Levi was in Egypt, a daughter, Jochebed, was born to him and she became the wife of Amram, son of Kohath. They were the parents of Aaron, Moses, and Miriam.

60   To Aaron were born Nadab, Abihu, Eleazar, and Ithamar.

61   But Nadab and Abihu died when they offered unholy fire before the Lord.

62   *The total number of Levites in the census* was 23,000, counting all the males a month old and upward. But the Levites were not included in the total census figure of the people of Israel, for the Levites were given no land when it was divided among the tribes.

63   So these are the census figures as prepared by Moses and Eleazar the priest, in the plains of Moab beside the Jordan River, across from Jericho.

64, 65   Not one person in this entire census had

been counted[1] in the previous census taken in the wilderness of Sinai! For all who had been counted then had died, as the Lord had decreed when He said of them, "They shall die in the wilderness." The only exceptions were Caleb (son of Jephunneh) and Joshua (son of Nun).

CHAPTER 27

One day the daughters of Zelophehad came to the entrance of the Tabernacle to give a petition to Moses, Eleazar the priest, the tribal leaders, and others who were there. These women were of the half-tribe of Manasseh (a son of Joseph). Their ancestor was Machir, son of Manasseh. Manasseh's son Gilead was their great-grandfather, his son Hepher was their grandfather, and his son Zelophehad was their father.

3, 4   "Our father died in the wilderness," they said, "and he was not one of those who perished in Korah's revolt against the Lord—it was a natural death, but he had no sons. Why should the name of our father disappear just because he had no son? We feel that we should be given property along with our father's brothers."

5   So Moses brought their case before the Lord.

6, 7   And the Lord replied to Moses, "The daughters of Zelophehad are correct. Give them land along with their uncles; give them the property that would have been given to their father if he had lived.

8   Moreover, this is a general law among you, that if a man dies and has no sons, then his inheritance shall be passed on to his daughters.

---

[1]Forty years earlier, at the time of the first census, they had been under twenty years of age, and so were not counted. All who at that time were older than twenty years of age were now dead.

9   And if he has no daughter, it shall belong to his brothers.

10   And if he has no brother, then it shall go to his uncles.

11   But if he has no uncles, then it shall go to the nearest relative."

12   One day the Lord said to Moses, "Go up into Mount Abarim and look across the river to the land I have given to the people of Israel.

13   After you have seen it, you shall die as Aaron your brother did,

14   For you rebelled against My instructions in the wilderness of Zin. When the people of Israel rebelled, you did not glorify Me[1] before them by following My instructions to order water to come out of the rock." He was referring to the incident at the waters of Meribah ("Place of Strife") in Kadesh, in the wilderness of Zin.

15   Then Moses said to the Lord,

16   "O Jehovah, the God of the spirits of all mankind, [before I am taken away[1]] please appoint a new leader for the people,

17   A man who will lead them into battle and care for them, so that the people of the Lord will not be as sheep without a shepherd."

18   The Lord replied, "Go and get Joshua (son of Nun), who has the Spirit in him,

19   And take him to Eleazar the priest, and as all the people watch, charge him with the responsibility of leading the people.

20   Publicly give him your authority so that all the people of Israel will obey him.

---

[1]Implied.

21 He shall be the one to consult with Eleazar the priest in order to get directions from the Lord. The Lord will speak to Eleazar through the use of the Urim, and Eleazar will pass on these instructions to Joshua and the people. In this way the Lord will continue to give them guidance."

22 So Moses did as Jehovah commanded, and took Joshua to Eleazar the priest. As the people watched,

23 Moses laid his hands upon him and dedicated him to his responsibilities, as the Lord had commanded.

CHAPTER 28

The Lord gave Moses these instructions to give to the people of Israel: "The offerings which you burn on the altar for Me are My food, and are a pleasure to Me; so see to it that they are brought regularly and are offered as I have instructed you.

3 When you make offerings by fire, you shall use yearling male lambs—each without defect. Two of them shall be offered each day as a regular burnt offering.

4 One lamb shall be sacrificed in the morning, the other in the evening.

5 With them shall be offered a grain offering of three quarts of finely ground flour mixed with three pints of oil.

6 This is the burnt offering ordained at Mount Sinai, to be regularly offered as a fragrant odor, an offering made by fire to the Lord.

7 Along with it shall be the drink offering, consisting of three pints of strong wine with each lamb, poured out in the holy place before the Lord.

8 Offer the second lamb in the evening with the

same grain offering and drink offering. It too is a fragrant odor to the Lord, an offering made by fire.

9, 10   On the Sabbath day, sacrifice two yearling male lambs—both without defect—in addition to the regular offerings. They are to be accompanied by a grain offering of six quarts of fine flour mixed with oil, and the usual drink offering.

11   Also, on the first day of each month there shall be an extra burnt offering to the Lord of two young bulls, one ram, and seven male yearling lambs—all without defect.

12   Accompany them with nine quarts of finely ground flour mixed with oil as a grain offering with each bull; and six quarts of finely ground flour mixed with oil as a grain offering for the ram;

13   And for each lamb, three quarts of finely ground flour mixed with oil for a grain offering. This burnt offering shall be presented by fire, and will please the Lord very much.

14   Along with each sacrifice shall be a drink offering—six pints of wine with each bull, four pints for a ram, and three pints for a lamb. This, then, will be the burnt offering each month throughout the year.

15   Also on the first day of each month you shall offer one male goat for a sin offering to the Lord. This is in addition to the regular daily burnt offering and its drink offering.

16   On the fourteenth day of the first month of each year, you shall celebrate the Passover—[when the death angel passed over the oldest sons of the Israelites in Egypt, leaving them unharmed.[1]]

17   On the following day, a great, joyous seven-day

---

[1]Implied.

festival will begin, but no leavened bread shall be served.

18 On the first day of the festival a holy assembly of all the people shall be called, and no hard work shall be done on that day.

19 You shall offer as burnt sacrifices to the Lord two young bulls, one ram, and seven yearling male lambs—all without defect.

20, 21 With each bull there shall be a grain offering of nine quarts of fine flour mixed with oil; with the ram there shall be six quarts; and with each of the seven lambs there shall be three quarts of fine flour.

22 You must also offer a male goat as a sin offering, to make atonement for yourselves.

23 These offerings shall be in addition to the usual daily sacrifices.

24 This same sacrifice shall be offered on each of the seven days of the feast; they will be very pleasant to the Lord.

25 On the seventh day there shall again be a holy and solemn assembly of all the people, and during that day you may do no hard work.

26 On the Day of First-fruits (also called the Festival of Weeks, or Pentecost), there must be a special, solemn assembly of all the people to celebrate the new harvest. On that day you are to present the first of the new crop of grain as a grain offering to the Lord; there is to be no hard work by anyone on that day.

27 A special burnt offering, very pleasant to the Lord, shall be offered that day. It shall consist of two young bulls, one ram, and seven yearling male lambs.

28, 29 These shall be accompanied by your grain offering of nine quarts of fine flour mixed with oil with each bull, six quarts with the ram, and three quarts with each of the seven lambs.

30 Also offer one male goat to make atonement for yourselves.

31 These special offerings are in addition to the regular daily burnt offerings and grain offerings and drink offerings. Make sure that the animals you sacrifice are without defect.

CHAPTER 29

T he Festival of Trumpets shall be celebrated on the fifteenth day of September[1] each year; there shall be a solemn assembly of all the people on that day, and no hard work may be done.

2 On that day you shall offer a burnt sacrifice consisting of one young bull, one ram, and seven yearling male lambs—all without defect. These are sacrifices which the Lord will appreciate and enjoy.

3, 4 A grain offering of nine quarts of fine flour mingled with oil shall be offered with the bull, six quarts with the ram, and three quarts with each of the seven lambs.

5 In addition, there shall be a male goat sacrificed as a sin offering, to make atonement for you.

6 These special sacrifices are in addition to the regular monthly burnt offering for that day,[2] and also in addition to the regular daily burnt sacrifices, which are to be offered with the respective grain offerings and drink offerings, as specified by the ordinances governing them.

---

[1]Literally, "upon the first day of the seventh month" (of the Hebrew calendar).
[2]Literally, "burnt offerings of the new moon."

7   Ten days later[3] another convocation of all the people shall be held. This will be a day of solemn humility before the Lord, and no work of any kind may be done.

8   On that day you shall offer a burnt sacrifice to the Lord—it will be very pleasant to Him—of one young bull, one ram, seven yearling male lambs—each without defect—

9, 10   And their accompanying grain offerings. Nine quarts of fine flour mixed with oil are to be offered with the bull; six with the ram; and three with each of the seven lambs.

11   You are also to sacrifice one male goat for a sin offering. This is in addition to the sin offering of the Day of Atonement [offered annually on that day[4]], and in addition to the regular daily burnt sacrifices, grain offerings, and drink offerings.

12   Five days later[5] there shall be yet another assembly of all the people, and on that day no hard work shall be done; it is the beginning of a seven-day festival before the Lord.

13   Your special burnt sacrifice that day, which will give much pleasure to the Lord, shall be thirteen young bulls, two rams, and fourteen male yearling lambs—each without defect—

14   Accompanied by the usual grain offerings—nine quarts of fine flour mingled with oil for each of the thirteen young bulls; six quarts for each of the two rams;

15   And three quarts for each of the fourteen lambs.

---

[3]Literally, "on the tenth day of the seventh month" (of the Hebrew calendar).
[4]Implied.
[5]Literally, "on the fifteenth day of the seventh month" (of the Hebrew calendar).

16   There must also be a male goat sacrificed for a sin offering, in addition to the regular daily burnt sacrifice with its accompanying grain offerings and drink offerings.

17   On the second day of this seven-day festival you shall sacrifice twelve young bulls, two rams, and fourteen male yearling lambs—each without defect—

18   Accompanied by the usual grain offerings and drink offerings.

19   Also, in addition to the regular daily burnt sacrifice, you are to sacrifice a male goat with its accompanying grain offering and drink offering for a sin offering.

20   On the third day of the festival, offer eleven yonug bulls, two rams, fourteen male yearling lambs— each without defect—

21   And the usual grain offering and drink offering with each sacrifice.

22   And in addition to the regular daily burnt sacrifices, sacrifice a male goat for a sin offering, with its accompanying grain offering and drink offering.

23   On the fourth day of the festival, you are to sacrifice ten young bulls, two rams, and fourteen male yearling lambs—each without defect—

24   Each with its accompanying grain offering and drink offering;

25   Also a male goat as a sin offering (along with the usual grain and drink offerings) in addition to the regular daily sacrifices.

26, 27   On the fifth day of the festival, sacrifice nine young bulls, two rams, and fourteen male yearling lambs—each without defect—accompanied by the usual grain offerings and drink offerings;

28   Also sacrifice a male goat with the usual grain

and drink offerings, as a special sin offering, in addition to the usual daily sacrifices.

29 On the sixth day of the festival, you must sacrifice eight young bulls, two rams, and fourteen male yearling lambs—each without defect—

30 Along with their usual grain and drink offerings.

31 In addition to the usual daily sacrifices, sacrifice a male goat and the usual grain and drink offerings as a sin offering.

32 On the seventh day of the festival, sacrifice seven young bulls, two rams, and fourteen male yearling lambs—each without defect—

33 Each with their customary grain and drink offerings;

34 Also sacrifice an extra sin offering of one male goat, with the usual grain and drink offerings, in addition to the regular daily sacrifices.

35 On the eighth day summon the people to another solemn assembly; you must do no hard work that day.

36 Sacrifice a burnt offering—they are very pleasant to the Lord—of one young bull, one ram, seven male yearling lambs—each without defect—

37 And the customary grain and drink offerings.

38 Sacrifice also one male goat with the usual grain and drink offerings for a sin offering, in addition to the regular daily sacrifices.

39 These offerings are compulsory at the times of your annual feasts, and are in addition to sacrifices and offerings you present in connection with vows, or as free will offerings, burnt sacrifices, grain offerings, drink offerings, or peace offerings."

40　So Moses gave all of these instructions to the people of Israel.

CHAPTER 30

Now Moses summoned the leaders of the tribes and told them, "The Lord has commanded that when anyone makes a promise to the Lord, either to do something or to quit doing something, that vow must not be broken: the person making the vow must do exactly as he has promised.

3　If a woman promises the Lord to do or not do something, and she is still a girl at home in her father's home,

4　And her father hears that she has made a vow with penalties, but says nothing, then her vow shall stand.

5　But if her father refuses to let her make the vow, or feels that the penalties she has agreed to are too harsh, then her promise will automatically become invalid. Her father must state his disagreement on the first day he hears about it; and then Jehovah will forgive her because her father would not let her do it.

6　If she takes a vow or makes a foolish pledge, and later marries,

7　And her husband learns of her vow and says nothing on the day he hears of it, her vow shall stand.

8　But if her husband refuses to accept her vow or foolish pledge, his disagreement makes it void, and Jehovah will forgive her.

9　But if the woman is a widow or is divorced, she must fulfill her vow.

10　If she is married and living in her husband's home when she makes the vow,

11   And her husband hears of it and does nothing, the vow shall stand;

12   But if he refuses to allow it on the first day he hears of it, her vow is void and Jehovah will forgive her.

13   So her husband may either confirm or nullify her vow,

14   But if he says nothing for a day, then he has already agreed to it.

15   If he waits more than a day and then refuses to permit the vow, whatever penalties to which she agreed shall come upon him—he shall be responsible."

16   These, then, are the commandments the Lord gave Moses concerning relationships between a man and his wife and between a father and his daughter who is living at home.

CHAPTER 31

Then the Lord said to Moses, "Take vengeance on the Midianites for leading you into idolatry, and then you must die."

3   Moses said to the people, "Some of you must take arms to wage Jehovah's war against Midian.

4, 5   Conscript 1,000 men from each tribe." So this was done; and out of the many thousands of Israel, 12,000 armed men were sent to battle by Moses.

6   Phinehas (son of Eleazar the priest) led them into battle, accompanied by the Ark,[1] with trumpets blaring.

7   And every man of Midian was killed in battle!

8   Among those killed were all five of the Midian-

---

[1]Literally, "with the vessels of the sanctuary."

ite kings—Evi, Rekem, Zur, Hur, and Reba. Balaam, the son of Beor, was also killed.

9, 10, 11 Then the Israeli army took as captives all the women and children, and seized the cattle and flocks and a lot of miscellaneous booty. All of the cities, towns, and villages of Midian were then burned.

12 The captives and other spoils of war were brought to Moses and Eleazar the priest, and to the rest of the people of Israel who were camped on the plains of Moab beside the Jordan River, across from Jericho.

13 Moses and Eleazar the priest and all the leaders of the people went out to meet the victorious army,

14 But Moses was very angry with the army officers and battalion leaders.

15 "Why have you let all the women live?" he demanded.

16 "These are the very ones who followed Balaam's advice and caused the people of Israel to worship idols on Mount Peor, and they are the cause of the plague that destroyed us.

17 Now kill all the boys and all the women who have had sexual intercourse.

18 Only the little girls may live; you may keep them for yourselves.

19 Now stay outside of the camp for seven days, all of you who have killed anyone or touched a dead body. Then purify yourselves and your captives on the third and seventh days.

20 Remember also to purify all your garments and everything made of leather, goat's hair, or wood."

21 Then Eleazar the priest said to the men who were in the battle, "This is the commandment Jehovah has given Moses:

22 'Anything that will stand heat—such as gold, silver, bronze, iron, tin, or lead—

23 Shall be passed through fire in order to be made ceremonially pure; it must then be further purified with the purification water. But anything that won't stand heat shall be purified by the water alone.'

24 On the seventh day you must wash your clothes and be purified, and then you may come back into the camp."

25 And the Lord said to Moses,

26 "You and Eleazar the priest and the leaders of the tribes are to make a list of all the booty, including the people and animals;

27 Then divide it into two parts. Half of it is for the men who were in the battle, and the other half is to be given to the people of Israel.

28 But first, the Lord gets a share of all the captives, oxen, donkeys, and flocks kept by the army. His share is one out of every five hundred.

29 Give this share to Eleazar the priest to be presented to the Lord by the gesture of waving before the altar.

30 Also levy a two percent tribute of all the captives, flocks, and cattle that are given to the people of Israel. Present these to the Levites in charge of the Tabernacle, for it is the Lord's portion."

31 So Moses and Eleazar the priest did as the Lord commanded.

32-35 The total booty (besides the jewelry, clothing, etc., which the soldiers kept for themselves) was 675,000 sheep; 72,000 oxen; 61,000 donkeys; and 32,000 young girls.

36, 37 So the half given to the army totaled:

337,500 sheep (of which 675 were given to the Lord):

38　　36,000 oxen (of which 72 were given to the Lord);

39　　30,500 donkeys (of which 61 were given to the Lord);

40　　16,000 girls (of whom 32 went to the Levites).[2]

41　All of the Lord's portion was given to Eleazar the priest, as the Lord had directed Moses.

42　The half of the booty assigned to the people of Israel—Moses had separated it from the half belonging to the warriors—amounted to:

43　　337,500 sheep,

44　　36,000 oxen,

45　　30,500 donkeys, and

46　　16,000 girls.

47　In accordance with the Lord's directions, Moses gave two percent of these to the Levites.

48, 49　Then the officers and battalion leaders came to Moses and said, "We have accounted for all the men who went out to battle, and not one of us is missing!

50　So we have brought a special thank-offering to the Lord from our booty—gold jewels, bracelets, anklets, rings, earrings, and necklaces. This is to make atonement for our souls before the Lord."

51, 52　Moses and Eleazar the priest received this special offering from the captains and battalion leaders and company commanders, and found its total value to be more than $300,000.

---

[2]Literally, "were the Lord's portion."

53   (The soldiers had also kept personal booty for themselves.)

54   The offering was taken into the Tabernacle and kept there before the Lord as a memorial of the people of Israel.

CHAPTER 32

When Israel arrived in the land of Jazar and Gilead, the tribes of Reuben and Gad (who had large flocks of sheep) noticed what wonderful sheep country it was.

2   So they came to Moses and Eleazar the priest and the other tribal leaders and said,

3, 4   "The Lord has used Israel to destroy the population of this whole countryside—Ataroth, Dibon, Jazer, Nimrah, Heshbon, Elealeh, Sebam, Nebo, and Beon. And it is all wonderful sheep country, ideal for our flocks.

5   Please let us have this land as our portion instead of the land on the other side of the Jordan River."

6   "You mean you want to sit here while your brothers go across and do all the fighting?" Moses demanded.

7   "Are you trying to discourage the rest of the people from going across to the land that the Lord has given them?

8   This is the same kind of thing your fathers did! I sent them from Kadesh-barnea to spy out the land,

9   But when they finished their survey and returned from the valley of Eshcol, they discouraged the people from going on into the Promised Land.

10, 11   And the Lord's anger was hot against them,

and He swore that of all those He had rescued from Egypt, no one over twenty years of age would ever see the land He promised Abraham, Isaac, and Jacob, for they had refused to do what He wanted them to.

12 The only exceptions were Caleb (son of Jephunneh the Kenizzite) and Joshua (son of Nun)—for they wholeheartedly followed the Lord and urged the people to go on into the Promised Land.

13 The Lord made us wander back and forth in the wilderness for forty years until all that evil generation died.

14 But here you are, a brood of sinners doing exactly the same thing! Only there are more of you, so Jehovah's anger against Israel will be even fiercer this time.

15 If you turn away from God like this, He will make the people stay even longer in the wilderness, and you will be responsible for destroying His people and bringing disaster to this entire nation!"

16 "Not at all!" they explained. "We will build sheepfolds for our flocks and cities for our little ones,

17 But we ourselves will go over armed, ahead of the rest of the people of Israel, until we have brought them safely to their inheritance. But first we will need to build walled cities here for our families, to keep them safe from attack by the local inhabitants.

18 We will not settle down here until all the people of Israel have received their inheritance.

19 We don't want land on the other side of the Jordan; we would rather have it on this side, on the east."

20 Then Moses said, "All right, if you will do what you have said and arm yourselves for Jehovah's war,

21 And keep your troops across the Jordan until the Lord has driven out His enemies,

22 Then, when the land is finally subdued before the Lord, you may return. Then you will have discharged your duty to the Lord and to the rest of the people of Israel. And the land on the eastern side shall be your possession from the Lord.

23 But if you don't do as you have said, then you will have sinned against the Lord, and you may be sure that your sin will catch up with you.

24 Go ahead and build cities for your families and sheepfolds for your sheep, and do all you have said."

25 "We will follow your instructions exactly," the people of Gad and Reuben replied.

26 "Our children, wives, flocks, and cattle shall stay here in the cities of Gilead.

27 But all of us who are conscripted will go over to battle for the Lord, just as you have said."

28 So Moses gave his approval by saying to Eleazar, Joshua, and the tribal leaders of Israel,

29 "If all the men of the tribes of Gad and Reuben who are conscripted for the Lord's battles go with you over Jordan, then, when the land is conquered, you must give them the land of Gilead;

30 But if they refuse, then they must accept land among the rest of you in the land of Canaan."

31 The tribes of Gad and Reuben said again, "As the Lord has commanded, so we will do—

32 We will follow the Lord fully armed into Canaan, but our own land shall be here on this side of the Jordan."

33 So Moses assigned the territory of King Sihon of the Amorites, and of King Og of Bashan—all the

land and cities—to the tribes of Gad, Reuben, and the half-tribe of Manasseh (son of Joseph).

34   The people of Gad built these cities:

Dibon,
Ataroth,
Aroer,

35   Atroth-shophan,
Jazer,
Jogbehah,

36   Beth-nimrah,
Beth-haran.

They were all fortified cities with sheepfolds.

37   The children of Reuben built the following cities:

Heshbon,
Elealeh,
Kiriathaim,

38   Nebo,
Baal-meon,
Sibmah.

(The Israelites later changed the names of some of these cities they had conquered and rebuilt.)

39   Then the clan of Machir of the tribe of Manasseh went to Gilead and conquered it, and drove out the Amorites who were living there.

40   So Moses gave Gilead to the Machirites, and they lived there.

41   The men of Jair, another clan of the tribe of Manasseh, occupied many of the towns in Gilead, and changed the name of their area to Havroth-jair.

42   Meanwhile, a man named Nobah led an army[1] to Kenath and its surrounding villages, and occupied

---

[1]Implied.

them, and he called the area Nobah, after his own
name.

CHAPTER 33

This is the itinerary of the nation of Israel from the
time Moses and Aaron led them out of Egypt.

2   Moses had written down their movements as
the Lord had instructed him.

3, 4   They left the city of Rameses, Egypt, on the
first day of April,[1] the day after the night of the Passover. They left proudly, hurried along by the Egyptians
who were burying all their eldest sons, killed by the
Lord the night before. The Lord had certainly defeated
all the gods of Egypt that night!

5, 6   After leaving Rameses, they stayed in Succoth, Etham (at the edge of the wilderness), and

7   Pihahiroth (near Baal-zephon, where they
camped at the foot of Mount Migdol).

8   From there they went through the middle of
the Red Sea and on for three days into the Etham
wilderness, camping at Marah.

9   Leaving Marah, they came to Elim, where there
are twelve springs of water and seventy palm trees;
they stayed there for quite a long time.

10   Leaving Elim, they camped beside the Red Sea,

11   And then in the Wilderness of Sihn.

12   Next was Dophkah,

13   And then Alush;

14   Then on to Rephidim (where there was no
water for the people to drink);

15   From Rephidim they went to the wilderness of
Sinai;

---

[1]Literally, "on the fifteenth day of the first month" (of the Hebrew
calendar).

16 From the wilderness of Sinai to Kibroth-hattaavah;

17 From Kibroth-hattaavah to Hazeroth;

18 From Hazeroth to Rithmah;

19 From Rithmah to Rimmon-parez;

20 From Rimmon-parez to Libnah;

21 From Libnah to Rissah;

22 From Rissah to Kehelathah;

23 From Kehelathah to Mount Shepher;

24 From Mount Shepher to Haradah;

25 From Haradah to Makheloth;

26 From Makheloth to Tahath;

27 From Tahath to Terah;

28 From Terah to Mithkah;

29 From Mithkah to Hashmonah;

30 From Hashmonah to Moseroth;

31 From Moseroth to Bene-jaakan;

32 From Bene-jaakan to Hor-haggidgad;

33 From Hor-haggidgad to Jotbathah;

34 From Jotbathah to Abronah;

35 From Abronah to Ezion-geber;

36 From Ezion-geber to Kadesh (in the wilderness of Zin);

37 From Kadesh to Mount Hor (at the edge of the land of Edom).

38, 39 While they were at the foot of Mount Hor, Aaron the priest was directed by the Lord to go up into the mountain, and there he died. This occurred during the fortieth year after the people of Israel had left Egypt. The date of his death was July 15,[2] when he was 123 years old.

---

[2]Literally, "the first day of the fifth month" (of the Hebrew calendar).

40   It was then that the Canaanite king of Arad, who lived in the Negeb, in the land of Canaan, heard that the people of Israel were approaching his land.

41   After dealing with him, the Israeli journeyed from Mount Hor and camped in Zalmonah,

42   Then at Punon,

43   Then at Oboth,

44   Then Iyeabarim (at the border of Moab).

45   From there they went to Dibon-gad,

46   And then to Almon-diblathaim,

47   And on into the mountains of Abarim, near Mount Nebo,

48   And finally to the plains of Moab beside the river Jordan, opposite Jericho.

49   While in that area they camped at various places along the Jordan River, from Beth-jeshimoth as far as Abel-shittim, on the plains of Moab.

50, 51   It was while they were camped there that the Lord told Moses to tell the people of Israel, "When you pass across the Jordan River into the land of Canaan,

52   You must drive out all the people living there and destroy all their idols—their carved stones, molten images, and the open-air sanctuaries in the hills where they worship their idols.

53   I have given the land to you; take it and live there.

54   You will be given land in proportion to the size of your tribes. The larger sections of land will be divided by lot among the larger tribes, and the smaller sections will be allotted to the smaller tribes.

55   But if you refuse to drive out the people living

there, those who remain will be as cinders in your eyes and thorns in your sides.

56   And I will destroy you as I had planned for you to destroy them."

CHAPTER 34

The Lord told Moses to tell the people of Israel, "When they come into the land of Canaan (I am giving you the entire land as your homeland),

3   The southern portion of the country will be the Wilderness of Zin, along the edge of Edom. The southern boundary will begin at the Dead Sea,

4   And will continue south past Scorpion Pass[1] in the direction of Zin. Its southernmost point will be Kadesh-barnea, from which it will go to Hazaraddar, and on to Azmon.

5   From Azmon the boundary will follow the Wadi-el-Arish[2] down to the Mediterranean Sea.

6   Your western boundary will be the coastline of the Mediterranean Sea.

7, 8, 9   Your northern border will begin at the Mediterranean Sea and will proceed eastward to Mount Hor, then to Lebo-Hamath, and on through Zedad and Ziphron to Hazar-enan.

10, 11   The eastern border will be from Hazar-enan south to Shepham, then on to Riblah at the east side of Ain. From there it will make a large half-circle, first going south and then westward until it touches the southernmost tip of the Sea of Galilee,

12   And then along the Jordan River, ending at the Dead Sea."

---

[1]Literally, "ascent of Akrabbim."
[2]Literally, "the brook of Egypt."

13 "This is the territory you are to apportion among yourselves by lot," Moses said. "It is to be divided up among the nine and one-half tribes,

14, 15 For the tribes of Reuben and Gad and the half-tribe of Manasseh have already been assigned land on the east side of the Jordan, opposite Jericho."

16, 17 And the Lord said to Moses, "These are the names of the men I have appointed to handle the dividing up of the land:

Eleazar the priest,
Joshua (son of Nun),

18 And one leader from each tribe, as listed below:

TRIBE	LEADER
19 Judah	Caleb (son of Jephunneh)
20 Simeon	Shemuel (son of Ammihud)
21 Benjamin	Elidad (son of Chislon)
22 Dan	Bukki (son of Jogli)
23 Manasseh	Hanniel (son of Ephod)
24 Ephraim	Kemuel (son of Shiphtan)
25 Zebulun	Elizaphan (son of Parnach)
26 Issachar	Paltiel (son of Azzan)
27 Asher	Ahihud (son of Shelomi)
28 Naphtali	Pedahel (son of Ammihud)

29 These are the names of the men I have appointed to oversee the dividing of the land among the tribes."

CHAPTER 35

While Israel was camped beside the Jordan on the plains of Moab, opposite Jericho, the Lord said to Moses,

2 "Instruct the people of Israel to give to the Levites as their inheritance certain cities and surrounding pasture lands.

3 These cities are for their homes, and the surrounding lands for their cattle, flocks, and other livestock.

4 Their pasture lands shall extend outward from the city walls for 1500 feet in each direction.

5 Thus there will be 3000 feet between the boundaries, with the city in the center.

6 You shall give the Levites the six Cities of Refuge where a person who has accidentally killed someone can run and be safe, and forty-two other cities besides.

7 In all, there shall be forty-eight cities with the surrounding pasture land given to the Levites.

8 These cities shall be in various parts of the nation: the larger tribes with many cities will give several to the Levites, while the smaller tribes will give fewer."

9, 10 And the Lord said to Moses, "Tell the people that when they arrive in the land,

11 Cities of Refuge shall be designated for anyone to flee into if he has killed someone accidentally.

12 These cities will be places of protection from the dead man's relatives who want to avenge his death; for the slayer must not be killed unless a fair trial establishes his guilt.

13, 14 Three of these six Cities of Refuge are to be located in the land of Canaan, and three on the east side of the Jordan River.

15 These are not only for the protection of Israelites, but also for foreigners and travelers.

16 But if someone is struck and killed by a piece of iron, it must be presumed to be murder, and the murderer must be executed.

17 Or if the slain man was struck down with a large stone, it is murder, and the murderer shall die.

18 The same is true if he is killed with a wooden weapon.

19 The avenger of his death shall personally kill the murderer when he meets him.

20 So, if anyone kills another out of hatred by throwing something at him, or ambushing him,

21 Or angrily striking him with his fist so that he dies, he is a murderer; and the murderer shall be executed by the avenger.

22, 23 But if it is an accident—a case in which something is thrown unintentionally, or in which a stone is thrown without anger, without realizing it will hit anyone, and without wanting to harm an enemy— yet the man dies,

24 Then the people shall judge whether or not it was an accident, and whether or not to hand the killer over to the avenger of the dead man.

25 If it is decided that it was accidental, then the people shall save the killer from the avenger; the killer shall be permitted to stay in the City of Refuge; and he must live there until the death of the High Priest.

26 If the slayer leaves the City,

27 And the avenger finds him outside and kills him, it is not murder,

28 For the man should have stayed inside the City until the death of the High Priest. But after the death of the High Priest, the man may return to his own land and home.

29 These are permanent laws for all Israel from generation to generation.

30 All murderers must be executed, but only if there is more than one witness; no man shall die with only one person testifying against him.

31 Whenever anyone is judged guilty of murder, he must die—no ransom may be accepted for him.

32 Nor may a payment be accepted from a refugee in a City of Refuge, permitting him to return to his home before the death of the High Priest.

33 In this way the land will not be polluted, for murder pollutes the land, and no atonement can be made for murder except by the execution of the murderer.

34 You shall not defile the land where you are going to live, for I, Jehovah, will be living there."

CHAPTER 36

Then the heads of the sub-clan of Gilead (of the clan of Machir, of the tribe of Manasseh, one of the sons of Joseph), came to Moses and the leaders of Israel with a petition: "The Lord instructed you to divide the land by lot among the people of Israel," they reminded Moses, "and to give the inheritance of our brother Zelophehad to his daughters.

3 But if they marry into another tribe, their land will go with them to the tribe into which they marry. In this way the total area of our tribe will be reduced,

4 And will not be returned at the year of Jubilee."

5 Then Moses replied publicly, giving them these instructions from the Lord: "The men of the tribe of Joseph have a proper complaint.

6 This is what the Lord has further commanded

concerning the daughters of Zelophehad: 'Let them be married to anyone they like, so long as it is within their own tribe.

7 In this way none of the land of the tribe will shift to any other tribe, for the inheritance of every tribe is to remain permanently as it was first allotted.

8 The girls throughout the tribes of Israel who are heiresses must marry within their own tribe, so that their land won't leave the tribe.

9 In this way no inheritance shall move from one tribe to another.' "

10 The daughters of Zelophehad did as the Lord commanded Moses.

11, 12 These girls, Mahlah, Tirzah, Hoglah, Milcah, and Noah, were married to men in their own tribe of Manasseh (son of Joseph); so their inheritance remained in their tribe.

13 These are the commandments and ordinances which the Lord gave to the people of Israel through Moses, while they were camped on the plains of Moab beside the Jordan River, across from Jericho.

Deuteronomy

CHAPTER 1

This book records Moses' address to the people of Israel when they were camped in the valley of the Arabah in the wilderness of Moab, east of the Jordan River. (Cities in the area included Suph, Paran, Tophel, Laban, Hazeroth, and Dizahab.) The speech was given on February 15,[1] forty years after the people of Israel left Mt. Horeb—though it takes only eleven days to travel by foot from Mt. Horeb to Kadesh-barnea,[2] going by way of Mt. Seir! At the time of this address, King Sihon of the Amorites had already been defeated at Heshbon, and King Og of Bashan had been defeated at Ashteroth, near Edre-i. Here, then, is Moses' address to Israel, stating all the laws God had commanded him to pass on to them:

6 "It was forty years ago, at Mt. Horeb, that Jehovah our God told us, 'You have stayed here long enough.

7 Now go and occupy the hill country of the Amorites, the valley of the Arabah, and the Negeb, and all the land of Canaan and Lebanon—the entire area from the shores of the Mediterranean Sea to the Euphrates River.

8 I am giving all of it to you! Go in and possess it, for it is the land the Lord promised to your ancestors

---

[1]Literally, "the first day of the eleventh month" (of the Hebrew calendar).
[2]Kadesh-barnea was at the southern edge of the Promised Land.

Abraham, Isaac, and Jacob, and all of their descendants.'

9 At that time I told the people, 'I need help! You are a great burden for me to carry all by myself,

10 For the Lord has multiplied you like stars!

11 And may He multiply you a thousand times more, and bless you as He promised,

12 But what can one man do to settle all your quarrels and problems?

13 So choose some men from each tribe who are wise, experienced, and understanding, and I will appoint them as your leaders.'

14 They agreed to this;

15 I took the men they selected, some from every tribe, and appointed them as administrative assistants in charge of thousands, hundreds, fifties, and tens to decide their quarrels and assist them in every way.

16 I instructed them to be perfectly fair at all times, even to foreigners!

17 'When giving your decisions,' I told them, 'never favor a man because he is rich; be fair to great and small alike. Don't fear their displeasure, for you are judging in the place of God. Bring me any cases too difficult for you, and I will handle them.'

18 And I gave them other instructions at that time, also.

19, 20, 21 Then we left Mount Horeb and traveled through the great and terrible desert, finally arriving among the Amorite hills to which the Lord our God had directed us. We were then at Kadesh-barnea [on the border of the Promised Land[3]] and I said to the people, 'The Lord God has given us this land. Go and

---
[3]Implied.

possess it as He told us to. Don't be afraid! Don't even doubt!'

22   But they replied, 'First let's send out spies to discover the best route of entry, and to decide which cities we should capture first.'

23   This seemed like a good idea, so I chose twelve spies, one from each tribe.

24, 25   They crossed into the hills and came to the Valley of Eshcol, and returned with samples of the local fruit. One look was enough to convince us that it was indeed a good land the Lord our God had given us.

26   But the people refused to go in, and rebelled against the Lord's command.

27   They murmured and complained in their tents and said, 'The Lord must hate us, bringing us here from Egypt to be slaughtered by these Amorites.

28   What are we getting into? Our brothers who spied out the land have frightened us with their report. They say that the people of the land are tall and power-ful, and that the walls of their cities rise high into the sky! They have even seen giants there—the descendants of the Anakim!'

29   But I said to them, 'Don't be afraid!

30   The Lord God is your leader, and He will fight for you with His mighty miracles, just as you saw Him do in Egypt.

31   And you know how he has cared for you again and again here in the wilderness, just as a father cares for his child!'

32   But nothing I said did any good. They refused to believe the Lord our God

33   Who had led them all the way, and had selected the best places for them to camp, and had guided them

by a pillar of fire at night and a pillar of cloud during the day.

34, 35　Well, the Lord heard their complaining and was very angry. He vowed that not one person in that entire generation would live to see the good land He had promised their fathers,

36　Except Caleb (the son of Jephunneh), who, because he had wholly followed the Lord, would receive as his personal inheritance some of the land he had walked over.

37　And the Lord was even angry with me because of them and said to me, 'You shall not enter the Promised Land!

38　Instead, your assistant, Joshua (the son of Nun), shall lead the people. Encourage him as he prepares to take over the leadership.

39　I will give the land to the children they said would die in the wilderness.

40　But as for you of the older generation, turn around now and go on back across the desert toward the Red Sea.'

41　Then they confessed, 'We have sinned! We will go into the land and fight for it as the Lord our God has told us to.' So they strapped on their weapons and thought it would be easy to conquer the whole area.

42　But the Lord said to me, 'Tell them not to do it, for I will not go with them; they will be struck down before their enemies.'

43　I told them, but they wouldn't listen. Instead, they rebelled again against the Lord's commandment and went on up into the hill country to fight.

44　But the Amorites who lived there came out

against them, and chased them like bees and killed them from Seir to Hormah.

45   Then they returned and wept before the Lord, but He wouldn't listen.

46   So they stayed there at Kadesh for a long time.

CHAPTER 2

Then we turned back across the wilderness toward the Red Sea, for so the Lord had instructed me. For many years we wandered around in the area of Mount Seir.

2   Then at last the Lord said,

3   'You have stayed here long enough. Turn northward.

4   Inform the people that they will be passing through the country belonging to their brothers the Edomites, the descendants of Esau who live in Seir; the Edomites will be nervous, so be careful.

5   Don't start a fight! For I have given them all the Mount Seir hill country as their permanent possession, and I will not give you even a tiny piece of their land.

6   Pay them for whatever food or water you use.

7   The Lord your God has watched over you and blessed you every step of the way for all these forty years as you have wandered around in this great wilderness; and you have lacked nothing in all that time.'

8   So we passed through Edom where our brothers lived, crossing the Arabah Road that goes south to Elath and Ezi-on-geber, and traveling northward toward the Moab desert.

9   Then the Lord warned us, 'Don't attack the Moabites either, for I will not give you any of their land; I have given it to the descendants of Lot.'

10 (The Emim used to live in that area, a very large tribe, tall as the giants of Anakim;

11 Both the Emim and the Anakim are often referred to as the Rephaim, but the Moabites call them Emim.

12 In earlier days the Horites lived in Seir, but they were driven out and displaced by the Edomites, the descendants of Esau, just as Israel would displace the peoples of Canaan, whose land had been assigned to Israel by the Lord.)

13 'Now cross Zered Brook,' the Lord said; and we did.

14, 15 So it took us thirty-eight years to finally get across Zered Brook from Kadesh! For the Lord had decreed that this could not happen until all the men, who thirty-eight years earlier were old enough to bear arms, had died. Yes, the hand of the Lord was against them until finally all were dead.

16, 17 Then at last the Lord said to me,

18 'Today Israel shall cross the borders of Moab at Ar,

19 Into the land of the Ammonites. But do not attack them, for I will not give you any of their land. I have given it to the descendants of Lot.'

20 (That area, too, used to be inhabited by the Rephaim, called 'Zamzummim' by the Ammonites.

21 They were a large and powerful tribe, as tall as the Anakim; but Jehovah destroyed them as the Ammonites came in, and the Ammonites lived there in their place.

22 The Lord had similarly helped the descendants of Esau at Mount Seir, for He destroyed the Horites who were living there before them.

23   Another similar situation occurred when the people of Caphtor invaded and destroyed the tribe of Avvim living in villages scattered across the countryside as far away as Gaza.)

24   Then the Lord said, 'Cross the Arnon River into the land of King Sihon the Amorite, king of Heshbon. War against him and begin to take possession of his land.

25   Beginning today I will make people throughout the whole earth tremble with fear because of you, and dread your arrival.'

26   Then from the wilderness of Kedemoth I sent ambassadors to King Sihon of Heshbon with a proposal of peace.

27   'Let us pass through your land,' we said. 'We will stay on the main road and won't turn off into the fields on either side.

28   We will not steal food as we go, but will purchase every bite we eat and everything we drink; all we want is permission to pass through.

29   The Edomites at Seir allowed us to go through their country, and so did the Moabites, whose capital is at Ar. We are on our way across the Jordan into the land the Lord our God has given us.'

30   But King Sihon refused because Jehovah your God made him obstinate, so that He could destroy him by the hands of Israel, as has now been done.

31   Then the Lord said to me, 'I have begun to give you the land of King Sihon; when you possess it, it shall belong to Israel forever.'

32   King Sihon then declared war on us and mobilized his forces at Jahaz.

33, 34   But the Lord our God crushed him, and

we conquered all his cities, and utterly destroyed everything, including the women and babies. We left nothing alive

35, 36 Except the cattle, which we took as our reward, along with the booty gained from ransacking the cities we had taken. We conquered everything from Aroer to Gilead—from the edge of the Arnon River valley, and including all the cities in the valley. Not one city was too strong for us, for the Lord our God gave all of them to us.

37 However, we stayed away from the people of Ammon and from the Jabbok River and the hill country cities, the places Jehovah our God had forbidden us to enter.

CHAPTER 3

Next we turned toward King Og's land of Bashan. He immediately mobilized his army and attacked us at Edre-i. But the Lord told me not to be afraid of him. 'All his people and his land are yours,' the Lord told me. 'You will do to him as you did to King Sihon of the Amorites, at Heshbon.'

3 So the Lord helped us fight against King Og and his people, and we killed them all.

4 We conquered all sixty of his cities, the entire Argob region of Bashan.

5 These were well-fortified cities with high walls and barred gates. Of course we also took all of the unwalled towns.

6 We utterly destroyed the kingdom of Bashan just as we had destroyed King Sihon's kingdom at Heshbon, killing the entire population—men, women, and children alike.

7 But we kept the cattle and loot for ourselves.

8 We now possessed all the land of the two kings of the Amorites east of the Jordan River—all the land from the valley of the Arnon to Mount Hermon.

9 (The Sidonians called Mount Hermon 'Sirion,' while the Amorites called it 'Senir.')

10 We had now conquered all the cities on the plateau, and all of Gilead and Bashan as far as the cities of Salecah and Edre-i.

11 Incidentally, King Og of Bashan was the last of the giant Rephaim. His iron bedstead is kept in a museum at Rabbah, one of the cities of the Ammonites, and measures thirteen and a half feet long by six feet wide.

12 At that time I gave the conquered land to the tribes of Reuben, Gad, and the half-tribe of Manasseh. To the tribes of Reuben and Gad I gave the area beginning at Aroer on the Arnon River, plus half of Mount Gilead, including its cities.

13 The half-tribe of Manasseh received the remainder of Gilead and all of the former kingdom of King Og, the Argob region. (Bashan is sometimes called 'The Land of the Rephaim.')

14 The clan of Jair, of the tribe of Manasseh, took over the whole Argob region (Bashan) to the borders of the Geshurites and Ma-acthites. They renamed their country after themselves, calling it Havvoth-jair (meaning 'Jair's Villages') as it is still known today.

15 Then I gave Gilead to the clan of Machir.

16 The tribes of Reuben and Gad received the area extending from the Jabbok River in Gilead (which was the Ammonite frontier) to the middle of the valley of the Arnon River.

17　　They also received the Arabah (or, wasteland), bounded by the Jordan River on the west, from Chinnereth to Mount Pisgah and the Salt Sea (also called the Sea of the Arabah).

18　　At that time I reminded the tribes of Reuben and Gad and the half-tribe of Manasseh, that although the Lord had given them the land, they could not begin settling down until their armed men led the other tribes across the Jordan to the land the Lord was giving them.

19　　'But your wives and children,' I told them, 'may live here in the cities the Lord has given you, caring for your many cattle

20　　Until you return after the Lord has given victory to the other tribes, too. When they conquer the land the Lord your God has given them across the Jordan River, then you may return here to your own land.'

21　　Then I said to Joshua, 'You have seen what the Lord your God has done to those two kings. You will do the same to all the kingdoms on the other side of the Jordan.

22　　Don't be afraid of the nations there, for the Lord your God will fight for you.'

23, 24, 25　　At that time I made this plea to God: 'O Lord God, please let me cross over into the Promised Land—the good land beyond the Jordan River with its rolling hills—and Lebanon. I want to see the result of all the greatness and power You have been showing us; for what God in all of heaven or earth can do what You have done for us?'

26　　But the Lord was angry with me because of you, and would not let me cross over. 'Speak of it no more,' He ordered,

27　　'But go to the top of Mount Pisgah where you

can look out in every direction, and there you will see
the land in the distance. But you shall not cross the
Jordan River.

28 Commission Joshua to replace you, and then
encourage him, for he shall lead the people across to
conquer the land you will see from the mountain top.'

29 So we remained in the valley near Beth-peor.

CHAPTER 4

And now, O Israel, listen carefully to these laws I
teach you, and obey them if you want to live and
enter into and possess the land given you by the Lord
God of your ancestors.

2 Do not add other laws or subtract from these;
just obey them, for they are from the Lord your God.

3 You have seen what the Lord did to you at
Baal-peor, where He destroyed many people for worshiping idols.

4 But all of you who were faithful to the Lord
your God are still alive today.

5 These are the laws for you to obey when you
arrive in the land where you will live. They are from
the Lord our God. He has given them to me to pass
on to you.

6 If you obey them they will give you a reputation
for wisdom and intelligence. When the surrounding
nations hear these laws they will exclaim, 'What other
nation is as wise and prudent as Israel!'

7 For what other nation, great or small, has God
among them, as the Lord our God is here among us
whenever we call upon Him?

8 And what nation, no matter how great, has laws
as fair as these I am giving you today?

9   But watch out! Be very careful never to forget what you have seen God doing for you. May His miracles have a deep and permanent effect upon your lives! Tell your children and your grandchildren about the glorious miracles He did.

10   Tell them especially about the day you stood before the Lord at Mount Horeb, and He told me, 'Summon the people before Me and I will instruct them, so that they will learn always to reverence Me, and so that they can teach My laws to their children.'

11   You stood at the foot of the mountain, and the mountain burned with fire; flames shot far into the sky, surrounded by black clouds and deep darkness.

12   And the Lord spoke to you from the fire; you heard His words but didn't see Him.

13   He proclaimed the laws you must obey—the Ten Commandments—and wrote them on two stone tablets.

14   Yes, it was at that time that the Lord commanded me to issue the laws you must obey when you arrive in the Promised Land.

15   But beware! You didn't see the form of God that day as He spoke to you from the fire at Mount Horeb,

16, 17   So do not defile yourselves by trying to make a statue of God—an idol in any form, whether of a man, woman, animal, bird,

18   A small animal that runs along the ground, or a fish.

19   And do not look up into the sky to worship the sun, moon, or stars. The Lord may permit other nations to get away with this, but not you.

20   The Lord has rescued you from prison—Egypt

—to be His special people, His own inheritance; this is what you are today.

21, 22 But He was angry with me because of you; He vowed that I could not go over the Jordan River into the good land He has given you as your inheritance. I must die here on this side of the river.

23 Beware lest you break the contract the Lord your God has made with you! You will break it if you make any idols, for the Lord your God has utterly forbidden this.

24 He is a devouring fire, a jealous God.

25 In the future, when your children and grandchildren are born and you have been in the land a long time, and you have defiled yourselves by making idols, and the Lord your God is very angry because of your sin,

26 Heaven and earth are witnesses that you shall be quickly destroyed from the land. Soon, now, you will cross the Jordan River and conquer that land. But your days there will be brief; you will then be utterly destroyed.

27 Jehovah will scatter you among the nations, and you will be but few in number.

28 There, far away, you will worship idols made from wood and stone, idols that neither see nor hear nor eat nor smell.

29 But you will also begin to search again for Jehovah your God, and you shall find Him when you search for Him with all your hearts and souls.

30 When those bitter days have come upon you in the latter times, you will finally return to the Lord your God and listen to what He tells you.

31 For the Lord your God is merciful—He will not

abandon you nor destroy you nor forget the promises He has made to your ancestors.

32 In all history, going back to the time when God created man upon the earth, search from one end of the heavens to the other to see if you can find anything like this:

33 An entire nation heard the voice of God speaking to it from fire, as you did, and lived!

34 Where else will you ever find another example of God's removing a nation from its slavery by sending terrible plagues, mighty miracles, war, and terror? Yet that is what the Lord your God did for you in Egypt, right before your very eyes.

35 He did these things so you would realize that Jehovah is God, and that there is no one else like Him.

36 He let you hear His voice instructing you from heaven, and He let you see His great pillar of fire upon the earth; you even heard His words from the center of the fire.

37 It was because He loved your ancestors and chose to bless their descendants that He personally brought you out from Egypt with a great display of power.

38 He drove away other nations greater by far than you, and gave you their land as an inheritance, as it is today.

39 This is your wonderful thought for the day: Jehovah is God both in heaven and down here upon the earth; and there is no God other than Him!

40 You must obey these laws that I will tell you today, so that all will be well with you and your children, and so that you will live forever in the land the Lord your God is giving you."

41 Then Moses instructed the people of Israel to

set apart three cities east of the Jordan River,

42   Where anyone who accidentally killed someone could flee for safety.

43   These cities were Bezer, on the plateau in the wilderness, for the tribe of Reuben; Ramoth, in Gilead, for the tribe of Gad; and Golan, in Bashan, for the tribe of Manasseh.

44, 45, 46   Listed below are the laws Moses issued to the people of Israel when they left Egypt, and as they were camped east of the Jordan River near the city of Beth-peor. (This was the land formerly occupied by the Amorites under King Sihon, whose capital was Heshbon; he and his people were destroyed by Moses and the Israeli.

47   Israel conquered his land and that of King Og of Bashan—they were two Amorite kings east of the Jordan.

48   Israel also conquered all the area from Aroer at the edge of the Arnon River Valley to Mount Sirion, or Mount Hermon, as it is sometimes called;

49   And all the Arabah east of the Jordan River over to the Salt Sea, below the slopes of Mount Pisgah.)

CHAPTER 5

Moses continued speaking to the people of Israel and said, "Listen carefully now to all these laws God has given you; learn them, and be sure to obey them!

2, 3   The Lord our God made a contract with you at Mount Horeb—*not with your ancestors, but with you who are here alive today.*

4   He spoke with you face to face from the center of the fire, there at the mountain.

5 I stood as an intermediary between you and Jehovah, for you were afraid of the fire and did not go up to Him on the mountain. He spoke to me and I passed on His laws to you. This is what He said:

6 'I am Jehovah your God who rescued you from slavery in Egypt.

7 Never worship any god but Me.

8 Never make idols; don't worship images, whether of birds, animals, or fish.

9, 10 You shall not bow down to any images nor worship them in any way, for I am the Lord your God. I am a jealous God, and I will bring the curse of a father's sins upon even the third and fourth generation of the children of those who hate Me; but I will show kindness to a thousand generations of those who love Me and keep My commandments.

11 You must never use My name to make a vow you don't intend to keep.[1] I will not overlook that.

12 Keep the Sabbath day holy. This is My command.

13 Work the other six days,

14 But the seventh day is the Sabbath of the Lord your God; no work shall be done that day by you or by any of your household—your sons, daughters, servants, oxen, donkeys, or cattle; even foreigners living among you must obey this law. Everybody must rest as you do.

15 Why should you keep the Sabbath? It is because you were slaves in Egypt, and the Lord your God brought you out with a great display of miracles.

16 Honor your father and mother (remember, this

---

[1]Literally, "You must not utter the name of the Lord your God to misuse it."

is a commandment of the Lord your God); if you do so, you shall have a long, prosperous life in the land He is giving you.

17   You must not murder.

18   You must not commit adultery.

19   You must not steal.

20   You must not tell lies.

21   You must not burn with desire for another man's wife, nor envy him for his home, land, servants, oxen, donkeys, nor anything else he owns.'

22   The Lord has given these laws to each one of you from the heart of the fire, surrounded by the clouds and thick darkness that engulfed Mount Sinai. Those were the only commandments He gave you at that time,[2] and He wrote them out on two stone tablets and gave them to me.

23   But when you heard the loud voice from the darkness, and saw the terrible fire at the top of the mountain, all your tribal leaders came to me

24   And pleaded, 'Today the Lord our God has shown us His glory and greatness; we have even heard His voice from the heart of the fire. Now we know that a man may speak to God and not die;

25   But we will surely die if He speaks to us again. This awesome fire will consume us.

26, 27   What man can hear, as we have, the voice of the living God speaking from the heart of the fire, and live? You go and listen to all that God says, then come and tell us, and we will listen and obey.'

28   And the Lord agreed to your request, and said to me, 'I have heard what the people have said to you, and I agree.

[2]Literally, "and He added no more."

29 Oh, that they would always have such a heart for Me, wanting to obey My commandments. Then all would go well with them in the future, and with their children throughout all generations!

30 Go and tell them to return to their tents.

31 Then you come back and stand here beside Me, and I will give you all My commandments, and you shall teach them to the people; and they will obey them in the land I am giving to them.' "

32 So Moses told the people, "You must obey all the commandments of the Lord your God, following His directions in every detail, going the whole way He has laid out for you;

33 Only then will you live long and prosperous lives in the land you are to enter and possess.

CHAPTER 6

The Lord your God told me to give you all these commandments which you are to obey in the land you will soon be entering, where you will live.

2 The purpose of these laws is to cause you, your sons, and your grandsons to reverence the Lord your God by obeying all of His instructions as long as you live; if you do, you will have long, prosperous years ahead of you.

3 Therefore, O Israel, listen closely to each command and be careful to obey it, so that all will go well with you, and so that you will have many children. If you obey these commands you will become a great nation in a glorious land 'flowing with milk and honey,' even as the God of your fathers promised you.

4 O Israel, listen: Jehovah is our God, Jehovah alone.

5 You must love Him with *all* your heart, soul, and might.

6 And you must think constantly about these commandments I am giving you today.

7 You must teach them to your children and talk about them when you are at home or out for a walk; at bedtime and the first thing in the morning.

8 Tie them on your finger, wear them on your forehead,

9 And write them on the doorposts of your house!

10, 11, 12 When the Lord your God has brought you into the land He promised your ancestors, Abraham, Isaac, and Jacob, and when He has given you great cities full of good things—cities you didn't build, wells you didn't dig, and vineyards and olive trees you didn't plant—and when you have eaten until you can hold no more, then beware lest you forget the Lord who brought you out of the land of Egypt, the land of slavery.

13 When you are full, don't forget to be reverent to Him and to serve Him and to use *His* name alone to endorse your promises.

14 You must not worship the gods of the neighboring nations,

15 For Jehovah your God who lives among you is a jealous God, and His anger may rise quickly against you, and wipe you off the face of the earth.

16 You must not provoke Him and try His patience as you did when you complained against Him at Massah.

17 You must actively obey Him in everything He commands.

18 Only then will you be doing what is right and

good in the Lord's eyes. If you obey Him, all will go well for you, and you will be able to go in and possess the good land which the Lord promised your ancestors.

19 You will also be able to throw out all the enemies living in your land, as the Lord agreed to help you do.

20 In the years to come when your son asks you, 'What is the purpose of these laws which the Lord our God has given us?'

21 You must tell him, 'We were Pharaoh's slaves in Egypt, and the Lord brought us out of Egypt with great power

22 And mighty miracles—with terrible blows against Egypt and Pharaoh and all his people. We saw it all with our own eyes.

23 He brought us out of Egypt so that He could give us this land He had promised to our ancestors.

24 And He has commanded us to obey all of these laws and to reverence Him so that He can preserve us alive as He has until now.

25 For it always goes well with us when we obey all the laws of the Lord our God.'

CHAPTER 7

When the Lord brings you into the Promised Land, as He soon will, He will destroy the following seven nations, all greater and mightier than you are:

> The Hittites,
> The Girgashites,
> The Amorites,
> The Canaanites,
> The Perizzites,
> The Hivites,
> The Jebusites.

2   When the Lord your God delivers them over to you to be destroyed, do a complete job of it—don't make any treaties or show them mercy; utterly wipe them out.

3   Do not intermarry with them, nor let your sons and daughters marry their sons and daughters.

4   That would surely result in your young people's beginning to worship their gods. Then the anger of the Lord would be hot against you and He would surely destroy you.

5   You must break down the heathen altars and shatter the obelisks and cut up the shameful images and burn the idols.

6   For you are a holy people, dedicated to the Lord your God. He has chosen you from all the people on the face of the whole earth to be His own chosen ones.

7   He didn't choose you and pour out His love upon you because you were a larger nation than any other, for you were the smallest of all!

8   It was just because He loves you, and because He kept His promise to your ancestors. That is why He brought you out of slavery in Egypt with such amazing power and mighty miracles.

9   Understand, therefore, that the Lord your God is the faithful God who for a thousand generations keeps His promises and constantly loves those who love Him and who obey His commands.

10   But those who hate Him shall be punished publicly and destroyed. He will deal with them personally.

11   Therefore, obey all these commandments I am giving you today.

12   Because of your obedience, the Lord your God

will keep His part of the contract which, in His tender love, He made with your fathers.

13 And He will love you and bless you and make you into a great nation. He will make you fertile and give fertility to your ground and to your animals, so that you will have large crops of grain, grapes, and olives, and great flocks of cattle, sheep, and goats when you arrive in the land He promised your fathers to give you.

14 You will be blessed above all the nations of the earth; not one of you, whether male or female, shall be barren, not even your cattle.

15 And the Lord will take away all your sickness and will not let you suffer any of the diseases of Egypt you remember so well; He will give them all to your enemies!

16 You must destroy all the nations which the Lord your God delivers into your hands. Have no pity, and do not worship their gods; if you do, it will be a sad day for you.

17 Perhaps you will think to yourself, 'How can we ever conquer these nations that are so much more powerful than we are?'

18 But don't be afraid of them! Just remember what the Lord your God did to Pharaoh and to all the land of Egypt.

19 Do you remember the terrors the Lord sent upon them—your parents saw it with their own eyes— and the mighty miracles and wonders, and the power and strength of Almighty God which He used to bring you out of Egypt? Well, the Lord your God will use this same might against the people you fear.

20 Moreover, the Lord your God will send hornets

to drive out those who hide from you!

21 No, do not be afraid of those nations, for the Lord your God is among you, and He is a great and awesome God.

22 He will cast them out a little at a time; He will not do it all at once, for if He did the wild animals would multiply too quickly and become dangerous.

23 He will do it gradually, and you will move in against those nations and destroy them.

24 He will deliver their kings into your hands, and you will erase their names from the face of the earth. No one will be able to stand against you.

25 Burn their idols and do not touch the silver or gold they are made of. Do not take it or it will be a snare to you, for it is horrible to the Lord your God.

26 Do not bring an idol into your home and worship it, for then your doom is sealed. Utterly detest it, for it is a cursed thing.

CHAPTER 8

You must obey all the commandments I give you today. If you do, you will not only live, you will multiply and will go in and take over the land promised to your fathers by the Lord.

2 Do you remember how the Lord led you through the wilderness for all those forty years, humbling you and testing you to find out how you would respond, and whether or not you would really obey Him?

3 Yes, He humbled you by letting you go hungry and then feeding you with manna, a food previously unknown to both you and your ancestors. He did it to help you realize that food isn't everything, and that

real life comes by obeying every command of God.

4 For all these forty years your clothes haven't grown old, and your feet haven't been blistered or swollen.

5 So you should realize that, as a man punishes his son, the Lord punishes you to help you.

6 Obey the laws of the Lord your God. Walk in His ways and fear Him.

7 For the Lord your God is bringing you into a good land of brooks, pools, gushing springs, valleys, and hills;

8 It is a land of wheat and barley, of grape vines, fig trees, pomegranates, olives, and honey;

9 It is a land where food is plentiful, and nothing is lacking; it is a land where iron is as common as stone, and copper is abundant in the hills.

10 When you have eaten your fill, bless the Lord your God for the good land He has given you.

11 But that is the time to be careful! Beware that in your plenty[1] you don't forget the Lord your God and begin to disobey Him.

12, 13 For when you have become full and prosperous and have built fine homes to live in, and when your flocks and herds have become very large, and your silver and gold have multiplied,

14 That is the time to watch out that you don't become proud, and forget the Lord your God who brought you out of your slavery in the land of Egypt.

15 Beware that you don't forget the God who led you through the great and terrible wilderness with the dangerous snakes and scorpions, where it was so hot and dry. He gave you water from the rock!

---

[1]Implied.

16 He fed you with manna in the wilderness (it was a kind of bread unknown before) so that you would become humble and so that your trust in Him would grow, and He could do you good.

17 He did it so that you would never feel that it was your own power and might that made you wealthy.

18 Always remember that it is the Lord your God who gives you power to become rich, and He does it to fulfill His promise to your ancestors.

19 But if you forget about the Lord your God and worship other gods instead, and follow evil ways, you shall certainly perish,

20 Just as the Lord has caused other nations in the past to perish. That will be your fate, too, if you don't obey the Lord your God.

CHAPTER 9

O Israel, listen! Today you are to cross the Jordan River and begin to dispossess the nations on the other side. Those nations are much greater and more powerful than you are! They live in high walled cities. Among them are the famed Anak giants, against whom none can stand!

3 But the Lord your God will go before you as a devouring fire to destroy them, so that you will quickly conquer them and drive them out.

4 Then, when the Lord has done this for you, don't say to yourselves, 'The Lord has helped us because we are so good!' No, it is because of the wickedness of the other nations that He is doing it.

5 It is not at all because you are such fine, upright people that the Lord will drive them out from before you! I say it again, it is only because of the

wickedness of the other nations, and because of His promises to your ancestors, Abraham, Isaac, and Jacob, that He will do it.

6 I say it yet again: *Jehovah your God is not giving you this good land because you are good, for you are not*—you are a wicked, stubborn people.

7 Don't you remember (oh, never forget it!) how continually angry you made the Lord your God out in the wilderness, from the day you left Egypt until now? For all this time you have constantly rebelled against Him.

8 Don't you remember how angry you made Him at Mount Horeb? He was ready to destroy you.

9 I was on the mountain at the time, receiving the contract which Jehovah had made with you—the stone tablets with the laws inscribed upon them. I was there for forty days and forty nights, and all that time I ate nothing. I didn't even take a drink of water.

10, 11 At the end of those forty days and nights the Lord gave me the contract, the tablets on which He had written the commandments He had spoken from the fire-covered mountain while the people had watched below.

12 He told me to go down quickly because the people I had led out of Egypt had defiled themselves, quickly turning away from the laws of God, and had made an idol from molten metal.

13, 14 'Let Me alone that I may destroy this evil, stubborn people!' the Lord told me, 'and I will blot out their name from under heaven, and I will make a mighty nation of you, mightier and greater than they are.'

15 I came down from the burning mountain, hold-

ing in my hands the two tablets inscribed with the laws of God.

16 There below me I could see the calf you had made in your terrible sin against the Lord your God. How quickly you turned away from Him!

17 I lifted the tablets high above my head and dashed them to the ground! I smashed them before your eyes!

18 Then, for another forty days and nights I lay before the Lord, neither eating bread nor drinking water, for you had done what the Lord hated most, thus provoking Him to great anger.

19 How I feared for you—for the Lord was ready to destroy you. But that time, too, He listened to me.

20 Aaron was in great danger because the Lord was so angry with him; but I prayed, and the Lord spared him.

21 I took your sin—the calf you had made—and burned it and ground it into fine dust, and threw it into the stream that cascaded out of the mountain.

22 Again at Taberah and once again at Massah you angered the Lord, and yet again at Kibroth-hattaavah.

23 At Kadesh-barnea, when the Lord told you to enter the land He had given you, you rebelled and wouldn't believe that He would help you; you refused to obey Him.

24 Yes, you have been rebellious against the Lord from the first day I knew you.

25 That is why I fell down before Him for forty days and nights when the Lord was ready to destroy you.

26 I prayed to Him, 'O Lord God, don't destroy

your own people. They are Your inheritance saved from Egypt by Your mighty power and glorious strength.

27 Don't notice the rebellion and stubbornness of these people, but remember instead Your promises to Your servants Abraham, Isaac, and Jacob. Oh, please overlook the awful wickedness and sin of these people.

28 For if You destroy them the Egyptians will say, "It is because the Lord wasn't able to bring them to the land He promised them," or "He destroyed them because He hated them: He brought them into the wilderness to slay them."

29 They are Your people and Your inheritance which You brought from Egypt by Your great power and Your mighty arm.'

CHAPTER 10

At that time the Lord told me to cut two more stone tablets like the first ones, and to make a wooden Ark to keep them in, and to return to God on the mountain.

2 He said He would rewrite on the tablets the same commandments that were on the tablets I had smashed, and that I should place them in the Ark.

3 So I made an Ark of acacia wood and hewed out two stone tablets like the first two, and took the tablets up on the mountain to God.

4 He again wrote the Ten Commandments on them and gave them to me. (They were the same commandments He had given you from the heart of the fire on the mountain as you all watched below.)

5 Then I came down and placed the tablets in the Ark I had made, where they are to this day, just as the Lord commanded me.

6 The people of Israel then journeyed from Beeroth of Bene-jaa-kan to Moserah, where Aaron died and was buried. His son Eleazar became the next priest.

7 Then they journeyed to Gudgodah, and from there to Jotbathah, a land of brooks and water.

8 It was there that Jehovah set apart the tribe of Levi to carry the Ark containing the Ten Commandments of Jehovah, and to stand before the Lord and to do His work and to bless His name, just as is done today.

9 (That is why the tribe of Levi does not have a portion of land reserved for it in the Promised Land, as their brother tribes do; for as the Lord told them, He Himself is their inheritance.)

10 As I said before, I stayed on the mountain before the Lord for forty days and nights the second time, just as I had the first, and the Lord again yielded to my pleas and didn't destroy you.

11 But He said to me, 'Arise and lead the people to the land I promised their fathers. It is time to go in and possess it.'

12, 13 And now, Israel, what does the Lord your God require of you except to listen carefully to all He says to you, and to obey for your own good the commandments I am giving you today, and to love Him, and to worship Him with all your hearts and souls?

14 Earth and highest heaven belong to the Lord your God.

15 And yet He rejoiced in your fathers and loved them so much that He chose you, their children, to be above every other nation, as is evident today.

16 Therefore, cleanse your sinful hearts and stop your stubbornness.

17   Jehovah your God is God of gods and Lord of lords. He is the great and mighty God, the God of terror who shows no partiality and takes no bribes.

18   He gives justice to the fatherless and widows. He loves foreigners and gives them food and clothing.

19   (You too must love foreigners, for you yourselves were foreigners in the land of Egypt.)

20   You must fear the Lord your God and worship Him and cling to Him and take oaths by His name alone.

21   He is your praise and He is your God, the one who has done mighty miracles you yourselves have seen.

22   When your ancestors went down into Egypt there were only seventy of them, but now the Lord your God has made you as many as the stars in the sky!

CHAPTER 11

You must love the Lord your God and obey every one of His commands.

2   Listen! I am not talking now to your children who have never experienced the Lord's punishments or seen His greatness and His awesome power.

3   They weren't there to see the miracles He did in Egypt against Pharaoh and all his land.

4   They didn't see what God did to the armies of Egypt and to their horses and chariots—how He drowned them in the Red Sea as they were chasing you, and how the Lord has kept them powerless against you until this very day!

5   They didn't see how the Lord cared for you time and again through all the years you were wandering in the wilderness, until your arrival here.

6   They weren't there when Dathan and Abiram

(the sons of Eliab, descendants[1] of Reuben) sinned, and the earth opened up and swallowed them, with their households and tents and all their belongings, as all Israel watched!

7   But *you* have seen these mighty miracles!

8   How carefully, then, you should obey these commandments I am going to give you today, so that you may have the strength to go in and possess the land you are about to enter.

9   If you obey the commandments, you will have a long and good life in the land the Lord promised to your ancestors and to you, their descendants—a wonderful land 'flowing with milk and honey'!

10   For the land you are about to enter and possess is not like the land of Egypt where you have come from, where irrigation is necessary.

11   It is a land of hills and valleys with plenty of rain—

12   A land that the Lord your God personally cares for! His eyes are always upon it, day after day throughout the year!

13   And if you will carefully obey all of His commandments that I am going to give you today, and if you will love the Lord your God with all your hearts and souls, and will worship Him,

14   Then He will continue to send both the early and late rains that will produce wonderful crops of grain, grapes for your wine, and olive oil.

15   He will give you lush pastureland for your cattle to graze in, and you yourselves shall have plenty to eat and be fully content.

---

[1]Literally, "sons."

16 But beware that your hearts do not turn from God to worship other gods.

17 For if you do, the anger of the Lord will be hot against you, and He will shut the heavens—there will be no rain and no harvest, and you will quickly perish from the good land the Lord has given you.

18 So keep these commandments carefully in mind. Tie them to your hand to remind you to obey them, and tie them to your forehead between your eyes!

19 Teach them to your children. Talk about them when you are sitting at home, when you are out walking, at bedtime, and before breakfast!

20 Write them upon the doors of your houses and upon your gates,

21 So that as long as there is sky above the earth, you and your children will enjoy the good life awaiting you in the land the Lord has promised you.[2]

22 If you carefully obey all the commandments I give you, loving the Lord your God, walking in all His ways, and clinging to Him,

23 Then the Lord will drive out all the nations in your land, no matter how much greater and stronger than you they might be.

24 Wherever you go, the land is yours. Your frontiers will stretch from the southern Negeb to Lebanon, and from the Euphrates River to the Mediterranean Sea.

25 No one will be able to stand against you, for the Lord your God will send fear and dread ahead of you wherever you go, just as He has promised.

26 I am giving you the choice today between God's blessing or God's curse!

---

[2]Literally, "your fathers."

27	There will be blessing if you obey the command-ments of the Lord your God which I am giving you today,

28	And a curse if you refuse them and worship the gods of these other nations.

29	When the Lord your God brings you into the land to possess it, a blessing shall be proclaimed from Mount Gerizim, and a curse from Mount Ebal!

30	(Gerizim and Ebal are mountains west of the Jordan River, where the Canaanites live, in the waste-land near Gilgal, where the oaks of Moreh are.)

31	For you are to cross the Jordan and live in the land the Lord is giving you.

32	But you must obey all the laws I am giving you today.

CHAPTER 12

These are the laws you must obey when you arrive in the land which Jehovah, the God of your fathers, has given you forever:

2	You must destroy all the heathen altars where-ever you find them—high in the mountains, up in the hills, or under the trees.

3	Break the altars, smash the obelisks, burn the shameful images, cut down the metal idols, and leave nothing even to remind you of them!

4, 5	You must not make sacrifices to your God just anywhere, as the heathen sacrifice to their gods. Rather, you must build a sanctuary for Him at a place He Himself will select as His home.

6	There you shall bring to the Lord your burnt offerings and other sacrifices—your tithes, your offer-ings presented by the gesture of waving before the altar, your offerings to fulfill your vows, your free-will offerings, and your offerings of the firstborn animals of your flocks and herds.

7   There you and your families shall feast before the Lord your God, and shall rejoice in all He has done for you.

8   You will no longer go your own way as you do now, everyone doing whatever he thinks is right;

9   (For these laws don't go into effect until you arrive in the place of rest the Lord will give to you.)

10   But when you cross the Jordan River and live in the Promised Land, and the Lord gives you rest and keeps you safe from all your enemies,

11   Then you must bring all your burnt sacrifices and other offerings to His sanctuary, the place He will choose as His home.

12   You shall rejoice there before the Lord with your sons and daughters and servants; and remember to invite the Levites to feast with you, for they have no land of their own.

13   You are not to sacrifice your burnt offerings just anywhere;

14   You may only do so in the place the Lord will choose. He will pick a place in the territory allotted to one of the tribes. Only there may you offer your sacrifices and bring your offerings.

15   However, the meat you eat may be butchered anywhere, just as you do now with gazelle and deer. Eat as much of this meat as you wish and as often as you are able to obtain it, because the Lord has prospered you. Those who are ceremonially defiled may eat it, too.

16   The only restriction is that you are not to eat

the blood—pour it out on the ground, like water.

17   But none of the offerings may be eaten at home. Neither the tithe of your grain and new wine and olive oil, nor the firstborn of your flocks and herds, nor anything you have vowed to give the Lord, nor your freewill offerings, nor the offerings to be presented to the Lord by waving them before His altar.

18   All these must be brought to the central altar where you, your children, and the Levites shall eat them before the Lord your God. He will tell you where this altar must be located. Rejoice before the Lord your God in everything you do.

19   (By the way, be very careful not to forget about the Levites. Share with them.)

20-23   If, when the Lord enlarges your borders, the central altar is too far away from you, then your flocks and herds may be butchered on your own farms, just as you do now with gazelle and deer. And even persons who are ceremonially defiled may eat them. The only restriction is never to eat the blood, for the blood is the life, and you shall not eat the life with the meat.

24, 25   Instead, pour the blood out upon the earth. If you do, all will be well with you and your children.

26, 27   Only your gifts to the Lord, and the offerings you have promised in your vows, and your burnt offerings need be taken to the central altar. These may only be sacrificed upon the altar of the Lord your God. The blood will be poured out upon the altar, and you will eat the meat.

28   Be careful to obey all of these commandments. If you do what is right in the eyes of the Lord your God, all will go well with you and your children forever.

29   When He destroys the nations in the land where you will live,

30   Don't follow their example in worshiping their gods. Do not ask, 'How do these nations worship their gods?' and then go and worship as they do!

31   You must not insult the Lord your God like that! These nations have done horrible things that He hates, all in the name of their religion. They have even roasted their sons and daughters before their gods.

32   Obey all the commandments I give you. Do not add or subtract from them.

CHAPTER 13

If there is a prophet among you, or one who claims to foretell the future by dreams,

2   And if his predictions come true but he says, 'Come, let us worship the gods of the other nations,'

3   Don't listen to him. For the Lord is testing you to find out whether or not you really love Him with all your heart and soul.

4   You must *never* worship any God but Jehovah; obey only His commands and cling to Him.

5   The prophet who tries to lead you astray must be executed, for he has attempted to foment rebellion against the Lord your God who brought you out of slavery in the land of Egypt. By executing him you will clear out the evil from among you.

6, 7   If your nearest relative or closest friend, even a brother, son, daughter, or beloved wife whispers to you to come and worship these foreign gods,

8   Do not consent nor listen, and have no pity: do not spare that person from the penalty; don't conceal his horrible suggestion.

9 Execute him! Your own hand shall be the first upon him to put him to death, then the hands of all the people.

10 Stone him to death because he has tried to draw you away from the Lord your God who brought you from the land of Egypt, the place of slavery.

11 Then all Israel will hear about his evil deed, and will fear such wickedness as this among you.

12, 13, 14 If you ever hear it said about one of the cities of Israel that some worthless rabble have led their fellow citizens astray with the suggestion that they worship foreign gods, first check the facts to see if the rumor is true. If you find that it is, that it is certain that such a horrible thing is happening among you in one of the cities the Lord has given you,

15 You must without fail declare war against that city and utterly destroy all of its inhabitants, and even all of the cattle.

16 Afterwards you must pile all the booty into the middle of the street and burn it, then put the entire city to the torch, as a burnt offering to Jehovah your God. That city shall forever remain a lifeless mound and may never be rebuilt.

17 Keep none of the booty! Then the Lord will turn from His fierce anger and be merciful to you, and have compassion upon you, and make you a great nation just as He promised your ancestors.

18 Of course, the Lord your God will be merciful only if you have been obedient to Him and to His commandments which I am giving you today, and if you have been doing that which is right in the eyes of the Lord.

CHAPTER 14

Since you are the people of God, never cut yourselves [as the heathen do when they worship their idols[1]] nor shave the front halves of your heads for funerals.

2 You belong exclusively to the Lord your God, and He has chosen you to be His own possession, more so than any other nation on the face of the earth.

3 You are not to eat any animal I have declared to be ceremonially defiled.

These are the animals you may eat:

      The ox,
      The sheep,
      The goat,

4, 5   The deer,
      The gazelle,
      The roebuck,
      The wild goat,
      The ibex,
      The antelope, and
      The mountain sheep.

6 Any animal that has cloven hooves and chews the cud may be eaten,

7 But if the animal doesn't have both, it may not be eaten. So you may not eat:

      The camel,
      The hare, or
      The coney.

They chew the cud but do not have cloven hooves.

8 Pigs may not be eaten because, although they have cloven hooves, they don't chew the cud. You may

---

[1]Implied.

not even touch the dead bodies of such animals.

9   Only sea animals with fins and scales may be eaten;

10   All other kinds are ceremonially defiled.

11, 12   You may eat any bird except the following:

> The eagle,
> The vulture,
> The osprey,

13   The buzzard,
> The falcon (any variety),

14   The raven (any variety),

15   The ostrich,
> The nighthawk,
> The sea gull,
> The hawk (any variety),

16   The screech owl,
> The great owl,
> The horned owl,

17   The pelican,
> The vulture,
> The cormorant,

18   The stork,
> The heron (any variety),
> The hoopoe,
> The bat.

19, 20   With certain exceptions,[2] winged insects are a defilement to you and may not be eaten.

21   Don't eat anything that has died a natural death. However, a foreigner among you may eat it. You may give it or sell it to him, but don't eat it yourself, for you are holy to the Lord your God.

---

[2]See Leviticus 11:20-23.

You must not boil a young goat in its mother's milk.

22 You must tithe all of your crops every year.

23 Bring this tithe to eat before the Lord your God at the place He shall choose as His sanctuary; this applies to your tithes of grain, new wine, olive oil, and the firstborn of your flocks and herds. The purpose of tithing is to teach you always to put God first in your lives.

24 If the place the Lord chooses for His sanctuary is so far away that it isn't convenient to carry your tithes to that place,

25 Then you may sell the tithe portion of your crops and herds and take the money to the Lord's sanctuary.

26 When you arrive, use the money to buy an ox, a sheep, some wine, or some strong drink, to feast there before the Lord your God, and to rejoice with your household.

27 Don't forget to share your income with the Levites in your community, for they have no property or crops as you do.

28 Every third year you are to use your entire tithe for local welfare programs:

29 Give it to the Levites who have no inheritance among you, or to foreigners, or to widows and orphans within your city, so that they can eat and be satisfied; and then Jehovah your God will bless you and your work.

CHAPTER 15

At the end of every seventh year there is to be a canceling of all debts!

2   Every creditor shall write "Paid in full" on any promissory note he holds against a fellow Israelite, for the Lord has released everyone from his obligation.

3   (This release does not apply to foreigners.)

4, 5   No one will become poor because of this, for the Lord will greatly bless you in the land He is giving you if you obey this command. The only prerequisite for His blessing is that you carefully heed all the commands of the Lord your God that I am giving you today.

6   He will bless you as He has promised. You shall lend money to many nations but will never need to borrow! You shall rule many nations, but they shall not rule over you!

7   But if, when you arrive in the land the Lord will give you, there are any among you who are poor, you must not shut your heart or hand against them;

8   You must lend them as much as they need.

9   Beware! Don't refuse a loan because the year of debt cancellation is close at hand! If you refuse to make the loan and the needy man cries out to the Lord, it will be counted against you as a sin.

10   You must lend him what he needs, and don't moan about it either! For the Lord will prosper you in everything you do because of this!

11   There will always be some among you who are poor; that is why this commandment is necessary. You must lend to them liberally.

12   If you buy a Hebrew slave, whether a man or woman, you must free him at the end of the sixth year you have owned him,

13   And don't send him away empty-handed!

14   Give him a large farewell present from your

flock, your olive press, and your wine press. Share with him in proportion as the Lord your God has blessed you.

15 Remember that you were slaves in the land of Egypt and the Lord your God rescued you! That is why I am giving you this command.

16 But if your Hebrew slave doesn't want to leave—if he says he loves you and enjoys your pleasant home and gets along well with you—

17 Then take an awl and pierce his ear into the door, and after that he shall be your slave forever. Do the same with your women slaves.

18 But when you free a slave you must not feel badly, for remember that for six years he has cost you less than half the price of a hired hand! And the Lord your God will prosper all you do because you have released him!

19 You shall set aside for God all the firstborn males from your flocks and herds. Do not use the first-born of your herds to work your fields, and do not shear the firstborn of your flocks of sheep and goats.

20 Instead, you and your family shall eat these animals before the Lord your God each year at His sanctuary.

21 However, if this firstborn animal has any defect such as being lame or blind, or if anything else is wrong with it, you shall not sacrifice it.

22 Instead, use it for food for your family at home. Anyone, even if ceremonially defiled at the time, may eat it, just as anyone may eat a gazelle or deer.

23 But don't eat the blood; pour it out upon the ground like water.

CHAPTER 16

A lways remember to celebrate the Passover during the month of April,[1] for that was when Jehovah your God brought you out of Egypt by night.

2 Your Passover sacrifice shall be either a lamb or an ox, sacrificed to the Lord your God at His sanctuary.

3 Eat the sacrifice with unleavened bread. Eat unleavened bread for seven days as a reminder of the bread you ate as you escaped from Egypt. This is to remind you that you left Egypt in such a hurry that there was no time for the bread to rise.[2] Remember that day all the rest of your lives!

4 For seven days no trace of yeast shall be in your homes, and none of the Passover lamb shall be left until the next morning.

5 The Passover is not to be eaten in your homes.

6 It must be eaten at the place the Lord shall choose as His sanctuary. Sacrifice it there on the anniversary evening just as the sun goes down.

7 Roast the lamb and eat it, then start back to your homes the next morning.

8 For the following six days you shall eat no bread made with yeast. On the seventh day there shall be a quiet gathering of the people of each city before the Lord your God. Don't do any work that day.

9 Seven weeks after the harvest begins,

10 There shall be another festival before the Lord your God called the Festival of Weeks. At that time bring to Him a freewill offering proportionate in size

---

[1]Literally, "Abib"—the first month of the Hebrew calendar.
[2]Literally, "For you left Egypt in hurried flight."

to His blessing upon you as judged by the amount of your harvest.

11 It is a time to rejoice before the Lord with your family and household. And don't forget to include the local Levites, foreigners, widows, and orphans. Invite them to accompany you to the celebration at the sanctuary.

12 Remember! You were a slave in Egypt, so be sure to carry out this command.

13 Another celebration, the Festival of Shelters, must be observed for seven days at the end of the harvest season, after the grain is threshed and the grapes have been pressed.

14 This will be a happy time of rejoicing together with your family and servants. And don't forget to include the Levites, foreigners, orphans, and widows of your town.

15 This feast will be held at the sanctuary, which will be located at the place the Lord will designate. It is a time of deep thanksgiving to the Lord for blessing you with a good harvest and in so many other ways; it shall be a time of great joy.

16 Every man in Israel shall appear before the Lord your God three times a year at the sanctuary for these festivals:

> The Festival of Unleavened Bread,
> The Festival of Weeks,
> The Festival of Shelters.

> On each of these occasions bring a gift to the Lord.

17 Give as you are able, according as the Lord has blessed you.

18 Appoint judges and administrative officials for

all the cities the Lord your God is giving you. They will administer justice in every part of the land.

19   Never twist justice to benefit a rich man, and never accept bribes. For bribes blind the eyes of the wisest and corrupt their decisions.

20   Justice must prevail. That is the only way you will be successful in the land which the Lord your God is giving you.

21   Never, under any circumstances, are you to erect shameful images beside the altar of the Lord your God.

22   And never set up an obelisk, for the Lord hates them!

CHAPTER 17

Never sacrifice a sick or defective ox or sheep to the Lord your God. He doesn't feel honored by such gifts!

2, 3   If anyone, whether man or woman, in any village throughout your land violates your covenant with God by worshiping other gods, the sun, moon, or stars—which I have strictly forbidden—

4   First check the rumor very carefully; if there is no doubt it is true,

5   Then that man or woman shall be taken outside the city and shall be stoned to death.

6   However, never put a man to death on the testimony of only one witness; there must be at least two or three.

7   The witnesses shall throw the first stones, and then all the people shall join in. In this way you will purge all evil from among you.

8   If a case arises that is too hard for you to

decide—for instance, whether someone is guilty of murder when there is insufficient evidence, or whether someone's rights have been violated—you shall take the case to the sanctuary of the Lord your God,

9 To the priests and Levites, and the chief judge on duty at the time will make the decision.

10 His decision is without appeal and is to be followed to the letter.

11 The sentence he imposes is to be fully executed.

12 If the defendant refuses to accept the decision of the priest or judge appointed by God for this purpose, the penalty is death. Such sinners must be purged from Israel.

13 Then everyone will hear about what happened to the man who refused God's verdict, and they will be afraid to defy the court's judgment a second time.

14 When you arrive in the land the Lord your God will give you, and have conquered it, and begin to think, 'We ought to have a king like the other nations around us'—

15 Be sure that you select as king the man the Lord your God shall choose. He must be an Israelite, not a foreigner.

16 Be sure that he doesn't build up a large stable of horses for himself, nor send his men to Egypt to raise horses for him there, for the Lord has told you, 'Never return to Egypt again.'

17 He must not have too many wives, lest his heart be turned away from the Lord, neither shall he be excessively rich.

18 And when he has been crowned and sits upon his throne as king, then he must copy these laws from the book kept by the Levite-priests.

19 That copy of the laws shall be his constant companion. He must read from it every day of his life so that he will learn to respect the Lord his God by obeying all of His commands.

20 This regular reading of God's laws will prevent him from feeling that he is better than his fellow citizens. It will also prevent him from turning away from God's laws in the slightest respect, and will ensure his having a long, good reign. His sons will then follow him upon the throne.

CHAPTER 18

Remember that the priests and all the other members of the Levite tribe will not be given property like the other tribes. So the priests and Levites are to be supported by the sacrifices brought to the altar of the Lord and by the other offerings the people bring to him.

2 They don't need to own property, for the Lord is their property! That is what He promised them!

3 The shoulder, the cheeks, and the stomach of every ox or sheep brought for sacrifice must be given to the priests.

4 In addition, the priests shall receive the harvest samples brought in thanksgiving to the Lord—the first of the grain, the new wine, the olive oil, and of the fleece at shearing time.

5 For the Lord your God has chosen the tribe of Levi, of all the tribes, to minister to the Lord from generation to generation.

6, 7 Any Levite, no matter where he lives in the land of Israel, has the right to come to the sanctuary at any time and minister in the name of the Lord, just like his brother Levites who work there regularly.

8 He shall be given his share of the sacrifices and offerings as his right, not just if he is in need.

9 When you arrive in the Promised Land you must be very careful lest you be corrupted by the horrible customs of the nations now living there.

10 For example, any Israeli who presents his child to be burned to death as a sacrifice to heathen gods, must be killed.[1] No Israeli may practice black magic, or call on the evil spirits for aid, or be a fortune teller,

11 Or be a serpent charmer, medium, or wizard, or call forth the spirits of the dead.

12 Anyone doing these things is an object of horror and disgust to the Lord, and it is because the nations do these things that the Lord your God will displace them.

13 You must walk blamelessly before the Lord your God.

14 The nations you replace all do these evil things, but the Lord your God will not permit you to do such things.

15 Instead, He will raise up for you a Prophet like me, an Israeli, a man to whom you must listen and whom you must obey.

16 For this is what you yourselves begged of God at Mount Horeb. There at the foot of the mountain you begged that you might not have to listen to the terrifying voice of God again, or see the awesome fire on the mountain, lest you die.

17 'All right,' the Lord said to me, 'I will do as they have requested.

18 I will raise up from among them a Prophet,

---

[1] Implied.

an Israeli like you. I will tell him what to say, and he shall be My spokesman to the people.

19   I will personally deal with anyone who will not listen to him and heed his messages from Me.

20   But any prophet who falsely claims that his message is from Me, shall die. And any prophet who claims to give a message from other gods must die.'

21   If you wonder, 'How shall we know whether the prophecy is from the Lord or not?'

22   This is the way to know: If the thing he prophesies doesn't happen, it is not the Lord who has given him the message; he has made it up himself. You have nothing to fear from him.

CHAPTER 19

When the Lord your God has destroyed the nations you will displace, and when you are living in their cities and homes,

2, 3   You must set apart three Cities of Refuge so that anyone who accidentally kills someone may flee to safety. Divide the country into three districts, with one of these cities in each district; and keep the roads to these cities in good repair.

4   Here is an example of the purpose of these cities:

5   If a man goes into the forest with his neighbor to chop wood, and the axe head flies off the handle and kills the man's neighbor, he may flee to one of those cities and be safe.

6, 7   Anyone seeking to avenge the death will not be able to. These cities must be scattered so that one of them will be reasonably close to everyone;

otherwise the angry avenger might catch and kill the innocent slayer, even though he should not have died since he had not killed deliberately.

8 If the Lord enlarges your boundaries as He promised your ancestors, and gives you all the land He promised,

9 (Whether He does this depends on your obedience to all these commandments I am giving you today—loving the Lord your God and walking His paths), then you must designate three additional Cities of Refuge.

10 In this way you will be able to avoid the death of innocent people, and you will not be held responsible for unjustified bloodshed.

11 But if anyone hates his neighbor and springs out of hiding and kills him, and then flees into one of the Cities of Refuge,

12 The elders of his home town shall send for him and shall bring him home and deliver him over to the dead man's avenger, to kill him.

13 Don't pity him! Purge all murderers from Israel! Only then will all go well with you.

14 When you arrive in the land the Lord your God is giving you, remember that you must never steal a man's land by moving the boundary marker.

15 Never convict anyone on the testimony of one witness. There must be at least two, and three is even better.

16 If anyone gives false witness, claiming he has seen someone do wrong when he hasn't,

17 Both men shall be brought before the priests and judges on duty before the Lord at the time.

18 They must be closely questioned, and if the witness is lying,

19 His penalty shall be the punishment he thought the other man would get. In this way you will purge out evil from among you.

20 Then those who hear about it will be afraid to tell lies on the witness stand.

21 You shall not show pity to a false witness. Life for life, eye for eye, tooth for tooth, hand for hand, foot for foot; this is your rule in such cases.

CHAPTER 20

When you go to war and see before you vast numbers of horses and chariots, an army far greater than yours, don't be frightened! The Lord your God is with you—the same God who brought you safely out of Egypt!

2 Before you begin the battle, a priest shall stand before the Israeli army and say,

3 'Listen to me, all you men of Israel! Don't be afraid as you go out to fight today!

4 For the Lord your God is going with you! He will fight for you against your enemies, and He will give you the victory!'

5 Then the officers of the army shall address the men in this manner: 'Has anyone just built a new house, but not yet dedicated it? If so, go home! For you might be killed in the battle, and someone else would dedicate it!

6 Has anyone just planted a vineyard but not yet eaten any of its fruit? If so, go home! You might die in battle and someone else would eat it!

7 Has anyone just become engaged? Well, go

home and get married! For you might die in the battle, and someone else would marry your fiancée.

8 And now, is anyone afraid? If you are, go home before you frighten the rest of us!'

9 When the officers have finished saying this to their men, they will announce the names of the battalion leaders.

10 As you approach a city to fight against it, first offer it a truce.

11 If it accepts the truce and opens its gates to you, then all its people shall become your servants.

12 But if it refuses and won't make peace with you, you must besiege it.

13 When the Lord your God has given it to you, kill every male in the city;

14 But you may keep for yourselves all the women, children, cattle, and booty.

15 These instructions apply only to distant cities, not to those in the Promised Land[1] itself.

16 For in the cities within the boundaries of the Promised Land you are to save no one; destroy every living thing.

17 Utterly destroy the Hittites, the Amorites, the Canaanites, the Perizzites, the Hivites, and the Jebusites. This is the commandment of the Lord your God.

18 The purpose of this command is to prevent the people of the land from luring you into idol worship and into participation in their loathsome customs, thus sinning deeply against the Lord your God.

19 When you besiege a city, don't destroy the fruit trees. Eat all the fruit you wish; just don't cut down

---

[1] Literally, "which are not of the cities of these nations."

the trees. They aren't enemies who need to be slaughtered!

20 But you may cut down trees that aren't valuable for food. Use them for the siege: [to make ladders, portable towers, and battering rams.²]

CHAPTER 21

If, when you arrive in the Promised Land, a murder victim is found lying in a field and no one has seen the murder,

2 The elders and judges shall measure from the body to the nearest city.

3 Then the elders of that city shall take a heifer that has never been yoked,

4 And lead it to a valley where there is running water—a valley neither plowed nor sowed—and there break its neck.

5 Then the priests shall come (for the Lord your God has chosen them to minister before Him and to pronounce His blessings and decide lawsuits and punishments),

6 And shall wash their hands over the heifer,

7 And say, 'Our hands have not shed this blood, neither have our eyes seen it.

8 O Lord, forgive Your people Israel whom You have redeemed, and do not charge them with murdering an innocent man. Forgive us the guilt of this man's blood.'

9 In this way you will put away the guilt from among you by following the Lord's directions.

---

²Implied.

10 When you go to war and the Lord your God delivers your enemies to you,

11 And you see among the captives a beautiful girl you want as your wife,

12 Take her home with you. She must shave her head and pare her nails

13 And change her clothing, laying aside that which she was wearing when she was captured, then remain in your home in mourning for her father and mother for a full month. After that you may marry her.

14 However, if after marrying her you decide you don't like her, you must let her go free—you may not sell her or treat her as a slave, for you have humiliated her.

15 If a man has two wives but loves one and not the other, and both have borne him children, and the mother of his oldest son is the wife he doesn't love,

16 He may not give a larger inheritance to his younger son, the son of the wife he loves.

17 He must give the customary double portion to his oldest son, who is the beginning of his strength and who owns the rights of a firstborn son, even though he is the son of the wife his father doesn't love.

18 If a man has a stubborn, rebellious son who will not obey his father or mother, even though they punish him,

19 Then his father and mother shall take him before the elders of the city

20 And declare, 'This son of ours is stubborn and rebellious and won't obey; he is a worthless drunkard.'

21 Then the men of the city shall stone him to death. In this way you shall put away this evil from among you, and all the young men of Israel will hear

about what happened and will be afraid.

22 If a man has committed a crime worthy of death, and is executed and then hanged on a tree,

23 His body shall not remain on the tree overnight. You must bury him the same day, for anyone hanging on a tree is cursed of God. Don't defile the land the Lord your God has given you.

CHAPTER 22

If you see someone's ox or sheep wandering away, don't pretend you didn't see it; take it back to its owner.

2 If you don't know who the owner is, take it to your farm and keep it there until the owner comes looking for it, and then give it to him.

3 The same applies to donkeys, clothing, or anything else you find. Keep it for its owner.

4 If you see someone trying to get an ox or donkey onto its feet when it has slipped beneath its load,[1] don't look the other way. Go and help!

5 A woman must not wear men's clothing, and a man must not wear women's clothing. This is abhorrent to the Lord your God.

6 If a bird's nest is lying on the ground, or if you spy one in a tree, and there are young ones or eggs in it with the mother sitting in the nest, don't take the mother with the young.

7 Let her go, and take only the young. The Lord will bless you for it.

8 Every new house must have a guardrail around the edge of the flat rooftop to prevent anyone from

---

[1]Implied.

falling off and bringing guilt to both the house and its owner.

9　Do not sow other crops in the rows of your vineyard. If you do, both the crops and the grapes shall both be confiscated by the priests.[2]

10　Don't plow with an ox and a donkey harnessed together.

11　Don't wear clothing woven from two kinds of thread: for instance, wool and linen.

12　You must sew tassels on the four corners of your cloaks.

13, 14　If a man marries a girl, then after sleeping with her accuses her of having had pre-marital intercourse with another man, saying, 'She was not a virgin when I married her,'

15　Then the girl's father and mother shall bring the proof of her virginity to the city judges.

16　Her father shall tell them, 'I gave my daughter to this man to be his wife, and now he despises her,

17, 18　And has accused her of shameful things, claiming that she was not a virgin when she married; yet here is the proof.' And they shall spread the garment before the judges. The judges shall sentence the man to be whipped,

19　And fine him one hundred dollars[3] to be given to the girl's father, for he has falsely accused a virgin of Israel. She shall remain his wife and he may never divorce her.

20　But if the man's accusations are true, and she was not a virgin,

21　The judges shall take the girl to the door of her

---

[2]Literally, "Lest the fulness of the fruit be consecrated."
[3]Literally, "a hundred shekels of silver." The exact value cannot be determined.

father's home where the men of the city shall stone her to death. She has defiled Israel by flagrant crime, being a prostitute while living at home with her parents; and such evil must be cleansed from among you.

22 If a man is discovered committing adultery, both he and the other man's wife must be killed; in this way evil will be cleansed from Israel.

23, 24 If a girl who is engaged is seduced within the walls of a city, both she and the man who seduced her shall be taken outside the gates and stoned to death —the girl because she didn't scream for help, and the man because he has violated the virginity of another man's fiancée.

25, 26, 27 In this way you will reduce crime among you. But if this deed takes place out in the country, only the man shall die. The girl is as innocent as a murder victim; for it must be assumed that she screamed, but there was no one to hear and rescue her out in the field.

28, 29 If a man rapes a girl who is not engaged, and is caught in the act, he must pay a fine[4] to the girl's father and marry her; he may never divorce her.

30 A man shall not sleep with his father's widow[5] since she belonged to his father.

CHAPTER 23

If a man's testicles are crushed or his penis cut off, he shall not enter the sanctuary.

2 A bastard may not enter the sanctuary, nor any of his descendants for ten generations.

3 No Ammonite or Moabite may ever enter the

[4]Literally, "shall pay her father fifty of silver."
[5]Literally, "his father's wife." The general law against adultery protected her and his other wives while their husband was living.

sanctuary, even after the tenth generation.

4 The reason for this law is that these nations did not welcome you with food and water when you came out of Egypt; they even tried to hire Balaam, the son of Beor from Pethor, Mesopotamia, to curse you.

5 But the Lord wouldn't listen to Balaam; instead, he turned the intended curse into a blessing for you, because the Lord loves you.

6 You must never, as long as you live, try to help the Ammonites or the Moabites in any way.

7 But don't look down on the Edomites and the Egyptians; the Edomites are your brothers and you lived among the Egyptians.

8 The grandchildren of the Egyptians who came with you from Egypt may enter the sanctuary of the Lord.

9, 10 When you are at war, the men in the camps must stay away from all evil. Any man who becomes ceremonially defiled because of a seminal emission during the night must leave the camp,

11 And stay outside until the evening; then he shall bathe himself and return at sunset.

12 The toilet area shall be outside the camp.

13 Each man must have a spade as part of his equipment; after every bowel movement he must dig a hole with the spade and cover the excrement.

14 The camp must be holy, for the Lord walks among you to protect you and to cause your enemies to fall before you; and the Lord does not want to see anything indecent lest He turn away from you.

15, 16 If a slave escapes from his master, you must not force him to return; let him live among you in whatever town he shall choose, and do not oppress him.

17, 18　No prostitutes are permitted in Israel, either men or women; you must not bring to the Lord any offering from the earnings of a prostitute or a homosexual, for both are detestable to the Lord your God.

19　Don't demand interest on loans you make to a brother Israelite, whether it is in the form of money, food, or anything else.

20　You may take interest from a foreigner, but not from an Israeli. For if you take interest from a brother, an Israeli, the Lord your God won't bless you when you arrive in the Promised Land.

21　When you make a vow to the Lord, be prompt in doing whatever it is you promised Him, for the Lord demands that you promptly fulfill your vows; it is a sin if you don't.

22　(But it is not a sin if you refrain from vowing!)

23　Once you make the vow, you must be careful to do as you have said, for it was your own choice, and you have vowed to the Lord your God.

24　You may eat your fill of the grapes from another man's vineyard, but do not take any away in a container.

25　It is the same with someone else's grain—you may eat a few handfuls of it, but don't use a sickle.

CHAPTER 24

If a man doesn't like something about his wife, he may write a letter stating that he has divorced her, give her the letter, and send her away.

2　If she then remarries,

3 And the second husband also divorces her, or dies,

4 The former husband may not marry her again, for she has been defiled; this would bring guilt upon the land the Lord your God is giving you.

5 A newly married man is not to be drafted into the army nor given any other special responsibilities; for a year he shall be free to be at home, happy with his wife.

6 It is illegal to take a millstone as a pledge, for it is a tool by which its owner gains his livelihood.

7 If anyone kidnaps a brother Israelite, and treats him as a slave or sells him, the kidnapper must die, in order to purge the evil from among you.

8 Be very careful to follow the instructions of the priest in cases of leprosy, for I have given him rules and guidelines you must obey to the letter:

9 Remember what the Lord your God did to Miriam as you were coming from Egypt.

10 If you lend anything to another man, you must not enter his house to get his security.

11 Stand outside! The owner will bring it out to you.

12, 13 If the man is poor and gives you his cloak as security, you are not to sleep in it. Take it back to him at sundown so that he can use it through the night and bless you; and the Lord your God will count it as righteousness for you.

14, 15 Never oppress a poor hired man, whether a fellow Israelite or a foreigner living in your town. Pay him his wage each day before sunset, for since he is poor he needs it right away; otherwise he may cry out to the Lord against you and it would be counted as a sin against you.

16   Fathers shall not be put to death for the sins of their sons nor the sons for the sins of their fathers; every man worthy of death shall be executed for his own crime.

17   Justice must be given to migrants and orphans and you must never accept a widow's garment in pledge of her debt.

18   Always remember that you were slaves in Egypt, and that the Lord your God rescued you; that is why I have given you this command.

19   If, when reaping your harvest, you forget to bring in a sheaf from the field, don't go back after it. Leave it for the migrants, orphans, and widows; then the Lord your God will bless and prosper all you do.

20   When you beat the olives from your olive trees, don't go over the boughs twice; leave anything remaining for the migrants, orphans, and widows.

21   It is the same for the grapes in your vineyard; don't glean the vines after they are picked, but leave what's left for those in need.

22   Remember that you were slaves in the land of Egypt—that is why I am giving you this command.

CHAPTER 25

If a man is guilty of a crime, and the penalty is a beating, the judge shall command him to lie down and be beaten in his presence with up to forty stripes in proportion to the seriousness of the crime; but no more than forty stripes may be given lest the punishment seem too severe, and your brother be degraded in your eyes.

4   Don't muzzle an ox as it treads out the grain.

5   If a man's brother dies without a son, his widow must not marry outside the family; instead, her husband's brother must marry her and sleep with her.

6   The first son she bears to him shall be counted as the son of the dead brother, so that his name will not be forgotten.

7   But if the dead man's brother refuses to do his duty in this matter, refusing to marry the widow, then she shall go to the city elders and say to them, 'My husband's brother refuses to let his brother's name continue—he refuses to marry me.'

8   The elders of the city will then summon him and talk it over with him, and if he still refuses,

9   The widow shall walk over to him in the presence of the elders, pull his sandal from his foot and spit in his face. She shall then say, 'This is what happens to a man who refuses to build his brother's house.'

10   And ever afterwards his house shall be referred to as 'the home of the man who had his sandal pulled off!'

11   If two men are fighting and the wife of one intervenes to help her husband by grabbing the testicles of the other man,

12   Her hand shall be cut off without pity.

13, 14, 15   In all your transactions you must use accurate scales and honest measurements, so that you will have a long, good life in the land the Lord your God is giving you.

16   All who cheat with unjust weights and measurements are detestable to the Lord your God.

17   You must never forget what the people of Amalek did to you as you came from Egypt.

18   Remember that they fought with you and struck down those who were faint and weary and lagging behind, with no respect or fear of God.

19   Therefore, when the Lord your God has given you rest from all your enemies in the Promised Land, you are utterly to destroy the name of Amalek from under heaven. Never forget this.

CHAPTER 26

W hen you arrive in the land and have conquered it and are living there,

2, 3   You must present to the Lord at His sanctuary the first sample from each annual[1] harvest. Bring it in a basket and hand it to the priest on duty and say to him, 'This gift is my acknowledgment that the Lord my God has brought me to the land He promised our ancestors.'

4   The priest will then take the basket from your hand and set it before the altar.

5   You shall then say before the Lord your God, 'My ancestors were migrant Arameans who went to Egypt for refuge. They were few in number, but in Egypt they became a mighty nation.

6, 7   The Egyptians mistreated us and we cried to the Lord God. He heard us and saw our hardship, toil, and oppression,

8   And brought us out of Egypt with mighty miracles and a powerful hand. He did great and awesome miracles before the Egyptians,

9   And has brought us to this place and given us this land "flowing with milk and honey!"

10   And now, O Lord, see, I have brought you a

---

[1]Implied.

token of the first of the crops from the ground You have given me.' Then place the samples before the Lord your God, and worship Him.

11 Afterwards, go and feast on all the good things He has given you. Celebrate with your family and with any Levites or migrants living among you.

12 Every third year is a year of special tithing. That year you are to give all your tithes to the Levites, migrants, orphans, and widows, so that they will be well fed.

13 Then you shall declare before the Lord your God, 'I have given all of my tithes to the Levites, the migrants, the orphans, and the widows, just as You commanded me; I have not violated or forgotten any of Your rules.

14 I have not touched the tithe while I was ceremonially defiled (for instance, while I was in mourning), nor have I offered any of it to the dead. I have obeyed the Lord my God and have done everything You commanded me.

15 Look down from Your holy home in heaven and bless Your people and the land You have given us, as You promised our ancestors; make it a land "flowing with milk and honey"!'

16 You must wholeheartedly obey all of these commandments and ordinances which the Lord your God is giving you today.

17 You have declared today that He is your God, and you have promised to obey and keep His laws and ordinances, and to heed all He tells you to do.

18 And the Lord has declared today that you are His very own people, just as He promised, and that you must obey all of His laws.

19   If you do, He will make you greater than any other nation, allowing you to receive praise, honor, and renown; but to attain this honor and renown you must be a holy people to the Lord your God, as He requires."

CHAPTER 27

Then Moses and the elders of Israel gave the people these further instructions to obey:[1]

2, 3, 4   "When you cross the Jordan River and go into the Promised Land—a land "flowing with milk and honey'—take out boulders from the river bottom and immediately pile them into a monument on the other side, at Mount Ebal. Face the stones with a coating of lime[2] and then write the laws of God in the lime.

5, 6   And build an altar there to the Lord your God. Use uncut boulders, and on the altar offer burnt offerings to the Lord your God.

7   Sacrifice peace offerings upon it also, and feast there with great joy before the Lord your God.

8   Write all of these laws plainly [upon the monument[3]]."

9   Then Moses and the Levite-priests addressed all Israel as follows:

"O Israel, listen! Today you have become the people of the Lord your God,

10   So today you must begin to obey all of these commandments I have given you."

11   That same day Moses gave this charge to the people:

12   "When you cross into the Promised Land, the

---

[1]Literally, "Keep all the commandments I enjoin on you today."
[2]Literally, "Plaster them with plaster."
[3]Implied. See verses 1-4.

tribes of Simeon, Levi, Judah, Issachar, Joseph, and Benjamin shall stand upon Mount Gerizim to proclaim a blessing,

13   And the tribes of Reuben, Gad, Asher, Zebulun, Dan, and Naphtali shall stand upon Mount Ebal to proclaim a curse.

14   Then the Levites standing between[4] them shall shout to all Israel,

15   'The curse of God be upon anyone who makes and worships an idol, even in secret, whether carved of wood or made from molten metal—for these hand-made gods are hated by the Lord.' And all the people shall reply, 'Amen.'

16   'Cursed is anyone who despises his father or mother.' And all the people shall reply, 'Amen.'

17   'Cursed is he who moves the boundary marker between his land and his neighbor's.' And all the people shall reply, 'Amen.'

18   'Cursed is he who takes advantage of a blind man.' And all the people shall reply, 'Amen.'

19   'Cursed is he who is unjust to the foreigner, the orphan, and the widow.' And all the people shall reply, 'Amen.'

20   'Cursed is he who commits adultery with one of his father's wives, for she belongs to his father.' And all the people shall reply, 'Amen.'

21   'Cursed is he who has sexual intercourse with an animal.' And all the people shall reply, 'Amen.'

22   'Cursed is he who has sexual intercourse with his sister, whether she be a full sister or a half sister.' And all the people shall reply, 'Amen.'

23   'Cursed is he who has sexual intercourse with

---

[4]Implied.

his widowed[5] mother-in-law.' And all the people shall reply, 'Amen.'

24 'Cursed is he who secretly slays another.' And all the people shall reply, 'Amen.'

25 'Cursed is he who accepts a bribe to kill an innocent person.' And all the people shall reply, 'Amen.'

26 'Cursed is anyone who does not obey these laws.' And all the people shall reply, 'Amen.'

CHAPTER 28

If you fully obey all of these commandments of the Lord your God, the laws I am declaring to you today, God will transform you into the greatest nation in the world.

2 These are the blessings that will come upon you:

3   Blessings in the city,
     Blessings in the field;

4   Many children,
     Ample crops,
     Large flocks and herds;

5   Blessings of fruit and bread;

6   Blessings when you come in,
     Blessings when you go out.

7 The Lord will defeat your enemies before you; they will march out together against you but scatter before you in seven directions!

8 The Lord will bless you with good crops and healthy cattle, and prosper everything you do when you arrive in the land the Lord your God is giving you.

---

[5]Implied. If she were still married, no special law would be needed to prohibit adultery.

9 He will change you into a holy people dedicated to Himself; this He has promised to do if you will only obey Him and walk in His ways.

10 All the nations in the world shall see that you belong to the Lord, and they will stand in awe.

11 The Lord will give you an abundance of good things in the land, just as He promised: many children, many cattle, and abundant crops.

12 He will open to you His wonderful treasury of rain in the heavens, to give you fine crops every season. He will bless everything you do; and you shall lend to many nations, but shall not borrow from them.

13 If you will only listen and obey the commandments of the Lord your God that I am giving you today, He will make you the head and not the tail, and you shall always have the upper hand.

14 But each of these blessings depends on your not turning aside in any way from the laws I have given you; and you must never worship other gods.

15 If you won't listen to the Lord your God and won't obey these laws I am giving you today, then all of these curses shall come upon you:

16   Curses in the city;
          Curses in the fields;
17   Curses on your fruit and bread;
18   The curse of barren wombs;
          Curses upon your crops;
          Curses upon the fertility of your cattle and
              flocks;
19   Curses when you come in;
          Curses when you go out.

20 For the Lord Himself will send His personal curse upon you. You will be confused and a failure

in everything you do, until at last you are destroyed because of the sin of forsaking Him.

21 He will send disease among you until you are destroyed from the face of the land which you are about to enter and possess.

22 He will send tuberculosis, fever, infections, plague, and war. He will blight your crops, covering them with mildew. All these devastations shall pursue you until you perish.

23 The heavens above you will be as unyielding as bronze, and the earth beneath will be as iron.

24 The land will become as dry as dust for lack of rain, and dust storms shall destroy you.

25 The Lord will cause you to be defeated by your enemies. You will march out to battle gloriously, but flee before your enemies in utter confusion; and you will be tossed to and fro among all the nations of the earth.

26 Your dead bodies will be food to the birds and wild animals, and no one will be there to chase them away.

27 He will send upon you Egyptian boils, tumors, scurvy, and itch, for none of which will there be a remedy.

28 He will send madness, blindness, fear, and panic upon you.

29 You shall grope in the bright sunlight just as the blind man gropes in darkness. You shall not prosper in anything you do; you will be oppressed and robbed continually, and nothing will save you.

30 Someone else will marry your fiancée; someone else will live in the house you build; someone else will eat the fruit of the vineyard you plant.

31 Your oxen shall be butchered before your eyes, but you won't get a single bite of the meat. Your donkeys will be driven away as you watch, and will never return to you again. Your sheep will be given to your enemies. And there will be no one to protect you.

32 You will watch as your sons and daughters are taken away as slaves. Your heart will break with longing for them, but you will not be able to help them.

33 A foreign nation you have not even heard of will eat the crops you will have worked so hard to grow. You will always be oppressed and crushed.

34 You will go mad because of all the tragedy you see around you.

35 The Lord will cover you with boils from head to foot.

36 He will exile you and the king you will choose, to a nation to whom neither you nor your ancestors gave a second thought; and while in exile you shall worship gods of wood and stone!

37 You will become an object of horror, a proverb and a byword among all the nations, for the Lord will thrust you away.

38 You will sow much but reap little, for the locusts will eat your crops.

39 You will plant vineyards and care for them, but you won't eat the grapes or drink the wine, for worms will destroy the vines.

40 Olive trees will be growing everywhere, but there won't be enough olive oil to anoint yourselves! For the trees will drop their fruit before it is matured.

41 Your sons and daughters will be snatched away from you as slaves.

42   The locusts shall destroy your trees and vines.

43   Foreigners living among you shall become richer and richer while you become poorer and poorer.

44   They shall lend to you, not you to them! They shall be the head and you shall be the tail!

45   All these curses shall pursue and overtake you until you are destroyed—all because you refuse to listen to the Lord your God.

46   These horrors shall befall you and your descendants as a warning:

47, 48   You will become slaves to your enemies because of your failure to praise God for all that He has given you. The Lord will send your enemies against you, and you will be hungry, thirsty, naked, and in want of everything. A yoke of iron shall be placed around your neck until you are destroyed!

49   The Lord will bring a distant nation against you, swooping down upon you like an eagle; a nation whose language you don't understand—

50   A nation of fierce and angry men who will have no mercy upon young or old.

51   They will eat you out of house and home until your cattle and crops are gone. Your grain, new wine, olive oil, calves, and lambs will all disappear.

52   That nation will lay siege to your cities and knock down your highest walls—the walls you will trust to protect you.

53   You will even eat the flesh of your own sons and daughters in the terrible days of siege that lie ahead.

54   The most tenderhearted man among you will be utterly callous toward his own brother and his beloved wife and his children who are still alive.

55 He will refuse to give them a share of the flesh he is devouring—the flesh of his own children—because he is starving in the midst of the siege of your cities.

56, 57 The most tender and delicate woman among you—the one who would not so much as touch her feet to the ground—will refuse to share with her beloved husband, son, and daughter. She will hide from them the afterbirth and the new baby she has borne, so that she herself can eat them: so terrible will be the hunger during the siege and the awful distress caused by your enemies at your gates.

58, 59 If you refuse to obey all the laws written in this book, thus refusing reverence to the glorious and fearful name of Jehovah your God, then Jehovah will send perpetual plagues upon you and upon your children.

60 He will bring upon you all the diseases of Egypt which you feared so much, and they shall plague the land.

61 And that is not all! The Lord will bring upon you every sickness and plague there is, even those not mentioned in this book, until you are destroyed.

62 There will be few of you left, though before you were as numerous as stars. All this if you do not listen to the Lord your God.

63 Just as the Lord has rejoiced over you and has done such wonderful things for you and has multiplied you, so the Lord at that time will rejoice in destroying you; and you shall disappear from the land.

64 For the Lord will scatter you among all the nations from one end of the earth to the other. There you will worship heathen gods that neither you nor

your ancestors have known, gods made of wood and stone!

65 There among those nations you shall find no rest, but the Lord will give you trembling hearts, darkness, and bodies wasted from sorrow and fear.

66 Your lives will hang in doubt. You will live night and day in fear, and will have no reason to believe that you will see the morning light.

67 In the morning you will say, 'Oh, that night were here!' And in the evening you will say, 'Oh, that morning were here!' You will say this because of the awesome horrors surrounding you.

68 Then the Lord will send you back to Egypt in ships, a journey I promised you would never need to make again; and there you will offer to sell yourselves to your enemies as slaves—but no one will even want to buy you."

CHAPTER 29

It was on the plains of Moab that Moses restated the covenant which the Lord had made with the people of Israel at Mount Horeb.

2, 3 He summoned all Israel before him and told them, "You have seen with your own eyes the great plagues and mighty miracles that the Lord brought upon Pharaoh and his people in the land of Egypt.

4 But even yet the Lord hasn't given you hearts that understand or eyes that see or ears that hear!

5 For forty years God has led you through the wilderness, yet your clothes haven't become old, and your shoes haven't worn out!

6 The reason He hasn't let you settle down to grow grain for bread or grapes for wine and strong

drink, is so that you would realize that it is the Lord your God who has been caring for you.

7   When we came here, King Sihon of Heshbon and King Og of Bashan came out against us in battle, but we destroyed them,

8   And took their land and gave it to the tribes of Reuben and Gad and to the half-tribe of Manasseh as their inheritance.

9   Therefore, obey the terms of this covenant so that you will prosper in everything you do.

10   All of you—your leaders, the people, your judges, and your administrative officers—are standing today before the Lord your God,

11   Along with your little ones and your wives and the foreigners that are among you—those who chop your wood and carry your water.

12   You are standing here to enter into a contract with Jehovah your God, a contract He is making with you today.

13   He wants to confirm you today as His people, and to confirm that He is your God, just as He promised your ancestors, Abraham, Isaac, and Jacob.

14, 15   This contract is not with you alone as you stand before Him today, but with all future generations of Israel as well.

16   Surely you remember how we lived in the land of Egypt, and how as we left, we came safely through the territory of enemy nations.

17   And you have seen their heathen idols made of wood, stone, silver, and gold.

18   The day that any of you—man or woman, family or tribe of Israel—begins to turn away from the Lord our God and desires to worship these gods of

other nations, that day a root will be planted that will grow bitter and poisonous fruit.

19 Let no one blithely think, when he hears the warnings of this curse, 'I shall prosper even though I walk in my own stubborn way!'

20 For the Lord will not pardon! His anger and jealousy will be hot against that man. And all the curses written in this book shall lie heavily upon him, and the Lord will blot out His name from under heaven.

21 The Lord will separate that man from all the tribes of Israel, to pour out upon him all the curses (which are recorded in this book) that befall those who break this contract.

22 Then your children and the generations to come and the foreigners that pass by from distant lands shall see the devastation of the land and the diseases the Lord will have sent upon it.

23 They will see that the whole land is alkali and salt, a burned over wasteland, unsown, without crops, without a shred of vegetation—just like Sodom and Gomorrah and Admah and Zeboiim, destroyed by the Lord in His anger.

24 'Why has the Lord done this to His land?' the nations will ask. 'Why was He so angry?'

25 And they will be told, 'Because the people of the land broke the contract made with them by Jehovah, the God of their ancestors, when He brought them out of the land of Egypt.

26 For they worshiped other gods, violating His express command.

27 That is why the anger of the Lord was hot against this land, so that all His curses (which are recorded in this book) broke forth upon them.

28 In great anger the Lord rooted them out of their land and threw them away into another land, where they still live today!'

29 There are secrets the Lord your God has not revealed to us, but these words which He has revealed are for us and our children to obey forever.

CHAPTER 30

When all these things have happened to you—the blessings and the curses I have listed—you will meditate upon them as you are living among the nations where the Lord your God will have driven you.

2 If at that time you want to return to the Lord your God, and you and your children have begun wholeheartedly to obey all of the commandments I have given you today,

3 Then the Lord your God will rescue you from your captivity! He will have mercy upon you and come and gather you out of all the nations where He will have scattered you.

4 Though you are at the ends of the earth, He will go and find you and bring you back again

5 To the land of your ancestors. You shall possess the land again, and He will do you good and bless you even more than He did your ancestors!

6 He will cleanse your hearts and the hearts of your children and of your children's children so that you will love the Lord your God with all your hearts and souls, and Israel shall come alive again!

7, 8 If you return to the Lord and obey all the commandments that I command you today, the Lord your God will take His curses and turn them against your enemies—against those who hate you and persecute you.

9 The Lord your God will prosper everything you do and give you many children and much cattle and wonderful crops; for the Lord will again rejoice over you as He did over your fathers.

10 He will rejoice if you but obey the commandments written in this book of the law, and if you turn to the Lord your God with all your hearts and souls.

11 Obeying these commandments is not something beyond your strength and reach;

12 For these laws are not in the far heavens, so distant that you can't hear and obey them, and with no one to bring them down to you;

13 Nor are they beyond the ocean, so far that no one can bring you their message;

14 But they are very close at hand—in your hearts and on your lips—so that you can obey them.

15 Look, today I have set before you life and death, depending on whether you obey or disobey.

16 I have commanded you today to love the Lord your God and to follow His paths and to keep His laws, so that you will live and become a great nation, and so that the Lord your God will bless you and the land you are about to possess.

17 But if your hearts turn away and you won't listen—if you are drawn away to worship other gods—

18 Then I declare to you this day that you shall surely perish; you will not have a long, good life in the land you are going in to possess.

19 I call heaven and earth to witness against you that today I have set before you life or death, blessing

or curse. Oh, that you would choose life; that you and your children might live!

20 Choose to love the Lord your God and to obey Him and to cling to Him, for He is your life and the length of your days. You will then be able to live safely in the land the Lord promised your ancestors, Abraham, Isaac, and Jacob."

CHAPTER 31

After Moses had said all these things to the people of Israel,

2 He told them, "I am now 120 years old! I am no longer able to lead you,[1] for the Lord has told me that I shall not cross the Jordan River.

3 But the Lord Himself will lead you, and will destroy the nations living there, and you shall overcome them. Joshua is your new commander, as the Lord has instructed.

4 The Lord will destroy the nations living in the land, just as He destroyed Sihon and Og, the kings of the Amorites.

5 The Lord will deliver over to you the people living there, and you shall destroy them as I have commanded you.

6 Be strong! Be courageous! Do not be afraid of them! For the Lord your God will be with you. He will neither fail you nor forsake you."

7 Then Moses called for Joshua and said to him, as all Israel watched, "Be strong! Be courageous! For you shall lead these people into the land promised by the Lord to their ancestors; see to it that they conquer it.

---

[1]Literally, "I am no longer able to go out and come in."

8 Don't be afraid, for the Lord will go before you and will be with you; He will not fail nor forsake you."

9 Then Moses wrote out the laws he had already delivered to the people and gave them to the priests, the sons of Levi, who carried the Ark containing the Ten Commandments of the Lord. Moses also gave copies of the laws to the elders of Israel.

10, 11 The Lord commanded that these laws be read to all the people at the end of every seventh year —the Year of Release—at the Festival of Tabernacles, when all Israel would assemble before the Lord at the sanctuary.

12 "Call them all together," the Lord instructed, "—men, women, children, and foreigners living among you—to hear the laws of God and to learn His will, so that you will reverence the Lord your God and obey His laws.

13 Do this so that your little children who have not known these laws will hear them and learn how to revere the Lord your God as long as you live in the Promised Land."

14 Then the Lord said to Moses, "The time has come when you must die. Summon Joshua and come into the Tabernacle where I can give him his instructions." So Moses and Joshua came and stood before the Lord.

15 He appeared to them in a great cloud at the Tabernacle entrance.

16 And said to Moses, "You shall die and join your ancestors. After you are gone, these people will begin worshiping foreign gods in the Promised Land. They will forget about Me and break the contract I have made with them.

17   Then My anger will flame out against them and I will abandon them, hiding My face from them, and they shall be destroyed. Terrible trouble will come upon them, so that they will say, 'God is no longer among us!'

18   I will turn away from them because of their sins in worshiping other gods.

19   Now write down the words of this song, and teach it to the people of Israel as My warning to them.

20   When I have brought them into the land I promised their ancestors—a land 'flowing with milk and honey'—and when they have become fat and prosperous, and worship other gods and despise Me and break My contract,

21   And great disasters come upon them, then this song will remind them of the reason for their woes. (For this song will live from generation to generation.) I know now, even before they enter the land, what these people are like."

22   So, on that very day, Moses wrote down the words of the song and taught it to the Israelites.

23   Then he charged Joshua (son of Nun) to be strong and courageous, and said to him, "You must bring the people of Israel into the land the Lord promised them; for the Lord says, 'I will be with you.'"

24   When Moses had finished writing down all the laws that are recorded in this book,

25   He instructed the Levites who carried the Ark containing the Ten Commandments

26   To put this book of the law beside the Ark, as a solemn warning to the people of Israel.

27   "For I know how rebellious and stubborn you are," Moses told them. "If even today, while I am still here with you, you are defiant rebels against the Lord,

how much more rebellious will you be after my death!

28   Now summon all the elders and officers of your tribes so that I can speak to them, and call heaven and earth to witness against them.

29   I know that after my death you will utterly defile yourselves and turn away from God and His commands; and in the days to come evil will crush you for you will do what the Lord says is evil, making Him very angry."

30   So Moses recited this entire song to the whole assembly of Israel:

CHAPTER 32

1   "Listen, O heavens and earth!
            Listen to what I say!

2   My words shall fall upon you
            Like the gentle rain and dew,
            Like rain upon the tender grass,
            Like showers on the hillside.

3   I will proclaim the greatness of the Lord.
            How glorious He is!

4   He is the Rock. His work is perfect.
            Everything He does is just and fair.
            He is faithful, without sin.

5   But Israel has become corrupt,
            Smeared with sin. They are no longer His,
            They are a stubborn, twisted generation.

6   Is this the way you treat Jehovah?
            O foolish people,
            Is not God your Father?
            Has He not created you?
            Has He not established you and made you
               strong?

7　　Remember the days of long ago!
　　(Ask your father and the aged men;
　　They will tell you all about it.)

8　　When God divided up the world among
　　　　the nations,
　　He gave each of them a supervising angel!

9　　But He appointed none for Israel;
　　For Israel was God's own personal posses-
　　　　sion!

10　　God protected them in the howling wilder-
　　　　ness
　　As though they were the apple of His eye.

11　　He spreads His wings over them,
　　Even as an eagle overspreads her young.
　　She carries them upon her wings—
　　As does the Lord His people!

12　　When the Lord alone was leading them,
　　And they lived without foreign gods,

13　　God gave them fertile hilltops,
　　Rolling, fertile fields,
　　Honey from the rock,
　　And olive oil from stony ground![1]

14　　He gave them milk and meat—
　　Choice Bashan rams, and goats—
　　And the finest of the wheat;
　　They drank the sparkling wine.

15　　But Israel[2] was soon overfed;
　　Yes, fat and bloated;
　　Then, in plenty, they forsook their God.
　　They shrugged away the Rock of their
　　　　salvation.

---

[1] Or, "oil from flinty rocks."
[2] Literally, "Jeshurun."

16   Israel began to follow foreign gods,
      And Jehovah was very angry;
      He was jealous of His people.

17   They sacrificed to heathen gods,
      To new gods never before worshiped.

18   They spurned the Rock who had made
        them,
      Forgetting it was God who had given them
        birth.

19   God saw what they were doing,
      And detested them!
      His sons and daughters were insulting Him.

20   He said, 'I will abandon them;
      See what happens to them then!
      For they are a stubborn, faithless genera-
        tion.

21   They have made Me very jealous of their
        idols,
      Which are not gods at all.
      Now I, in turn, will make them jealous
      By giving My affections
      To the foolish Gentile nations of the world.

22   For My anger has kindled a fire
      That burns to the depths of the underworld,
      Consuming the earth and all of its crops,
      And setting its mountains on fire.

23   I will heap evils upon them
      And shoot them down with My arrows.

24   I will waste them with hunger,
      Burning fever, and fatal disease.
      I will devour them! I will set wild beasts
        upon them,
      To rip them apart with their teeth;

And deadly serpents
Crawling in the dust.

25 Outside, the enemies' sword—
Inside, the plague[3]—
Shall terrorize young men and girls alike;
The baby nursing at the breast,
And aged men.

26 I had decided to scatter them to distant lands,
So that even the memory of them
Would disappear.

27 But then I thought,
'My enemies will boast,
"Israel is destroyed by our own might;
It was not the Lord
Who did it!" '

28 Israel is a stupid nation;
Foolish, without understanding.

29 Oh, that they were wise!
Oh, that they could understand!
Oh, that they would know what they are getting into!

30 How could one single enemy chase a thousand of them,
And two put ten thousand to flight,
Unless their Rock had abandoned them,
Unless the Lord had destroyed them?

31 But the rock of other nations
Is not like our Rock;
Prayers to their gods are valueless.

32 They act like men of Sodom and Gomorrah:

---

[3]Implied.

Their deeds[4] are bitter with poison;

33   They drink the wine of serpent venom.

34   But Israel[5] is My special people,

Sealed as jewels within My treasury.

35   Vengeance is Mine,

And I decree the punishment of all her enemies:

Their doom is sealed.

36   The Lord will see His people righted,

And will have compassion on them when they slip.

He will watch their power ebb away,

Both slave and free.

37   Then God will ask,

'Where are their gods—

The rocks they claimed to be their refuge?

38   Where are these gods now,

To whom they sacrificed their fat and wine?

Let those gods arise,

And help them!

39   Don't you see that I alone am God?

I kill and make live.

I wound and heal—

No one delivers from My power.

40, 41   I raise My hand to heaven

And vow by My existence,

That I will whet the lightning of My sword!

And hurl My punishments upon My enemies!

42   My arrows shall be drunk with blood!

---

[4]Literally, "grapes."
[5]Implied.

> My sword devours the flesh and blood
> Of all the slain and captives.
> The heads of the enemy
> Are gory with blood.'

43   Praise His people,
> O Gentile nations,
> For He will avenge His people,
> Taking vengeance on His enemies,
> Purifying His land
> And His people."

44, 45   When Moses and Joshua had recited all the words of this song to the people,

46   Moses made these comments:

"Meditate upon all the laws I have given you today, and pass them on to your children.

47   These laws are not mere words—they are your life! Through obeying them you will live long, plentiful lives in the land you are going to possess across the Jordan River."

48   That same day, the Lord said to Moses,

49   "Go to Mount Nebo in the Abarim mountains, in the land of Moab across from Jericho. Climb to its heights, and look out across the land of Canaan, the land I am giving to the people of Israel.

50   After you see the land you must die and join your ancestors, just as Aaron your brother died in Mount Hor and joined them.

51   For you dishonored Me among the people of Israel at the springs of Meribath-kadesh, in the wilderness of Zin.

52   You will see spread out before you the land I am giving the people of Israel, but you will not enter it."

CHAPTER 33

This is the blessing that Moses, the man of God, gave to the people of Israel before his death:

2   "The Lord came to us at Mount Sinai,
         And dawned upon us from Mount Seir;
         He shone from Mount Paran,
         Surrounded by ten thousands of holy angels,[1]
         And with flaming fire at His right hand.

3   How He loves His people—
         His holy ones are in His hands.
         They followed in Your steps, O Lord.
         They have received their directions from You.

4   The laws I have given
         Are your precious possession.

5   The Lord became king in Jerusalem,
         Elected by a convocation of the leaders of the tribes!

6   Let Reuben live forever
         And may his tribe increase!"

7 And Moses said of Judah:
         "O Lord, hear the cry of Judah
         And unite him with Israel;
         Fight for him against his enemies."

8 Then Moses said concerning the tribe of Levi:
         "Give to godly Levi
         Your Urim and Your Thummim.
         You tested Levi at Massah and at Meribah;

9   He obeyed Your instructions
         [and destroyed many sinners[1]],

---

[1]Literally, "holy ones."
[1]Implied.

Even his own children, brothers, fathers,
and mothers.

10   The Levites shall teach God's laws to Israel
And shall work before You at the incense
altar
And the altar of burnt offering.

11   O Lord, prosper the Levites
And accept the work they do for You.
Crush those who are their enemies;
Don't let them rise again."

12   Concerning the tribe of Benjamin, Moses said:
"He is beloved of God
And lives in safety beside Him.
God surrounds him with His loving care,
And preserves him from every harm."

13   Concerning the tribe of Joseph, he said:
"May his land be blessed by God
With the choicest gifts of heaven
And of the earth that lies below.

14   May he be blessed
With the best of what the sun makes grow;
Growing richly month by month,

15   With the finest of mountain crops
And of the everlasting hills.

16   May he be blessed with the best gifts
Of the earth and its fullness,
And with the favor of God who appeared
In the burning bush.
Let all these blessings come upon Joseph,
The prince among his brothers.

17   He is a young bull in strength and splendor,
With the strong horns of a wild ox

To push against the nations everywhere;
This is my blessing on the multitudes of
    Ephraim
And the thousands of Manasseh."

18 Of the tribe of Zebulun, Moses said:
"Rejoice, O Zebulun, you outdoorsmen,
And Issachar, you lovers of your tents;

19 They shall summon the people
To celebrate their sacrifices with them.
Lo, they taste the riches of the sea
And the treasures of the sand";

20 Concerning the tribe of Gad, Moses said:
"A blessing upon those who help Gad.
He crouches like a lion,
With savage arm and face and head.

21 He chose the best of the land for himself
Because it is reserved for a leader.
He led the people
Because he carried out God's penalties for
    Israel."

22 Of the tribe of Dan, Moses said:
"Dan is like a lion's cub
Leaping out from Bashan."

23 Of the tribe of Naphtali, Moses said:
"O Naphtali, you are satisfied
With all the blessings of the Lord;
The Mediterranean coast and the Negeb
Are your home."

24 Of the tribe of Asher:
"Asher is a favorite son,
Esteemed above his brothers;
He bathes his feet in soothing olive oil.

25 May you be protected with strong bolts

> Of iron and bronze,
> And may your strength match the length
> of your days!

26   There is none like the God of Jerusalem—
> He descends from the heavens
> In majestic splendor to help you.

27   The eternal God is your Refuge,
> And underneath are the everlasting arms.
> He thrusts out your enemies before you;
> It is He who cries, 'Destroy them!'

28   So Israel dwells safely,
> Prospering in a land of corn and wine,
> While the gentle rains descend from heaven.

29   What blessings are yours, O Israel!
> Who else has been saved by the Lord?
> He is your shield and your helper!
> He is your excellent sword!
> Your enemies shall bow low before you,
> And you shall trample on their backs!"

CHAPTER 34

Then Moses climbed from the plains of Moab to Pisgah Peak in Mount Nebo, across from Jericho. And the Lord pointed out to him the Promised Land, as they gazed out across Gilead as far as Dan:

2 "There is Naphtali; and there is Ephraim and Manasseh; and across there, Judah, extending to the Mediterranean Sea;

3 There is the Negeb; and the Jordan Valley; and Jericho, the city of palm trees; and Zoar," the Lord told him.

4 "It is the Promised Land," the Lord told Moses. "I promised Abraham, Isaac, and Jacob that I would

give it to their descendants. Now you have seen it, but you will not enter it."

5 So Moses, the disciple of the Lord, died in the land of Moab as the Lord had said.

6 The Lord buried him in a valley near Beth-Peor in Moab, but no one knows the exact place.

7 Moses was 120 years old when he died, yet his eyesight was perfect and he was as strong as a young man.

8 The people of Israel mourned for him for thirty days on the plains of Moab.

9 Joshua (son of Nun) was full of the spirit of wisdom, for Moses had laid his hands upon him; so the people of Israel obeyed him, and followed the commandments that the Lord had given to Moses.

10 There has never been another prophet like Moses, for the Lord talked to him face to face.

11, 12 And at God's command he performed amazing miracles which have never been equalled. He did great and terrifying wonders before Pharaoh and his entire court in Egypt, and before the people of Israel in the wilderness.